Conditional Fees

THIRD EDITION

Other titles available from Law Society Publishing:

Civil Litigation Handbook (2nd Edition)
General Editor: District Judge Suzanne Burn, Consultant Editor: Professor John Peysner

Personal Injury Handbook
Nicholas Waller

Fatal Accidents: Law and Practice
Clive Thomas

Civil Costs Assessment Handbook (2nd Edition)
Peter Burdge

Enforcement and Debt Recovery: A Guide to the New Law
Peter Levaggi, David Marsden and Peter Mooney

All books from Law Society Publishing can be ordered through good bookshops or direct from our distributors, Prolog, by telephone 0870 850 1422 or email **lawsociety@prolog.uk.com**. Please confirm the price before ordering.

For further information or a catalogue, please contact our editorial and marketing office by email **publishing@lawsociety.co.uk**.

CONDITIONAL FEES

A Guide to CFAs and Litigation Funding

THIRD EDITION

Gordon Wignall

Consultant Editor: Steven Green

with contributions from
Matthew Amey and Robert Rose

The Law Society

Appendices 11–14 are reproduced with the kind permission of the Bar Council.

© Law Society 2008

ISBN 978-1-85328-992-7

First published in 1995
2nd edition published in 2001
This 3rd edition published in 2008
by the Law Society
113 Chancery Lane, London WC2A 1PL

Typeset by J&L Composition Ltd, Filey, North Yorkshire
Printed by MPG Books Ltd, Bodmin, Cornwall

Contents

Contributors

Matthew Amey has been a Director of The Judge Limited which is the largest independent specialist after-the-event insurance broker. Matthew has had an uninterrupted career in litigation insurance which includes roles in claims handling, underwriting and brokerage. As an underwriter, he specialised in complex commercial litigation and group actions and as a broker deals with risk transfer solutions for all type of litigation. Matthew has given oral evidence in SCCO and assists clients, with routine success, in providing expert evidence for the purposes of premium recoverability. Matthew writes regularly for the Law Society's *Litigation Funding* magazine and frequently speaks at litigation funding conferences and seminars, including Central Law Training.

Steven Green is the Costs Manager at Irwin Mitchell and is a fellow of the Association of Law Costs Draftsmen. A regular speaker at conferences relating to costs issues, he has a particular interest in CFAs and their development in the personal injury and commercial marketplace.

Robert Rose has headed up the PI/Clinical Negligence Team at Harvey Ingram LLP since 1996, and will be appointed the firm's first Deputy Managing Partner on 1 April 2008. The firm has used CFAs since the mid 1990s and has seen a tenfold expansion in the instructions it receives over that period of time. Robert is on the Law Society's clinical negligence panel, and has taken a particular interest in obstetric negligence. He is currently studying for an MBA in Legal Practice at the Nottingham Trent University.

Gordon Wignall is a barrister at No5 Chambers who specialises in costs and CFA law, as well as in environmental and other group actions. He is a former scholarship prizewinner of Gray's Inn and a part-time employment judge.

Preface

This book is primarily about CFAs. CFAs began in the 1990s as a funding vehicle intended to encourage access to the courts. The new scheme put in place by reason of the Access to Justice Act 1999, in particular the CFA Regulations 2000, brought about a period of mayhem which will not subside for years. A malevolent word about CFAs has now been uttered by every category of person who has had to have professional dealings with them. The judiciary's time has been spent on technical arguments about regulatory consumer care provisions, whilst their historical objection to 'no win, no fee' arrangements (that the winning side might suppress or fabricate evidence) never seems to have troubled the legislature. Claimants' lawyers are exasperated by what they see as the crocodile tears of defendant interests apparently seeking to champion the claimants' own rights against their lawyers' lack of interest in client care. Defendants are frustrated by what they consider to be excessive uplifts and the ability by claimants to fund litigation in an environment free of any concern about the costs.

The extensive and complicated technical challenges which have been made to CFAs entered into prior to the revocation of the 2000 Regulations (with effect from 1 November 2005) have made it necessary to produce a book which considers these challenges in detail. There will come a time in the future when such a detailed exegesis of the law relating to CFAs will not be necessary. By then, however, the courts will have explored in even greater detail than they have done recently other rules and procedures which facilitate the funding of litigation, and the Civil Justice Council is currently working on various novel proposals. Whilst this is primarily a book about CFAs, therefore, some brief guidance is given in this edition about other means of litigation funding, and it is likely that these areas will expand in any future editions.

It is necessary to acknowledge the assistance of a number of practitioners expert in their own fields. Steven Green, the Consultant Editor, is the Costs Manager at Irwin Mitchell, and possesses a full knowledge of the law relating to CFAs and costs, and in daily practice is a fine tactician. He is responsible for the final version of large parts of this book. Matthew Amey from The Judge has contributed the chapter about insurance, and Robert Rose of

Harvey Ingram is responsible for the chapters about CFA litigation practice. Neil Stockdale and Gwen Evans of Hugh James made useful contributions in relation to environmental and group actions. Alastair Brett at News International was kind enough to discuss the difficulties faced in media proceedings. Simon Trees of Else Commercial Solicitors contributed to the chapter which touches on commercial cases. There are many others. Sadly, the blame for undoing their good work, and indeed generally, must remain my own.

The librarians at No5 Chambers, especially Hilary Boucher and Lindsay Higgs, have spent many hours tracing authorities, and indeed I am grateful for the help of all staff and barrister colleagues at No5. Paul Bleasdale QC made some detailed suggestions about the final text.

As to the Law Society, Jennifer Cowan and Janet Noble have always been very generous with their help. There can be absolutely no one who requires a greater degree of patience in her working life than the legal publisher. In matters of private life that requirement falls to one's family.

The attempt has been made to describe CFA law and practice as of 1 January 2008.

Gordon Wignall
London
22 February 2008

Table of cases

Table of statutory instruments and European legislation

Table of statutes

EUROPEAN LEGISLATION

Abbreviations

ADR	alternative dispute resolution
APIL	Association of Personal Injury Lawyers
ATE	after-the-event legal expenses insurance
AVMA	Action for the Victims of Medical Accidents
BMIF	Bar Mutual Indemnity Fund
BTE	before-the-event legal expenses insurance
ChBA	Chancery Bar Association
CFA	conditional fee agreement
CFA (Miscellaneous Amendments) Regulations 2003	Conditional Fee Agreements (Miscellaneous Amendments) Regulations 2003, SI 2003/1240
CFA (Miscellaneous Amendments) (No.2) Regulations 2003	Conditional Fee Agreements (Miscellaneous Amendments) (No.2) Regulations 2003, SI 2003/3344
CFA (Revocation) Regulations 2005	Conditional Fee Agreements (Revocation) Regulations 2005, SI 2005/2305
CFA Regulations 1995	Conditional Fee Agreements Regulations 1995, SI 1995/1675
CFA Regulations 2000	Conditional Fee Agreements Regulations 2000, SI 2000/692
CCFA	collective conditional fee agreement
CCFA Regulations 2000	Collective Conditional Fee Agreements Regulations 2000
CLAF	Contingency Legal Aid Fund
CoLAF	Conditional Legal Aid Fund
CPD	Costs Practice Direction
CPR	Civil Procedure Rules 1998
GLO	group litigation order

LEI	legal expense insurance
LMS	The Law Society's Law Management Section
PI	personal injury
PIBA	Personal Injuries Bar Association
RPI	Retail Prices Index
SRA	Solicitors Regulation Authority
WIP	work in progress

PART I

Underlying legal principles

CHAPTER 1

Basic principles

1.1   INTRODUCTION

Overview

In this chapter an explanation will be offered as to what is meant by a '*conditional* fee agreement' and why such an agreement (referred to throughout this book as a 'CFA') needs the protection of Parliament to be enforceable. In order to achieve these aims, it will be necessary to give an account of the relevant underlying common law principles of maintenance and champerty and also the indemnity principle. Maintenance and champerty will be dealt with in a little detail since it is hoped that by doing so it will be possible to provide some assistance for those wishing to explore other funding options, for instance the extent to which a funder who has no connection with litigation can fund a party. Whilst this is primarily a book about CFAs, various summary accounts of other non-CFA litigation funding options will be found in **Chapter 12**. It is likely that in any future editions these topics will be expanded upon as they continue to gain in importance.

A 'conditional fee agreement' at common law: champerty and the indemnity principle

In summary, a conditional fee agreement is one where the extent of the fees which a client agrees to pay to his lawyer is conditional on a specified outcome being achieved. At common law a retainer on these terms is considered champertous. This derives from the notion that the lawyer is ultimately seeking a share of the spoils of litigation, so that such an arrangement is potentially inimical to justice and contrary to public policy. Putting it bluntly, the lawyer might be tempted to interfere with the evidence in order to ensure success. A champertous retainer has always been considered unlawful and void for this reason, and the result is that a lawyer working under such terms cannot claim any costs from the client. The further consequence is that a successful litigant who has engaged a lawyer on champertous terms cannot recover any costs from his opponent. This is because the indemnity principle prohibits a litigant from recovering more from his opponent than he is liable to pay to his lawyer.

Parliamentary intervention

By enacting Courts and Legal Services Act 1990, s.58, the legislature definitively barred a judge from declaring a lawyer's retainer unenforceable should payment be conditional only in the event of specified circumstances. Section 58 operates as a statutory bar prohibiting the judiciary from declaring public policy to be such as to render this type of agreement void. So long as certain conditions are satisfied, then a conditional agreement is declared by s.58(1) to be 'enforceable'. If it does not comply with those conditions, then it will be 'unenforceable'.

Challenges by paying parties

It will be immediately understood why it is so attractive to a losing party which has to pay costs to be able to demonstrate that the conditions required to render a conditional arrangement 'enforceable' are not satisfied. If the arrangement can be stripped of its cloak of enforceability, then the effect of the rule against champerty and the indemnity principle is that no costs are payable.

The statutory conditions with which statutory CFAs must comply and the various challenges to which they have been subject will be dealt with in other chapters, in particular in **Chapter 3**.

Is statutory protection now needed?

A debate which rumbles on and which rears its head from time to time is the question whether statutory protection in the form of the 1990 Act (as amended) is still needed. Champerty is only a rule of public policy, and there is a good argument that public policy has moved on. If we no longer accept that there is any wrong in a conditional arrangement, then why should anyone need to appeal to Parliament's protection? If a judge, reflecting society's view at large, considers that a 'no win, no fee' arrangement is not in principle objectionable, which was indeed the view of Millett J in *Thai Trading* and the Vice Chancellor in *Bevan Ashford*, then Courts and Legal Services Act 1990, s.58 is redundant (but see *Awward* v. *Geraghty* [2001] QB 570).

This shift in perception is reflected by the courts' growing reluctance automatically to prohibit agreements which are suggestive of maintenance and champerty, preferring today to examine the nature of the agreements in detail and to determine the nature of the wrong which might in practice result from them. It is reflected too by the revocation of the CFA Regulations 2000, and also by this statement from the Privy Council in *Kenneth Kellar* v. *Stanley Williams* 24 June 2004 (para.31), when it gave its advice as follows:

4

It . . . has to be considered whether the fee agreement, whether in its original form or as varied in 2000, constituted a conditional fee agreement. In approaching this issue their Lordships wish to make it plain that they are not to be taken as accepting without question the traditional doctrine of the common law that all such agreements are unenforceable on grounds of public policy. The content of public policy can change over the years, and it may now be time to reconsider the accepted prohibition in the light of modern practising conditions.

As other chapters of this book will show, the statutory provisions enacted by Parliament which render conditional fees enforceable have been concerned almost entirely with consumer protection. They have never made any provision against the risks associated with the engagement of lawyers on terms which at common law are considered champertous and therefore offensive. The dangers portrayed so vividly by Lord Denning and others (see **1.5** below) that, for personal gain, lawyers might be tempted 'to inflame the damages, to suppress evidence, or even to suborn witnesses', have not crossed Parliament's radar screen.

It is a remarkable result (in the case of pre-November 2005 CFAs at least) that although a lawyer might succeed for his client and obtain substantial damages, the fact that he has failed in some aspect solely of consumer protection (and *not* because Parliament thought that he might interfere with the course of justice) means that a judge is then obliged as a matter of common law precedent to declare the retainer unlawful on the very grounds with which Parliament is not concerned (the theoretical risk of interference with justice) and, as a consequence, to permit the original wrongdoer to escape paying any of the lawyer's costs. The result is all the more remarkable since it is the paying party which is entitled in certain circumstances to set in motion the inquiry as to whether the winning party's lawyer complied with the consumer protection provisions designed only to protect the winning party himself (see further at **Chapter 4**).

1.2 WHAT IS A 'CONDITIONAL FEE' FOR THE PURPOSES OF THE COURTS AND LEGAL SERVICES ACT 1990?

A 'conditional fee', then, is a means of remuneration for a lawyer which can only be determined according to the outcome of the task which the lawyer has agreed to undertake.

By Courts and Legal Services Act 1990, s.58(2)(a) (as substituted now by Access to Justice Act 1999, s.27):

(a)   a conditional fee agreement is an agreement with a person providing advocacy or litigation services which provides for his fees and expenses, or any part of them, to be payable only in specified circumstances.

5

(A similar provision existed in the unamended Act.) This definition embraces both individual CFAs and collective agreements (known as CCFAs). Save for the regulations which were contained in the Collective Conditional Fee Agreements Regulations 2000 (now revoked), a CCFA is not recognised as a separate and distinct entity either under the legislative provisions or under the costs rules of the Civil Procedure Rules (CPR).

Section 58A(4) 'Advocacy and Litigation services' includes 'any sort of proceedings for resolving disputes (and not just proceedings in a court), whether commenced or contemplated'. 'Advocacy services' and 'litigation services' are defined at Courts and Legal Services Act 1990, s.119 as follows:

> 'Advocacy services' means any services which it would be reasonable to expect as person who is exercising, or contemplating exercising, a right of audience in relation to any proceedings, or contemplated proceedings, to provide;
> 'Litigation services' means any services which it would be reasonable to expect as person who is exercising, or contemplating exercising, a right to conduct litigation in relation to any proceedings, or contemplated proceedings, to provide.

While 'proceedings' is also defined at s.119, it has a more restricted sense than that given to it in s.58A(4) ('proceedings in any court').

In *Gaynor* v. *Central West London Buses Ltd* [2006] EWCA 1120 28 July 2006 the Court of Appeal was faced with the question whether a letter of retainer which contained the following words was thereby a CFA within the meaning of s.58(2)(a):

> If your claim is disputed by your opponent and you decide not to pursue your claim then we will not make a charge for the work we have done to date.

The retainer was agreed between the client and solicitor within weeks of the client's accident and the defendant admitted liability shortly thereafter. The letter had stated that the client would be offered a CFA if the claim was disputed and the client subsequently wished 'to pursue her claim through litigation'. The Court of Appeal held that that work done pursuant to the letter could not constitute 'litigation services' within the meaning of CLSA 1990, s.119 or s.58(2)(a). These were 'pre-litigation services'. Therefore this was not a CFA caught by s.58(1) of the 1990 Act and the rigours of the 2000 Regulations did not apply. The oddity of the case was that 15 months later the claimant (as she had become) issued proceedings and subsequently claimed costs on the back of this initial letter. This fact did not cause the Court of Appeal to resile from its view that when the letter was entered into there were not even any contemplated proceedings, so that the basic advice which was intended to be given at the time was only as to whether the client had a good claim. *Gaynor* demonstrates that not all retainers where there is some payment condition contingent on success will fall within s.58(2)(a). The services to be provided under the retainer must be litigation or advocacy services as defined within s.119 in the context of the wider definition of proceedings as set out in s.58A(4).

It is convenient to note here that a CFA as understood and defined by s.58 of the 1990 Act may be contained in more than one instrument, so that in *Jones* v. *Wrexham B.C.* [2007] EWCA 1356, 19 December 2007, both the CFA document itself and a client care letter were held to constitute the CFA (see para.86).

'Payable only in specified circumstances': 'success'

It will be noted that the statutory definition embraces all conditional arrangements whether or not they provide for a success fee. What determines whether or not an agreement is a CFA within the terms of the statute (thereby potentially meriting the protection afforded by s.58(1)) is the fact that the client's fees and expenses are payable 'only in specified circumstances', meaning the circumstances specified in the written agreement (s.58(3)(a) requires a CFA to be in writing).

There are numerous different methods by which fees can be determined on a conditional basis. In the most typical form a lawyer will be paid nothing unless 'success' has been achieved, although the meaning of this expression might be very widely drawn so that, for instance, it might encompass the recovery of damages or of costs or possibly even 'any benefit' to the client. If there is a 'success', then the lawyer will receive his basic charges together with a success fee (by s.58(6)). In commercial litigation it is not uncommon for a lawyer to agree to be paid his normal rate on success along with a percentage uplift, but to be paid a discounted hourly rate where there is a failure (see for instance *Aratra Potato Co Ltd* v. *Taylor Johnson Garrett* [1995] 4 All ER 695 and now *Gloucestershire County Council* v. *Evans* [2008] EWCA Civ 21, 31 January 2008). In more generous arrangements a lawyer may agree to receive only his normal rate in the event of success (i.e. without mark-up) and nothing at all in the event of failure. The permutations are considerable, so that a pyramid agreement allowing a lawyer a greater share of his client's damages in proportion to the increasing amounts recovered by the client was considered to be within the ambit of the 1990 Act (*Benaim UK Ltd*, Rich J).

In order to be able to calculate what fees need to be paid over where a lawyer acts on conditional terms, there are two critical factors. The first is what constitutes success under the agreement, and the second the means by which payment is to be assessed.

Other nomenclatures: 'differential fees', 'contingent fees'

'Conditional' fees have gone by a number of different descriptions in the recent past. Distinctions have been drawn, for instance between 'differential fees' and 'differential normal fees' (see *Awwad* v. *Geraghty* [2001] QB 570). What we would recognise today as 'conditional fees' have sometimes been described as 'contingent fees'. A contingent arrangement entails handing over a share of the proceeds to the lawyer and is not lawful in England and Wales as a means of funding litigation, save for a non-contentious business agreement permitted by Solicitors Act 1974, s.57 (but see recommendation 4 of the Civil Justice Council papers 'Improved Access to Justice – Funding Options and Proportionate Costs' (June 2007). The effect of Courts and Legal Services Act 1990, s.58(5) is that a lawful non-contentious business agreement is not unenforceable because of s.58(1) on the ground that it does not comply with the conditions otherwise applicable to conditional agreements by reason of that subsection.

1.3 STATUTORY PROTECTION GIVEN TO CFAs: COURTS AND LEGAL SERVICES ACT 1990, s.58(1)

By virtue of the development of a series of common law principles summarised in the introductory paragraphs of this chapter and explained in more detail in the following sections, it took an Act of Parliament in 1990 to render conditional fees lawful.

By Courts and Legal Services Act 1990, s.58(1) (as substituted by Access to Justice Act 1999, s.27):

> 58. – (1) A conditional fee agreement which satisfies all of the conditions applicable to it by virtue of this section shall not be unenforceable by reason only of its being a conditional fee agreement; but (subject to subsection (5)) any other conditional fee agreement shall be unenforceable.

Section 58(2)(a) intends to encompass all conditional agreements which are not contingent arrangements and which are do not fall within the definition of 'non-contentious business agreements' under Solicitors Act 1974, s.57 (see s.58(5)).

Parliament found itself required to give express statutory protection to conditional arrangements in order to render them lawful by reason of the residual rule prohibiting champerty and the applicable of the indemnity principle, but only if they comply with the conditions applicable under the Act. Something further must briefly be said on a preliminary basis about the relevant common law doctrines since they will explain why a lawyer who is acting under a CFA will be so very concerned if the agreement is for some reason declared unenforceable: he will not be paid anything, not even a *quantum meruit* for the services that he has provided (see *Awwad* v. *Geraghty* [2001] QB 570 at 596C–E).

1.4   THE INDEMNITY PRINCIPLE

Gundry v. *Sainsbury*

The clearest modern statement of the rule known as the indemnity principle ('modern' being a word still to be used advisedly in costs law) stems from the dangerous dog case of *Gundry* v. *Sainsbury* [1910] 1 KB 645. As the headnote tells us: 'The action was brought in the Wandsworth County Court to recover damages for injuries alleged to have been sustained by the plaintiff through having been bitten by the defendant's dog'. The plaintiff's solicitor suffered four misfortunes. The most serious was that his client gave evidence that he had reached an agreement with the solicitor that he would not have to pay anything for his costs. Secondly, G's barrister was not quite alive to what the judge meant when the judge declared that he would consider the question of costs subsequently, so that the barrister did not make a prompt application to call further evidence in relation to the costs. Then, thirdlly, the judge refused a late application to call further evidence by the solicitor as to the nature of the retainer. Fourthly, the Court of Appeal decided not to intervene in the judge's exercise of his discretion to permit this further evidence to be called.

The Court of Appeal held that the judge had been right to prohibit the recovery of costs from the losing party since costs were awarded only as an indemnity for the costs payable by the winning party to his solicitor and there had been an agreement that the claimant would not have to pay those costs.

The nature of the indemnity principle is explained by two well-known passages from the judgments of Cozens-Hardy MR and Buckley LJ. At 649 the Master of the Rolls said:

> What are party and party costs? They are not a complete indemnity, but they are only given in the character of an indemnity. I cannot do better than read the opinion expressed by Bramwell B. in *Harold v. Smith* (1): 'Costs as between party and party are given by the law as an indemnity to the person entitled to them; they are not imposed as a punishment on the party who pays them, nor given as a bonus to the party who receives them. Therefore, if the extent of the damnification can be found out, the extent to which costs ought to be allowed is also ascertained'.

And Buckley LJ ruled at 653, whilst expressing his 'regret that the solicitor was not allowed to go into the box and state the real facts relating to the agreement', that:

> The client comes to the Court and says 'This is a matter in respect of which I am entitled to get costs because I have been put to expense, and the law as administered in this Court allows me in that state of things to be indemnified by the defendant to the extent of party and party costs.' But he having come to assert that right, the Court says 'True, you are entitled to such indemnity, but inasmuch as you have nothing to pay by reason of your agreement with your solicitor there is nothing for which to indemnify you.'

There are many statements of the principle in a modern context. For instance, in *Butt* v. *Nizami* [2006] 1 WLR 3307, 3309D–E (para.8), Simon J stated that 'at its simplest the indemnity principle provides that an unsuccessful party cannot be liable to pay more to a successful party that the successful party is himself legally liable to pay' (para.8). In *Kenneth Kellar* v. *Stanley Williams*, unreported, 24 June 2004 the Privy Council ruled that the indemnity principle provides that 'the costs recoverable by the receiving party are limited to those which he is liable to pay to his own solicitor, subject to the limitation that they were reasonably incurred and were reasonable in amount' (para.17).

The purpose and effect of the indemnity principle

The indemnity principle is the mainstay of costs law in England and Wales. It prohibits a litigant from obtaining more from a paying party than he is legally bound to pay to his solicitors.

The common law rule is now 'enshrined in statute' by Solicitors Act 1974, s.60(3):

> A client shall not be entitled to recover from any other person under an order for the payment of any costs to which a contentious business agreement relates more than the amount payable by him to his solicitor in respect of those costs under the agreement.

As the Court of Appeal stated in *General of Berne Insurance Co* v. *Jardine Reinsurance Management Ltd* [1998] 1 WLR 1231, 1234G the rule ensures that an order for costs 'is not punitive and should not enable the receiving party to make a profit'.

The statutory power to override the indemnity principle

It should be noted that Supreme Court Act 1981, s.51, the ultimate source of the entitlement to the costs of litigation, has now been amended by Access to Justice Act 1999, s.31. The new s.51(2) states:

> Without prejudice to any general power to make rules of court, such rules may make provision for regulating matters relating to the costs of those proceedings including, in particular, prescribing scales of costs to be paid to legal *or other representatives or for securing that the amount awarded to a party in respect of the costs to be paid by him to such representatives is not limited to what would have been payable by him to them if he had not been awarded costs.*

The words in italics were given effect on 2 June 2003 by the Access to Justice Act (Commencement No.10) Order 2002, SI 2003/1241. The amended s.51(2) expressly allows rules to be made which will make provision for costs to be paid without reference to the indemnity principle, although at the time of writing none have been made.

The indemnity certificate on the Bill of Costs: a prima facie entitlement to costs

The indemnity principle has an important status relevant to CFA challenges. One of the three certificates as to accuracy is required to be placed on a Bill of Costs (see CPD, para.4.15). The indemnity certificate states that 'I certify that this bill is both accurate and complete and . . . the costs claimed herein do not exceed the costs which the receiving party is required to pay me/my firm' (see Precedent F to the Schedule of Costs Precedents annexed to the Costs Practice Direction). It is the signature to this certificate which was described by Henry LJ in *Bailey* v. *IBC Vehicles* [1998] 3 All ER 570, 575g as 'no empty formality', and which is intended, in the absence of a real issue being raised as to the receiving party's entitlement to costs, to prevent skirmishes designed to attack the receiving party's costs on the grounds that the costs as claimed are in excess of the costs due to the receiving party's legal representative. This is a starting point in an attack on the validity of a CFA retainer since it raises the presumption that the costs of a matter funded by a CFA do not breach the indemnity principle. In order to be able to mount a challenge, the paying party must be able to demonstrate by evidence that the certificate is unreliable and that the CFA is unenforceable. There is a discussion of the method by which a challenge can be made to the presumption that a Bill is accurate below at **4.5**.

1.5 MAINTENANCE AND CHAMPERTY

In the context of CFAs, a conditional agreement which is unenforceable because it does not comply with the formalities of the Courts and Legal Services Act 1990 (as amended) loses statutory protection and offends against the public policy rule outlawing champerty. If a CFA is unenforceable for this reason then there is no legal obligation requiring the receiving party to pay his solicitor because of the breach of the indemnity principle. As has been said above, this is the ultimate goal to which paying parties strive when considering whether there is a breach of the formalities laid down by statute. It is for the very purpose of preventing judges automatically declaring CFAs unenforceable as a result of the effect of the rule against champerty that Parliament brought about the statutory declaration as to the enforceability of CFAs set out in s.58(1) of the Act.

Maintenance consists in the provision of financial support to a litigant, and champerty is 'only a particular form of maintenance, namely, where the person who maintains takes as a reward a share in the property recovered' (Scrutton LJ in *Ellis* v. *Torrington* [1920] 1 KB 399, 412). These are considered further in the following paragraphs.

Criminal Law Act 1967

Until 1967 both maintenance and champerty were both torts and crimes. This was brought to an end by Criminal Law Act 1967, ss.13(1) and 14(1), but by a reservation in s.14(2):

> The abolition of criminal and civil liability under the law of England and Wales for maintenance and champerty shall not affect any rule of that law as to the cases in which a contract is to be treated as contrary to public policy or otherwise illegal.

Public policy

At common law, therefore, both maintenance and champerty are capable of rendering a contract unenforceable and void on the ground of illegality. But as to exactly what contracts should be considered unenforceable on these grounds is entirely a matter of public policy, and this has been left to the judges.

Perceptions as to what should be considered an unlawful form of maintenance has varied considerably in recent years. Lord Denning MR described maintenance as 'improperly stirring up litigation and strife by giving aid to one party to bring or defend a claim without just cause or excuse' (*In re Trepca Mines Ltd (No.2)* [1963] Ch 199, 219), but there have always been forms of maintenance which have been permitted by the courts. See *Giles* v. *Thompson* [1994] 1 AC 142, 161:

> even in former times maintenance was permissible when the maintainer had a legitimate interest in the outcome of the suit. This was not confined to cases where he had a financial or commercial interest in the result. It extended to other cases where social, family or other ties justified the maintenance in supporting the litigation. In *Neville v London 'Express' Newspaper Ltd* [1919] AC 368, 389 Lord Haldane said: 'Such an interest is held to be possessed when in litigation a master assists his servant, or a servant his master, or help is given to an heir, or a near relative, or to a poor man out of charity, to maintain a right which he might otherwise lose.'

Thus Millett LJ (as he then was) decided in *Trading Co* v. *Taylor* [1998] QB 781 that it was impossible for the losing party to complain about unlawful maintenance of the successful party by her solicitor since the solicitor was her husband and employer (see further below).

By the time of *Hamilton* v. *Fayed (No.2)* [2002] 3 All ER 641, the effect of the Access to Justice Act 1999 and of the availability of CFAs was that the Court of Appeal could find nothing wrong with an arrangement by which a pure funder agreed to pay for the legal expenses of one of the parties. As Chadwick LJ put it:

> 69. [The appellant] relies heavily on what is said to be the unfairness inherent in a funding arrangement which has the consequence that, if the claim succeeds, the funders will be reimbursed out of costs which the claimant will recover from him but that, if the claim fails, he will not recover his costs from the funders. But that is a feature inherent also in a conditional fee agreement. And it is accepted that it is in the public interest to facilitate access to justice by an agreement which has that effect. Indeed, it is accepted that it remains in the public interest to fund litigation by that means notwithstanding that the other party to the proceedings – usually a defendant – is exposed to the risk of liability for the uplifted fees payable under the conditional fee agreement if the claim succeeds.
>
> 70. For my part I can see no difference in principle, in the context of facilitating access to justice, between the lawyer who provides his services pro bono or under a conditional fee arrangement, the expert (say an accountant, a valuer or a medical practitioner) who provides his services on a no win no fee basis and the supporter who – having no skill which he can offer in kind – provides support in the form of funding to meet the fees of those who have. In each case the provision of support – whether in kind or in cash – facilitates access to justice by enabling the impecunious claimant to meet the defendant on an equal footing.

A change of great significance in the court's assessment as to what should and what should not be unlawful on grounds both of maintenance and champerty is that a court no longer approaches this issue as thought it is a matter of the automatic application of public policy. Rather, the court will consider all the relevant factors to determine whether there would be some real prejudice to justice in the instant case (see further at **12.2**).

Champerty

As to champerty, described by Lord Mustill in *Giles* v. *Thompson* [1994] 1 AC 142, 161 as a form of maintenance to which 'there must be added the notion of a division of spoils', this has always been inimical to the notions of justice as a pronounced by the judges of England and Wales. In *In re Trepca Mines Ltd (No.2)* [1963] Ch 199, 219–20, Lord Denning MR provided a succinct explanation of the courts' aversion to champerty:

> The reason why the common law condemns champerty is because of the abuses to which it may give rise. The common law fears that the champertous maintainer might be tempted, for his own personal gain, to inflame the damages, to suppress evidence, or even to suborn witnesses.

Indeed the prohibition against champertous retainers has always been particularly strongly expressed because of the special position of solicitors. See for instance the condemnations by Lord Denning MR in two subsequent cases. The first is taken from *Wallersteiner* v. *Moir (No.2)* [1975] QB 373, 393:

13

English law has never sanctioned an agreement by which a lawyer is remunerated on the basis of a 'contingency fee', that is that he gets paid the fee if he wins, but not if he loses. Such an agreement was illegal on the ground that it was the offence of champerty.

The second is from *Trendtex Trading Corporation* v. *Credit Suisse* [1980] QB 629, 654:

[Champerty] exists when the maintainer seeks to make a profit out of another man's action – by taking the proceeds of it, or a part of them, for himself. Modern public policy condemns champerty in a lawyer whenever he seeks to recover – not only his proper costs – but also a portion of the damages for himself: or when he conducts a case on the basis that he is to be paid if he wins but not if he loses.

These pronouncements by Lord Denning MR were applied in *British Waterways Board* v. *Norman* (1993) 26 HLR 232 (DC) and in *Aratra Potato Co Ltd* v. *Taylor Joynson Garrett* [1995] 4 All ER 695 (in which the solicitors agreed to waive 20 per cent of their fees in unsuccessful cases).

Thai Trading

On 27 February 1998 the Court of Appeal caused great excitement in *Thai Trading Co* v. *Taylor* [1998] QB 781 when it held that both *Wallersteiner* and *Trendtex* had been wrongly decided and that a retainer by which a solicitor agreed to act for his client (his wife) without a fee if she lost was not unlawful on grounds of public policy (see Millett LJ at 790):

Where the solicitor contracts for a reward over and above his proper fees if he wins, it may well be that the whole retainer is unlawful and the solicitor can recover nothing. But where he contracts for no more than his proper fees if he wins, this result does not follow. There is nothing unlawful in the retainer or in the client's obligation to pay the solicitor's proper costs if he wins the case.

In this action (fought over a bed worth some £2,500) Millett LJ considered it 'fanciful to suppose that a solicitor will be tempted to compromise his professional integrity because he will be unable to recover his ordinary profit costs in a small case if the case is lost'. The court was influenced by the recent passage of the Courts and Legal Services Act 1990 which showed, so the judge thought, that:

the fear that lawyers may be tempted by having a financial incentive in the outcome of litigation to act improperly is exaggerated, and that there is a countervailing public policy in making justice readily accessible to persons of modest means.

Excitement caused by *Thai Trading* was short-lived. Orthodoxy returned as a result of the Divisional Court's ruling in *Hughes* v. *Kingston upon Hull City*

Council [1999] QB 1193, which decided that the Court of Appeal had been in error in *Thai Trading* because the Solicitors' Practice Rules in force at the time of that decision did indeed prohibit CFAs, and moreover the Court of Appeal had failed to observe that the Practice Rules have the force of statute (*Swain* v. *The Law Society* [1983] 1 AC 598). This decision was supported by another Divisional Court in *Leeds City Council* v. *Carr* [2000] Env LR 522. Then, in *Awwad* v. *Geraghty* [2001] QB 570, the Court of Appeal decided that a retainer dated 1993 which provided that the client would pay the solicitor's standard fees in the event of success but a lower rate of fees in the event of failure was indeed contrary to public policy. All the factors operating in favour of, and against, the retainer in question were considered by the court (at 588–9), which ultimately was not at all sanguine about the absence of risks connected with a conditional arrangement since such an agreement 'does expose him to temptations to which he would not be exposed if he had not entered into it'. As to the Courts and Legal Services Act 1990, those judges who expressed a view about the matter considered that in such a fiercely contested area it was for Parliament to determine what should be and what should not be contrary to public policy without parallel intervention by the judges (see Schiemann LJ at 593 and May LJ at 600).

No quantum meruit entitlement where a retainer is champertous

The Court of Appeal in *Awwad's* case, in one very short paragraph, went on finally to settle the position that where a lawyer's retainer is unlawful because it is champertous and therefore unlawful, then there are no grounds for the lawyer to recover any fees at all, even on a *quantum meruit* basis (at 596):

> If the court, for reasons of public policy refuses to enforce an agreement that a solicitor should be paid it must follow that he cannot claim on a *quantum meruit*.

The court was not impressed by comparisons with *Mohamed* v. *Alaga & Co* [2000] 1 WLR 1815. In that case an interpreter entered into an agreement with a solicitor for the payment of a share of the legal aid fees which were earned by the solicitors as a result of the introduction of Somali clients introduced by the interpreter. Notwithstanding the unenforceability of this arrangement, the interpreter was entitled to remuneration for the services he provided under the agreement including his translations and interpretations.

The Solicitors' Practice Rules and Solicitors' Code of Conduct 2007

Something should be said finally in this introductory chapter about the legislation governing solicitors. By Solicitors Act 1974, s.31(1):

> the Council [of the Law Society] may . . . make rules, with the concurrence of the Master of the Rolls, for regulating in respect of any matter the professional practice, conduct and discipline of solicitors . . .

The Solicitors' Practice Rules 1990, rule 8(1) states:

> A solicitor who is retained or employed to prosecute or defend any action, suit or other contentious proceeding shall not enter into any arrangement to receive a contingency fee in respect of that proceeding, save one permitted under statute or by the common law.

And as from 1 July 2007 the Solicitors' Code of Conduct 2007, rule 2.04(1) contains the following:

> You must not enter into an arrangement to receive a contingency fee for work done in prosecuting or defending any contentious proceedings before a court of England and Wales, a British court martial or an arbitrator where the seat of the arbitration is in England and Wales, except as permitted by statute or the common law.

Rule 18(2) of the Practice Rules set out various definitions including a definition of 'contingency fee' under rule 18(2)(c):

> any sum (whether fixed, or calculated either as a percentage of the proceeds or otherwise howsoever) payable only in the event of success . . .

This provision is now reproduced in rule 24.01 of the Solicitors' Code of Conduct 2007.

The effect of these rules is expressly to prohibit a solicitor from entering into a differential fee arrangement to govern contentious business which is not a conditional fee agreement sanctioned by statute.

PART II

CFA law and practice

CHAPTER 2

The regulatory framework

2.1 INTRODUCTION

This chapter is intended to chart the development of the statutory provisions governing CFAs since they first became possible on 5 July 1995. This is, therefore, mainly a narrative, or historical, account of the regulatory framework established by the Courts and Legal Services Act 1990 in its original form and as amended by the Access to Justice Act 1999, although explanations will be provided as to some of the key underlying policy considerations. These statements of policy made by both government and the courts can be extremely useful in considering challenges made to CFA retainers and in understanding the extent to which additional liabilities are recoverable.

It is important to note that this chapter needs to be considered in conjunction with **Chapters 3** and **4**, which examine the recoverability of additional liabilities (in **Chapter 3**) and enforceability (**Chapter 4**). For a detailed consideration of the legislative provisions, in particular of the meaning and effect of s.58 and of the CFA Regulations 2000 (which continue even now to be the subject of many challenges designed to demonstrate the unenforceability of CFAs) it will be necessary to turn to **Chapter 4**. **Chapter 4** also considers the enforceability of collective CFAs (CCFAs) in some detail.

As to the interpretation and effect of Access to Justice Act 1999, s.29 (recovery of insurance premiums), the reader is directed to **Chapter 3** and also to the practical guidance on insurance given in **Chapter 11**.

Section 30 of the Access to Justice Act 1999 ('recovery where body undertakes to meet costs liabilities') is concerned with the provision by which prescribed bodies (such as trade unions and other membership organisations) can recover notional insurance premiums. This chapter also looks at the mechanisms in place by which a membership organisation receives the requisite 'prescribed' status in order for it to be able to recover these valuable amounts, as well as the principles governing their recoverability (see **2.12**).

2.2 THE STATUTORY SCHEMES IN OUTLINE

Introduction

Section 58 of the Courts and Legal Services Act 1990 first made it possible to permit litigation funding by means of the use of CFAs. In 1995 their use was sanctioned in proceedings concerning personal injury, insolvency and bankruptcy, and also under the European Convention on Human Rights where proceedings were commenced in Strasbourg. A second Order which came into force in 1998 sanctioned the use of CFAs in all matters (save for criminal and family proceedings). A detailed account of these early developments is set out below (see **2.3**).

Recovery of additional liabilities from paying parties

The principal characteristic of these early arrangements was that there was no mechanism which allowed success fees or after-the-event (ATE) premiums to be recovered from the losing side. This changed after the coming into force of the Access to Justice Act 1999, which substituted a replacement s.58, and inserted a new s.58A into the Courts and Legal Services Act 1990 and which by ss.29 and 30 allowed ATE premiums (and the equivalent in the case of membership organisations) to be recovered from the paying party. A new set of regulations was created in 2000 (and amended in 2003 primarily to accommodate 'simplified' CFAs and CCFAs), and additional costs rules were introduced into the Civil Procedure Rules (CPR) which provided the means by which 'additional liabilities' (uplifts and ATE premiums and their equivalents) could be recovered (see **2.5** and **2.6**).

'Trench warfare'

The changes brought about by the Access to Justice Act 1999 instigated the fierce trench warfare which will continue to rage until at least the time at which those CFAs which were entered into prior to the revocation of the CFA Regulations 2000 have come to an end (i.e. those Access to Justice Act CFAs which were entered into prior to 1 November 2005).

The effect of the revocation of the CFA Regulations 2000

Since the revocation of the CFA Regulations 2000 with effect from 1 November 2005 (as a result of the Conditional Fee Agreements (Revocation) Regulations 2005, SI 2005/2305), solicitors and their clients intending to work on CFA terms only have the conditions set out in the Act itself about which to be concerned. The client care provisions which – even prior to the enactment of the Access to Justice Act 1999 – many had thought would be best left to the internal discipline of solicitor regulation, are now solely within the ambit of the regulatory machinery, and should no longer be available for costly scrutiny by paying parties.

Why the Courts and Legal Services Act 1990 was necessary

In both of its forms (whether pre- or post-Access to Justice Act 1999) s.58 renders lawful what would otherwise, at common law, be unlawful champertous arrangements. At the risk of covering too much ground which is repeated elsewhere in this book (in particular in **Chapter 1**), s.58 achieves this end in both cases by stating that a CFA 'shall not be unenforceable by reason only of its being a conditional fee agreement' (see s.58(3) in the original section and s.58(1) in the substituted version). This wording prohibits a judge from declaring an agreement which complies with the statutory requirements unenforceable as a matter of public policy, the common law considering any fee arrangement which is contingent on success being prone to serious risks of abuse (see *In re Trepca Mines Ltd (No.2)* [1963] Ch 199, 219–20, Lord Denning MR):

> The common law fears that the champertous maintainer might be tempted, for his own personal gain, to inflame the damages, to suppress evidence, or even to suborn witnesses.

The protection of s.58 is required since without it there would necessarily be a breach of the indemnity principle: if a retainer is void and unenforceable, then a solicitor cannot compel his client to pay him anything, and a receiving party cannot recover in costs what he is not required to pay to his solicitor. This is also the effect of Solicitors Act 1974, s.60(3).

Failure to regulate against the risks to the administration of justice

As will be seen below, the statutory requirements set out in the various regulations which have been made are not concerned to any degree with the risks of interference with the administration of justice as perceived by the common law courts (for instance, by Lord Denning in *In re Trepca Mines* as set out above), but almost entirely with matters of consumer protection. No provision was made by Parliament in respect of the risks which the judges perceived might compromise the course of justice – these were simply ignored.

No change in the common law as a result of the Access to Justice Act 1999

Notwithstanding the fact that Parliament did not address the concerns of judges held over the centuries when it permitted conditional fee agreements (suggesting that Parliament does not perceive them to carry those risks), the judges have felt it impossible to hold that public policy has changed and that the protection expressly afforded by s.58(1) is no longer required to render a conditional retainer lawful (see *Awwad* v. *Geraghty* and **1.1** above).

2.3   THE ORIGINAL SCHEME OF THE COURTS AND LEGAL SERVICES ACT 1990

The change in the law permitting the use of conditional fees was first set out in the Lord Chancellor's Department's Green Paper *Contingency Fees* (January 1989, HMSO Cmnd 571). The perception was that the law was the preserve of the poor (who were eligible for legal aid) or for the well-off and that a system of conditional fees would facilitate increased access to the courts. Indeed the implementation of a system of funding by way of conditional fee agreements is consistent with the 'general objective' of the 1990 Act set out in s.17(1):

> 17(1) The general objective of this Part is the development of legal services in England and Wales (and in particular the development of . . . litigation . . . services) by making provision for new or better ways of providing such services and a wider choice of persons providing them, while maintaining the proper and efficient administration of justice.

This section is still relevant today in the post-Access to Justice Act regime.

The White Paper which followed the original Green Paper in July 1989 went on to announce the government's proposal to 'remove the existing prohibitions to enable clients to agree with any or all of their lawyers payment of a conditional fee on the speculative basis already permitted in Scotland'.

The mechanism by which CFA funding is rendered lawful

Section 58 of the Courts and Legal Services Act 1990, which first permitted the use of CFAs, came into force, therefore, on 1 October 1993 as a direct result of the 1989 White Paper. It set out key provisions in s.58 itself, but left other important provisions to be determined by statutory instrument. The mechanism by which CFAs became part of the litigation funding landscape in England and Wales was the statutory declaration prohibiting judges from declaring such agreements unenforceable. If the prohibition did not exist, then conditional fee retainers would be unenforceable on public policy grounds since they represent a clear breach of the rule against champerty.

This is explained in detail in **Chapter 1** at **1.1–1.3**. Section 58(1) provided that an enforceable CFA had to comply with any requirements made by the Lord Chancellor (s.58(1)(c)).

The ambit and extent of CFA funding

Section 58 went on to allow the Lord Chancellor to make provision by secondary legislation for CFAs to be used in 'specified proceedings' (s.58(3)), defined by s.58(4) as 'proceedings of a description specified by order made by the Lord Chancellor for the purposes of subsection (3)'. The statute expressly prohibited their use in all criminal proceedings and in most family proceedings (s.58(1)(a), (10)). By para.2(2) of the Conditional Fee Agreements Order 1995 (see below) Parliament ensured that litigation services supplied before the issue of a Claim Form would be remunerated under a CFA even if the case settles before the Claim Form is issued.

Conditional Fee Agreements Order 1995

The first Order which went on to specify those proceedings which could be funded by way of a CFA was the Conditional Fee Agreements Order 1995, SI 1995/1674 which came into force on 5 July 1995. The effect of the Order was to allow CFAs to be used in proceedings concerning personal injury (personal injury being defined to include 'any disease and any impairment of a person's physical or mental condition'), various insolvency and bankruptcy proceedings, and proceedings before the European Commission or European Court of Human Rights. The Order is set out at **Appendix 2**.

Conditional Fee Agreements Order 1998

A second Order, the Conditional Fee Agreements Order 1998, SI 1998/1860 came into force on 30 July 1998. By this Order the 1995 Order was revoked and 'all proceedings' were expressed to be specified proceedings for the purposes of s.58 of the 1990 Act (para.3(1)). Section 58(10) of the 1990 Act of course made it impossible for 'all proceedings' to encompass either criminal proceedings or the family proceedings listed in that subsection. This Order is set out at **Appendix 2**.

CFAs and arbitrations

In *Bevan Ashford* v. *Geoff Yeandle (Contractors) Ltd (In Liquidation)* the Vice Chancellor was faced with the question whether or not a case which was to be concluded by way of arbitration could be concluded by an enforceable CFA. He held that arbitration proceedings could not be brought within the definition of 'specified proceedings', reasoning as follows (245F–H):

Section 119(1) of the Act of 1990 contains a number of important definitions. 'Advocacy services' and 'litigation services' are defined so as to be limited to services 'in relation to any proceedings, or contemplated proceedings.' And 'proceedings' means 'proceedings in any court.' It seems to me to be clear from these definitions, first, that section 58 of the Courts and Legal Services Act 1990 does not apply to advocacy services or litigation services in relation to proceedings that are not 'proceedings in court' and, second, that 'specified proceedings' in subsection (3) means proceedings in court of a description specified by order made by the Lord Chancellor. It follows, in my opinion, that section 58 of the Act of 1990 does not apply to advocacy services or litigation services in relation to arbitration proceedings. Arbitration proceedings can properly be described as litigation but are not proceedings in court.

The judge went on to decide, however, that although ostensibly champertous, there was no reason why such an agreement should be declared unenforceable as a matter of public policy (251H–252A):

> if a conditional fee agreement relating to a particular cause of action is sanctioned for proceedings in court by section 58 of the Act of 1990 and by the Order of 1995 and the Regulations of 1995, the conditional fee agreement is free from any public policy objection in relation to arbitration proceedings in pursuance of that cause of action.

A new s.58A subsequently inserted into the 1990 Act by Access to Justice Act 1999, s.27 redefined 'proceedings' so that 'it includes any sort of proceedings for resolving disputes (and not just proceedings in a court)' (s.58A(6)). The circumstances of *Bevan Ashford*'s case now have statutory approval.

The uplift

By s.58(5), the statutory instrument which was to prescribe those proceedings which might be funded by a CFA could also state the maximum permitted percentage by which the fees of each class of specified proceedings could be increased. By s.58(6), if the maximum permitted uplift was exceeded, then the CFA would remain unenforceable. Section 58(8) expressly prevented a costs order made against a paying party from including an element to reflect the percentage increase.

The maximum permitted uplift was 100 per cent in all classes of proceedings covered first by the original 1995 and then the 1998 Orders (see para.3 of each). The success fee came out of a client's damages, but voluntary arrangements observed by both branches of the lawyers' professions meant that the amount of the deduction was capped at 25 per cent.

The CFA Regulations 1995

In addition to the Orders made under s.58(4) of the 1990 Act, a set of regulations, namely the Conditional Fee Agreement Regulations 1995, SI 1995/1675, was brought into force on the same date as the first Order (5 July 1995). Made under s.58(1), these Regulations expressly stated that an agreement which did not comply with their requirements would not be a CFA within the meaning of the Act (the effect of reg.2). Foreshadowing the difficulties caused by the CFA Regulations 2000, the requirements of a CFA are set out in reg.3 in mandatory form. That is to say that by reg.3 a CFA '*shall* state' the various matters which follow, including the proceedings to which the CFA relates (reg.3(a)), the 'circumstances in which the legal representative's fees and expenses or part of them are to be payable' (reg.3(b)), and what payment is due in other circumstances (including on partial failure and on termination) (see reg.3(c)). By reg.4 a solicitor was required to 'draw the client's attention' to other specified matters, namely whether the client might be entitled to legal aid and any conditions which might attach to that legal aid, the circumstances in which the client may have to meet either his own legal representative's, or his opponent's, costs, and the circumstances in which the client might obtain an assessment of his own legal representative's costs. By reg.3(c) this regulation did not apply to a CFA between two legal representatives (i.e. barrister and solicitor). By reg.6 a statutory CFA had to be in writing and signed by the parties (again this provision did not apply to a CFA between two lawyers), and by reg.7 all of the requirements relating to the original CFA had to be observed all over again if it is extended to other proceedings. See **Appendix 2**.

2.4   TRANSITIONAL ARRANGEMENTS PRIOR TO THE ACCESS TO JUSTICE ACT 1999 REFORMS

Introduction

The continuation of the CFA programme was the result of the Access to Justice Act 1999, the effect of which was that the success fee and the cost of the provision of ATE insurance were to become recoverable from the losing side. Difficulties were perceived to exist in the sudden transfer of funding arrangements from non-recoverable instruments on to CFAs where uplifts (and also premiums) might then become payable by defendants who would not have made provision for their potential recovery at the commencement of proceedings. In order to prevent this, transitional provisions were put in place.

Additional transitional arrangements was necessary because of the time lag between the coming into force of the Access to Justice Act provisions on 1 April 2000 (after which new-style CFAs could be entered into) and the provisions in the CPR which allowed for the recovery of additional liabilities. These were only brought into force on 3 July 2000 by virtue of the Civil Procedure (Amendment No.3) Rules 2000, SI 2000/1317 and were incorporated into the CPR by Update 16. The different transitional provisions are summarised at rules 57.8(1) and 57.9(1) of the Costs Practice Direction, section 57. The following sections provide further detail.

Transitional arrangements required to stop claimants claiming additional liabilities for which defendants had not had an opportunity to make provision

First, as to the provisions which made it impossible to convert an old-style CFA into a post-Access to Justice Act CFA, these were comprehensive. They are contained in the Access to Justice (Transitional Provisions) Order 2000, SI 2000/900 which came into force on 1 April 2000. This Order made it impossible (by para.2(1)) for a lawyer to transfer the funding of proceedings which had already been issued on to a CFA which provided for a recoverable success fee (see Sumner J in *Cowley* v. *Merseyside Regional Ambulance Service NHS Trust* [2003] EWHC 250 (Fam), 28 February 2003). It also provided (by para.2(2)) that CFAs entered into before 1 April 2000 would continue to have effect as though a new s.58 had not been inserted into the 1999 Act (preserving the enforceability of old-style arrangements). At the same time, by CPR Part 51, rules 51.1A and 51PD.18, any assessment of costs taking place after 26 April 1999 (the date of the commencement of the CPR) would be in accordance with CPR Parts 43–8.

Transitional arrangements required as a result of the delay in introducing the CPR

The second species of transitional provisions required by the CPR were contained in the Civil Procedure (Amendment No.3) Rules 2000, SI 2000/1317. CFAs had been left in limbo after they were introduced by the Access to Justice Act and related statutory materials, since no rules governing recoverability were in force until 3 July 2000 when the Amendment No.3 Rules amended the CPR and incorporated the bulk of the rules which exist today. Paragraph 39 of the same statutory instrument gave solicitors who had already entered into new-style CFAs and who had also commenced proceedings by 3 July 2000 until 31 July 2000 to comply with the new rules. In practice this meant that they had to comply with the requirement to provide information about funding arrangements as set out in CPR 44.15 and the accompanying part of the Costs Practice Direction.

2.5 CFAs AND OTHER FUNDING ARRANGEMENTS AFTER THE ACCESS TO JUSTICE ACT 1999 – POLICY CONSIDERATIONS

The rationale for the Access to Justice Act 1999 changes

The main purpose of this oddly named Act was the creation of the Legal Services Commission to replace the Legal Aid Board, the government intending for the first time to cap the budget available to fund the provision of public legal services. The net result was the effective removal of legal aid altogether from large categories of legal services and from ever greater numbers of people. The decline in spending provision on legal aid continues apace to the present day. Its effect is particularly keenly felt in civil proceedings, the criminal legal aid budget having been ring-fenced because of concerns arising out of the effect of the European Convention on Human Rights.

The lengthy Access to Justice Act 1999 (which runs to 110 sections and 15 dense schedules) included a modest five sections dealing with CFA funding. The government's stated aim in introducing these sections and in the development of CFA funding was to increase access to the courts with the apparent belief that it could do so while reforming legal aid. The perception was that lawyers had been keen to advocate the use of legal aid because they were paid win or lose, and that it would benefit a client to have the lawyer share the risks in the outcome. There is no expression that by sharing the risks there might be some concomitant risk to justice itself (see **1.1** above), no concern that by inviting lawyers to share the risks of litigation the lawyers might refuse to do so altogether if there was some real prospect that a case might be lost (for instance, because of the personal inadequacies of the client), and nothing to protect clients from the danger that a lawyer might be tempted to advise the acceptance of an unreasonably low offer to compromise an action in order to secure payment of his fees.

Developments and purposes in the regime as charted by senior judges

The history of CFAs has been set out in numerous authorities, including the Court of Appeal in *Callery* v. *Gray* [2001] 1 WLR 2112 and in *Hollins* v. *Russell* [2003] 1 WLR 2487. In *Callery* v. *Gray* [2002] 1 WLR 2000 at 2006E Lord Hoffmann described the Court of Appeal as 'traditionally and rightly responsible for supervising the administration of civil procedure', and it is to the Court of Appeal that we must look for accounts of the correct operation of the CFA scheme. However, Lords Bingham, Hoffmann and Hope in *Callery*'s case and Lord Hoffmann again in *Campbell* v. *MGN* [2005] 1 WLR 3394 did provide their own explanations of the development of CFAs, Lord Hope tracing the new post-Access to Justice scheme back to a September

1999 consultation paper from the LCD, 'Conditional Fees: Sharing the Risks of Litigation'.

Consultation papers

Ultimately, however, the reason for the use of recoverable success fees in all forms of civil litigation probably goes back to an LCD consultation paper dated March 1998: 'Access to Justice with Conditional Fees'. Some of the principal paragraphs give a true flavour of government's thinking:

> 1.2. A huge swathe of ordinary people on modest incomes are deterred from starting a legal action by the potential costs of litigation – their own costs, and the risk of ending up paying the costs of the other side. That is why the Government has embarked on a programme of wide ranging reform of the system to make it quicker, simpler and more certain.
>
> 1.3. The current system does not encourage lawyers – who are paid the same, win, lose or draw – to weed out weak cases. This means that too many people undergo the strain of lengthy legal disputes for nothing.
>
> 1.4. At the same time the cost of the Legal Aid Fund goes up and up. Net expenditure in 1990–91 was £682 million. Only six years later, expenditure had more than doubled to £1,477 million. That is an increase of 115%. On civil alone the cost has almost tripled.
>
> 1.5. This Government was elected with a modernising agenda, and there could be no clearer case for radical reform than Legal Aid. When it was set up 50 years ago, it was a great step forward. It brought the opportunity of access to justice within the reach of the majority of the population. Now it is failing the people it was supposed to help, and stands in the way of the modernisation of the legal profession and the justice system as a whole.
>
> 1.6. That is why the Lord Chancellor, Lord Irvine, has announced a radical programme of reform to achieve change. The programme will be delivered in two stages. This paper looks at the first stage. The Government intends to: promote access to justice for the majority of the population in England and Wales through the wider availability of conditional fee agreements. This will make access to the courts a reality for the majority of the population of England and Wales. Conditional fees ensure that the risks of litigation are shared between the lawyer and the client: clients do not pay their lawyers fees unless they win; and lawyers, when they win, receive a level of fees that recognises the risk they have taken.

Legal aid was therefore largely withdrawn apparently in order to promote access to justice, and recoverable success fees were intended to encourage lawyers to share the risks of litigation with their clients. Quite how the provision of legal aid stood in the way of modernisation of justice, and exactly what that modernisation may have been intended to be, does not admit of an obvious explanation. As to whether the experiment has been a success, it is a matter of some concern perhaps that the Civil Justice Council in its paper 'Improved Access to Justice – Funding Options & Proportionate Costs' (June 2007) has identified a 'sandwich class' of litigant who is 'somewhat above legal aid eligibility limits' and 'does not have effective access to other funding mechanisms' (paras.62(b) and 66).

Shifting the burden of meeting claimants' costs from the government to defence insurers and ultimately to the premium-paying public

The burden of paying a receiving party's success fee under the new regime is a burden ultimately borne by unsuccessful defendants. This process was achieved in part by changes to the statutory scheme brought about by the Access to Justice Act 1999 and various statutory instruments (as described below), but also by important changes to court rules which permitted recovery of additional liabilities (success fees and insurance premiums). The court rules which permit recovery of these additional liabilities are described in **Chapter 3**.

The overall effect on unsuccessful defendants is set out by the Court of Appeal in *Callery* v. *Gray* [2001] 1 WLR 2112 at para.93:

> Including success fees in recoverable costs has the general effect of shifting from the legal aid fund to defendants, or their insurers, the costs incurred by litigants whose claims fail. In the first instance the claimants' solicitors shoulder the risks in relation to these costs, in exchange for uplift. But the fact that the uplift in successful cases is transferred to unsuccessful defendants results, if one takes a global view, in the burden of unsuccessful claimants' costs being [borne] by unsuccessful defendants.

Lord Hoffmann in the House of Lords at [2002] 1 WLR 2000, para.31, described this as 'a perfectly rational social and economic policy'.

A concomitant desire on the part of defence insurers to fight back

This change in policy, transferring the burden of having to pay for unsuccessful cases from the taxpayer to liability defendants (and their premium-paying public), led to an understandable interest by paying parties in seeing whether they might pray in aid the consumer protection provisions of the statutory regime which were intended to protect the receiving parties so that they might avoid meeting their ordinary costs obligations. As it was put in *Hollins* v. *Russell* [2003] 1 WLR 2487 at paras.22–3:

> 22. Defendant liability insurers, who have viewed with disfavour the increased financial burden imposed on them by a combination of the 'front-end loading' of the Woolf reforms and the new liability to pay ATE premiums and success fees to successful claimants pursuant to other provisions contained in Part II of the 1999 Act, have seized the opportunity of challenging the enforceability of many CFAs by pointing to breaches of one or more of the 'conditions applicable to it'. They argued that, even if they only succeeded in establishing a single breach, they could escape liability to pay any of the costs (and possibly also the disbursements) that were referable to

the unenforceable CFA. In other words, it is not only the solicitor's success fee which is at risk, but the cost of all the solicitor's services (or the services of counsel, if rendered under an enforceable CFA), which may on occasion run to many thousands of pounds.

23. Liability insurers were able to take this course through the operation of the indemnity principle (for which see *Harold v Smith* 5 H&N 381, 385; *Gundry v Sainsbury* [1910] 1 KB 645, 649 and 653; and *General of Berne Insurance Co Ltd v Jardine Reinsurance Management Ltd* [1998] 1 WLR 1231).

The heady effect of the combination of the rule against champerty and the indemnity principle resulting in the ability to avoid totally any liability to pay costs is explained variously in this chapter and in **Chapter 1**.

2.6   CFAs AFTER THE ACCESS TO JUSTICE ACT 1999 – LEGISLATIVE MATERIAL

Courts and Legal Services Act 1990, ss.58, 58A (as substituted and inserted by Access to Justice Act 1999, s.27) and the CFA Order 2000

A new s.58 of the Courts and Legal Services Act 1990 was substituted by s.27 of the Access to Justice Act 1999 and supplemented by a new s.58A (also by reason of s.27 of the 1999 Act), and these provisions were brought into force on 1 April 2000. These two sections together expanded the provisions previously contained in the original s.58, which rendered conditional fee arrangements lawful.

As has been pointed out elsewhere, s.58(1) acts as a statutory prohibition against judges declaring a CFA unenforceable so long as the agreement 'satisfies all of the conditions applicable to it'. What is meant by that expression and the extent to which non-compliance with the provisions of subsections (3) and (4) and the conditions to which they refer can render a CFA unlawful on the grounds of non-compliance are set out in detail in **Chapter 4**. In summary, however, in *Hollins* v. *Russell* [2003] 1 WLR 2387 the Court of Appeal decided that (para.107):

> The key question, therefore, is whether the conditions applicable to the CFA by virtue of section 58 of the 1990 Act have been sufficiently complied with in the light of their purposes. Costs judges should accordingly ask themselves the following question: 'Has the particular departure from a regulation pursuant to section 58(3)(c) of the 1990 Act or a requirement in section 58, either on its own or in conjunction with any other such departure in this case, had a materially adverse effect either upon the protection afforded to the client or upon the proper administration of justice?' If the answer is 'yes' the conditions have not been satisfied. If the answer is 'no' then the departure is immaterial and (assuming that there is no other reason to conclude otherwise) the conditions have been satisfied.

The question whether a breach represents a material departure is entirely fact-specific and it is not helpful to consider whether there has been a breach solely by reference to adjectival phrases such as 'trivial' or 'technical'.

Section 58(2)(a) sets out a definition as to what a CFA is. If a paying party can bring an agreement within that definition then it will be unenforceable if the conditions of s.58 are not satisfied (see the attempt to elevate a retainer letter to the status of CFA in *Gaynor* v. *Central West London Buses Limited* [2007] 1 WLR 1045).

The meaning of s.58(3)(a) is clear: a CFA must be in writing.

The proceedings which 'cannot be the subject of an enforceable conditional fee agreement' for the purposes of s.58(3)(b) are those proceedings described in s.58A(1), (2). These are all criminal proceedings (save for those brought under the Environmental Protection Act 1990, s.82) and most types of family proceedings.

Section 58(3)(c) is in effect a reference to the contents of the CFA Regulations 2000 (as amended), which are considered further below and at **4.3**. See also s.58A(3), which at 58A(3)(c) allows the Lord Chancellor to make different arrangements in respect of different descriptions of CFAs. This is a power which could be used to set up different regulations for different classes of proceedings. These could be used to accommodate the legitimate ends of litigants in disparate fields. The balance of what is acceptable between the parties in media cases, for instance (where freedom of speech is enshrined in the European Convention on Human Rights) may be very different from that appropriate in standard personal injury litigation.

Section 58(4) concerns only those CFAs which make provision for the recovery of a success fee, and s.58(4)(a) allows the Lord Chancellor by order to place a limit on which categories of proceedings can be permitted to make provision for any uplift. The relevant Order to date continues (even after the Revocation Regulations have come into force) to be the CFA Order 2000, SI 2000/823. This allows (by para.3) an uplift to be recovered on any class of proceedings save for proceedings under Environmental Protection Act 1990, s.82. The same Order (by para.4) specifies the maximum percentage by which base fees can be increased for the purposes of s.58(4)(c): it is 100 per cent in respect of all categories of proceedings.

Section 58(4)(b) expressly requires a CFA to state the percentage uplift payable on a solicitor's base fees.

Section 58(5) allows a non-contentious business agreement to be enforceable without having to comply with the conditions of s.58. 'Contentious business' is defined by the Solicitors Act 1974, s.87 as 'business done, whether as solicitor or advocate . . . in or for the purposes of proceedings begun before a court or before an arbitrator not being business which falls within the definition of a non-contentious or common form probate business contained in s.128 of the Supreme Court Act 1981'. All business done prior to the commencement of proceedings if it was done with a view to the commencement of those proceedings and they were in fact commenced is considered to be contentious business (*In re Simpkin Marshall Limited* [1959] Ch 229). The definition of s.58(A)(4) is important in this context.

By s.58A(4) 'proceedings' includes 'any sort of proceedings for resolving disputes (and not just proceedings in a court) whether commenced or contemplated' (for instance, the Claims Handling Agreement at the centre of VWF litigation). This reverses the effect of *Bevan Ashford* v. *Geoff Yeandle (Contractors) Ltd* [1999] Ch 239. Solicitors must be cautious to make sure that they are entitled to enter into non-contentious business agreements given the statutory definitions of 'proceedings' in s.119 of the 1990 Act and the extended meaning of 'proceedings' in s.58A(4).

Section 58A(6), (7) allows a costs order in any proceedings to include provision for the payment of a success fee and allow rules of court to be made which govern the recoverability of costs due under CFAs. The recoverability of such costs is considered in detail in **Chapter 3**.

The CFA Regulations 2000

The CFA Regulations 2000, SI 2000/692 came into force on 1 April 2000 and were made by the Lord Chancellor in the exercise of his powers under the Courts and Legal Services Act 1990, ss.58(3)(c), 58A(3) and 119. These Regulations contain a body of client care provisions which were otherwise contained within the Solicitors' Costs Information and Client Care Code 1999 dated 3 September 1999 (and subsequently amended from time to time) and made under the Solicitors' Practice Rules, rule 15 ('Costs Information and Client Care'). See now the Solicitors' Code of Conduct 2007. It was the mandatory nature of the Regulations (the obligations on the part of the solicitor being expressed in terms of 'must' and 'shall') which led to such great interest on the part of paying parties as to compliance by claimants' legal representatives. The mixture of these mandatory conditions and the mandatory requirements of s.58(3), (4), which, when taken together with the wording of s.58(1), rendered any non-compliant CFA unenforceable, necessarily meant that no costs were payable under the retainer. This was because of the effect of the indemnity principle which allows a party to recover from an opponent only those costs which are required to be paid to the lawyer.

The 2000 Regulations were amended twice. The first occasion was by the CFA (Miscellaneous Amendments) Regulations 2003, SI 2003/1240 (which came into force on 2 June 2003), making express provision for a 'simplified' CFA, the purpose of which was to relieve the client of any liability for costs which could not be recovered from an opponent (save in the event of non-cooperation by the client and for similar conduct). These provisions (which inserted a reg.3A into the 2000 Regulations) are dealt with below under the heading 'Simplified CFAs' (see **2.8**) and are considered in detail in *Jones* v. *Wrexham B.C.* [2007] EWCA 1356, 19 December 2007. They have the distinct advantage in that reg.4 (as well as regs.2 and 3) had no application, rendering the possibility of challenges much less likely. The second set of amendments was contained in the CFA (Miscellaneous Amendments) (No.2) Regulations 2003, SI 2003/3344 (which came into force on 2 February 2004), and made some amendments to the Simplified CFA regime (further considered below).

The enforceability of a CFA subject to the 2000 Regulations and the meaning and effect of those individual regulations which have been the subject of judicial scrutiny are the subjects of **Chapter 4**. In the following paragraphs a brief outline will be set out as to the contents of the individual regulations. The 2000 Regulations are now revoked by the Conditional Fee Agreements (Revocation) Regulations 2005, SI 2005/2305 (see **2.9**).

The individual regulations in outline

Regulation 1(3) makes it clear that a 'client' for the purpose of CFA arrangements includes either the person giving instructions or a person who has agreed to indemnify the fees incurred by that person. It also defines 'legal representative' as the person providing advocacy or litigation services. This means the firm of solicitors acting for the client. A CFA should be signed in the name of the firm rather than the individual fee earner.

Regulation 2 set out the general requirements for the contents of CFAs. These set out the core provisions that a CFA must make it clear to the client the circumstances in which payment of the solicitor's fees and expenses are to be paid in relation to the proceedings covered by the CFA. Regulation 2(1)(c) expressly requires the CFA to set out what payment is due (i) in the event of partial success, (ii) in any event, (iii) on termination. Regulation 2(1)(d) was the subject of discussion by the courts during the process of enforceability challenges and is dealt with in **Chapter 4.** Finally, this regulation requires any agreement to which reg.4 applies ('Information to be given before conditional fee agreements made') to contain a statement confirming that reg.4 has been observed.

Regulation 3 set out the 'Requirements for contents of conditional fee agreements providing for success fees'.

Regulation 3(1)(a) requires the reasons why an uplift has been set at the percentage stated in the CFA to be expressly rehearsed in the agreement. This is for the purpose of ascertaining the reasonableness of the claim to the particular success fee by the application of the factors set out in CPR rule 44.5 as further explained by CPD, s.11 (see **3.6**).

Regulation 3(1)(b) necessitates a recital in the CFA what element of the percentage uplift 'relates to the cost to the legal representative of the postponement of the payment of his fees and expenses'. This regulation is concerned with the proper application of CPR rule 44.3B(a) which prohibits a party from recovering the 'postponement' element of the uplift.

The effect of reg.3(2)(a) is to ensure that any risk assessment by which a percentage uplift is calculated can be disclosed (either by a client or his solicitor) at a costs assessment.

Regulation 3(2)(b) ensures that a solicitor cannot recover any part of an uplift which is disallowed in a claim against an opposing party on the grounds that it is 'unreasonable' under CPR rule 44.5 unless the solicitor makes an application to the Court under CPR rule 44.16 for the disallowed part to be paid by the client (see **3.4**).

Regulation 3(2)(c) ostensibly contains a corresponding provision to reg.3(2)(b) in the event that there is a compromise with a receiving party. This was the conclusion to which Master Hurst came in *Oyston* v. *Royal Bank of Scotland* plc (16 May 2006). Master Seager-Berry reached a different decision in *Ghannouchi* v. *Houni Ltd* (4 March 2004), holding that the wording of this regulation is wider than that of reg.3(2)(b) since it relates to the totality of a solicitor's fees and not just to the percentage uplift.

Regulation 4 has been the subject of very many extensive challenges and is considered in detail in **Chapter 4**. Regulation 4 represents the core of the client care provisions contained in the statutory instrument.

Regulation 5 requires a CFA to be signed by both the client and the solicitor. A CFA between solicitor and barrister, or between any two legal representatives, does not need to be signed (reg.5(2)).

Regulation 6 concerns amendments made to a CFA. In the event of an amendment, reg.6(a) states that regs.2, 3, 3A (in respect of a Simplified CFA) and reg.5 apply to the amended agreement, so that the amended documents must be drafted accordingly. By reg.6(b) the regulations under reg.4 must be gone over again if the effect of the amendments is such that it would be necessary to give the reg.4 client care information again.

2.7 COLLECTIVE CONDITIONAL FEE AGREEMENTS (CCFAs)

The CCFA Regulations 2000, SI 2000/2988 came into force on 30 November 2000. By reason of Courts and Legal Services Act 1990, s.3(3)(c) it was obligatory for an agreement which fell within the definition of a CCFA at reg.3(1)(b) to comply with the CCFA Regulations, reg.3(1)(b) stating as follows:

3(1) Subject to paragraph (2) of this regulation, a collective conditional fee agreement is an agreement which – . . .

(b) does not refer to specific proceedings, but provides for fees to be payable on a common basis in relation to a class of proceedings, or, if it refers to more than one class of proceedings, on a common basis in relation to each class.

Regulation 2 specified that the Regulations could not apply to agreements entered into before that date.

Regulation 3(1)(a) states that a CCFA is an 'agreement which ... disregarding section 58(3)(c) of the Courts and Legal Services Act 1990, would be a conditional fee agreement'. This cryptic wording appears to be the only hint that a CCFA might possibly be considered a different animal from an individual CFA. Both individual and collective agreements fall within the definition of Courts and Legal Services Act 1990, s.58(2)(a). Regulation 3(1)(a) was presumably an attempt to specify the CCFA Regulations, rather than the CFA Regulations, as the regulatory conditions which must be met in order for a collective conditional fee agreement to obtain the statutory protection conveyed to an otherwise champertous agreement by s.58(1). Save for reg.3(1)(a), neither the 1990 Act nor the Costs Rules distinguish between CFAs and CCFAs in any material degree. There is no reference to any such entity as a 'collective conditional fee agreement' in s.58(2) of the Courts and Legal Services Act 1990 (as inserted by the Access to Justice Act 1999).

An account of the theoretical basis for the validity of CCFAs based on previous case law protecting third party funding arrangement (going back to the trade union case of *Adams* v. *London Improved Motor Coach Builders Ltd* [1921] 1 KB 495 (CA)) will be found in **Chapter 4** at **4.4**.

The central requirement under reg.3(1)(b) is that a CCFA is an agreement which 'does not refer to specific proceedings, but provides for fees to be payable on a common basis in relation to a class of proceedings, or, if it refers to more than one class of proceedings, on a common basis in relation to each class'. It is important for the 'class of proceedings' to be clearly identified, but this is a matter of drafting and should not pose insuperable difficulties, even if it is intended that the CCFA should encompass all of the litigation of one particular funder.

The CCFA Regulations 2000 expressly provided that a collective agreement could be entered into whether or not the funder was a client (reg.3(2)(a)) and without the necessity to name any individual clients in the agreement (reg.3(2)).

As with individual arrangements under the CFA Regulations 2000, the CCFA Regulations contain separate provisions applicable whether or not a success was to be claimed. Regulation 4(1) required a CCFA to 'specify the circumstances in which the legal representative's fees and expenses, or part of them, are payable'.

Insofar as the regulations governed the process to take place between solicitor and the clients being funded, all that was expressly required was that the CCFA would state that (a) the client would be told when he might be liable to pay the lawyer's costs and (b) the client would be provided with any further explanation, advice or other information that he might reasonably require (reg.4(2)). If any explanation, advice or other information were not in fact supplied, then the structure of the Regulations is not such as to deprive the agreement of its statutory protection in the same way that, for instance, a material breach of CFA Regulations 2000, reg.4 might result in a declaration of unenforceability. By reg.4(4) the CCFA Regulations also required the agreement to state that when instructions were received by the funder to represent an individual client then the legal representative would confirm his receipt of instructions to the client.

In practical terms and for the purposes of preserving the apparent effect of the indemnity principle (as well as in order to observe the relevant client care provisions), it has been necessary to send out a letter of retainer to the client.

As to CCFAs whereby an uplift was to be claimed, then reg.5 comes into operation. Regulation 5(1) required the CCFA to provide that when instructions were accepted, the legal representative had to prepare and retain a written statement containing an assessment of the risks affecting the likelihood of payment being required by the client (the 'risk assessment' – reg.5(1)(a)), a written statement as to the amount of the percentage uplift (reg.5(1)(b)) and a statement explaining why the uplift is justified by reference to the risks assessed (reg.5(1)(c)).

Regulation 5(2), (3) concern disclosure of the written reasons why the percentage uplift was assessed at the level at which it was assessed, the effect of non-recovery of fees at an assessment or compromise of the costs claimed, and a definition of 'percentage increase'. These are in identical terms to the CFA Regulations 2000, reg.3(2), (3).

The CCFA Regulations are now revoked by the Conditional Fee Agreements (Revocation) Regulations 2005, SI 2005/2305 (see **2.9**).

The CCFA Regulations (as amended)

Collective CFAs are lawful in exactly the same way that standard CFAs are lawful. So long as an agreement complies with the CCFA Regulations 2000 (as amended), it will enjoy statutory protection by virtue of the Courts and Legal Services Act 1990, s.58 (as amended by the Access to Justice Act 1999).

2.8 SIMPLIFIED CFAs AND CCFAs

The CFA (Miscellaneous Amendments) Regulations 2003, SI 2003/1240 (which came into force on 2 June 2003), made express provision for 'simplified' CFAs and CCFAs, and these were further amended (in minor ways as explained below) by the CFA (Miscellaneous Amendments) (No.2) Regulations 2003, SI 2003/3344 (see para.2.6). The Civil Procedure (Amendment No.2) Rules 2003, SI 2003/1242 made amendments to CPR rule 43.2 which made it clear that the costs under such arrangements were recoverable and these also came into effect on 2 June 2003.

The 'Simplified CFA' enables a retainer to be entered into which frees the client from any liability to pay the shortfall on the costs recovered from the opponent. Parliamentary sanction was not strictly needed for this type of arrangement which was approved by Master Hurst in his decision on the *TAG Tranche 2* cases given on 15 May 2003 (paras.380–5). That a Simplified CFA has not changed the costs rules relating to the recovery of CFA costs was clarified by the inclusion of CPR rule 43.2(3) into the definitions section of the Costs Rules. However, the use of a Simplified CFA as sanction by the amendment to the Regulations, does have the dramatic consequence that by reg.3A(3) neither regs.2, 3 or 4 apply to the agreement. Regulation 3A(6) does require the solicitor to explain what payment may be due in the residual circumstances in which payment can be required (as explained below).

A Simplified CFA furthers the aim of Parliament in facilitating access to the courts. At the same time it would surely confirm the fears expressed by the Court of Appeal and the House of Lords that it is possible for clients to be able to gain legal representation in an entirely risk-free environment. These fears were summarised, for instance, by the Court of Appeal in *Hollins* at para.49:

> the House of Lords in *Callery v Gray (Nos 1 and 2)* [2002] UKHL 28; [2002] 1 WLR 2000 in relation to the opportunities for abuse opened up by the new legislative regime. These stemmed largely from the fact that the client is unlikely to be very concerned about the details of a CFA because no liability will fall on her. If she wins, she will recover her costs, plus any additional liabilities, from the defendants. If she loses, she will be protected from paying the other side's costs by ATE insurance, which will often cover her own costs as well. If it does not, her solicitors will not charge her anything.

A Simplified CFA is very satisfactory not only from the client's perspective, but at least in a successful case, also from the lawyer's. The client may well find that the use of a CFA on simplified terms together with an ATE policy means that the solicitor is on a more advantageous package than he would get from a modest before-the-event (BTE) arrangement giving him, say, £25,000 or £50,000 cover. The CFA will give the client access to unlimited funding of his own costs whereas BTE cover has to be apportioned between his own and the other side's costs. From the solicitor's point of view the added risk justifies a higher uplift. What constitutes a Simplified CFA has been examined in detail in *Jones* v. *Wrexham B.C.* [2007] EWCA 1356, 19 December 2007.

The amendment to the 2000 Regulations brought about by the two sets of Amendment Regulations 2003 also has the useful consequence that by a new reg.3A(5) the lawyer's right to recover fees in their entirety from the client was preserved where the client:

(a)   failed to cooperate with the lawyer;
(b)   failed to attend any medical or expert examination or court hearing which the lawyer reasonably requests him to attend;
(c)   failed to give necessary instructions to the lawyer;
(d)   withdrew instructions from the lawyer;
(e)   'is an individual who is adjudged bankrupt or enters into an arrangement or a composition with his creditors, or against whom an administration order is made'; or
(f)   'is a company for which a receiver, administrative receiver or liquidator is appointed'.

The Amendment (No.2) Regulations also caused the CFA Regulations to provide that a CFA might specify that the client's estate could be the responsible for the client's fees and expenses in the event of his death (reg.3A(5A)).

Simplified CCFAs

The CCFA Regulations 2000 were also amended by the CFA (Miscellaneous Amendments) Regulations 2003, SI 20043/1240 which made it clear that it was lawful to enter into 'simplified' CCFA terms, i.e. terms by which no fee would be recovered from the client which was not paid by the losing party (as with individual CFAs). This was effected by the insertion of a new reg.4(1A).

As set out above, the Amendment Regulations were further amended by the CFA (Miscellaneous Amendments) (No.2) Regulations 2003, SI 2003/3344. The effect of these Amendment Regulations was the same as for individual CFAs, so that notwithstanding that a CCFA had been drafted on 'simplified' terms, costs could still be recovered from the client if the client:

(a)   failed to cooperate with the legal representative;
(b)   failed to attend any medical or expert examination or court hearing which the legal representative reasonably requests him to attend;
(c)   failed to give necessary instructions to the legal representative;
(d)   withdrew instructions from the legal representative;
(e)   'is an individual who is adjudged bankrupt or enters into an arrangement or a composition with his creditors, or against whom an administration order is made'; or
(f)   'is a company for which a receiver, administrative receiver or liquidator is appointed'.

The CCFA Regulations were further amended by the CFA (Miscellaneous Amendments) (No.2) Regulations 2003, SI 2003/3344 (which came into force on 2 February 2004). As with individual CFAs, a new reg.5(7) permitted a CFA to provide that the client's estate could be responsible for the client's fees and expenses in the event of his death (reg.3A(5A)).

2.9 REVOCATION: THE CFA (REVOCATION) REGULATIONS 2005

The CFA Regulations 2000 were made by Parliament notwithstanding very substantial lobbying on the lines that clients were adequately protected by the Practice Rules and the Costs Information and Client Care Code. By deciding that it was appropriate to give the contents of the Code statutory protection in the form of the Regulations, Parliament opened the way for the regulatory challenges referred to above and which are covered in some detail in **Chapter 4**. These challenges have substantially driven the increasing prevalence of costs litigation (and its concomitant costs) over recent years. Parliament must have seen the error of its ways, for the Conditional Fee Agreements (Revocation) Regulations 2005, SI 2005/2305 revoked the 2000 Regulations (and the CCFA Regulations 2000) in their entirety.

CFAs made after 1 November 2005 are not subject to the rigours of the 2000 Regulations and their mandatory provisions. It is widely thought that having been given protection from the prying eyes of paying parties by the transfer of the client care provisions into the regulatory scheme which governs the profession (see now the Solicitors' Code of Conduct 2007), it will be impossible for paying parties to make the same regulatory challenges to the same dramatic effect. This is because, while a breach of the professional Code may given rise to financial and other disciplinary sanctions at the instigation of the client, such a breach cannot give rise to a direct claim by a paying party or to an allegation that there has been a breach of the indemnity principle (N.B. *Garbutt* v. *Edwards* [2006] 1 WLR 2907). The 'conditions' applicable to every CFA by s.58(3)(c) which are required to be satisfied for a CFA to be declared enforceable simply no longer exist.

2.10 CLAF/CoLAF: s.58B

A new s.58B was inserted by s.28 of the 1999 Act. This provision made possible the creation of a 'litigation funding agreement'. Section 58B was enacted to please the Law Society and Bar Council, which had both made strenuous efforts to persuade the government that a CFA system should be established on a mutual basis. Dominic Grieve MP described this provision in the Access to Justice Bill as 'a little golden nugget in the middle of what frankly resembles a large dunghill'. By such a scheme, successful litigants would make payments into a Conditional or Contingency Legal Aid Fund (CoLAF or CLAF) to fund further cases. Even in May 2005, the Chairman of the Bar had this as the first idea in his 'Menu for Justice' to plug 'real gaps' in civil justice and it remains part of the Bar Council's Strategic Plan for 2006–8 as the basis for establishing fair remuneration for publicly funded work.

The establishment of such a mutual fund stalled because of a dispute between the professions and the government about who should provide the money to start one. The professions have insisted that it should be a government-driven scheme, but the government, by enacting s.58B, threw the gauntlet down to the professions inviting them to set up such a scheme if they thought that it could be viable. The government's view was that such a scheme was not likely to be successful since, without an element of compulsion forcing litigants to enter a CLAF, the lawyers would cherry-pick winning cases and run them on individual CFAs (see Hansard, Standing Committee E, 13 May 1999). The element of compulsion was considered objectionable since at the time of the Bill 'the Government [did] not think it right to prevent the further development of conditional fees which are proving to be so successful' (see para.4.9: 'Access to Justice with Conditional Fees', LCD, March 1998).

The Civil Justice Council temporarily placed the establishment of a Conditional Legal Aid Scheme to be run by the Legal Services Commission back on the agenda in cases where ATE insurance is unavailable (see Recommendation 10: 'Improved Access to Justice – Funding Options & Proportionate Costs', September 2005). The updated set of recommendations in 'Improved Access to Justice – Funding Options & Proportionate Costs' (June 2007) expressly states that a CLAF should not be established in England and Wales, but proposes the establishment of a 'SLAS', a 'Supplementary Legal Aid Scheme' designed to introduce a measure of self-funding into the current public funding scheme.

2.11   RECOVERABLE ATE PREMIUMS

Access to Justice Act 1999, s.29, introduced a new provision which, subject to rules of court, enabled ATE insurance provisions to be recovered from unsuccessful parties. The meaning and effect of this section is set out at **3.9**.

2.12   MEMBERSHIP ORGANISATIONS

Section 30 is a section of the Access to Justice Act 1999 still shrouded by a certain element of mystery. The effect is to allow a prescribed organisation (described only in the title to the relevant regulations as 'Membership Organisations'), so long as it has complied with certain limited client care formalities, to recover the equivalent of a full commercial insurance premium on the fictional basis that the organisation would have had to set aside the equivalent of the premium in order to self-insure the risk of failure. Section 30 was supplemented by the Access to Justice (Membership Organisations) Regulations 2000, SI 2000/693 made pursuant to s.30(1). These Regulations have now been revoked by the Access to Justice (Membership Organisation) Regulations 2005, SI 2005/2306.

Section 30 ('Recovery where body undertakes to meet costs liabilities') reads straightforwardly enough. It applies by s.30(1) where a 'body of a prescribed description' undertakes to meet liabilities which members of the body 'or other persons who are parties to proceedings' may incur to pay the costs of other parties to the proceedings. In other words, it covers circumstances where, if there were no such membership organisation, the individual to any particular proceedings might have chosen to take out an ATE policy to insure against the risk that he would have to pay his opponent's costs.

Achieving 'membership organisation' status

This section does rather beg the question of who is a prescribed organisation. Section 30(1), (5) allows for regulations to be made to answer this question.

Regulation 5 of the Access to Justice (Membership Organisations) Regulations 2005 ('Bodies of a prescribed description') states simply that prescribed bodies are 'those bodies which are for the time being approved by the Lord Chancellor for that purpose') (the same wording was to be found in the Access to Justice (Membership Organisations) Regulations 2000, reg.2). In other words, we do not get much help from the Act or the Regulations.

At the time of writing the best information which can be obtained publicly about prescription is from the Department of Constitutional Affairs website which contains a document headed 'How to apply for Prescription as an Approved Membership Organisation under Section 30 of the Access to Justice Act 1999' (last updated in October 2003: **www.dca.gov.uk/confeeagr/presapp.htm**). This tells us that the Lord Chancellor issued a press notice on 30 March 2000 by which all trade unions listed by the Certification Officer as of 31 March automatically became prescribed bodies. Should anyone wish to know what criteria apply on an application for prescription then he will discover that:

> Rather than set down rigid criteria for prescription in regulations it was announced that the Lord Chancellor would adopt a flexible approach with each application for approval treated on its merits.

The following criteria are relevant when representations for approval are made, namely:

whether the organisation in question:

(a)   exists to protect, defend, represent and promote the interest of its members;
(b)   has an exclusive range of benefits for members;
(c)   offers litigation funding as one of those benefits and on a discretionary basis, at no additional charge;

41

(d) publishes annual accounts;
(e) invests its membership payment within the organisation for the benefit of the members and the organisation;
(f) covers all those deemed eligible by the organisation (not only members).

In other words, the process whether or not an application for prescribed status might succeed is opaque rather than transparent. This is surprising given the advantage which this status confers as further described below.

This amended (2003) document discloses that the following organisations were approved membership organisations for the purposes of s.30 along with trade unions listed by the certification officer as of 31 March 2000:

- AA Legal Services
- British Cycling Federation
- Defence Police Federation
- Durham Colliery Overmen Deputies & Shotfirers Retired Members Group
- Engineering Employers' Federation
- Police Federation of England and Wales
- RAC Motoring Services
- The Cyclist Touring Club
- The London Cycling Campaign
- British Triathlon Federation
- The Co-operative Group
- The National Union of Students

The fact that s.30(1) applies where a membership organisation covers the risk not only of members but also 'other persons who are parties to proceedings' is of some interest. This enables an organisation such as one of the above to offer funding to meet the risk of paying an adverse costs order not only to those who contribute to the organisation's funds, but also to those who are connected with them, for instance to family or friends.

Section 30(2) allows rules of court to provide that where a costs order is made it can include 'an additional amount in respect of any provision made by or on behalf of the body in connection with the proceedings against the risk of having to meet such liabilities'. Section 30(3) limits that additional amount so that it 'shall not exceed a sum determined in a prescribed manner', and the formula by which that limitation is to be determined is set out in reg.5 of the Membership Organisations Regulations 2005, in particular reg.5(2). The sum which cannot be exceeded is:

> the likely cost to the member of the body or, as the case may be, the other person who is a party to the proceedings in which the costs order is made of the premium of an insurance policy against the risk of incurring a liability to pay the costs of other parties to the proceedings.

It appears then that when a claim for costs is made the amount which can be recovered by virtue of s.30 is to be assessed by reference to the amount which could be recovered by way of an ATE premium. Since the membership organisation is very likely to be self-insuring out of its own funds, it can be seen that this entitlement can be a very useful source of income.

The client care formalities required for the recovery of a membership organisation premium are limited and are to be found in the Membership Organisations Regulations 2005, reg.4. Formerly the Membership Organisations Regulations 2000 required the organisation which has agreed to supply the individual with the benefit of cover to provide, as soon as possible after the agreement, written information specifying when the individual may be required to pay the costs of the proceedings in different circumstances (broadly reflecting CFA Regulations 2000, reg.2) and the procedure for seeking an assessment of costs (reg.3). Regulation 4(1) now requires only that the arrangements be in writing and that they 'contain a statement specifying the circumstances in which the member may be liable to pay the costs of the proceedings'.

Section 31 and the indemnity principle

Section 31 is a provision amending Supreme Court Act 1981, s.51(2), the underlying rule which allows the CPR to make rules as to costs. When in force, rules made under the amended s.51(2) will expressly allow costs to be awarded without reference to the indemnity principle (see **1.4**).

CHAPTER 3

Recoverability

3.1 INTRODUCTION

This chapter examines the means by which, and the extent to which, a successful receiving party is entitled to recover the costs of any additional liabilities (success fees, after-the-event (ATE) and membership organisation premiums), save that something is also said in an initial section about the extent to which a CFA can be drafted retrospectively to accommodate any pre-CFA costs liabilities. This chapter should be read in conjunction with **Chapters 2** and **4**. **Chapter 2** seeks to provide an account of the relevant primary and secondary legislation, and also looks at some of the relevant policy considerations which led to the introduction of CFAs and the Access to Justice Act 1999 regime. **Chapter 4** is reserved for challenges to CFAs, but also provides more details as to how the individual statutory conditions which were applicable to CFAs under the CFA Regulations 2000 (and other legislative provisions) have been interpreted.

This chapter inevitably focuses on the Civil Procedure Rules 1998 (CPR) since it is the CPR which provide the mechanics by which additional liabilities are awarded. The structure of this chapter is as follows:

- *Backdating and retrospectivity:* **3.2** considers the contractual question of whether a CFA can be 'backdated' or given retrospective effect in order to absorb pre-CFA costs.
- *The rules: an overview:* **3.3** gives an account of the statutory and costs rules which allow a costs order to make provision for the recovery of additional liabilities. It also recounts the relevant definitions used in the CPR.
- *A limit on recovery of general application – the need to provide information:* **3.4** describes the limitations on recovery which are applicable in respect of all additional liabilities where the requisite information has not been provided to an opponent.
- *Summary and detailed assessments:* **3.5** discusses the time and manner in which assessments of additional liabilities may be undertaken – in other words the relevant rules relating to summary and detailed assessments.

- *Additional liabilities are assessed by reference to CPR Part 45*: **3.6** looks briefly at the application of CPR rule 44.5 and the role of proportionality as applied generally to additional liabilities.
- *Percentage uplifts*: **3.7–3.8** examine the rules relating to success fees and how they are to be assessed.
- *Insurance premiums*: **3.9** seeks to provide an account as to the rules governing the recoverability of ATE and notional membership organisation premiums.
- *Fixed recoverable costs*: **3.10** considers fixed recoverable success fees under CPR Part 45.

Both the relevant substantive law and matters of practice and procedure will be considered, so that it is hoped that this chapter will assist anyone intending to manufacture his own agreement.

3.2   BACKDATING AND RETROSPECTIVITY

CFAs between solicitors and clients are contractual agreements which are subject to legislative control. A question which arises from time to time is the extent to which they can be used as a vehicle for the recovery of costs incurred prior to the making of the CFA. So long as a final costs order has not been made there is nothing to prohibit the parties from agreeing that the CFA includes the costs incurred from a date prior to the date on which the CFA was made in the expectation that these costs can be recovered from a paying party (see *Kenneth Kellar* v. *Stanley Williams* 24 June 2004 although the relevance of this case to English and Welsh CFAs is doubtful). It is a different matter to 'backdate' the CFA to make it appear that a CFA had been entered into on a date prior to that on which it had in fact been made. The difference is set out in the judgment of Stanley Burnton J in *Holmes* v. *Alfred McAlpine Homes (Yorkshire) Ltd* [2006] EWCA 110 7 February 2006 (at para.25):

> 'back-dating' has a connotation of impropriety suggesting an intention deliberately to mislead, whilst a 'retrospective' agreement is one which 'should be correctly dated with the date on which it is signed and expressed to have retrospective effect, i.e. to apply to work done before its date (para.25).

As to the recovery of a success fee where provision has been made for the incorporation of retrospective costs, see the decision of Master Hurst in *Musa King* v. *Telegraph Group Limited* [2005] EWHC 90015 (Costs), 2 December 2005. In that decision Master Hurst did in fact refer to a retrospective provision as a 'backdated' element, but the jurisprudential wording used by Stanley Burnton J is to be preferred for the reasons which he gives. See **3.7** below (uplift not recoverable on retrospective costs).

3.3 WHAT MAKES ADDITIONAL LIABILITIES RECOVERABLE?

Statute

The basic statutory provisions which give the court power to make orders for the payment of additional liabilities derive ultimately from the Access to Justice Act 1999, and are set out in the following paragraphs. All of these provisions defer to the CPR when it comes to describing the extent to which additional liabilities as claimed in a contractual agreement (the CFA, policy or otherwise) are recoverable. For the purposes of the CFA regime, at least, the Act came into force on 1 April 2000.

Uplifts: Courts and Legal Services Act 1990, s.58A(6), (7) (as amended)

As to success fees, the Courts and Legal Services Act 1990, 58A(6), (7) (as inserted by Access to Justice Act 1999, s.27) provides:

> (6) A costs order made in any proceedings may, subject in the case of court proceedings to rules of court, include provision requiring the payment of any fees payable under a conditional fee agreement which provides for a success fee.
> (7) Rules of court may make provision with respect to the assessment of any costs which include fees payable under a conditional fee agreement (including one which provides for a success fee).

See further at **3.7–3.8**.

ATE premiums: Access to Justice Act 1999, s.29

In respect of ATE premiums, s.29 provides:

> **Recovery of insurance premiums by way of costs**
>
> Where in any proceedings a costs order is made in favour of any party who has taken out an insurance policy against the risk of incurring a liability in those proceedings, the costs payable to him may, subject in the case of court proceedings to rules of court, include costs in respect of the premium of the policy.

See further at **3.9**.

Notional membership organisation premiums: Access to Justice Act 1999, s.30

Section 30 is the enabling section by which membership organisation premiums can be recovered:

Recovery where body undertakes to meet costs liabilities

(1) This section applies where a body of a prescribed description undertakes to meet (in accordance with arrangements satisfying prescribed conditions) liabilities which members of the body or other persons who are parties to proceedings may incur to pay the costs of other parties to the proceedings.

(2) If in any of the proceedings a costs order is made in favour of any of the members or other persons, the costs payable to him may, subject to subsection (3) and (in the case of court proceedings) to rules of court, include an additional amount in respect of any provision made by or on behalf of the body in connection with the proceedings against the risk of having to meet such liabilities.

Access to Justice (Membership Organisations) Regulations 2005, SI 2005/2306, reg.5(2) states that additional amount cannot exceed:

the likely cost to the member of the body or, as the case may be, the other person who is a party to the proceedings in which the costs order is made of the premium of an insurance policy against the risk of incurring a liability to pay the costs of other parties to the proceedings.

The regulatory framework describing what a 'membership organisation' is will be found in **Chapter 2** at **2.12**. See further at the conclusion of **3.9**.

Civil Procedure Rules

CPR Part 43 includes certain definitions which are used throughout the remainder of the costs rules and they must be clarified at the start of this chapter.

'Funding arrangement'

CPR Part 43 contains provisions which define success fees, ATE premiums and membership organisation premiums. These are CPR rule 43.2(1)(k)(i), (ii), (iii) which define each of these additional claims for recoverable costs as a 'funding arrangement'. It follows that a CFA which has been entered into which provides for a success fee, therefore, is a 'funding arrangement', as is an arrangement by which someone has taken out an ATE policy the premium of which is recoverable by virtue of s.29 of the 1999 Act, as is an arrangement where an individual has entered into an agreement with a membership organisation whereby the organisation has agreed to meet his costs. A CFA may consist of several separate documents, including a client care letter (see *Jones v. Wrexham B.C.* [2007] EWCA 1356, 19 December 2007 at para.86).

'Additional liability'

The success fee ('percentage uplift'), premium and membership organisation premium are each an 'additional liability' by virtue of CPR rule 43.2(1)(o), and the definition of 'costs' in rule 43.2(1)(a) expressly includes 'any additional liability incurred under a funding arrangement'.

Statutory power to make costs orders and the Costs Practice Direction

The enabling provisions effected by the Access to Justice Act 1999 are complemented by the following two provisions in the Costs Practice Direction (CPD):

> CPD para.2.1:
>
> Where the court makes an order for costs and the receiving party has entered into a funding arrangement . . . the costs payable by the paying party include any additional liability';
>
> CPD para.11.4:
>
> Where a party has entered into a funding arrangement the costs claimed may . . . include an additional liability.

Section 2 of the CPD contains some further provisions describing the scope of the costs rules and definitions insofar as they concern funding arrangements. These paragraphs do little more than summarise the relevant rules.

CFAs without additional liabilities

For the most part CFAs which do not attract success fees are not treated as anything different from ordinary retainers. There are very few special provisions which relate to them.

3.4 LIMITS ON RECOVERY: PROVIDING INFORMATION ABOUT FUNDING ARRANGEMENTS

It should be noted that the CPR contain detailed provisions restricting the recovery of additional liabilities where the paying party has not been sent specified information showing that a claim for costs is based on a funding arrangement. Since additional liabilities may not be recoverable at all under these rules it seems appropriate to deal with them at the commencement of this section. In some circumstances it may be possible to apply for relief from the sanction of irrecoverability imposed where the requisite information has not been provided, and an account is given here as to the means by which to apply for that relief. In addition to the provisions in the CPR the courts have added a further gloss requiring information to be given in order for staged insurance premiums to be payable at the end of proceedings (see 'Staged/stepped and other increasing premiums' at **3.9** below).

Information required to be given during the transitional stage

First, it should be remembered the Civil Procedure (Amendment No.3) Rules 2000, SI 2000/1317 contained transitional provisions to cater for the fact that CFAs had been left in limbo after they were introduced by the Access to Justice Act reforms in 2000, since no rules governing recoverability were in force until 3 July 2000 (when the Amendment No.3 Rules amended the CPR incorporating the bulk of the rules which exist today). Paragraph 39 of this statutory instrument gave solicitors who had already entered into new-style CFAs and who had also commenced proceedings by 3 July 2000 until 31 July 2000 to comply with the new rules. In practice this meant that they had to comply with the requirement to provide information about funding arrangements as set out in CPR rule 44.15 and the accompanying part of the CPD.

As we shall see (below) a party who fails to provide information about funding arrangements may apply for relief from the sanction of irre-coverability of additional liabilities and relief may be possible in these circumstances.

CPR rules 44.15 and 44.3B: providing information and limits on recovery

The obligation to provide information about additional liabilities

In order for additional liabilities to be recoverable, a party who may seek to recover them at the conclusion of a case must have provided information about the nature of the funding arrangement in accordance with CPR rule 44.15 and section 19 of the CPD. Rule 44.3B(1)(c) prohibits the recovery of an additional liability if the requisite information has not been provided, although it is possible to apply for relief from this sanction. Practice and procedure relating to these issues are set out in the following paragraphs.

Providing information at the Pre-Action Protocol stage

It is good practice to inform an opposing party about the existence of a funding arrangement during the pre-action protocol process, and indeed many firms do make sure that the Letter of Claim does include this wording. However, para.4A.1 of the Practice Direction-Protocols states that a person who has entered into a funding arrangement 'should' inform the other parties that he has done so, but this has not been interpreted in the SCCO as imposing a mandatory obligation on the client (see the discussion by Master Roger in *Choudhury* v. *Kingston Hospital NHS Trust*, 2 May 2006, and the decision of Master Campbell in *Cullen* v. *Chopra*, 21 December 2007). A failure to provide information therefore does not of itself result in any sanction (see *Metcalfe* v. *Clipston*, 6 April 2004 (Master Campbell)). The draft letters of claim annexed to certain of the Pre-Action Protocols (for instance, for personal injury claims and disease and illness claims) do expressly make reference to the existence of additional liabilities.

It is broadly the case that judges are sympathetic to applications for relief from sanction, normally because a paying party cannot escape the inference that even if it had known about the likelihood of a claim for an additional liability it would not have done anything differently: it would not have compromised proceedings at an earlier stage in order to avoid having to meet these additional liabilities. It should be noted that it is not usually enough to inform an opponent as to the mere existence of a CFA retainer. What is necessary is that the other party must be warned about the possible claim to a success fee or ATE premium.

What information must be provided?

The effect of section 19.2(1) of the CPD is that the information which is contained on form N251 must be provided to the opponent at the prescribed stages. Form N251 itself does not have to used, and the information which has to be supplied which is set out on the form is itemised at para.19.4(1) of the CPD. A copy of form N251 is included at **Appendix 6**.

When must the information be provided?

By para.19.2(2)(a) of the CPD the notice of funding must be provided to the court by a claimant by filing the notice together with the claim form. If the court serves the claim form then it will serve any notice of funding with which it has been provided at the same time (a good reason for using form N251), otherwise it must be served by the claimant (CPD para.19.2(2)(b)). In the case of the defendant, then it must provide notice to the court at the time at which it files its 'first document' (for instance an acknowledgement of service) (CPD para.19.2(3)(a)). By CPD para.19.2(3)(b) the court will serve copies on the other parties if provided with sufficient numbers and if it is to serve the first document, otherwise service must be effected by the defendant. In 'all other circumstances' (meaning primarily occasions in which a party enters into a funding arrangement after these express trigger points by which notice must be served) a party must file and serve notice within seven days of entering into the CFA (CPD para.19.2(4)).

CPR rule 44.15(2) and CPD para.19.3(1) require a notice of change of information to be filed and served if the notice previously supplied is inaccurate. CPD para.19.3(2)(a) clarifies that 'further notification' is not needed where a new CFA is entered into with an additional legal representative (for instance, a barrister). If a solicitor has not entered into a funding arrangement but a barrister subsequently does, then of course a notice of funding does need to be provided. CPD para.19.3(2)(b) demonstrates that notice is not required if top-up insurance is obtained from the same insurer. Additional notice is only needed if 'cover is cancelled or unless new cover is taken out with a different insurer'.

If a notice of change of information is required but an allocation or listing questionnaire has already been filed, then by CPD para.19.15(3) a new estimate of costs must also be filed and served.

Consequences of the failure to provide information about funding arrangements and relief from sanction

If notice of funding is not provided to an opponent in accordance with CPR rule 44.15, then by rule 44.3B the client as receiving party is prohibited from recovering any additional liability for the period during which it was in default. However, it is open to the party in default to apply for relief, as CPD para.10.1 reminds us (see also CPR rule 3.8). An application for relief must be made in accordance with CPR Part 23, rule 3.9 reflecting the circumstances to which the court will have regard when considering the application (as discussed in *Woodhouse* v. *Consignia* [2002] 1 WLR 2558 as interpreted in this context by Langley J. in *Montlake & Ors* v. *Lambert Smith Hampton* [2004] 4 Costs LR 650). Section 10 of the CPD emphasises the need to act promptly. It is probably better practice to send the draft application and supporting evidence to a paying party with seven days' notice prior to issuing the application to see whether any agreement can be reached. There is always the temptation not to apply for relief during proceedings since this may needlessly put a party on notice as to the error, but to wait for a detailed assessment. The best course is surely to make the application straightaway.

Experience shows that district judges take a somewhat flexible approach as to when to deal with an application for relief. Judges have accepted variously that so long as the application has been made promptly it is acceptable to list the matter as a preliminary issue on a detailed assessment, or even that an application for relief may be made orally without notice during a detailed assessment (see CPR rule 23.3(2)(b) and the decision of Master Rogers in *Choudhury* v. *Kingston Hospital NHS Trust* 2 May 2006).

There is an unreported decision of a Circuit Judge in *Connor* v. *Birmingham City Council* 16 March 2005 which, in the writers' experience, runs contrary to many judges' approach to applications for relief. However, this did concern an application for a success fee which was made at trial without there having been such application for relief (although there was judicial speculation about what the result might have been if there had been such an application).

As to the evidence required to support an application for relief, the starting point is to ascertain whether or not some indication was provided to the opponent that the proceedings are being funded by way of a funding arrangement involving a claim to an additional liability. The initial question is whether the opposing party was or should have been aware that the funding arrangements in question did make provisions for an additional liability. Such evidence, especially if combined with material to show that the opposing party would not have compromised the proceedings (for instance where a heavy-handed and detailed defence has been filed), is often compelling when seeking to persuade the judge that relief should be granted.

CPD para.10.2 requires notice of an application for relief to be provided to counsel at least two days before the hearing and permits counsel to make written or oral submissions in reply.

What is the position if a party fails to apply for relief from sanction at a first instance hearing? Can the application be made on an appeal? The 'initial view' of Sumner J in *Cowley* v. *Merseyside Regional Ambulance Service NHS Trust* [2003] EWHC 250 (Fam) 28 February 2003 was that in such circumstances the receiving party should have the matter relisted at a further first instance hearing (ultimately the judge did not have to decide the issue).

Providing information about staged and other increasing ATE premiums

Where a party has taken out an insurance policy with staged or other increasing premiums, then an obligation arises which is in addition to the basic requirement of CPR rule 44.15(1) and paras.19.1(1) and 19.4 of the CPD. Where a party has such a policy he is required to inform his opponent that the policy is staged and to specify the trigger moments at which the second or later stages will be reached. This is the effect of the decision in *Rogers* v. *Merthyr Tydfi* (see further below), although that case does not make it clear what information will have to be disclosed in relation to every form of increasing premium. If this rule of good practice is not followed, it does not seem that any formal Part 23 application for relief from sanction is required. It is likely to be a matter for argument at the detailed assessment whether or not the final (assessed) stages of the premium should be recoverable. A sensible approach is to provide sufficient information at the pre-action protocol stage.

3.5 TIME AND MANNER OF THE ASSESSMENT OF ADDITIONAL LIABILITIES: SUMMARY AND DETAILED ASSESSMENTS

Knowledge as to the amount of a success fee or an ATE premium is considered highly confidential. It is thought that if an opponent were to have possession of this information, then inferences could be drawn as to the legal representative's assessment of the client's prospects of success. This is a reason why the prospective receiving party cannot find out the amount of the success fee or the value of an ATE premium when notice of funding is provided.

Additional liabilities to be assessed at the conclusion of proceedings

For the same reason CPR Part 44 contains express rules proving for the occasions at which additional liabilities will be assessed. CPR rule 44.3A(1) prevents an additional liability from being assessed until the conclusion of the part of the proceedings to which the funding arrangement relates. Where costs are summarily assessed before the conclusion of the case (i.e. at an interim stage) then the base costs should be assessed separately from the additional liability (CPD para.14.2). There will be an order that the amount of any additional liability will be determined at a detailed assessment (CPR rule 44.3A(2)). CPD para.9.2(1) requires the base costs, counsel's fees, other disbursements and VAT to be separately identified. This enables the court carrying out the assessment of the appropriate uplift to ensure that it knows what those base costs were. In default of an assessment on these lines the judge at a detailed assessment is entitled to make an apportionment between these items (CPD para.9.2(2)). CPD para.2.4 of the CPD sets out a definition as to when proceedings can be said to have been 'concluded' for the purpose of CPR rule 44.3A, namely 'when the court has finally determined the matters in issue in the claim', providing in addition that the making of an award of provisional damages under CPR Part 41 'will also be treated as a final determination of the matters in issue'.

The court can of course summarily assess the costs as required in the circumstances set out in para.13.2 of the CPD (at the end of fast-track trials, or one-day hearings). It may then assess the base costs and additional liability at the summary assessment or order them to go to a detailed assessment (CPR rule 44.3A). In *Burton* v. *Kingsley* [2005] EWHC 1034 (25 May 2005) Richards J assessed the uplift at the conclusion of the liability trial and adjourned the base costs to a detailed assessment.

Costs-only proceedings

In the event of disagreement about the level of any additional liabilities then costs-only proceedings under CPR rule 44.12A (and CPD section 17) are a suitable vehicle for obtaining a ruling to settle the dispute (see the guidance given by Master Hurst in *Bensusan* v. *Freedman* (unreported) 20 September 2001).

Whether or not costs-only proceedings attract an uplift depends on the construction of the underlying CFA. *Halloran* v. *Delaney* [2003] 1 WLR 28 concerned the original Law Society model agreement which expressly covered enforcement proceedings. While costs-only proceedings were not enforcement proceedings, they were a means of quantifying the legal representative's fees and expenses and, at the same time, a process whereby a 'win' was achieved under the terms of the agreement (since a 'win' meant recovering fees and expenses). They were therefore an ancillary stage prior to any enforcement proceedings and part of the 'claim'.

The detailed assessment process

This book is not intended to stray into the full process of detailed assessments. It is important to remember however that section 52 of the CPD does contain rules relevant to claims for costs where the costs include additional liabilities. Paragraph 32.4 therefore requires a detailed assessment only of additional liabilities to include at (c) 'the relevant details of an additional liability', which are further defined at para.32.5. These are set out in **Appendix 4** of this book and include a statement of reasons justifying the success fee and certain details of any ATE cover provided. Where there is to be a detailed assessment of additional liabilities and of base costs, para.32.7 also requires 'the relevant details of an additional liability' to be supplied as defined by para.32.5. When there is to be a detailed assessment hearing of any additional liability, then CPR rule 40.12 requires the papers 'relevant to the issues raised by the claim for additional liability' to be filed along with any other papers.

3.6 THE UNDERLYING BASIS FOR THE ASSESSMENT OF THE RECOVERABLE AMOUNT OF ADDITIONAL LIABILITIES: CPR PART 45 AND THE ROLE OF PROPORTIONALITY

Additional liabilities are 'costs' within the meaning of CPR rule 43.2(1)(a) so that it follows that they are part of the costs to be assessed according on the two bases set out in rule 44.4 (the standard and the indemnity bases). Whilst the factors ordinarily set out in CPR rule 44.5 ('factors to be taken into account in deciding the amount of costs') might be relevant at least on the assessment of an ATE premium, the starting point in assessing the amount of a success fee is always the risks as they reasonably appeared to the solicitor entering into the CFA, and these must be carefully determined and recorded when the CFA is made. A great deal of costs may depend on this short document. It must be noted that even though the CFA Regulations 2000 have been revoked, CPD paras.32.4(c) and 32.5 require the details of an additional liability to be provided to the paying party at the commencement of detailed assessment proceedings. Section 11 of the CPD provides express guidance as to some of the circumstances which the court should consider.

Proportionality

Ultimately, on a standard assessment the question is whether the additional liability was reasonably and proportionately incurred and proportionate and reasonable in amount (see CPR rule 44.5(1)(a)). In determining these questions the amount of any additional liability will be considered separately from the base costs (CPD para.11.5), but there is no doubt that proportionality is a matter which is intended to be applied in the case of funding arrangements. Indeed in the context of the protection to be afforded to the right of free speech enjoyed by defendant media interests, Lord Hope in *Campbell* v. *MGN (No.2)* [2005] 1 WLR 3394 described the test of proportionality as applied to the uplift as the 'ultimate controlling factor' (see para.47).

In the context of percentage uplifts, CPD para.11.9 expressly provides that:

> a percentage uplift will not be reduced simply on the ground that, when added to base costs which are reasonable and proportionate, the total appears disproportionate.

Thus in the detailed assessment in *Musa King* v. *Telegraph Group Ltd* [2005] EWHC 90015 (Costs), 2 December 2005, at paras.12–19, Master Hurst rejected a submission by counsel for the paying party that the court should address the proportionality of the total sum of base costs and uplift considered together. See:

> 19. Both the base costs and the success fee separately must be assessed at reasonable and proportionate figures but, if the two figures taken together appear, as they inevitably will, to be disproportionate, that is not a factor to be taken into account.

This was because the intention of Parliament was that litigants who are represented on CFA terms 'should be able to recover a reasonable and proportionate success fee in addition to the reasonable and proportionate base costs' (Master Hurst at para.15). It is difficult, however, to see how proportionality can be applied to a success fee, since section 11 of the CPD so clearly anticipates an examination of the risks as they seemed at the time at which the agreement was made. The task is made more complicated by the need to avoid hindsight when examining the solicitor's contemporary assessment of the risks involved. See **3.7** and **3.8** below in which the recoverability of uplifts is considered.

In relation to ATE premiums, a wide interpretation of the law relating to proportionality has provided a successful vehicle for the recovery of staged ATE premiums where the final (assessed as opposed to initial block-rated) premium is ostensibly disproportionate to the amount of the damages. (See further at **3.9** below which concerns the recoverability of ATE premiums.)

3.7   SUCCESS FEES: WIDER CONSIDERATIONS

This section is concerned with the wider rules regulating the amount of the percentage uplift which is recoverable (if any), whether under the terms of a CFA or of a collective CFA (CCFA). To this extent at least CFAs and CCFAs are one and the same: identical rules apply to the assessment of the success fee. In the initial section consideration is given to the question whether a success fee can be recovered at all in respect of the retrospective period of a CD; work done by agents; and work done by the in-house solicitor. Other wider questions which are examined are the express limitations and restrictions affecting the recovery of success fees; whether it is reasonable to incur a success fee at all; the requirement that the court must examine the risks as they appeared to the legal representative when the CFA was entered into; whether a judge can reduce an agreed success fee; whether a success fee can extend to detailed assessment proceedings; the correct standard by reference to which the success fee is to be determined (being the standard of the reasonable careful solicitor); and certain underlying policy considerations. Section **3.8** sets out some specific circumstances which affect how the amount of an uplift is to be determined.

How may a success fee be defined in a CFA?

Section 58(2)(b) of the Courts and Legal Services Act 1990 (as substituted by the Access to Justice Act 1990) provides the only statutory guidance as to what a success fee is. It is in very wide terms and follows s.58(2) of the Act in its original form in that a CFA is stated to provide for a success fee if it 'provides for the amount of any to which it applies to be increased, in specified circumstances, above the amount which would be payable if it were not a conditional fee agreement'.

This expression is given a wide interpretation. In *Benaim UK Ltd* v. *Davies Middleton & Davies Ltd* (26 March 2004) Rich J. sanctioned an arrangement whereby the amount of the uplift was staged according to the amount of damages recovered. Thus the uplift was 25 per cent if the recovery was £200,000, but it was 100 per cent if the recovery was £1 million. There are numerous different methods by which uplifts can be calculated, and it is intended that these paragraphs should give some assistance as to how to they might be defined. See also *Gloucestershire County Council* v. *Evans* [2008] EWCA Civ 21, 31 January 2008, and the end of **1.2**.

Retrospective agreements

Can a success fee be recovered on the retrospective costs included in a CFA (i.e. where there is provision that the retainer includes costs from a date which is a date prior to that on which the CFA was made)? Master Hurst came to the unequivocal conclusion in *Musa King* v. *Telegraph Group Limited* [2005] EWHC 90015 (Costs) that a success fee could not be included in the pre-CFA costs since this would 'fly in the face of the CFA Regulations and the CPR' (para.89). Indeed this may be one area in which para.11.8(2) of the CPD might have had proper effect where there was an attempt to recover a pre-contract uplift (for doubts about the lawfulness of this paragraph of the CPD and its removal from the CPD see 'Can a judge reduce the amount of a success fee from that ageeed in a CFA?' below).

There is an argument, perhaps, that it may be possible to claim a success fee at least for a short period prior to the making of the agreement if it has not been possible (or perhaps necessary) to provide the paying party with information about the existence of the CFA, and if the risks have not altered in the intervening period. An example might be where it was necessary to wait for a police or medical report before the risks could properly be assessed. Where a claimant who has reached his or her 18th birthday chooses not to ratify the CFA with a litigation friend but enters into a new agreement, is there really no scope for including the uplift set out in the agreement with the litigation friend in respect of the earlier work? The recovery of retrospective uplifts is likely to become a contested issue in the future.

Work done by agents

Where work has been done by agents rather than by external organisations who must be treated as disbursements, then it is possible to claim a success fee on that work. See *Guy* v. *Castle Morpeth* BC, HHJ Hewitt, 9 January 2006, *Crane* v. *Canons Leisure Centre*, 1 March 2006, Master Wright (both concerning costs draftsmen), and *Stringer* v. *Copley*, 11 June 2002, HHJ Cook and *Woollard* v. *Fowler*, 24 May 2006, Master Hurst (both being about medical agencies). In *Crane* v. *Canons Leisure Centre* [2007] EWCA Civ 1352, 19 December 2007, May LJ felt that the real question is whether or not the solicitors remain directly responsible to the client for the work done, even though it has been delegated to another. The Court of Appeal overturned the decision of Master Wright and held that the work done by the costs draftsmen counted as 'base costs' and not 'disbursements' under the CCFA.

What is the position in respect of solicitor agents, and does it matter if the agents undertake wholesale the conduct of a raft of cases in which the first solicitor has signed up many clients under CFAs?

The old authorities derive from a time when a London solicitor had to be used to commence proceedings. *Pomeroy* v. *Tanner* [1897] 1 Ch 284 makes it clear that a solicitor engaged on another solicitor's behalf is engaged as an agent. See at 287:

> It is well settled that between the client and the London agent of the country solicitor there is no privity. The relationship of solicitor and client does not exist between the client and the London agent. What is done by the London agent is part of the work done by country solicitor for the client . . . It follows, therefore, that that the items which make up the London agent's bill are not mere disbursements, but are items taxable in the strictest sense as between the client and the country solicitor personally, or by the clerk whom he employs in the country.

See also *Cobb* v. *Becke* 6 QB 930: 'the general rule undoubtedly is, that there is no privity between the agent in town and the client in the country'.

Prior to the CPR this position was reflected by para.1.16, *Practice Direction (Taxation: Practice) No.2 of 1992* [1993] 1WLR 12:

> Charges as between a principal solicitor and a solicitor agent will continue to be dealt with on the established principle that such charges . . . form part of the principal solicitor's charges.

Now CPD paras.4.6(9) and 4.16(6) continue the same rule into the CPR.

The modern authorities are unequivocal, so that Master Hurst at para.80, *Claims Direct Test Cases, Tranche 2 Issues* [2003] EWHC 9005 stated, when discussing what payments might constitute agency charges/disbursements:

> In my view the solicitor can charge as profit costs only that work undertaken by him or a member of his firm in the capacity of solicitor. If a task is delegated to a solicitor agent that too is chargeable as part of the principal solicitors profit costs.

So too in the *Accident Group Test Cases* (27 November 2002) he held that:

> [*Stringer* and *Smith*'s cases] merely confirm the well-established principle that where solicitors in litigation . . . delegate certain tasks they are entitled to charge for the work done and to make a profit rather than charge for the delegated work at cost.

See also para.74, *Agassi* v. *Robinson (No.2)* [2006] 1 WLR 2126 to the same effect.

Whether or not a solicitor can engage another as his agent to conduct the proceedings covered by a CFA will be governed by the terms and conditions of the agreement. In the former Law Society model, condition 6 set out the following:

> The cost of advocacy *and other work* by us, or by any solicitor agent on our behalf, forms part of our basic charges.

In principle, the common law, for the reasons set out above, supports the use of a solicitor agent, even across a tranche of cases.

In conclusion, it appears that a success fee can be claimed on work undertaken under the terms of a CFA where the work has been done by a solicitor agent, even though contractually the success fee may not be payable to the agent.

Success fees and the in-house solicitor

There are generally considered to be obstacles which prohibit the recovery of success fees by an in-house solicitor. One obstruction is thought to be the fact that a court might consider that any arrangement by which an in-house solicitor is engaged cannot satisfy the statutory definition of s.58(2)(a), in particular the requirement that there must be any arrangement by which the fees and expenses of the in-house department would be payable 'only in specified circumstances'. A further objection is the presumption by which an in-house firm is permitted to recover costs from an opposing party, namely the presumption that there is no breach of the indemnity principle. The benefit of this presumption is that the in-house solicitor would be entitled to his reasonable costs as though he were an independent solicitor, notwithstanding that his salary and overheads are in fact provided as a matter of course by his employer (see *Re Eastwood* [1975] Ch 112). It would be open to a paying party to argue that a claim for a percentage uplift, even if the difficulty posed by s.58(2)(a) could be overcome, was an unusual element of additional costs and would not fall within the presumption, so that the indemnity principle was infringed.

But what if an organisation providing legal assistance to members had a membership agreement stipulating for payment only in the event of success? It might perhaps be possible then to draft an agreement which did fall within s.58(2)(a), and in addition it might also be possible to argue such an arrangement is in line with public policy so that the uplift should be recoverable and could no longer be considered an unusual element of costs. The Vibration White Finger litigation as reported at (2007) PIQR P8 (CA) supports this as a possibility. In that case the 'costs' which were permitted to be recovered under the VWF compromise agreement were held to include success fees even though this was not in the contemplation of the parties when the agreement was reached. The Access to Justice agenda can be said to be promoted if a membership organisation is allowed to recover success fees. If the organisation itself is prepared (and contractually required) to act on conditional fee terms, then it would be sharing the risks with clients and aiding access to the courts. The success fees would enable the organisation to pursue more cases in the courts.

Express limitations and restrictions on the recovery of a success fee

Before considering the factors which are to be taken into account in determining the extent of the uplift (and providing that the uplift in question is not one which is fixed by CPR Part 45, which is discussed at the end of this chapter) those rules which either limit or restrict the amount of an uplift should first be considered.

The cost of the delay in payment of the legal representative's fees and expenses cannot be recovered

Rule 44.3B(1)(a) prohibits any recovery of that proportion of a success fee which is attributable to the delay in payment of the legal representatives' fees and expenses. This provision mirrors the rule as it was set out in the CFA Regulations 2000, reg.3(1)(b) (as amended), which requires a CFA to specify how much of the uplift relates to the postponement element. There is no discretionary rule which allows the postponement element of a success fee to be recovered: it will come out of a client's damages. For this reason many firms do not make provision for a postponement element since they prefer to leave the client's damages as intact as possible. Where there is a postponement element it is unlikely to be more than about 5 to 10 per cent.

Failure to give information about a funding arrangement

Rule 44.3B(1)(c) limits *any* additional liability from being recovered if there has been a breach of the rule requiring notice of funding to be given. Relief from sanction is available where notice has not been provided in accordance with the rules. The application and effect of rule 44.3B(1)(c) and the means by which relief can be obtained are set out at **3.4**.

Failure to comply with an order to disclose a statement of reasons

Rule 44.3B(1)(d) provides that a success fee cannot be recovered where a party has not complied with a requirement in the CPD or a court order requiring a statement of reasons to be disclosed explaining why a percentage uplift has been assessed at the level stated in the CFA. This reflects the former CFA Regulations 2000, reg.3(2)(a) (as amended), which required a CFA to state that either the legal representative or client must disclose to the court, when required to do so, the reasons why the success fee was as stated in the agreement (see also CCFA Regulations 2000, reg.5(2)(a) (as amended)). Relief from sanction is also available in such a case. CPD para.10.2 requires notice of an application for relief to be provided to counsel at least two days before the hearing and permits counsel to make written or oral submissions in reply. CPD paras.32.4 to 32.7 set out the requirements which must be satisfied in order to give details of any additional liabilities when detailed assessment proceedings are commenced.

Is it reasonable to incur a success fee at all?

When it comes to determining whether or not it is reasonable to incur a success fee, CPD para.11.8(1)(c) allows an assessing judge to consider 'what other methods of financing the costs were available to the receiving party'. If a solicitor, whilst advising a client as to the existence of other means of funding litigation did discover, for instance, that the client had before-the-event (BTE) insurance, but the client insisted nevertheless on using a CFA, this paragraph of the CPD would be an appropriate basis on which to challenge the success fee on the ground that the decision not to use the BTE was unreasonable. Such cases do occur when a client finds that he is being offered a solicitor who is on a BTE insurer's panel but wants to use a different firm, or alternatively has been using a panel solicitor who demonstrates a lack of competence. Depending on the facts, for instance as to whether the panel firm has in fact done a very poor job, the need to use a CFA (together with an uplift) may or may not be accepted by a costs judge. The insurance ombudsman has adopted the position that up to the time at which proceedings have to be issued a client is obliged to use a panel firm, notwithstanding the wording of Council Directive 87/344/EEC and the Insurance Companies (Legal Expenses Insurance) Regulations 1990, SI 1990/1159 (see para.26, *Sarwar* v. *Alam* [2002] 1 WLR 125).

The circumstances in which it might be reasonable not to make use of a BTE policy on the grounds, for instance, of the desire on the part of a client to employ the solicitor of one's choice are discussed in *Sarwar* at paras.3.7–3.8. This was a case concerned with a pre-1999 Act CFA entered into without a success fee and with the question whether it was reasonable to be able to recover an ATE premium by virtue of the CPD para.11.10. The same principles apply to the recovery of an uplift in such circumstances as they do to the question whether the ATE premium was recoverable. If there is pre-existing BTE which would have funded the action, then why is it reasonable to enter into funding arrangements with expensive additional liabilities? The conclusion of the Court of Appeal in *Sarwar* was that a passenger in a straightforward road traffic accident should ordinarily be expected to make use of a BTE if intending to take proceedings against a negligent driver of the car in which the passenger was travelling. See the discussion at **3.9** below.

When considering the amount of the uplift, the court must consider the facts as they appeared to the legal representative at the time of the CFA (or at the time of any variation)

CPD para.11.7 is clear:

> When considering the factors to be taken into account in assessing an additional liability, [the Court] will have regard to the facts and circumstances as they reasonably appeared to the solicitor or counsel when the funding arrangement was entered into and at the time of any variation of the arrangement.

The plain reading of this paragraph was supported by the decision in *Atack* v. *Lee* [2006] RTR 11 (CA) at para.51: 'The reasonableness of the success fee has to be assessed as at the time the CFA was agreed'. This means that hindsight is not an appropriate test to apply in assessing whether the amount of a success fee was reasonable. This is a principle of general application in costs law (see *Francis* v. *Francis and Dickerson* [1956] P 87, 95 as cited in para.20 of *Ku* v. *Liverpool CC* [2005] 1 WLR 2657) which has been sanctioned in the context of the assessment of CFA uplifts by Master Hurst in *Bensusan* v. *Freedman* (unreported, 20 September 2001) and approved by the Court of Appeal in *Halloran* v. *Delaney* [2003] 1 WLR 28 at para.30. In *Smiths Dock* v. *Edwards* [2004] EWHC 1116 Mr Justice Crane made the concessions (at para.12) that the fact that a defendant had fought a claim hard showed that a receiving party's pessimistic assessment of the risks had been justified. Paragraph 11.7 demonstrates that there should be a separate assessment of the risks on the variation of a CFA.

Can a judge reduce the amount of a success fee from that agreed in a CFA?

What is the case if, as a claim progresses, it becomes more and more apparent that the claimant is going to succeed? CPD para.11.8(2) formerly stated that:

> The court has the power, when considering whether a percentage increase is reasonable, to allow different percentages for different items of costs or for different periods during which costs were incurred.

On the face of it this gave a judge a discretion to reduce a success fee to accommodate changing circumstances. It was relied on without success in *Ku* v. *Liverpool CC* [2005] 1 WLR 2657 in which the Court of Appeal concluded:

> 42. Nowhere in the statute, the regulations, or the rules is there any indication that the court is to have any power to subvert the statutory scheme by determining that although the level of a success fee was reasonable in view of the facts which were or should have been known to the legal representative at the time it was set, he is only entitled to recover a different, much lower, success fee in respect of some later period when different facts were or should have been known to him.

47. ... Once it is clear (in the absence of any later consensual variation which provides for a different success fee) that a CFA may only carry one success fee, and that the task of a costs judge is to determine whether that success fee was a reasonable one in the light of the matters that the legal representative knew or should have known when it was made, there is simply no room for a costs judge to substitute different percentage increases for different items of costs, or for different periods when costs were incurred. He could only do this with the benefit of hindsight, which is prohibited, and the rules and the regulations give him no power to remake the parties' agreement. His powers of interference are limited to altering the success fee to a more reasonable one when he considers the size of the additional liability the paying party should bear. This is because there is nothing in the statute or the regulations to suggest that he is required to do anything other than carry out his usual function of deciding whether an item on a bill is reasonable, and if he decides it is not, of substituting a reasonable amount or deleting the item altogether.

As for CPD para.11.8(2):

56. ... The court has no power to direct that a success fee is recoverable at different rates for different periods of the proceedings. In so far as para 11.8(2) of the Costs Practice Direction suggests otherwise, it is wrong.

This is in part because a practice direction has no legislative force. Practice directions provide 'invaluable guidance to matters of practice in the civil courts, but in so far as they contain statements of the law which are wrong they carry no authority at all' (see Hale LJ in *Re C (Legal Aid: Preparation of Bill of Costs)* [2001] FLR 602 at para.21 and other cases cited at para.55 of *Ku*). The district judge in *Ku* had been wrong to reduce the success fee on the ground that it would have been 'appropriate' to fund the case under a two-stage success fee.

CPD para.27.3 expressly rehearses the wording of para.11.8(2) in the context of fast track trial costs and continues to survive. This section of the CPD has not been considered by the courts, but it must surely be interpreted in the same way as para.11.8(2) was formerly interpreted (see above).

Does a success fee extend to detailed assessment proceedings?

As with costs-only proceedings it is a question of the construction of the CFA whether a success fee extends to detailed assessment proceedings. It would be a very unusual CFA which did not allow a success fee to be claimed on the costs of the detailed assessment. *Ku* v. *Liverpool CC* [2005] 1 WLR 2657 (see above) demonstrates that is single-stage success fee will apply to the detailed assessment proceedings and is not to be reduced (whether under the former CPD para.11.8(2) or otherwise). Where a client has died after the final order in the substantive litigation and a new CFA has been entered into with the executors it will not be possible to recover a success fee unless there is a

Wood v. *Worthing* provision (see below at **3.8** 'Waiving post-Part 36 costs'): there is no 'win' to be achieved.

What is the correct standard by reference to which the assessment of a success fee is to be determined – the 'reasonably careful solicitor'

In *Atack* v. *Lee* [2006] RTR 11 (CA) the receiving party's solicitor had prepared a matrix to stand as his risk assessment. The district judge found the matrix 'of no value at all'. The Court of Appeal held that the judge had been correct 'to consider the matter from the standpoint of a reasonably careful solicitor assessing the risk on the basis of what was known to the claimant's solicitor at the time'.

Atack's case on this issue is a judgment which is in accordance with CPD para.11.7 which is concerned with the facts and circumstances 'as they reasonably appeared to the solicitor or counsel'. The contents of the risk assessment are important and they will be scrutinised to determine whether the uplift claimed was reasonable. But while *Callery* v. *Gray* [2001] 1 WLR 2112 tells us that a CFA can be entered into when a solicitor first takes instructions, the assessment of risk need not be an altogether passive matter. It may be reasonable to expect some limited inquiries to be made at the time of the CFA which will affect the assessment of risk. Thus in *Atack* the Court of Appeal decided that the claimant's solicitor could have made a quick inquiry of the police who would have been able to supply the details of the defendant driver.

Underlying policy considerations

To understand how the rules for the assessment of success fees are operated in practice, it may be useful to go back to some of the policy formulations which preceded the Access to Justice Act 1999.

During the process of consultation leading up to the recoverability provisions contained in the 1999 Act (which amended the original statutory scheme) the view was widely promoted that success fees had to be recoverable because they allowed a legal representative to make up on successful cases the costs which would be lost on unsuccessful cases. In other words the effect of success fees overall would be entirely cost-neutral. Indeed this was the position of both the Law Society and APIL, and anyone interested in the way in which a recoverability of 100 per cent against a losing party made its way into the new funding regime will see a short discussion at section 8 of *Callery* v. *Gray* [2001] 1 WLR 2112 (para.60ff). A ready reckoner (included at **Appendix 9**) has gained general acceptance by costs judges, which was thought to accommodate this arrangement. The Court of Appeal in *Callery* attributed it to *Cook on Costs* (see para.101) although it was also promoted in the first edition of this book. His Honour Michael Cook explains that the table is based on the view that if prospects of success of a case are 75 per cent, then the appropriate uplift is 33 per cent since one of four such cases is likely to settle. Where the prospects of success are 50 per cent, then the appropriate success fee is 100 per cent (see para.4 of *Atack* v. *Lee* [2006] RTR 11 (CA)).

Unfortunately the validity of this type of basic statistical assessment can be skewed by the propensity of some claimant lawyers to do what both defendants and academics asserted would happen after additional liabilities became recoverable, namely 'cherry pick' those cases which were more likely to succeed. There are many public spirited firms which will use CFAs as a vehicle to promote worthy and difficult cases, but there is a concern that for a few claimant lawyers success fees have become primarily a significant extra income stream rather than a vehicle for promoting access to justice: success fees are generally not always used to cushion the effect of cases which are lost. If this is correct, then the question must be asked why the ready reckoner figures should be taken as a sensible starting-point for the assessment of uplifts. Indeed the higher courts have been inviting judges to take account of the more detailed statistical material which has become available over the years since additional liabilities first became recoverable (see the discussion of the use of the Fenn/ Rickman report in RTA cases in *Atack* v. *Lee* [2006] RTR 11 now overtaken by CPR Part 45 and the reference to the data used in the slip/trip case of *Ku* v. *Liverpool CC* [2005] 1 WLR 2657). At a standard detailed assessment level, however, district judges rarely have time to consider such material, and defendants are not geared up to put this material before them. The ready reckoner remains the norm.

In considering whether success fees really do reflect a proper spreading of risk amongst those who need acess to justice, it is worth observing that in 'Improved Access to Justice – Funding Options & Proportionate Costs' (June 2007) the Civil Justice Council has gone to some lengths to uncover new forms of funding to assist the wider policy agenda. These include the development of a 'SLAS', a Supplementary Legal Aid Scheme. This is intended to be of assistance in group actions, but also in individual claims such as clinical negligence, actions against the police, education damages or housing disrepair cases. The CJC identifies a 'sandwich' class of litigant who are above eligibility limits and who apparently cannot obtain access to other funding models. At one point it offers a 'more radical option for a SLAS which would tackle the problem of adverse selection head on' (para.88), an acknowledgment perhaps that success fees are not spreading risk as much as Parliament envisaged. If adverse selection is taking place then why exactly is the ready reckoner approach always the norm?

Deferring the assessment of risk

A ready reckoner approach may be inappropriate for some solicitors in some circumstances. At para.85 of *Callery* for instance, the court observed that:

These comments are not, of course, directed to solicitors who choose, as they reasonably may, to defer agreeing a CFA until they know more about the claim than they have learned from the claimant. Nor are they apposite in the case of a solicitor who does not specialise in litigation, but who on occasion conducts a piece of litigation for a client. Such a solicitor is likely to decide on the uplift by asking himself what reward he requires to induce him to take the risk that he may not recover his fees from the case in question.

This is an acknowledgement that a solicitor does not have to demonstrate a risk-sharing approach in furtherance of the access to justice agenda, but that it is open to a solicitor to specify an uplift on commercial grounds as a species of speculative profit-making. Where a success fee is assessed on this basis, however, experience shows that the court will nevertheless make use of the ready reckoner as a means of testing whether the claimed uplift is reasonable, primarily for want of any other starting point.

3.8 ASSESSING THE SUCCESS FEE

Introduction

Where the fixed recoverable success fee provisions of CPR Part 45 do not apply, the amount of the uplift which will be payable will be determined primarily by reference to section 11 of the CPD and especially to para.11.8(1). This paragraph refers expressly to '(a) the risk that the circumstances in which the costs, fees or expenses would be payable might or might not occur' and '(b) the legal representative's liability for any disbursements' (which will be considered below).

Save for these broad guidelines and for the assistance provided by recent authorities (also considered below), cases are far too fact-specific to make it helpful to run through the individual circumstances of each, and such an approach is likely to irritate a costs judge. On the other hand, when embarking on a consideration what uplift may be appropriate on grounds of principle, a good starting-point is what is recoverable at the very end of proceedings (if the claim gets to trial) as well those other circumstances which have been taken to justify a high success fee.

It is in accordance with the policy considerations which underlie the Access to Justice Act 1999 that CFAs which properly attract high success fees will be those in which a solicitor takes all the risk, ring-fencing the damages which should end up in the client's pocket under 'Simplified' CFA terms. This is contrary to the reservations felt by many judges in the higher courts. Lord Hoffmann, for instance, said of such arrangements in *Callery* that:

> 25. . . . Since the client will in no event be paying the success fee out of his pocket or his damages, he is not concerned with economic rationality. He has no

interest in what the fee is. The only persons who have such an interest are the solicitor on the one hand and the liability insurer who will be called upon to pay it on the other. And their interest centres entirely upon whether the agreed success fee will or will not exceed what the costs judge is willing to allow.

In practice, however, submissions based on the policy approach supporting Parliament's intention to encourage access to justice have generally produced very favourable results for claimants. Only in media cases where the impact of the Human Rights Act 1998 is truly felt is the lack of 'economic rationality' relevant. In such cases the media must be protected from the 'ransom' and 'chilling' effects brought about by litigants able to use the threat of high uplifts together with high base costs. These are discussed in **Chapter 6**.

An arrangement in reasonably common form which justifiably merits a high success fee because it promotes access to the courts is one under the terms of which the solicitor agrees (a) on 'Simplified' CFA terms to restrict his costs to those recovered from the other side; (b) to finance all the disbursements; (c) not to charge anything because of the delay in payment of his costs; and (d) not to charge basic fees (as well as the success fee) in the event that a Part 36 payment or offer is not beaten at trial. Some of these elements are considered further below in the following paragraphs. Some caution is now needed because there must be a risk that notwithstanding Lord Woolf's statement in *Hodgson* v. *Imperial Tobacco* [1998] 1 WLR 1056 that 'there is no reason why the circumstances in which a lawyer, acting under a CFA, can be made personally liable for the costs of a party other than his client should differ from those in which a lawyer who is not acting under a CFA would be so liable', the effect of *Myatt* v. *NCB (No.2)* [2007] 1 WLR 1559 is that a solicitor may end up paying a paying party's costs personally on the basis that he is the one who would have benefited substantially from the proceedings if they had succeeded.

100 per cent uplift appropriate if the matter goes to trial

By the time of trial, at least, it is generally agreed that if there is to be a contested hearing then each side must think that it has a good chance of success. In *Designer Guild Ltd* v. *Russell Williams (Textiles) Ltd (trading as Washington DC) (No.2)* 20 February 2003 (No.4 of 2003 on the SCCO website), Mr Brendon Keith (Principal Judicial Clerk) and Chief Master Hurst (Senior Costs Judge sitting as a Judicial Taxing Officer) decided that:

> There is an argument for saying that in any case which reached trial a success fee of 100 per cent is easily justified because both sides presumably believed that they had an arguable and winnable case.

While hindsight may be irrelevant in many ways, the fact that a case has reached a contested hearing may support the contents of the original risk assessment (cf. Crane J in *Smith Docks* v. *Edwards* at para.12). The canny legal representative who has not entered into a two-stage success fee will conclude his agreement to allow him the option of entering into a new agreement just for trial. This enables a 100 per cent success fee to be claimed.

In *Callery* v. *Gray* [2001] 1 WLR 2112 the Court of Appeal was willing to sanction a 100 per cent success fee in low value RTAs (subject to a reduction if the matter settled during the pre-action protocol period). This was on the basis that 'if the other party is not prepared to settle, or not prepared to settle upon reasonable terms, there is a serious defence'. As a matter of record the continuing expectation that 100 per cent was appropriate in such circumstances was brought to an end by *Halloran* v. *Delaney* [2003] 1 WLR 28 at para.36 (when it was said that 5 per cent was appropriate at all stages), and these cases have now been overtaken by the fixed recoverable success fees of CPR Part 45. However, *Callery*, *Designer Guild*, and indeed the fixed recoverable costs rules, do support a contractual agreement in a CFA for a 100 per cent success fee if the matter gets to trial. In some CFAs lawyers successfully stipulate that 100 per cent is appropriate a certain number of weeks prior to trial, for instance where there has to be a large-scale costs commitment some time before a hearing (reflecting the staged approach in CPR Part 45).

Costs judges will be more willing to approve what appear to be high success fees in cases which have gone a long distance towards trial if the maker of the CFA has agreed that a much lower success fee should be payable if the claim settles at an early stage. See *Re Claims Direct Test Cases* [2003] EWCA Civ 136, [2003] 4 All ER 508 at para.101 for an earlier exposition of this principle.

Simplified CFAs

A 'Simplified CFA' is one under the terms of which a solicitor agrees to waive any costs which are not recovered from the other side. Costs under a simplified agreement are expressly recoverable by reason of CPR rule 43.2(3), (4) which contains amendments to rule 43.2 effected by the Civil Procedure (Amendment No.2) Rules 2003, SI 2003/1242, and which came into effect on 2 June 2003 CFAs on such terms are discussed in some detail in **Chapter 2** (at **2.8**). A Simplified CFA is Access to Justice friendly insofar as it is likely to have the effect of encouraging access to the courts. See *Jones* v. *Wrexham B.C.* [2007] EWCA 1356, 19 December 2007, for a detailed account of what constitutes a Simplified CFA.

Funding the disbursements

The fact that a solicitor agrees to meet the disbursements is expressly recognised as a reason for increasing a success fee (see CPD para.11.8(1)(a)). The opposite, the provision for a disbursement funding loan under a regulated consumer credit agreement (often requiring the client to meet uninsured interest payments) has frequently been treated with grave suspicion by costs judges (see, for instance, the housing disrepair cases of *Bowen* v. *Bridgend CBC,* 25 March 2004 (Master Hurst) and of *Hussain* v. *Leeds CC*, 16 December 2005 (Master O'Hare) and also the decisions of Master Wright at first instance in *Myatt* v. *NCB* 5 August and of Master Hurst in *Richards* v. *Davis* [2005] EWHC 90014 (Costs)). The rules relating to the cost to a lawyer in delay in payment of his fees (which are not recoverable from a paying party in any event) are considered above at **3.7** under 'Express limitations'.

Waiving post-Part 36 costs

As to any provisions in a CFA by which a legal representative agrees not to charge basic fees (rather than just the uplift) in the event that a Part 36 payment or offer is not beaten at trial, these have impressed costs judges. They are risky for a solicitor, especially where the costs of the litigation are likely to be very high and the solicitor can fairly say (as is often the case) that there was a real risk that a defendant might make an early tactical payment-in by way of a well-judged offer which will require careful assessment. An uplift of 100 per cent may well be recoverable where this provision is included in the retainer. In *Wood* v. *Worthing & Southlands Hospitals NHS Trust* (Case no. 23 of 2004 on the SCCO website), Hodge J decided that Master Wright was wrong to have construed a CFA drafted in such terms so that the receiving party was not entitled to any success fee at all, and remitted the matter back to the same judge. Master Wright at a hearing on 26 November 2004 (unreported) decided that the 100 per cent mark-up properly represented the risks in a clinical negligence case where there had been a payment-in in excess of £200,000 prior to the making of the CFA. Even where there has been an admission of liability before the date on which the CFA was made, it is the writer's experience that a 100 per cent uplift can be recovered, for instance where difficulties in causation or quantum make the assessment of damages difficult. At the time of writing, however, it seems that judges in the SCCO have become less impressed by this provision in a CFA since there is likely to be a period before a Part 36 offer is made when the basic costs will not be at risk. *Wood* is distinguishable because there was already a payment-in. It is best to be able to supply evidence to demonstrate that there were real risks in respect of the individual case. For instance, was this a paying party with a particular reputation for making early Part 36 offers?

Two-stage success fees

In *Ku* v. *Liverpool CC* [2005] 1 WLR 2657 the Court of Appeal decided that the Access to Justice Act scheme, in particular s.58(2)(b) (as substituted by the 1999 Act) and the CFA Regulations 2000, reg.3 showed that Parliament envisaged that a CFA when made would include only one uplift, an assumption reflected by para.11.7 of the Practice Direction.

In *Callery* v. *Gray* [2001] 1 WLR 2112, however, the court had already suggested (at para.106ff.) the use of an alternative type of arrangement, namely a 'two-stage' success fee:

> 107. A success fee can be agreed which assumes the case will not settle, at least until after the end of the protocol period, if at all, but which is subject to a rebate if it does in fact settle before the end of that period. Thus, by way of example, the uplift might be agreed at 100 per cent, subject to a reduction to 5 per cent should the claim settle before the end of the protocol period.
>
> 108. The logic behind a two-stage success fee is that, in calculating the success fee, it can properly be assumed that if, notwithstanding the compliance with the protocol, the other party is not prepared to settle, or not prepared to settle upon reasonable terms, there is a serious defence. By the end of the protocol period, both parties should have decided upon their positions. If they are prepared to settle, they should make an offer setting out their position clearly and providing the level of costs protection which they determine is appropriate.

This type of arrangement was enthusiastically welcomed by the professions and is in common use in various permutations. It forms the basis for the fixed recoverable success fee now contained in CPR Part 45. There are discussions of the benefits of two-stage success fees in *Halloran* v. *Delaney* [2003] 1 WLR 28 and in *Atack* v. *Lee* [2006] RTR 11. In *Ku* v. *Liverpool CC* [2005] 1 WLR 2657 the Court of Appeal held that the district judge had not been entitled to reassess a success fee on the basis that it would have been 'appropriate' to have entered into a two-stage, rather than a single-stage, CFA.

Recovery of success fees under CCFAs

A CCFA is not an entity distinct from a CFA under the Access to Justice Act 1999. The statutory provision which allows for the recovery of a success fee won pursuant to the terms of a CCFA under the Act is therefore the same as that which applies for individual CFAs, namely s.58A(6). The legislative framework governing CCFAs is to be found in **Chapter 2**, and an explanation as to the reasons for their lawfulness and enforceability (in particular that the claim to a success fee does not breach the indemnity principle) is to be found in **Chapter 4**.

So far as the costs rules are concerned, the want of any distinction between CFAs and CCFAs is reflected by the definition section of CPR rule 43.2(k)(i) ('funding arrangement') which expressly includes under the one subparagraph any CFA or CCFA so long as that agreement provides for a success fee. In other words success fees are recoverable as part of a party's costs under rule 44.5 in exactly the same way as success fees are recoverable where they are claimed under individual CFAs. The costs rules distinguish between, on the one hand, CFAs and CCFAs which do not provide for success fees (these being treated as ordinary private retainers) and 'funding arrangements' on the other, namely CFAs (including CCFAs) which do provide for success fees.

A few express references to CCFAs do exist in the costs rules. Thus they are found in rule 44.16 ('Adjournment where legal representative seeks to challenge disallowance of any amount of percentage increase') and in the corresponding part of the CPD (section 20). They are also to be found in Part 45 (fixed costs). However, these express references do not set up any difference in the treatment of CCFAs separately from individual CFAs.

The consequence of the want of any distinction between individual CFAs and collective arrangements in the costs rules is that all of the rules concerning the recovery of success fees apply to uplifts earned under CCFA terms in just the same way that they do in the case of individual arrangements. This means that there are no special rules which apply, for instance, in respect of either the obligations to supply information about a CCFA which provides for a success fee, the stage of the proceedings at which a CCFA success fee will be assessed, or the limitations and restrictions which apply to the recovery of a CCFA success fee, or the basis for the assessment of a success fees payable under the terms of a CCFA. All of the relevant rules will be found in the preceding paragraphs of this chapter, where any reference to a success fee means any success fee whether it is payable by reason of an individual CFA or a CCFA. The rules bite in respect of the arrangements made for the individual case funded by the CCFA.

3.9 RECOVERY OF INSURANCE PREMIUMS

'Insurance premium'

Section 29 of the Access to Justice Act 1999 ('Recovery of insurance premiums by way of costs') is the main power by which an order as to costs may include an order for the payment of an ATE premium. Section 29, and the corresponding provisions anticipating the recovery of additional liabilities as they appear in the CPD, are set out at **Appendix 4**.

It is the definition of 'insurance premium' at CPR rule 43.2(m) which perhaps provides a rather clearer definition of the nature of the 'insurance premium' which is recoverable by virtue of Access to Justice Act 1999, s.29 than that provided by s.29 itself. This rule defines an 'insurance premium' as:

> a sum of money paid or payable against the risk of incurring a costs liability in the proceedings, taken out after the event that is the subject matter of the claim.

In other words, what is recoverable is the premium incurred by the purchase of an ATE policy. This does not mean that the ATE policy has to be bought to sit alongside a CFA. Section 29 allows an ATE premium to be entirely free-standing, for instance a policy which will meet both sides' costs in a commercial action. In *Callery* v. *Gray (No.2)* the Court of Appeal decided that 'insurance . . . against the risk of incurring a costs liability in the proceedings' should be interpreted to read 'insurance against the risk of incurring a costs liability in the proceedings that cannot be passed on to the opposing party', to make the wider ambit of s.29 clear.

Rules common to ATE premiums as one form of 'additional liability'

Summary and detailed assessments

It follows by virtue of the definition sections at rule 43.2 and the wording of CPR rule 44.3A ('costs orders relating to funding arrangements') that the rules as set out in rule 44.3A (which govern the relevant assessment process and the time of the assessment) apply where a claim includes an insurance premium. Rule 44.3A and the corresponding parts of the CPD set out the provisions which govern the time when an additional liability will be assessed and whether by way of a summary or detailed assessment, and they are explained at **3.5**.

Limits on the recovery of insurance premiums

Also by reason of the definition sections and by reason of the wording of CPR rule 44.3B ('limits on recovery under funding arrangements'), a receiving party is subject to the same limitation on recovering an ATE premium where he has failed to provide information about it as he would be if he had failed to provide information about a CFA which made provision for a success fee. This is the effect of rule 44.3B(c). The rules governing such cases and the means by which and the circumstances in which relief from sanction may be obtained are set out at **3.4**.

The assessment of the recoverable amount of insurance premiums: CPR Part 45

The underlying basis for the assessment of an insurance premium is either the indemnity or standard basis as set out in CPR rule 44.5 according to the relevant order giving rise to the entitlement to costs. In this respect, insurance premiums are no different from other additional liabilities.

The role of proportionality in justifying the amount of an ATE

Proportionality as an element of rule 44.5 has attracted the attention of judges as a means of justifying the higher levels of 'staged' or 'stepped' premiums, a matter examined by the Court of Appeal in *Rogers* v. *Merthyr Tydfil*. In that case an ATE policy provided for a premium of £450 payable at the outset, a further £900 when proceedings were issued and a further £3,510 60 days before trial. At trial damages were awarded in the sum of £3,105 (exclusive of interest).

The Court of Appeal in *Rogers* went back to the well-known statement of the role and function of proportionality in a costs context in *Lownds* v. *Home Office (Practice Note)* [2002] 1 WLR 2450 when Lord Woolf MR said:

> 31. ... [W]hat is required is a two-stage approach. There has to be a global approach and an item by item approach. The global approach will indicate whether the total sum claimed is or appears to be disproportionate having particular regard to the considerations which Part 44.5(3) states are relevant. If the costs as a whole are not disproportionate according to that test then all that is normally required is that each item should have been reasonably incurred and the cost for that item should be reasonable. If on the other hand the costs as a whole appear disproportionate then the court will want to be satisfied that the work in relation to each item was necessary and, if necessary, that the cost of the item is reasonable. If, because of lack of planning or due to other causes, the global costs are disproportionately high, then the requirement that the costs should be proportionate means that no more should be payable than would have been payable if the litigation had been conducted in a proportionate manner. This is turn means that reasonable costs will only be recovered for the items which were necessary if the litigation had been conducted in a proportionate manner.

In the context of the premium of an insurance policy within the meaning of Access to Justice Act 1999, s.29, the Court of Appeal decided that questions of proportionality were not limited to issues of quantum (see para.105):

> If the court concludes that it was *necessary* to incur the staged premium, then as this court's judgment in *Lownds* shows, it should be adjudged a proportionate expense. Necessity here is, we think, not some absolute litmus test. It may be demonstrated by the application of strategic considerations which travel beyond

the dictates of the particular case. Thus it may include, as we are persuaded it does, the unavoidable characteristics of the market in insurance of this kind. It does so because this very market is integral to the means of providing access to justice in civil disputes in what may be called the post-legal aid world.

A similarly wide approach to proportionality in the context of ATE premiums was expressed in *Callery* v. *Gray (No.2)* [2001] 1 WLR 2142 at para.70 in which the court decided, when considering the question whether a premium was proportionate, that it was proper to ask whether the amount of the premium was manifestly disproportionate to the risk.

'Proportionality' in the context of an ATE premium therefore is not limited to issues of pure expense, and by this route it becomes easier to justify the cost of an ATE premium. Ultimately, 'principle and pragmatism' drove the Court of Appeal in *Rogers* to the conclusion that the premium was necessarily incurred and that it was therefore a proportionate expense. Further, the choice of this particular policy had been a reasonable one in the circumstances given the background advanced by the solicitor to show how he had gone about finding a reliable insurer. His evidence had been that he had sought to find a policy provided by an insurer which would benefit his clients, and after investigating the market he had made a rational and reasonable choice in selecting this particular one. He had been badly let down by a previous provider (who had baulked at paying out when required to do so under the terms of the policy) and when he had invited several insurers to show him their products, this one had taken the trouble to come and visit him.

In addition to these wider considerations, the figures advanced to the court demonstrated that it was 'impossible to say that a total premium of £4,860 was unreasonable' (para.110). This was because the estimated loss (£6,500) had compared favourably with the actual outcome, and the estimated prospect of success at 51 per cent was not unreasonable in all the circumstances.

It was clear that as a matter of policy the court was attracted to the staged premium model since (a) it mirrored the two-stage success fee; (b) it was appropriate for an insurer to block-rate its risk in the early stages and then to seek to recover a premium which truly reflected the risks nearer to trial; and (c) exposure to the risks at trial 'required a defendant to think very seriously about the merits of his position before a trial takes place' (para.107).

In *Ashworth* v. *Peterborough* UFC, 10 June 2002, Master Wright noted that the proportionality of an item of costs must be determined under CPR rule 44.4(2)(a) by reference to the 'matters in issue' when allowing an ATE premium of £45,937.50 in a commercial matter in which the receiving party had had difficulty in securing insurance but had nevertheless done the best he could in order to obtain it. (The amount of damages recovered was some £66,000 and the total bill of costs was a little over £100,000.)

CPD para.11.10 ('factors to be taken into account in deciding the amount of costs')

Paragraph 11.10 of the CPD sets out some express circumstances which are to be taken into account by reason of rule 44.5 in assessing whether the cost of insurance cover is reasonable. These are:

(a) where the insurance cover is not purchased in support of a conditional fee agreement with a success fee, how its cost compares with the likely cost of funding the case with a conditional fee agreement with a success fee and supporting insurance cover;
(b) the level and extent of the cover provided;
(c) the availability of any pre-existing insurance cover;
(d) whether any part of the premium would be rebated in the event of early settlement;
(e) the amount of commission payable to the receiving party or his legal representatives or other agents.

The availability of pre-existing insurance

Paragraph 11(3) above, which requires the court to take into consideration the availability of any pre-existing insurance cover, occupies a central role in the assessment of what insurance premium may be recoverable. This is by reason of the fact that in an appropriate case a court may decide that no ATE premium should be recoverable at all (see the facts of *Richards* v. *Davis* [2005] EWHC 90014, although the same result was reached by a different route). While the client care provisions formerly set out in CFA Regulations 2000, reg.4 and now contained in the Solicitors' Code of Conduct 2007 require a solicitor to provide the requisite information, advice and explanation as to the existence of BTE, the client was not required inevitably to make use of any BTE which was unearthed. On the other hand, an unreasonable refusal to make use of that cover might result in any ATE policy (or success fee) being disallowed on an assessment.

In an early case, *Sarwar* v. *Alam* [2002] 1 WLR 125, which concerned a CFA to which the CFA Regulations 2000 did not apply (because they were not in force at the time at which it was made), the Court of Appeal set out a determination when a client might be expected to make use of a BTE and not take out a separate ATE policy. This was an RTA which settled for £2,250, the claimant passenger having sued the driver of the car in which he was travelling. There was no dispute as to liability. The claimant took out an ATE policy without realising that the driver had BTE DAS insurance cover which would have covered his passenger.

The central question was whether it was reasonable in all the circumstances for Mr Sarwar, acting on his solicitor's advice, to incur the cost of the ATE premium without making any further inquiries into the possible existence of

BTE cover. The matter was in reality a contest between BTE and ATE insurers. As it was put in para.39:

> Liability insurers believe that if BTE cover is available for these small motor accident claims the claimants should use it, and should not saddle them with the cost ... of an ATE premium and a success fee uplift. BTE insurers wish to hold onto and expand their business. ATE insurers are worried that, if they lose business to BTE insurers, their premiums may have to rise or they may have to go out of business altogether. While wishing to hold the ring between the different insurance interests which are members of the association, the ABI believes that in a case like the present the BTE insurer should be given precedence. It believes, however, that there is a market for both BTE and ATE insurance, which should complement but not duplicate each other, and that each should be allowed to develop in response to public demand.

The Court of Appeal ultimately decided as a matter of principle and of public policy that it would be better in such cases (where the value of the claim was less than £5,000 and so long also as the claim possessed no special features or unusual difficulties) for the BTE policy to be used.

At the same time the fact of the prior existence of the BTE policy was dependent on discovery by the client's solicitor that such a policy existed, leading to guidance being provided by the court as to the existence of such cover. This is to be found at paras.45–51. The court held that:

45. ... Proper modern practice dictates that a solicitor should normally invite a client to bring to the first interview any relevant motor insurance policy, any household insurance policy and any stand-alone BTE insurance policy belonging to the client and/or any spouse or partner living in the same household as the client. It would seem desirable for solicitors to develop the practice of sending a standard form letter requesting a sight of these documents to the client in advance of the first interview. At the interview the solicitor will also ask the client, as required by paragraph 4(j)(iv) of the Client Care Code (see paragraph 14 above) whether his/her liability for costs may be paid by another person, for example an employer or trade union.

46. ... The solicitor will then be able to read through the policy, and if BTE cover is available ... the solicitor should refer the client to the BTE insurer without further ado. The solicitor's inquiries should be proportionate to the amount at stake. The solicitor is not obliged to embark on a treasure hunt, seeking to see the insurance policies of every member of the client's family in case by chance they contain relevant BTE cover which the client might use.

47. Now that motor insurance often contains provision for BTE cover for a claim brought by a passenger, the solicitor should ordinarily ask the client passenger to obtain a copy of the driver's insurance policy, if reasonably practicable. Whether it is reasonably practicable to comply with the solicitor's request is likely to be fact-sensitive. At one end of the spectrum is the driver who is a member of the same family or the same household, as with Mr Sarwar and Mr Alam. At the other is the unknown driver who gave a lift to a hitchhiker who got hurt in an accident and the driver then disappeared into the night.

48. If the solicitor sees that the BTE cover contains a stipulation, like the BTE cover in this case, that the driver should consent to its use by the passenger, the solicitor should tell the client to obtain the driver's consent before making a claim on the BTE insurer. . . . If the driver refuses consent for reasons of his/her own, then it is common ground that the BTE cover would not be available.

49. So far as credit cards and charge cards are concerned, we have received no evidence of the terms of LEI cover offered by the companies marketing these cards, and we do not know how easy it is for the cardholders to avail themselves of such cover in a case like the present. We are inclined to think that the time taken by a solicitor in assisting a client to identify and pursue such cover would at present be likely to result in this course proving more expensive than an ATE premium in this class of case. If, at some time in the future, credit card or charge card companies decide as a matter of business practice to make the extent of any BTE cover they provide readily available to solicitors, either through one of their professional journals or guides or on a publicly accessible website, then the client should also be asked to bring to the first interview any credit card or charge card belonging to him/her and/or any spouse or partner living in the same household.

50. The guidance we have given in this part of our judgment should not be treated as an inflexible code. The overriding principle is that the claimant, assisted by his/her solicitor, should act in a manner that is reasonable. The availability of ATE cover at a modest premium will inevitably restrict the extent to which it will be reasonable for a solicitor's time to be used in investigating alternative sources of insurance.

These are principles which are likely still to be applied in similar circumstances where a claim for fixed recoverable costs under Part 45 includes a claim for an insurance policy or notional membership organisation premium. They are to be distinguished from the guidance given in *Garrett* v. *Halton B.C.* [2007] 1 WLR 554 as to the test relevant to the reg.4 client care inquiries which were required to be given under the CFA Regulations 2000 (see **Chapter 4**).

On the facts of the case, and notwithstanding the general advice it gave, the Court of Appeal held that the insurance premium was not recoverable. This was because DAS, ostensibly the managers of insurance provided by CIS, were also the reinsurers, a fact which would not have been clear to the claimant. The arrangements in place did not enjoy the transparency expected by Council Directive (EEC) 87/344 as reproduced in the Insurance Companies (Legal Expenses Insurance) Regulations 1990, SI 1990/1159: the insurers had not 'financed some transparently independent organisation to handle such claims [as those made by Mr Sarwar], and [had not] made it clear in the policy that this is what they were doing' (para.53).

Freedom to instruct a solicitor of one's choice; panel arrangements; public funding

In some circumstances the decision not to make use of BTE cover known to be available may be quite legitimate and reasonable, for instance where the solicitor has some special expertise or the client has been badly served by a previous lawyer. While the Court of Appeal in *Sarwar* was not persuaded that a claimant has an unfettered right to the lawyer of his choice (applying *R* v. *Legal Aid Board, ex p. Duncan* [2000] COD 159), there is a suggestion in the same case (para.46) that in respect of a matter which is not straightforward it may be appropriate not to take up BTE insurance where the cover has a limit of £25,000. This is not a lot of protection for both sides' costs in a large case, and CFA terms, for instance on an 'Access to Justice friendly' model, may well be more advantageous than the use of a BTE policy.

This problem whether the legal representative can be utilised without putting a claim for additional liabilities in jeopardy is particularly acute where a panel solicitor is available under the terms of BTE insurance.

Regulation 6 of the Insurance Companies (Legal Expenses Insurance) Regulations 1990, SI 1990/1159 ('freedom to choose lawyer') provides:

(1)   Where under a legal expenses insurance contract recourse is had to a lawyer (or other person having such qualifications as may be necessary) to defend, represent or serve the interests of the insured in any inquiry or proceedings, the insured shall be free to choose that lawyer (or other person).

The Insurance Ombudsman 'has consistently interpreted reg.6(1) as meaning that the obligation to permit the insured to select a lawyer of his choice is triggered at the time when efforts to settle a claim by negotiation have failed and legal proceedings have to be initiated' (*Sarwar* para.26).

The Ombudsman in a newsletter dated March 2003 (issue 26) has stated that he would expect a BTE insurer to fund an insured's claim in the event that it is a serious or complex matter such as a large personal injury matter, an allegation of medical negligence, especially if there is a 'considerable history to investigate and assess'. But judges on detailed assessments have not stood too closely with the theoretical possibilities. Thus in the detailed assessment proceedings in *White* v. *Revell*, 8 September 2006, a refusal by DAS to allow a non-panel firm to act was sufficient to justify an ATE of modest cost.

Where a client has instructed solicitors on Simplified CFA terms the client may be better off than if the client had the benefit of a public funding certificate (because of the effect of the statutory charge), so that the use of an ATE premium may be an entirely reasonable option.

When is a premium unreasonably high given the level and extent of the cover?

CPD para.11.10(2) states that material considerations for determining the reasonableness of a recoverable premium include the level and extent of the cover provided. The amount of cover and the circumstances which may restrict or limit its availability can be determined from the policy wording without difficulty. What is a much more difficult, even an impossible, task, in present circumstances, is effectively to be able to compare the cost of one policy with that of another, a problem in particular for paying parties wishing to challenge ATE premiums.

This has become a problem because of several factors. First, there is the simple practical fact that there is no convenient means of getting a straightforward comparison before a judge on a detailed assessment, the Court of Appeal having dismissed the ways in which use was being made by defendants of indicative information periodically set out in *Litigation Funding* or to be found on the website of *The Judge*. Indeed Master Hurst had already said the following in the *Re RSA Pursuit Test Cases* (at para.235):

> As to the information contained in Litigation Funding and The Judge website, this is no more than an indication of policies which might be available in certain circumstances. As [counsel] points out, the premiums on his website are 'indicative only' and the website contains further warnings. Litigation Funding has similar warnings and reservations.

The second explanation is because of the concern that judges are not insurance experts and cannot be expected to be familiar with this particular market. Thirdly (see *Rogers* at para.117):

> the viability of the ATE market will be imperilled if they regard themselves (without the assistance of expert evidence) as better qualified than the underwriter to rate the financial risk the insurer faces.

Fourthly, the burden of demonstrating that there is an alternative policy available is firmly on the shoulders of the paying party (see *Tyndall* v. *Battersea Dogs' Home* (16 December 2005, Master Wright) at para.77 and *Rogers* at para.112). While Master Hurst has stated in the *RSA Pursuit Test Cases* [2005] EWHC 90003 that in considering the recoverability of a premium 'the court should look both at the costs risks and the size of the claim' (para.261), the result of these practical difficulties is that district judges and costs judges will be required to judge the reasonableness of a premium only on a 'very broad brush' basis and they are likely to reduce a premium which is claimed by a respectable provider with considerable reservation (see *Tyndall* at para.79). In *Winmill* v. *Doncaster MBC*, 8 November 2007, Master Roger took a very broad-brush view when reducing ATE premiums claimed in sums in excess of £77,000.

It is difficult to see how the courts do expect a market in proportionate and reasonable ATE premiums to be encouraged. Many judges have expressed reservations. Lord Hoffmann in *Callery* v. *Gray* said, for instance:

> 25. The difficulty is that while, in principle, it may be rational to agree a success fee at the earliest moment, it is extremely difficult to say whether the actual

'premium' paid by the client was reasonable or not. This is because the client does not pay the 'premium', whether the success fee is agreed at an earlier or later stage. The transaction therefore lacks the features of a normal insurance, in which the transaction takes place against the background of an insurance market in which the economically rational client or his broker will choose the cheapest insurance suited to his needs. Since the client will in no event be paying the success fee out of his pocket or his damages, he is not concerned with economic rationality. He has no interest in what the fee is. The only persons who have such an interest are the solicitor on the one hand and the liability insurer who will be called upon to pay it on the other. And their interest centres entirely upon whether the agreed success fee will or will not exceed what the costs judge is willing to allow.

See too the Addendum in *Rogers* written by Smith LJ with which the other judges agreed:

127. . . . I do not think it was the intention of Parliament that would-be claimants should be able to litigate weak cases without any risk whatsoever to themselves. But it seems to me that this is what is happening. ATE premiums are set on the basis of a high expected failure rate at trial. Even cases that are assessed at a prospect of success of only 51% receive ATE insurance. Thus the premiums have to be significantly higher than they would be if a more rigorous standard were applied. Often no premium has to be paid upfront. If the case is lost the premium is rarely paid. That practice inevitably increases the premiums even further. If the case is won, the premium is in principle recoverable from the liability insurer and, as this court has held in the instant case, if it was necessary for the claimant to take out ATE insurance and the solicitor has acted reasonably, the whole premium will be recovered.

128. Two things concern me about this situation. One is that there is very little incentive for solicitors to look for the best value in ATE insurance. One can understand the position of someone like [the claimant's solicitor] whose primary concern is to protect his client from the kind of problem that he had experienced with his previous provider. He can quite sensibly justify opting for a more expensive product. His client will never have to pay the premium regardless of the outcome. As the judgement of the court acknowledges, there is a pressure on insurers to keep their premiums at a reasonable level in order to avoid challenges such as has occurred in this case . . .

129. As the judgment of court observes, the proper use of a three stage premium should require a defendant to take a second, more rigorous, look at the merits of the case before it proceeds to trial. What concerns me is that the ATE system does not provide any incentive for the claimant's side to have a second and more rigorous look at the merits, often even after a Part 36 offer has been made and refused. It appears that the claimant can just carry on. The only assessment that is made is as to the size of the premium; the lower the chances of success, the higher the premium. I have the impression that the insurer does not ask whether the claim should be stopped. It seems to me that if, at the third stage, when much more information should be available than at the time of issue, solicitors and ATE insurers were to make a careful assessment of the prospects of success, and were to stop the weak ones, the proportion of cases which fail at trial would be much reduced. All sensible private clients would insist on such an assessment. At present, the insured claimant can notionally pay the high premium which reflects his poor chances of success,

secure in the knowledge that, if he wins, the premium will be recovered and, if he loses, he can walk away unscathed. I find it hard to believe that Parliament intended that claimants should be in so much better a position than a private litigant.

As she also noted (at para.128), the decision in *Rogers* is likely to have made the position worse since the effect is now that only where the premium is clearly unreasonable will it be possible for a judge to intervene (see for instance paras.109 and 115 of *Rogers*).

Staged/stepped and other increasing premiums

For the reasons set out in the preceding paragraphs (see **3.9**), the Court of Appeal in *Rogers* decided that for sound public policy reasons the premium of an ATE insurance policy requiring payment of a staged/stepped premium with an assessed element for the last (trial) stage is recoverable. So too in *Tyndall* Master Wright held that the choice of the particular staged policy had been reasonable. On the other hand, there are additional forms of increasing premium policies which are available (see **Chaper 11**) and the assumption should not be made that the decision in *Rogers* will necessarily apply to all.

Providing information to an opponent as to staged premiums

Good practice requires that where a party has the benefit of a policy with staged premiums, then he should inform his opponent that the policy is staged and specify the trigger moments at which the second or later stages will be reached. This is an obligation to be undertaken in addition to the obligations set out in CPR rule 44.15(1) and in paras 19.1(1) and 19.4 of the CPD. By observing this practice 'the opponent has been given fair notice of the staging, and unless there are features of the case that are out of the ordinary, his liability to pay at the second or third stage a higher premium than he would have had to pay if the claim had been settled at the first stage should not prove to be a contentious issue' (see *Rogers* at para.116).

Good practice where there is a challenge to a staged premium

The Court of Appeal in *Rogers* considered what should be done 'if an issue arises about the size of a second or third stage premium' (para.117), deciding that:

it will ordinarily be sufficient for a claimant's solicitor to write a brief note for the purposes of the costs assessment explaining how he came to choose the particular ATE product for his client, and the basis on which the premium is rated – whether block rated or individually rated.

This will ordinarily enable a judge on an assessment to decide whether or not what will probably appear a disproportionately large premium can be justified on broad terms as an appropriate selection. This is surely a matter of good practice where any challenge is made to the size of an ATE premium.

Deferred premiums and the Consumer Credit Act 1974

Deferred premiums are perfectly acceptable and a normal part of an ATE premium. In *Tilby* v. *Perfect Pizza*, 28 February 2002, Master Hurst held that an ATE premium payable on deferred terms did not fall within the ambit of the Consumer Credit Act 1974.

Self-insuring premiums

Rogers v. *Merthyr* itself demonstrates that it is permissible for an element of an ATE policy to include provision for insurance of the premium in the event that the case is lost and the premium is not recoverable from the opponent.

Premiums assessed as a proportion of the damages

It is not champertous to fix the size of an ATE premium by reference to the amount of damages recovered (*Pirie* v. *Ayling*, 18 February 2003 Master Hurst).

Panel/delegated/bulk schemes

An arrangement by which a legal representative agrees to source insurance products from one source is not unlawful, although notice of such an arrangement must be provided to the client. See r.8A and Appendix 1 of the Solicitors' Financial Services (Conduct of Business) Rules 2001 made by the Law Society under the Financial Services and Markets Act 2000:

> a solicitor who proposes that his client should enter into an ATE insurance policy, and who recommends a particular policy because it is the only policy which, consistently with his firm's membership of a panel, he is allowed to recommend, must tell the client that he is contractually obliged to recommend a policy with that insurer. That would give the client notice of the particular interest which the firm has in recommending the policy, whereas just to tell the client that the firm is on a particular panel does not convey that information.

Unbundling the elements of an insurance premium

Where there is a serious challenge to the nature and extent of an ATE premium, in particular on the basis that what is being sought to be recovered are collateral benefits which should not be part of a recoverable premium, the course adopted by the Court of Appeal is for it to sit as a court rehearing the matter when it will invite evidence to be submitted from all interested parties. A report is likely to be obtained from a Costs Judge sitting as an assessor. Such an approach was adopted in, for instance, the *Claims Direct* and *TAG* cases, as well as in *Callery* v. *Grey (No.2)* and *Rogers*. An account of the detailed process of 'unbundling' and the conclusions is not within the scope of this book.

Membership organisations

Access to Justice Act 1999, s.30 ('recovery where body undertakes to meet costs liabilities') allows a 'body of a prescribed description' to recover 'an . . . amount in respect of any provision made by or on behalf of the body in connection with the proceedings against the risk of having to meet such liabilities' (s.30(2)).

This rule was originally introduced for the benefit of trades unions but it has now been made available to a wider range of prescribed organisations (such as the AA). How prescribed organisation status can be obtained is set out at **2.12**.

Section 30(3) prohibits the amount recoverable from exceeding that set out in regulations, and the effect of Access to Justice (Membership Organisations) Regulations 2005, SI 2005/2306, reg.5 is that a recognised body can recover the equivalent (but no more than the equivalent) of an ATE premium, even though no such premiums may ever have to be collected or set aside.

The CPD and the Costs Rules make it clear that the notional insurance premium which can be recovered by a prescribed membership organisation is to be assessed by the rules which apply to ATE premiums. See CPD para.11.11:

> Where the court is considering a provision made by a membership organisation, rule 44.3B(1) (b) provides that any such provision which exceeds the likely cost to the receiving party of the premium of an insurance policy against the risk of incur-ring a liability to pay the costs of other parties to the proceedings is not recover-able. In such circumstances the court will, when assessing the additional liability, have regard to the factors set out in paragraph 11.10 above, in addition to the factors set out in rule 44.5.

The reader is therefore directed to the principles and rules which concern the recovery of ATE premiums as set out in the foregoing paragraphs.

CPR rule 44.3B(1)(b) expressly repeats the limit to be imposed on the amount of an ATE which is recoverable by reason of reg.4. The effect of this rule is that a costs judge may not permit the recovery of a membership organ-isation premium to the extent that it exceeds the likely cost of an ATE premium. There is no discretionary rule which allows an additional liability calculated in excess of the statutory formula to be recovered.

3.10   FIXED RECOVERABLE SUCCESS FEES

CPR Part 45 contains provisions as to fixed costs in certain categories of proceedings. The amounts which can be recovered are set out variously in section II of Part II (fixed recoverable costs in RTAs), Part III (fixed percentage uplifts in RTAs), Part IV (fixed percentage uplifts in employers' liability claims) and Part V (fixed percentage uplifts in employers' liability disease claims). Additional parts to Part 45 can be expected.

The automatic calculation of fixed recoverable success fees in Part 45 marks a revolution against the requirements which ordinarily have to be satisfied in the case of a statutory CFA. See *Nizami* v. *Butt* [2006] 1 WLR 3307 in which Simon J held (para.26):

> the receiving party does not have to demonstrate that there is a valid retainer between the solicitor and client, merely that the conditions laid down under the Rules have been complied with.

This is not the place for a detailed examination of these various rules, but a broad account is given setting out the amount of the percentage uplifts recoverable at different stages. It will be noted that the maximum percentage uplift is 100 per cent to be awarded if the matter gets to trial (the precise boundaries as to whether the matter has got to trial are important). This reflects the understanding (discussed below) that if a matter gets all the way to trial then each side must have thought that it stood a good chance of winning.

Part II of Part 45 applies in costs-only proceedings under rule 44.12A and in proceedings for approval or settlement under rule 21.10(2). The total of the agreed damages must not exceed £10,000 and the appropriate track must not have been the small claims track (rule 45.7(2)(c), (d)). The claim must have arisen out of a road traffic accident which occurred on or after 6 October 2003, and the 'agreed damages' may be either personal injury or property damage or both.

In addition to providing a formula for the recovery of costs generally, the rules in Part II specify how success fees are to be calculated. The amount of the percentage uplift is fixed by rule 45.11(2) as 12.5 per cent of the fixed recoverable costs calculated according to the formula set out in rule 45.9(1) (£800 plus 20 per cent of the damages agreed up to £5,000 and 15 per cent of the damages agreed between £5,000 and £10,000). In calculating the success fee any 'weighting allowance' (rules 45.9(2), 45.11(2)) will not be taken into consideration; neither will any additional discretionary award of costs under rule 45.12(1).

As to Part III, which concerns only fixed uplifts, this Part can only apply to road traffic accidents occurring on or after 6 October 2003 where the proceedings were not, or would not have been, allocated to the small claims track (rule 45.15(3)). Separate provisions apply to solicitors' and counsel's fees. Rule 45.16 permits a solicitor to recover 100 per cent to be recovered by way of an uplift where the claim concludes at trial, and 12.5 per cent in any other circumstances (including settlement before the issue of proceedings (rule 45.16). Counsel is permitted different uplifts depending on the appropriate form of allocation and the time at which the matter is concluded, the uplifts being fixed variously at 12.5 per cent, 50 per cent, 75 per cent and 100 per cent. The rules are set out comprehensively and clearly in rule 45.17. Where the damages (broadly speaking) exceed £500,000 either the solicitor or counsel may apply for an assessment of the success fee outside the fixed formulas (rule 45.18). On the assessment of the uplift the amount awarded must be greater than 20 per cent for it to be recovered at a rate other than 12.5 per cent (12.5 per cent by rule 45.19(3)(a) being the default rate if the 20 per cent is not beaten), save that if the amount of the uplift when assessed is less than 7.5 per cent, then this is the amount which the legal representative must be awarded (rule 45.19(2)). There is an additional sanction, which is that if the alternative uplift is assessed at between 7.5 per cent and 20 per cent, then the costs of the application and of the assessment must be paid by the applicant (rule 45.19(3)(b)).

Part IV concerns employers liability claims in which the dispute relates to an injury sustained on or after 1 October 2004. Certain claims are expressly excluded by rule 45.20 (being claims which fall within other categories of fixed recoverable costs or which would normally be allocated to the small claims track). The same mechanisms apply for the calculation of fixed percentage uplifts to be awarded either to solicitors or counsel as apply under rules 45.16 and 45.17, save that in the case of solicitors the percentage uplift in a case which does not proceed to trial is 27.5 per cent if a membership organisation is funding the claim, otherwise it is 25 per cent (rule 45.21(a)). In the case of counsel the mechanism in rule 45.17 applies save that the minimum fixed amount is 25 per cent, not 12.5 per cent (rule 45.21(b)). As in Part I, it is possible to apply for an alternative percentage uplift where the damages exceed £500,000, but a similar range of sanctions applies in the event that the stated range is not achieved (rule 45.22).

Part V concerns employers' liability disease claims which are not caught by other fixed percentage arrangements under Part 45 and in respect of which a letter of claim was sent on or after 1 October 2005. The dispute must relate to a disease alleged to have been contracted 'as a consequence of the employer's alleged breach of statutory or common law duties of care in the course of the employee's employment (see rule 45.23). The types of claim are further broken down according to whether they relate to asbestos exposure ('Type A' claims), psychiatric illness or work-related upper-limb disorders caused by physical stress or strain (excluding hand/arm vibration injuries) ('Type B' claims) or other diseases ('Type C' claims). There is a non-exhaustive list of the conditions falling within Types A and B in CPD para.25B.1. There are then a series of mechanisms for the calculation of success fees – and sanctions – as for Part IV. These are set out in the tables annexed to this Part.

CHAPTER 4

Enforceability

4.1 INTRODUCTION

This chapter examines the meaning of Access to Justice Act 1999, s.58(1) and the circumstances in which a CFA or a CCFA might be declared unenforceable. While the Act, the CFA and CCFA Regulations 2000 have already been discussed and placed in their historical and political context in **Chapter 2**, they will be scrutinised in more detail in the following paragraphs. The basis on which the courts have found that CCFAs are not contrary to the operation of the indemnity principle is also examined below (see **4.4**). In addition, this chapter also offers some guidance as to how to approach a substantive challenge made to the enforceability of a CFA or CCFA, typically at a detailed assessment. Finally, the chapter contains comments on the extent to which it may be possible to cure any defects in a CFA.

As noted previously, s.58(1) of the Courts and Legal Services Act 1990 was brought into force to prevent judges from declaring CFAs void and unenforceable on the grounds that they breach the rule against champerty and therefore the indemnity principle as enshrined in Solicitors Act 1974, s.60(3) (see **Chapter 1**). Any retainer which can be classified as a CFA under s.58(2)(a) (as substituted by Access to Justice Act 1999, s.27) must comply with the 'conditions applicable to it'. If it does not, then it is expressly stated by s.58(1) to be 'unenforceable' and the costs pertaining to it will be irrecoverable, since any claim for those costs would amount to a breach of the indemnity principle (see **Chapter 1**).

To the date of writing, the legal issues surrounding the interpretation of the Act and of its underlying Regulations have been those which arose once the Access to Justice Act and the Civil Procedure Rules (CPR) permitted additional liabilities to be recovered from losing parties. The battleground has been one between the rival camps of claimant lawyers (and their ATE providers) and defence interests (primarily indemnity insurers). It is generally thought that these challenges will begin to subside now that the CFA Regulations 2000 have been revoked and as cases funded by CFAs governed by these regulations work their way to a conclusion.

In examining the meaning and effect of this primary and secondary legislation, therefore, the unashamed focus of this chapter is the overarching question whether or not a CFA may be enforceable or not. Years after these CFAs were made, judges started to interpret them along robust lines which had not entirely been foreseen by claimant lawyers. Admittedly also, some representatives had seen the main chance to profit by the new arrangements without full regard for the protection which was owed to their clients. This chapter, then, has 'enforceability' as its focus, not only because that is the primary question with which professional advisers are still preoccupied by reason of the 2000 Regulations, but because ultimately that is what s.58(1) is about: is the CFA under examination 'unenforceable' because it does not satisfy the conditions applicable to it by virtue of s.58 (and s.58A) and the Regulations?

4.2 DETERMINING ENFORCEABILITY: s.58(1) AND COMPLIANCE WITH MANDATORY CONDITIONS

Section 58(1)(c) of the Courts and Legal Services Act 1990 in its original form defined a CFA as one which (among other basic provisions) 'complies with such requirements (if any) as may be prescribed by the Lord Chancellor'. So long as it complied with these requirements, then, by s.58(3) 'it shall not be unenforceable by reason only of its being a conditional fee agreement'.

Section 27 of the Access to Justice Act 1999 substituted and inserted a new s.58 into the Courts and Legal Services Act 1990 which commences:

> 58(1) A conditional fee agreement which satisfies all of the conditions applicable to it by virtue of this section shall not be unenforceable by reason only of its being a conditional fee agreement; but ... any other conditional fee agreement shall be unenforceable.

The applicable conditions as set out in s.58 itself (which apply whether or not a percentage uplift is to be claimed are as follows (emphasis added):

> (3) The following conditions are applicable to every conditional fee agreement –
>
> (a) it *must* be in writing;
> (b) it *must* not relate to proceedings which cannot be the subject of an enforceable conditional fee agreement; and
> (c) it *must* comply with such requirements (if any) as may be prescribed by the Lord Chancellor.

By s.58(4), further conditions apply if the agreement provides for a success fee (emphasis added):

> (4) The following conditions are applicable to a conditional fee agreement which provides for a success fee –

(a) it *must* relate to proceedings of a description specified by order made by the Lord Chancellor;

(b) it *must* state the percentage by which the amount of the fees which would be payable if it were not a conditional fee agreement is to be increased; and

(c) that percentage *must not* exceed the percentage specified in relation to the description of proceedings to which the agreement relates by order made by the Lord Chancellor.

It will be immediately apparent that the conditions as set out in the Act itself are cast in unequivocally mandatory terms. The same is true of the CFA Regulations 2000 (now revoked). For instance, the key provision in reg.4(1) which has probably given rise to the vast majority of challenges is (emphasis added):

4. – (1) Before a conditional fee agreement is made the legal representative *must* –

(a) inform the client about the following matters, and

(b) if the client requires any further explanation, advice or other information about any of those matters, provide such further explanation, advice or other information about them as the client may reasonably require.

(The 'following matters' are issues of client care and are set out in reg.4(2)(a)–(e) and are discussed more fully in the paragraphs below.)

It was realised by paying parties at an early stage that if it would be possible to demonstrate a breach of the applicable mandatory conditions (which on their face appear to admit neither of any exception nor of the possibility of the exercise of any discretion), then the effect of s.58(1) and the indemnity principle would be that the whole Bill of Costs would be 'unenforceable' so that there would be nothing to pay. As it was said in *Spencer* v. *Wood* [2004] EWCA Civ 352 (para.10):

Unlike, for example, the Consumer Credit Act 1974, there is no graduated response to different kinds of breach: it is all or nothing.

(See also *Garrett* v. *Halton B.C.*; *Myatt* v. *NCB* [2007] 1 WLR 554 discussed below ('How and when is materiality to be determined?').)

The Court of Appeal set out an explanation of defence interests' position in *Hollins* v. *Russell* [2003] 1 WLR 2487 at para.22:

Defendant liability insurers, who have viewed with disfavour the increased financial burden imposed on them by a combination of the 'front-end loading' of the Woolf reforms and the new liability to pay ATE premiums and success fees to successful claimants pursuant to other provisions contained in Part II of the 1999 Act, have seized the opportunity of challenging the enforceability of many CFAs by pointing to breaches of one or more of the 'conditions applicable to it'. They argued that, even if they only succeeded in establishing a single breach, they could escape liability to pay any of the costs (and possibly also the disbursements) that were referable to the unenforceable CFA. In other words, it is not only the solicitor's success fee which is at risk, but the cost of all the solicitor's services (or the services of counsel, if rendered under an enforceable CFA), which may on occasion run to many thousands of pounds.

Inevitably, these challenges became more and more technical until the Court of Appeal was invited to find a way through in *Hollins*.

Satisfaction and 'materiality'

In *Hollins* the court had to consider the extent to which a breach of any of the mandatory conditions set out in the CFA Regulations 2000 would result in a declaration of unenforceability:

> 89. The new section 58(1) was clearly intended to leave it to Parliament to decide what further inroads might be made into the principle that contingency or conditional fee agreements are unenforceable: see *Awwad v Geraghty & Co* [2001] QB 570 (para 14 above). It also reflected Parliament's assessment of the state of public policy in this area: see *R (Factortame Ltd) v Secretary of State for Transport (No 8)* [2002] EWCA Civ 932 at [61]; [2002] 3 WLR 1104. The question for us is whether it was also intended to render unenforceable a CFA which did not comply in every particular with the requirements of the section and of regulations made under powers contained in the section.

Hollins itself was not concerned with breaches of the primary legislation as such (cf. *Jones* v. *Caradon Catnic*), but with breaches of the individual regulations which constituted the conditions applicable to it and which were required to be satisfied in order for the agreements to remain enforceable.

Leaving aside the question whether or not the parliamentary draftsman did in fact appreciate the consequence of his piece of drafting (a matter conventionally purely for statutory interpretation, but the answer to which it would be interesting to know), the court found a way to exonerate some breaches even though ostensibly they amounted to breaches of the mandatory conditions under consideration. This was by concentrating on the word 'satisfies' in s.58(1), a word which does admit of questions of degree, as the Court of Appeal vividly demonstrated at para.106:

> The question whether something is 'satisfied' inevitably raises questions of degree. What is enough to satisfy? There can be different degrees of satisfaction. A court may be satisfied beyond reasonable doubt or on the balance of probabilities but it is still satisfied. Different things can be satisfied in different ways. Hunger is satisfied by enough to eat. Greed may only be satisfied by more than enough. Sufficiency produces satisfaction. Conditions are satisfied when they have been sufficiently met. How sufficiently must depend upon the purpose of the conditions. It is not impossible to imagine conditions which would only be sufficiently met if

they were observed in every minute particular: the specifications for precision machinery might be an example. But in general conditions are sufficiently met when there has been substantial compliance with, or in other words no material departure from, what is required.

What the court created was a test of 'substantial compliance', to be tested by a convenient question which could be applied to the consequences of the breach.

Has there been a breach which has had a materially adverse effect either upon the protection afforded to the client or upon the proper administration of justice?

The test to be applied is set out in the following passage from *Hollins* (at para.107):

> The key question, therefore, is whether the conditions applicable to the CFA by virtue of section 58 of the 1990 Act have been sufficiently complied with in the light of their purposes. Costs judges should accordingly ask themselves the following question: 'Has the particular departure from a regulation pursuant to section 58(3)(c) of the 1990 Act or a requirement in section 58, either on its own or in conjunction with any other such departure in this case, had a materially adverse effect either upon the protection afforded to the client or upon the proper adminis-tration of justice?' If the answer is 'yes' the conditions have not been satisfied. If the answer is 'no' then the departure is immaterial and (assuming that there is no other reason to conclude otherwise) the conditions have been satisfied.

Whether or not a particular breach of the applicable conditions would fail the materiality test so that the CFA should be declared unenforceable under s.58(1) is a fact-sensitive issue: 'sufficiency or materiality will depend upon the circumstances of each case' (para.109).

This test of 'materiality' is repeated in the conclusions to the case at para.221, making it clear in this passage that whether or not a breach is 'material' depends on the circumstances of the case:

> A CFA will only be unenforceable if in the circumstances of the particular case the conditions applicable to it by virtue of section 58 have not been sufficiently complied with in the light of their statutory purposes (see paras 105–110 above). Costs judges should ask themselves the following question: 'Has the particular departure from a regulation or requirement in section 58, either on its own or in conjunction with any other such departure in this case, had a materially adverse effect either upon the protection afforded to the client or upon the proper administration of justice?

Cases in which it has been alleged, sometimes successfully and sometimes not, that the whole CFA should be impugned because there has been either a 'materially adverse effect either upon the protection afforded to the client or upon the proper administration of justice' arising out of a breach of the conditions applicable to it are set out at **4.3** below.

'Triviality', 'technicality', 'minor shortcoming', 'marginal breach'

In *Garrett* v. *Halton BC*; *Myatt* v. *NCB*, the Court of Appeal described *Hollins* as having been concerned with 'trivial' breaches, but this is not a description which appears at any point in any of the *Hollins* cases, although the court does refer to 'minor shortcomings' (see for instance para.109). A fuller summary of the right approach is found, for instance, at para.39 of *Garrett*:

> The importance of *Hollins v Russell* is that it dealt a fatal blow to challenges that were being made by defendants' insurers to the enforceability of CFAs on the grounds of minor technical breaches of the statutory requirements. The court explained that Parliament did not intend that such breaches should render CFAs unenforceable. The breaches had to be material in the sense that they had a materially adverse effect on the protection afforded to the client or on the proper administration of justice. The primary statutory purpose of the requirements was to provide protection to claimants

Brooke LJ does use the word 'trivial' in *Jones* v. *Caradon Catnic Ltd*, in which Laws LJ referred to 'marginal' violations. While such epithets may have some use by providing a shorthand account of what has occurred, it is not helpful to test the question whether or not there has been a 'material breach' by reference solely to a simple adjectival phrase. It could be said that an attempt to turn an investigation into materiality into a search for a 'trivial' breach or similar without reference to the fuller account, would be to subvert the test established in *Hollins* which the Court in *Garrett* expressly approved.

How and when is materiality to be determined?

In *Hollins* the Court of Appeal recommended that the judge conducting the assessment 'should first consider the position as between solicitor and client' (para.222):

> If the court considers that as between solicitor and client the client would have just cause for complaint because some requirement introduced for his protection was not satisfied . . . the CFA will be unenforceable.

What of the solicitor–client position where the parties have made their way successfully through to the end of the litigation and the client has not felt the need to make any complaint or has not suffered any prejudice? Should it matter that by the time of a detailed assessment the client has suffered no detriment?

These were the questions of principle considered by the Court of Appeal in *Garrett & Myatt* (para.7):

The principal question that arises is whether the test of 'materiality' referred to in para 107 of *Hollins v Russell* requires the court to consider whether the client has suffered actual prejudice as a result of an alleged failure to satisfy the conditions referred to section 58(3) of the 1990 Act. A related question is whether the enforceability of a CFA is to be judged by reference to the circumstances existing at the time when it is entered into, or by reference to the circumstances known to exist at the time when the question arises for decision.

While approving *Hollins*, the Court of Appeal had little difficulty in resolving these issues contrary to the submissions of the receiving parties, for the reasons given in the following paragraphs.

In respect of the assertion that it should be possible to determine whether there had been a materially adverse effect on the client by reference to the actual outcome, the court in *Garrett & Myatt* considered (para.21) that:

> if there has been a departure from a regulation which has had a materially adverse effect on client protection, the client 'would have just cause for complaint' even if he chooses not to complain because he has not in fact suffered any detriment.

The court was impressed by the submission that by the mandatory language of s.58(1), (3) of the 1990 Act, Parliament's intention was 'clear and uncompromising: if one or more of the applicable conditions is not satisfied, then the CFA is unenforceable' (para.27). The judges considered that the legislature intended to effect a policy which was 'tough but ... not irrational' and which had the useful effect of 'punishing solicitors pour encourager les autres'. There was strong emphasis throughout on the potential threat to the administration of justice, a statement of principle which indeed emanated ultimately from the Court of Appeal in *Hollins*. It has subsequently proved a strong card for paying parties at detailed assessments in the absence of any real threat of prejudice to the client. It is odd, however, that the Court of Appeal in *Garrett & Myatt* should have considered that the danger to the administration of justice was the risk that solicitors might develop too lax an attitude to questions of client care, not the dangers which judges had previously thought it necessary to protect by the application of the principle of champerty, namely that there might be the temptation to suppress evidence or to suborn witnesses (see **Chapter 1**).

Accordingly, while it might be a harsh result that the consequence of a declaration of unenforceability would be that the solicitor would not be entitled to payment for his services, even though a successful outcome had finally been achieved. Parliament 'must be taken to have deliberately decided not to distinguish between cases of non-compliance which are innocent and those which are negligent or committed in bad faith, nor between those which cause prejudice (in the sense of actual loss) and those which do not'. The court concluded (para.32) that:

The principal question that arises on these appeals is whether there is substantial compliance with (or no material departure from) a requirement if a breach does not in fact cause the client to suffer detriment. If it had been intended that a CFA should only be enforceable where the client suffered actual damage, it would have been easy enough so to provide. But the focus of the scheme was on whether the CFA satisfied the applicable conditions, not on the actual consequences of a breach of one of the requirements of the scheme. In our view, it is fallacious to say that a breach is trivial or not material because it does not in fact cause loss to the client in the particular case. The scheme has the wider purpose of providing for client protection (as well as the proper administration of justice).

What actually happened during the progress of a case might be relevant only because 'that may shed light on the *potential* consequences of a breach (if the matter is judged at the date of the CFA) and therefore on the extent to which the breach had a material adverse effect on the protection afforded to the client' (para.39).

Materiality after Hollins and Garrett & Myatt

There is very little merit now in trying to unpick the effect of *Garrett & Myatt*. Argument on the part of claimant receiving parties was extensive and did not advance the claimant cause to any material extent. An assessing court should be reminded that the ultimate question is ultimately one of 'sufficiency', and that its inquiry will be very fact sensitive. 'Materiality' is generally not best considered to be part of a distinct two-stage process. The questions whether there has been a breach and whether any breach caused prejudice either to the client or to the administration of justice are likely to be very much enmeshed, as indeed they were in the case of *Pratt* v. *Bull* (see below), which was one of the conjoined *Hollins* appeals and which was expressly approved by the Court of Appeal in *Garrett & Myatt*.

Breaches of conditions contained in s.58(3), (4)

All of subsections 58(3), (4) of the Act are in mandatory terms and the test of materiality is to be applied to alleged breaches of all of these subsections. The CFA Regulations 2000, however, are perhaps seen as being one step removed from the conditions relevant to CFAs which are otherwise contained in s.58(3), (4). Succeeding in demonstrating the test of materiality in respect of breaches of these other subsections is likely to be much more difficult to achieve. This is the result of *Jones* v. *Caradon Catnic Ltd.*

Jones concerned a trade union CCFA in which the solicitor had prepared a risk assessment in an individual case in which the stated success fee was 100 per cent. This is ultimately a breach of s.58(3)(c) which prohibits the percentage uplift in a CFA from exceeding the maximum uplift prescribed by order made by the Lord Chancellor. Throughout the period during which

CFAs have been lawful, 100 per cent has always been the maximum permitted outcome, and this is the amount stated in the CFA Order 2000. Mr Jones was never at risk of having to pay more than 100 per cent: the costs rules prevented this. The Court of Appeal, however, decided that to consider the breach immaterial would be 'acting flat against the grain of the legislature's substantial policy objectives' (para.36). What was at stake was the proper administration of justice (para.32), so that for instance the result might be countless preliminary issue hearings which would consume the resources of the courts unnecessarily.

Such is very likely to be the ultimate result of a breach of s.58(3)(a) which requires a CCFA to be in writing. It is very difficult to see a court accepting either that a client suffered no prejudice to the protection this subsection is intended to afford him or that there was no prejudice to the administration of justice. The same is true of s.58(3)(b) which prevents an enforceable CFA from being made in relation to certain classes of proceedings which are set out in s.58A(1),(2). The same is also likely to be true of a breach of s.58(4)(a) which requires a CFA to 'relate to proceedings of a description specified by order made by the Lord Chancellor'. Of all the proceedings which can be funded by way of an enforceable CFA para.3, the CFA Order prohibits only proceedings under the Environmental Protection Act 1990, s.82 from attracting a success fee. Notwithstanding that no uplift could possibly be recovered from a client in such a case, the reasoning in *Jones* would surely be held to apply. It is also difficult, for broadly similar reasons, to see why a CFA should not be declared unenforceable if it fails to specify the amount of the percentage uplift (see s.58(4)(b)).

In the *Jones* case the Court of Appeal was content to restate the applicability of the 'materiality' test as set out in *Hollins*, but while this might theoretically provide an avenue of escape for a unique case, the possibility of its application where there is a breach of a requirement set out in the primary legislation (including for these purposes s.58(4)(b), (c)), must be remote.

4.3   ENFORCEABILITY AND THE CFA REGULATIONS 2000

The CFA Regulations as client care provisions

The CFA Regulations 2000 came into force on 1 April 2000. They contain purely client care provisions which were derived from the Solicitors' Costs Information and Client Care Code 1999, and made under rule 15 of the Solicitors' Practice Rules (Costs Information and Client Care). They were amended with effect from 2 June 2003 to allow for Simplified CFAs (CFAs where a shortfall in costs cannot be recovered from the client). The legislative history of the 2000 Regulations (as amended) and a basic account of their meaning and effect is contained in **Chapter 2**.

The 2000 Regulations are considered further in this chapter (on a regulation by regulation basis) to the extent that they have been considered by the courts during the course of challenges to the validity of CFA retainers. **Chapter 2** also contains a brief account of their contents. The 2000 Regulations were revoked with effect from 1 November 2005, and it is hoped that as a result, technical challenges will thereafter die a death, clients being appropriately protected by the new Solicitors' Code of Conduct 2007. However, challenges based on the CFA Regulations are very much alive, so that the remainder of this section is drafted as though they are still in operation.

Advantages of Simplified CFAs

It is important to recall that by reg.3A(3) of the 2000 Regulations (as amended) Simplified CFAs are not subject to regs.2, 3 or 4 of the 2000 Regulations. Challenges to Simplified CFAs should be rare. There are similar advantages in the case of CCFAs by reg.3A(5).

Whether or not a CFA can be categorised as a Simplified CFA is discussed in detail in *Jones* v. *Wrexham B.C.* [2007] EWCA Civ 1356.

Regulation 2

Regulation 2 requires a CFA to 'specify' certain matters. The Court of Appeal considered the meaning of the word 'specify', observing (para.125) that 'the ordinary meaning of "specify" is to state explicitly' (see, for example *BWE International Ltd* v. *Jones* [2003] EWCA Civ 298 at [27] cited in *Hollins* at para.125). This had relevance to its further considerations under the regulations falling within reg.2 (see below).

Regulation 2(1)(d)

Regulation 2(1)(d) requires a CFA to specify:

> the amounts which are payable in all the circumstances and cases specified or the method to be used to calculate them *and, in particular, whether the amounts are limited by reference to the damages which may be recovered on behalf of the client.*

The passage in italics is a reference to the cap applied on a voluntary basis by solicitors and barristers under the pre-Access to Justice Act 1999 scheme when additional liabilities could not be recovered as part of a solicitor's costs from the other side.

However, the meaning of the word 'specify' (see above) is such that (paras.125–6):

> The operative requirement in regulation 2(1)(d) is that the CFA must 'specify' the matters listed in regulation 2(1)(a) to (d), including in particular, whether the amounts are limited by reference to the damages which may be recovered on behalf of the client. . . . To fulfil precisely the requirements of the regulations, the CFA . . . should [say] in terms that basic charges and disbursements (as well as the success fee) were not limited by reference to the damages which might be recovered on behalf of the client.

The CFAs in both *Hollins* and in the conjoined appeal of *Tichband* v. *Hurdman* failed to make such an explicit statement. The CFA in *Hollins* followed an April 2000 model which stated that the amount of a client's *success fee* (rather than all fees and disbursements) was not limited by reference to the damages (the position was rectified by the July 2000 model agreement). The CFA in *Tichband* said nothing at all to reflect this regulation. The court decided in both cases that since the true position was perfectly clear the materiality test was satisfied in the receiving party's favour.

Regulation 3(1)(b)

In *Tichband* v. *Hurdman* (see *Hollins*) the CFA itself failed to specify how much of the percentage increase (by way of success fee) related to the cost to the legal representative of the postponement of the payment of his fees and expenses. The effect of CPR rule 44.3B(1)(a) is that the postponement element cannot be recovered from the paying party. The terms and conditions of the CFA in question made it clear that the postponement element would not be recovered from the client and the risk assessment demonstrated that the postponement element of the uplift was 5 per cent. The defendant raised an argument which the Court of Appeal described (para.132) as 'as unattractive as it is unmeritorious', namely that the CFA was unenforceable because it failed to specify the element of the postponement element. The court held (para.134) that by reason of the written terms and conditions 'on its true construction the CFA in this case complies with the Regulations'. In *Brennan* v. *Associated Asphalt* (18 May 2006, Master Hurst) it was held to be an immaterial breach that the CFA did not specify how much of percentage uplift related to the cost of postponement. A note on the report on the Lawtel database states that an appeal from this decision was allowed by consent.

In *Spencer* v. *Wood* [2004] EWCA Civ 552 the CFA made no reference at all to which proportion of the 75 per cent success fee was attributable to the postponement element, although the risk assessment stated that the deferment element was 50 per cent. The judge found that the claimant did not know which part of the 75 per cent uplift could not be recovered from his opponent and the Court of Appeal agreed that the CFA was unenforceable. See also *Utting* v. *McBain*, 17 August 2007, in which Master Campbell held a CFA to be unenforceable because, notwithstanding that there was no postponement charge, the regulation required this expressly to be stated.

Regulation 3(1)(b) has quite regularly given rise to difficulties. It is an easy mistake to make, to confuse the postponement and non-postponement elements or to fail to insert the correct sum. It is worth checking all attendance notes and other documents going to the client since this is one area where rectification of a CFA may be possible (see **4.7** below).

Regulation 3(2)(c)

The meaning of this regulation was explored first by Master Seager Berry in *Ghannouchi* v. *Houni Ltd* and then by Master Hurst in *Oyston* v. *Royal Bank of Scotland plc* [2006] 16 May. In *Ghannouchi* Master Seager Berry was invited to compare reg.3(2)(c) with reg.3(2)(b) and to determine whether the Law Society model then in force breached the regulations because it did not accurately explain the meaning and effect of reg.3(2)(c). The Costs Judge concluded that while reg.3(2)(b) required a CFA to state what amount of the success fee ceased would be recoverable against the client in the event that it was reduced on an assessment (unless the court was satisfied that it should continue to be payable), reg.3(2)(c) required the CFA to state that *both* the base fees and the success fee would be reduced in the event of compromise (unless the court was satisfied that they should continue to be payable). The judge held that the model then in force was deficient in making the true position under reg.3(2)(c) clear, but that the breach was not material since:

(a)   on any explanation as to the terms of a settlement the solicitor was obliged to explain the costs consequences to the client and it was to be assumed that this had taken place; and

(b)   by reason of CPR rule 44.16 ('adjournment where legal representative seeks to challenge disallowance of any amount of percentage increase'):

> the court is the guardian available to protect the Claimant in respect of any further recovery of base costs and success fee where there has been a settlement and the further recovery of the success fee where there has been a reduction at a detailed assessment.

Master Hurst came to a different conclusion about the interpretation of reg.3(2)(c) in *Oyston*, holding that it was intended to refer to success fees in the event of a compromise and was intended to reflect reg.3(2)(b).

Regulation 4

Challenges brought alleging a breach of reg.4 are probably the most common type of enforceability challenge. They allow the paying party scope to delve into the pre-CFA client care discussions between solicitor and client in the hope that it may be possible to establish that the correct information was not given. See the discussions below.

Regulation 4 and BTE

A particular focus is the question whether BTE insurance existed, since by failing to make the right inquiries, a potential breach of reg.4(1), (2)(c), (d), (e) may be established.

It is important when a challenge is faced for the receiving party to make proper preparations and to address all of the potential breaches of reg.4. This is because a challenge is likely to be unfocused and because an assessing judge may be tempted to widen the scope of an inquiry beyond what is immediately set out in the Points of Dispute and Replies (see further below).

Regulation 4(2)(c) and (d) and BTE

A court will consider the question whether there has been substantial compliance with reg.4(2)(c) and (d) by reference to an implied duty to take reasonable steps to ascertain what BTE insurance cover the client has, and that what is reasonable will depend on all the circumstances of the case (see *Garrett* at paras.55 and 65). The court went on to provide the following guidance as to how this duty should be observed, rejecting the submission that the guidance previously set out in *Sarwar* v. *Alam* provided an appropriate test which should automatically be adopted when it came to a reg.4 challenge based on the possible existence of BTE cover (para.69). *Sarwar* itself was concerned with the question whether it was reasonable for a premium to be recovered in respect of very low value RTA claims without unusual features (claims of up to £5,000), not with the issue of enforceability, see **3.9**.

It is worth quoting the relevant passage from *Garrett & Myatt* in full:

71   So what guidance can be given as to the steps that a solicitor should reasonably take to discharge his obligation under regulation 4(2)(c)? A number of factors are relevant. What follows is not intended to be an exhaustive list. We emphasise that what is reasonably required of a solicitor depends on all the circumstances of the case.

72   First, the nature of the client. If the client is evidently intelligent and has a real knowledge and understanding of insurance matters, it may be reasonable for the solicitor to ask him not only (i) whether he has credit cards, motor insurance or household insurance or is a member of a trade union, (ii) whether he has legal expenses insurance, but also (iii) the ultimate question of whether the legal expenses policy covers the proposed claim and, if so, whether it does so to a sufficient extent. Litigants such as the *Myatt* claimants and Ms Garrett plainly do not fall into this category: few litigants will. If the solicitor does ask such questions, he will have to form a view as to whether the client's answers to the questions can reasonably be relied upon.

73   Secondly, the circumstances in which the solicitor is instructed may be relevant to the nature of the enquiries that it is reasonable to expect the solicitor to undertake in order to establish the BTE position. A good example of the application of this factor is to be found in *Pratt v Bull,* which was one of the five cases that was heard together with *Hollins v Russell.* In that case, the 80-year old claimant was injured in a road accident. A solicitor visited her while she was

in hospital and a CFA was made. At the assessment of her costs, it was argued on behalf of the defendant that the possibility of legal expenses insurance under her home insurance policy had not been fully explored. At para 138, the court said that there were limits to what can reasonably be expected of the interchange between solicitor and client in such circumstances: 'It would be ridiculous to expect a solicitor dealing with a seriously ill old woman in hospital to delay making a CFA while her home insurance policy was found and checked.' It was sufficient that the solicitor had discussed it with her and formed a view on the funding options.

74 Thirdly, the nature of the claim may be relevant. If the claim is one in respect of which it is unlikely that standard insurance policies would provide legal expenses cover, this may be a further reason why it may be reasonable for the solicitor to take fewer steps to ascertain the position than might otherwise be the case.

75 Fourthly, the cost of the ATE premium may be a relevant factor. This is the point made at para 50 of *Sarwar*. In our judgment, it is as relevant to a question of breach of regulation 4(2)(c) as to a question of the reasonableness of the premium for the purposes of an assessment of costs pursuant to CPR 44.4.

76 Fifthly, if the claim has been referred to solicitors who are on a panel, it may be relevant that the referring body has already investigated the question of the availability of BTE. Whether it is reasonable to rely on any conclusion already reached will be a matter on which the panel solicitor must exercise his own judgment.

77 It follows from the calibrated approach that we have suggested at paras.72–76 above that we do not consider that it is possible to give rigid guidance as to the questions a solicitor should ask in every case. In particular, in our judgment a solicitor is not required in every case to ask the client who says that he has a home, credit card or motor insurance or is a member of a trade union to send him the policy or trade union membership document (the first of the three approaches suggested by Mr McCue: see para.56 above). In some circumstances, it is reasonable for the solicitor to ask the further question whether the insurance covers legal expenses and to rely on the answer given by the client without further ado. In yet other cases, it is even reasonable to ask the client to answer what we have called the ultimate question.

78 We acknowledge that to require the solicitor to ask the client to send the policies in all cases has the merit of certainty and would minimise the risk of satellite litigation. In *Adair v Cullen*, Judge Holman said that the *Sarwar* approach should be adopted to breach of regulation cases and that it 'suggests a question along the lines of 'Do you have motor insurance' and if the answer is 'Yes', the next question is 'can I see the policy document please?' In some cases, such an approach is reasonable and necessary to enable the solicitor to discharge his regulation 4(2)(c) duty. But for the reasons that we have given, we do not accept that it is required in all cases.

In detailed assessments following *Garrett & Myatt* costs judges have been reasonably flexible in applying this guidance. As to the question whether a client is sophisticated enough to understand whether he has BTE available to him, in *White* v. *Revell* Master Wright accepted that a man who had left school at 16 but who went on to take two university degrees and to qualify as a chartered surveyor could appropriately be asked this question. The claimant's job had involved a consideration of the expense of projects and he had shown a particular interest in the costs of the litigation. In a pre-*Garrett & Myatt* case, *Choudhury* v. *Kingston Hospital Trust*, Master Rogers accepted that it was sufficient to ask a consultant anaesthetist whether she had BTE insurance. Moreover, the questions had been put by a past president of APIL. See also *Kashmiri* v. *Ejaz* [2007] EWHC 90074 (Costs), which concerned an allegation of unenforceability, and where it was said that inadequate advice was given as to BTE funding. Master Simons decided that after a discussion of five hours between a 'sophisticated businessman' and his solicitor, the businessman could be relied on to know whether he had ATE for what 'proved to be an unmeritorious claim for damages in respect of a dilapidations claim relating to their former occupancy of business premises which they had vacated more than two years earlier'.

In *Myatt* itself however the claimants failed. Of the four ex-miner clients evidence was adduced as to what inquiries were made of one of them. The evidence showed however that that claimant was asked whether he had BTE insurance which would cover him in respect of a claim 'for noise-induced hearing loss against his former employer the National Coal Board'. In other words he was asked the 'ultimate' question, a question which he could not adequately answer. It certainly did not help his case that he was asked this question over the telephone without any forewarning that he should be prepared with his documentation. The reg.4 inquiries were inadequate.

Breaches of reg.4(2)(c) are not uncommon in connection with 'scheme' arrangements where a solicitor has sought to make use of pre-drafted oral checklists by which their staff or agents are intended to ensure that clients (usually living far off and spoken with only over the telephone) have obtained appropriate reg.4 advice and information. Thus in one of the housing scheme cases, *Bowen* v. *Bridgend CBC*, 25 March 2004 (Master Hurst), the clients were asked to do the following:

> You should consider the alternative methods of funding this claim which including private funding, Community Legal Service funding (formally known as legal aid), payment of costs on an hourly rate basis, legal expenses insurance, trade union funding or any other possible source of funding. Once you have considered these alternatives, you must advise your legal representative whether you wish to pursue the claim on a CFA funded basis.

The responsibility for considering the insurance question was wrongly placed on the client.

The *Pratt* v. *Bull* example in *Hollins* is also worth remembering when applying the *Garrett & Myatt* guidance and indeed when considering what the Court of Appeal considered amounts to a material breach and what does not. *Pratt* was one of the *Hollins* conjoined appeals and it concerned an alleged breach of reg.4(2)(c). Again, it is worth quoting in full (see *Hollins* at paras.137–8). It was a case in which the court refused to order disclosure of funding documentation because it did not think that any case alleging non-compliance could be made out.

137 In *Pratt v Bull*, the 80 year old claimant was severely injured when she was struck by the defendant's car when using a pedestrian crossing. Initial instructions were given by relatives while she was in intensive care. The following month, when she had recovered enough to give instructions, a solicitor visited her in hospital and a standard CFA was made. When her solicitors sought to recover their costs, the defendant's solicitors demanded to be provided, not only with the CFA, but also with attendance notes and documents to show that she had been given all the oral and written information required by regulation 4. They expressed concern that other methods of funding might not have been properly explored. They seized upon one reply given to their questions as indicating that the possibility of legal expenses insurance under her home insurance policy had not been fully explored. The claimant's solicitor's response was that other funding possibilities had indeed been discussed. 'Evidently our client did not think she had cover . . . Of course there was consideration of the point but to a reasonable degree where this lady was still lying in her hospital bed recovering from the horrific injuries inflicted by your insured'.

138 For the reasons given earlier (see paras 81 to 86 above) we do not consider that documents such as these should ordinarily be disclosed, nor should the costs judge require this unless there is a genuine compliance issue. In our view, this is a classic case in which there was no good reason to think that the conditions applicable to this CFA had not been sufficiently satisfied. There are limits to what can reasonably be expected of the interchange between solicitor and client in circumstances such as these. It would be ridiculous to expect a solicitor dealing with a seriously ill old woman in hospital to delay making a CFA while her home insurance policy was found and checked. It is sufficient to satisfy section 58 that he had discussed it with her and formed a view on the funding options.

It is quite possible to imagine a variety of submissions being made about the issue of compliance in such circumstances. If there was no limitation problem, for instance, it might have been possible to wait longer; the relatives might have looked for the insurance policies; the solicitor could have been authorised to write to any buildings/contents insurers. So long as the court considered this to be a proper example of the application of its guidance as to how a solicitor makes reasonable inquiries into the existence of BTE, then this does show that the court will approach the individual circumstances of each case with some flexibility. The question is always whether the CFA has 'satisfied' the relevant requirements.

Regulation 4(2)(d) and legal aid

In a series of housing disrepair cases the courts found that there had been a failure to advise housing tenants that they could (or indeed should) fund their litigation by way of legal aid. A good example is the decision of Master Hurst in *Bowen* v. *Bridgend CBC* 25 March 2004 who held (para.87) that:

> The proper test for me to apply here is whether the Claimants acted reasonably in instructing a solicitor on CFA terms with insurance rather than instructing a legal aid solicitor. If their choice of funding was reasonable, the reasonable costs they incur would be recoverable even if it would lead to extra expense for the Defendant. I should not approach this topic by considering whether a legally aided solicitor could reasonably have conducted these cases (*cf R v Dudley Magistrates Court ex p. Power City Stores Ltd* (1990) 154 J.P.654, DC).

Further instances are the decisions of Master O'Hare in *Hughes* v. *Newham LBC*, 28 July 2005, and in *Hussain* v. *Leeds CC*, 16 December 2005 (Master O'Hare).

Where a client has instructed a solicitor on Simplified CFA terms then the use of a CFA may be preferable to legal aid with the burden of the statutory charge.

Regulation 4(2)(e)(ii)

In *Dunn* v. *Ward*, one of the conjoined *Hollins* appeals, it was argued that when a solicitor provides information as to whether a particular form of (ATE) insurance is appropriate for the purposes of financing an opponent's costs order under reg.4(1), (2)(e)(ii) and makes a specific recommendation to that effect, the information which is also required to be given 'whether he has an interest in doing so' is to be construed as though 'whether' reads 'whether or not'. The Court of Appeal dismissed this interpretation (para.144). There was no reason to construe 'whether' as meaning anything other than 'if' since 'the mischief which this regulation was introduced to remedy was the risk that the client's legal representative might induce the client to enter into insurance arrangements in which he had an interest'. If he had no interest, then there was no identified mischief and nothing had to be said.

Garrett was also concerned with reg.4(2)(e)(ii). This was a case in which the case had been referred by a claims management company to solicitors who were members of its panel. The solicitors told the client that they had no interest in the NIG insurance policy which they recommended to her while they were on the AA panel. The Points of Dispute made the allegation that failure to comply with an obligation to recommend the NIG policy would lead to termination of panel membership. The assessing judge decided that a genuine issue of compliance had been raised by the paying party and that this was the 'crunch' averment. The lack of response to the allegation made in the Points of Dispute meant that the inference had to be drawn that in fact the solicitors would have been thrown off the panel.

The Court of Appeal rejected a submission that (a) the word 'interest' was ambiguous since it could mean either a direct or an indirect interest and (b) the latter meaning was to be preferred. It held (para.92) that:

> In our judgment, the Regulations should be construed by giving the plain language in which they are expressed its normal and natural meaning. We do not accept that

the word 'interest' is ambiguous. For the reasons that we shall give, it seems to us to be clear that it includes membership of a panel.

The court also held (para.94) that:

> The obligation in regulation 4(2)(e)(ii) is to inform the client if he recommends a particular insurance contract 'whether he has an interest in doing so'. The obligation is not to inform the client whether he believes that he has an interest in doing so; it is to inform the client whether he has an interest in doing so *in fact*.

The court also noted that in a February 2000 consultation paper issued by the Lord Chancellor it was expressly proposed that panel membership should be disclosed to a client. Moreover, the court went on to observe (para.103) that after 14 January 2005 and by reason of rule 8A and Appendix 1 of the Solicitors' Financial Services (Conduct of Business) Rules 2001 made by the Law Society under the Financial Services and Markets Act 2000:

> a solicitor who proposes that his client should enter into an ATE insurance policy, and who recommends a particular policy because it is the only policy which, consistently with his firm's membership of a panel, he is allowed to recommend, must tell the client that he is contractually obliged to recommend a policy with that insurer. That would give the client notice of the particular interest which the firm has in recommending the policy, whereas just to tell the client that the firm is on a particular panel does not convey that information.

As long as that obligation is observed after 14 January 2005, then the problem which arose in the *Garrett* appeal should not arise again.

As to pre-November 2005 CFAs, several cases have been decided at Circuit Judge/SCCO level which merit consideration.

Garrett itself was a second tier appeal from a judgment of HHJ Stewart QC. He had accepted what the DJ had said as to the crunch averment in the Points of Dispute which had never been satisfactorily answered. In another case decided by HHJ Stewart QC (*O'Driscoll* v. *Liverpool CC*, 8 May 2007 (a TAG/NIG matter)), he held that there was 'no positive averment, unlike in the *Garrett* case, that the claimant's solicitors would lose panel membership and, therefore, no basis for such an inference to be drawn as was drawn in *Garrett*'. He held that by the Points of Dispute the claimant's solicitors had simply been 'put to proof as to whether they had an interest in recommending the after the event policy'. The judge described the case as 'exceptional'. A salutary lesson is to take stock of exactly what the detailed assessment pleadings assert before deciding whether further evidence is needed.

A further Ashley Ainsworth panel case (as in *Garrett*) was decided by Master Hurst on 9 February 2007 (*Andrews* v. *Harrison Taylor Scaffolding*). The evidence was that 95 per cent of the solicitors' work has been referred to them by Ashley Ainsworth. There was no evidence that by failing to recommend the NIG ATE they would have been taken off the panel, but Master

Hurst described this as the 'inescapable' conclusion. The solicitors had told the claimant that they were on the panel but this was not enough. Where a disbursement funding loan was offered to a claimant the Operations Manual required the NIG policy to be recommended. No other policy was ever in fact recommended to a client.

A worrying case from a claimant's point of view in this context is *Myers* v. *Bonnington (Cavendish Hotel) Ltd* (6 July 2007, Master Rogers). This concerned the Accident Line Protect (ALP) policy issued by the Law Society and considered generally to be a very sound arrangement. The ALP manual required the solicitor as part of his duties 'to issue an Accident Line Protect Insurance policy in all eligible CFA cases'. Where a breach of duty was established the sanction was termination of membership. Master Rogers decided on the facts of the case that there was no *material* breach: (a) the claimant had been an established client of the firm; (b) he had won a personal injury claim previously with these solicitors and would have instructed the firm even if he had been told of the firm's interest in recommending the policy; and (c) less than 1 per cent of the firm's income came from ALP referrals. On the other hand, he had no hesitation in deciding that there had otherwise been a failure to comply with reg.4(2)(e)(ii) since the solicitors had simply stated that they recommended the policy. He found that the solicitors had done an excellent job for their client.

It is clear that the Court of Appeal intends to take a very restrictive (wide) view as to what constitutes an interest. It has therefore become extremely important, if possible, to demonstrate that the CFA is a Simplified agreement, since if this can achieved, reg.4(2)(e)(ii) does not apply. See *Jones* v. *Wrexham B.C.* [2007] EWCA Civ 1356.

Regulation 4(3)

This regulation was considered in the case of *Ghannnouchi* discussed above.

Regulation 4(5)

Regulation 4(5) requires some reg.4 client care information to be given orally (namely that which is contained at reg.4(2)(a)–(d)), while other information must be given both orally and also in writing (namely that contained within regs.4(2)(e), (3)).

The Law Society model CFA has always contained a written provision advising the client to read the Law Society Conditions and asking the client to explain whatever may not be clear. The Court of Appeal held (paras.152–4) that this statement when read in conjunction with the Law Society conditions adequately complied with the regulation.

This regulation was considered in the case of *Ghannnouchi* discussed above.

In *Preece* v. *Caerphilly CDC* (unreported, 15 August 2007) it was held by the Circuit Judge on an appeal that it is a material breach of a CFA if it is not signed.

4.4 COLLECTIVE CONDITIONAL FEE AGREEMENTS (CCFAs)

CCFAs are third-party funding arrangements on CFA terms. While they may seem exotic beasts within the CFA firmament, there is nothing extraordinary about them. They are but a species of CFA to which s.58(1) applies and indeed are treated as such by the Costs Rules. A general account of the CCFA Regulations 2000 will be found in **Chapter 2** at **2.7**. An explanation of Simplified CCFAs will be found at **2.8**.

There have been few challenges to CCFAs. At least that is to say that there have been few challenges which have been contested in the courts and the results then published in any widely available form of law report.

To understand the jurisprudential basis on which CCFAs are considered lawful, it is helpful to place them in their proper context at the end of a long line of third-party funding arrangements validated by cases decided in the twentieth century. These had all been cases in which defendants had sought to establish that third-party funding arrangements in question breached the indemnity principle.

The first of these cases, namely *Adams* v. *London Improved Motor Coach Builders Ltd* [1921] 1 KB 495 (CA) has been the model used by the courts in respect of subsequent challenges which have been made to third-party funding arrangements, and indeed this case has also been the model used by the courts to explain why CCFAs themselves are valid. It was a case in which a member of a trade union received financial backing for litigation (his claim for wrongful dismissal). There was no written retainer either between the client and the solicitors. The defendant argued that this was a breach of the indemnity principle since the solicitors were not in fact the client's solicitors. The court held that in order to establish a breach of the indemnity principle in these circumstances the court would have to find that there had been some agreement that in no circumstances would the client be liable for the solicitors' costs.

Similar arguments by defendants were lost for substantially the same reasons in the context of legal assistance provided by an employer (*R* v. *Miller* [1983] 1 WLR 1056) and also by insurers (see *Davies* v. *Taylor (No.2)* [1974] 1 AC 225 and *Lewis* v. *Averay (No.2)* [1973] 1 WLR 510 (CA)). The latter case concerned the AA in which the insurer had written a letter stating: 'We make it clear that Mr. Averay was indemnified in all respects by the Automobile Association so that no part of the costs of the appeal has or would have fallen on him.'

CCFAs and the indemnity principle: are they an exception to it?

During the currency of the CCFA Regulations 2000 (that is, until their revocation by the Revocation Regulations 2005), there was perceived to be a particular form of difficulty caused by the fact that there was nothing in the Regulations which placed a primary liability on the client to incur a success fee. It was thought by some that the right to claim a success fee could only arise under the terms of an individual CFA under the CFA Regulations 2000. Ostensibly this might be classed as a breach of the indemnity principle.

In *Gliddon* v. *Lloyd Maunder Ltd*, 31 January 2003, Master O'Hare, this apparent difficulty was sought to be circumvented by the submission that a CCFA represented an exception to the indemnity principle, the government's conclusions to the Collective Conditional Fee Agreement Consultation Paper (published in September 2000) being cited:

> Although the introduction of CCFA Regulations under Section 58 of the Courts and Legal Services Act 1990 (as amended) abrogates the indemnity principle for CCFAs, the Government is persuaded that there is no longer any justification for the operation of the principle when assessing costs no matter how funded.

Master O'Hare rejected this argument, finding this particular agreement unenforceable by reason of correspondence adduced by the paying party which suggested that the claimant union's solicitors would never expect the client to be personally liable for the uplift. No doubt for reasons of confidentiality and of sensitivity the CCFA was not disclosed to the judge, and this judgment was not made at the end of the detailed assessment proceedings so that it is of somewhat limited assistance.

Thornley v. *Lang* [2003] EWCA Civ 1484 was decided at first instance by Field J. He accepted the argument that any enforceable agreement by which a success fee was to be recoverable from a client had to be a CFA under the CFA Regulations 2000. However, he went on to hold that an uplift was recoverable under a CCFA which complied with the CCFA Regulations 2000 by reason of CLSA 1990, s.58A(6) since this subsection expressly states that if a costs order is made in proceedings it may make provision for a success fee (see further below).

CCFAs as an extension of the authorities permitting third-party funding arrangements

The Court of Appeal in *Thornley* decided on a Respondent's Notice that Field J had been wrong. It was also clear that the court would not have been prepared to have accepted any submission that an agreement which complied with the CCFA Regulations could be considered an exception to the indemnity principle (see para.19). Accepting that an agreement regulated by the CCFA Regulations could not be confused with the CFA Regulations 2000 and that the two were mutually exclusive (para.13), they compared a CCFA with the third-party funding arrangements such as those in *Adams* v. *London Improved Motor Coach Builders Ltd* [1921] 1 KB 495 and on similar lines (see above). The union had been acting as the client's agent when entering into the CCFA, or alternatively by accepting the services of the solicitors the client had ratified the agreement between the union and his solicitors.

This interpretation as expressed by the Court of Appeal in *Thornley* had been the basis of Master O'Hare's explanation as to the connection between client and solicitors in *Gliddon*. It went on to be applied in *Kitchen* v. *Burwell & Reed Kinghorn Ltd* (3 August 2005, Gray J). In that case the claimant had received union support prior to the making of a CCFA in May 2001. A year later he was told by his solicitors that they had accepted his instructions on CCFA terms, and notwithstanding his silence it was held that he had agreed to a variation of the terms with his solicitors so that they were engaged under the terms of the CCFA terms. He had either ratified or accepted by his conduct the variation in the terms of the retainer (see para.16).

In *Kitchen* the CCFA contained the following clause:

> 5.8   The Solicitors shall not seek to recover direct from the member their charges in respect of any period during which the member was covered by the Union's legal assistance unless that legal assistance has been annulled.

In a careful examination of the way in which third-party funding arrangements have been applied by the courts since *Adams*, the judge held (observing the guidance governing the construction of a contract given by Lord Hoffmann in *Investors Compensation Scheme* v. *West Bromwich Building Society* [1998] 1 WLR 896 at pp.912–3), that the CCFA did not offend the indemnity principle. Clause 5.8 did not mean and was not intended to mean that the claimant would in no circumstances be liable to pay the costs of the defendant.

The Court of Appeal also held in *Thornley* that the necessary liability on the part of the client to meet the costs of his solicitors had been established so that he could recover them without breaching the indemnity principle. The court did not perceive a need to meet head-on the further question by what mechanism the success fee was then recoverable and whether and how it might be recoverable from the individual client alone rather than from a funder. Moreover, during its judgment the court also referred to Courts and Legal Services Act 1990, s.58A(6) and Access to Justice Act 1999, s.30(2) (which allows additional amounts for insurance to be recoverable as the costs of proceedings by Membership Organisations) as constituting a 'derogation' from the indemnity principle, a tantalising *obiter* remark the effect of which it might have been helpful to have heard more about.

In summary, CCFAs when properly drafted are a conditional fee variant of the third-party funding permitted by the courts to date, and are not unenforceable on the ground that they breach the indemnity principle.

CCFA Regulations 2000, reg.5(1)

In *Various Claimants* v. *Gower Chemicals Ltd* (28 February 2007) Field J. had to consider the meaning and effect of CCFA Regulations 2000, reg.5(1) ('requirements for contents of collective conditional fee agreements providing for success fees'), which states that:

> 5. – (1) Where a collective conditional fee agreement provides for a success fee the agreement must provide that, when accepting instructions in relation to any specific proceedings the legal representative must prepare and retain a written statement containing –
>
> (a) his assessment of the probability of the circumstances arising in which the percentage increase will become payable in relation to those proceedings ('the risk assessment');
> (b) his assessment of the amount of the percentage increase in relation to those proceedings, having regard to the risk assessment; and
> (c) the reasons, by reference to the risk assessment, for setting the percentage increase at that level.

Field J. adopted the plain and ordinary meaning of this subsection which, he held, required only that the CCFA itself had to provide a 'written statement' of the items set out in paragraphs (a)–(c). The Regulations did not require that these provisions had in fact to be performed. The actual preparation and retention of conforming risk assessments, therefore, was not a requirement prescribed by Courts and Legal Services Act 1990, s.58(3)(c) (as substituted). The failure to prepare such a written statement could lead to a contractual right either to terminate the agreement or to claim damages or abate the amount of any costs due, but it could not deprive a CCFA of the statutory protection enjoyed by virtue of s.58(1).

CCFAs unenforceable in respect of single specific proceedings

While the Court of Appeal may have established the theoretical basis on which a correctly drawn CCFA is lawful and not a breach of the indemnity principle, it may still be possible for a CCFA to be unenforceable in respect of an individual client whose legal services were funded by the agreement.

This was the result in *Jones* v. *Caradon Catnic Ltd*. In this case a trade union CCFA made it clear that the maximum success fee payable under the CCFA was 100 per cent. The client could never have been required to pay the uplift. However, the legal representative had set out a success fee of 120 per cent in the written statement of the amount of the uplift required by CCFA Regulations 2000, reg.5(1) (and indeed this was claimed in the Bill of Costs). While there was no risk to consumer protection, this was a breach of Access to Justice Act 1999, s.58(4)(c) and CFA Order 2000, para.4 which was so serious that it materially prejudiced the proper administration of justice. The

CCFA was unenforceable in the sense that the costs of the particular client were not recoverable.

CCFAs after the Revocation Regulations 2005

The revocation of the CCFA Regulations 2000 has left a new problem as to enforceability, which is how a CFA can be drafted to comply with s.58(4)(b), which requires that a CFA:

> must state the percentage by which the amount of the fees which would be payable if it were not a conditional fee agreement is to be increased.

How can one original agreement by which a funder has agreed terms with a solicitor in advance for all future classes of proceedings caught by the agreement possibly anticipate and then 'state' the appropriate percentage uplift for all future specific proceedings?

A satisfactory device to accommodate this drafting difficulty left by the revocation of the CCFA Regulations appears to be to draft the agreement so that any statement of the amount of the uplift payable in respect of future specific proceedings becomes annexed to the CCFA and forms part of it as a Schedule incorporated into the agreement.

4.5 CHALLENGING A CFA/CCFA RETAINER

Introduction

Satellite litigation about costs is not intended by the higher courts to be made easy. On the other hand, while an unsuccessful opponent may have 'no legitimate interest in seeking to avoid his proper obligations by seizing on an apparent breach of the requirements which is immaterial in the context of the other two purposes of the statutory regulation' (*Hollins* at para.105), the extra burden of the additional liabilities means that 'The court is entitled and bound to have regard to the interests of paying parties, and those to whom they pass on the costs . . . as well as those of receiving parties' (para.71).

Going behind the certificate on the Bill: a presumption as to accuracy

The conventional position is that the indemnity certificate placed at the end of a Bill of Costs (see CPD para.4.15) creates a presumption that the Bill is accurate and that a claim is not being made which offends against the indemnity principle. This certificate states that 'I certify that this bill is both accurate and complete and . . . the costs claimed herein do not exceed the costs which the receiving party is required to pay me/my firm' (see Precedent F to

110

the Schedule of Costs Precedents annexed to the Costs Practice Direction). It is the signature to this certificate which was described by Henry LJ in *Bailey* v. *IBC Vehicles* [1998] 3 All ER 570 as 'no empty formality', and which is intended, in the absence of a real issue being raised as to the receiving party's entitlement to costs, to prevent skirmishes designed to attack the receiving party's costs on the grounds that the costs as claimed are in excess of the costs due to the receiving party's legal representative.

Disclosure of a CFA

The validity of the presumption as set out in *Bailey* was distinguished in *Hollins* (para.64ff), at least insofar as the question of non-disclosure of the CFA retainer was concerned. Disclosure of a CFA is regularly required by paying parties and it is inviting some order for costs against a paying party who, in the absence of a very good reason, does not hand over the agreement. This is commented on at para.71:

> As we see it, where there is a CFA, a costs judge should normally exercise his discretion … so as to require the receiving parties (subject to their right of election preserved by paragraph 40.14 of the Costs Practice Direction … to produce a copy of their CFAs to the paying parties in order that they can see whether or not the Regulations were complied with and (where a CFA provides for a success fee) whether the liability of the receiving party to pay that success fee is indeed enforceable.

Confidential passages can be redacted (para.72). It should be added that if the Court of Appeal intended by this passage to distinguish *Bailey* to the extent that the presumption is supposed not to operate in the context of CFA challenges (for instance where there are allegations of breaches of the CFA Regulations 2000), then it failed. It still requires a genuine issue or genuine issue to be raised (which is a matter of evidence and not mere assertion) before a judge will launch into a lengthy inquiry into the validity of a CFA, especially where the allegation involves a breach of reg.4 (necessitating an inquiry beyond what can be argued from the written words of the CFA itself). At para.82 of *Hollins* the Court of Appeal set out its expectation that in a normal case a receiving party would disclose a CFA 'without more ado'.

It seems more likely than not that the expectation will continue to be that CFAs should be disclosed to a paying party even now that the CFA Regulations 2000 have been revoked. There are a sufficient number of mandatory requirements in the Act to make this the ordinary rule.

Raising a 'genuine issue'

The position in relation to ordinary retainers still applies in practice where funding is by way of a CFA. In this respect, *Hazlett* v. *Sefton Metropolitan Borough Council* [2000] 4 All ER 887 at p.893c–d is relevant:

The need for a complainant to give evidence to prove his entitlement to costs rather than relying on the presumption in his favour will not . . . arise if the defendant simply puts the complainant to proof of his entitlement to costs. The complainant would be justified in relying on the presumption in his favour. It would be necessary for the defendant to raise a genuine issue as to whether the complainant is liable for his solicitors' costs before the complainant would be called upon to adduce evidence to show that he is entitled to his costs.

See also the useful exegesis in *Ilangartne* v. *BMA* (2005) EWHC 2096 (Ch), Warren J, 4 October 2005 (unreported).

Examples of first-instance cases in which assessing judges reached decision whether or not to go behind the solicitors' certificate are *Culshaw* v. *Goodliffe*, 24 November 2003, HHJ Stewart QC, *Adair* v. *Cullen*, 14 June 2004, HHJ Holman, *Samonini* v. *London Gen Trans Services Ltd*, 19 January 2005, Master Hurst, *Garrett* v. *Halton BC*, 5 April 2005, HHJ Stewart QC and *Myatt* v. *NCB*, 12 August 2005 Master Wright. These all concerned either grossly disproportionate and unfair costs liabilities (for instance in the case of scheme arrangements where the claimants were likely to receive disproportionately little as compared with the costs, or cases where pre-existing BTE insurance in fact existed). The exception is the decision of Master Wright in *Myatt*. Other examples of 'scheme' arrangements in which the damages are very low and the claimants are drawn into taking out disproportionately expensive funding loans are to be found in the housing disrepair cases, for instance *Bowen* v. *Bridgend CBC*, Master Hurst, 25 March 2004, *Hughes* v. *Newham LBC*, 28 July 2005, Master O'Hare, and *Hussain* v. *Leeds CC*, 16 December 2005, Master O'Hare.

A summary process

Hazlett anticipates that an inquiry into the indemnity principle is very much a summary process. The Divisional Court expected that a trial judge would consider the matter at the conclusion of the hearing, and that so long as the potential receiving party had 'prior notice' as to the paying party's claim that there was a genuine issue to be tried, the receiving party would have to have made a judgement itself prior to the end of the hearing as to whether or not it was necessary to call evidence for the purpose of proving a retainer.

The summary nature of this process is prevalent among costs judges. It is very unusual to find that a costs judge will make a ruling as to whether the presumption set up by the certificate can be relied upon, but then adjourn the matter so that a receiving party can call its evidence. This creates a difficulty for receiving parties. Almost inevitably an explanation in a witness statement intended to explain the issue thrown up by a paying party creates additional queries. The receiving party is very likely to fall foul of Master Wright's decision in *Myatt*, the effect of which is that now that everything is out in the open, the court might as well carry on with the inquiry.

Obtaining client care material in addition to the CFA: Part 18 requests for information

A further question is the extent to which a paying party can obtain material other than the CFA. This will be particularly relevant where a reg.4 challenge is contemplated since many paying parties would like to know what pre-CFA information was provided in the hope that this might reveal a breach of the regulation, for instance, whether there was a breach of the duty to take reasonable steps to inquire into the existence of BTE insurance which is the cornerstone of reg.4(2)(c). While the Court of Appeal was satisfied in *Hollins* that a CFA should normally be disclosed, it was not prepared to sanction the disclosure of other material (see para.81):

> The appellants in the present cases also seek disclosure of the attendance notes prepared by the receiving parties' solicitors showing compliance with regulation 4. We do not consider that these should ordinarily be disclosed. We consider that the costs judge should not require these to be disclosed unless there is a genuine issue as to whether there was compliance with regulation 4.

There was a period when very extensive Part 18 requests were being made by paying parties. Where a receiving party claims an additional liability, para.35.7 of the Costs Practice Direction expressly permits a Part 18 request to be made by a paying party as to 'other methods of financing costs which were available to the receiving party'. Proper practice in relation to the application of this rule has been definitively provided by the Senior Costs Judge in *Hutchings* v. *British Transport Police*, 11 October 2006, Master Hurst who allowed three questions to be asked which could be considered reasonable and proportionate: (a) does the claimant have any insurance; (b) with whom; (c) does the claimant have any legal expense insurance? The breadth of these questions, however, is so wide as to have a potentially devastating effect. If the answer is 'yes' (as it often is) then it opens a wide range of potential issues depending on what is revealed in the Bill.

Evidence: witness statements

How then does a receiving party fight off a challenge to its retainer on the basis that the CFA does not satisfy the applicable conditions as required by s.58(1)?

The best means for achieving this is by preparing a witness statement from the solicitor concerned. After all, the exercise is in essence one designed to establish what the reasonable and prudent solicitor did. Judges do not require an Order permitting reliance on a witness statement. CPR rules 32.2(1)(b) and 32.6 apply so that the witness statement will be relied on unless the other party makes an application for the maker's cross examination under rule 32.7 (requiring a Part 23 application). The witness statement should be served to give the paying party a reasonable time to consider it and to make its application for cross-examination. Giving more than one week's notice is being slightly too generous to a paying party. The formalities of 32PD11–15 ('Exhibits') and of 32PD.17–22 ('Witness Statements') must be observed.

4.6 ENFORCEABILITY AFTER 1 NOVEMBER 2005

CFAs made after 1 November 2005 are not subject to the rigours of the 2000 Regulations and their mandatory provisions. This is the effect of the CFA (Revocation) Regulations 2005, SI 2005/2305 which revoked the old regulations as from (i.e. including) 1 November 2005. The client care provisions are now those which govern solicitors by reason of their general obligations under the Practice Rules, whether the Client Case and Costs Information Code under rule 15, or (from 1 July 2007) the Solicitors' Code of Conduct 2007.

It is widely thought that by the transfer of the client care provisions into the regulatory scheme which governs the profession, it will be impossible for paying parties to make the same regulatory challenges to the same dramatic effect. This is because mandatory 'conditions' applicable to every CFA by s.58(3)(c) which are required to be satisfied for a CFA to be declared enforceable simply no longer exist by reason of the Revocation Regulations. Moreover, *Garbutt* v. *Edwards* [2006] 1 WLR 2907 is authority for the proposition that while a breach of a professional code may have given rise to financial and other disciplinary sanctions at the instigation of the client (such as a finding of Inadequate Professional Services), such a breach cannot give rise to a direct claim by a paying party that there has been a breach of the indemnity principle.

4.7 CAN A 'DEFECTIVE' CFA BE CURED?

The question whether the defects in a retainer can be put right and the CFA protected from being declared unenforceable will depend on the circumstances, in particular the time at which the defect becomes apparent and whether the CFA properly records what the parties thought they had agreed. There are two principal difficulties. The first is the fact that defects tend not to appear prior to the costs order which gives rise to the entitlement to costs, and at this stage it has been held to be too late to vary a retainer. The second is that the weight of public policy is against trying to put right after the event that which otherwise prejudiced the administration of justice or the protection afforded to the client. On the other hand, rectification is possible where the contents of the CFA itself run contrary to the true intentions of the parties and where wording has been entered or omitted by mistake, for instance where the wording fails to specify correctly what proportion of the success fee is attributable to postponement of the legal representative's fees and expenses and what does not for the purposes of reg.3(1)(b). These issues and the potential remedies are considered further below.

Variation

In *Kellar* v. *Carib West Limited* (Privy Council Appeal No.13 of 2003, 24 June 2004), the Privy Council stated, in a discussion about a variation to a retainer, that:

> It was quite open to the respondent and his attorneys to vary the fee agreement to an hourly charging arrangement if they so wished, and their Lordships consider that there was clearly good consideration for such a variation. When the bills are taxed, they could be prepared, if the respondent's attorneys choose, on the hourly charging basis and then be subject to the normal process of ascertainment of the hours properly to be charged and of the applicable rates or rates to be applied to the work done. If, however, it were likely to produce a larger costs bill than the original framework, an amalgam of hourly rates and brief fees (which appears to be unlikely from the terms of the letter), the appellants' attorneys would be entitled simply to refuse to accept the amended basis and require the respondent to revert to the original framework. They could do so on the ground, as the Chief Justice correctly held, that that amendment had come into existence subsequent to the making of the costs basis and so could be disregarded by the paying party if he wished.

This statement of principle, that a variation cannot be used to impose a greater burden on the paying party than existed before final judgment (see Master Hurst in *Oyston*), has confounded any attempts to date to make good, retrospectively, defects found to exist in a CFA notwithstanding that on careful examination of *Kellar* its application should be restricted to the practice of lawyers in the Turks and Caicos islands.

Oyston concerned a case in which a costs order had been made in an action in the Mercantile Court on 25 July 2005. On 16 August 2005 the claimant and his solicitors had entered into a deed of variation removing the requirement that in the event of success the claimant would pay a lump sum of £50,000 in addition to the 100 per cent uplift. Master Hurst held that this was a breach like that in *Jones* v. *Caradon Catnic* which was considered 'central to the regime' (see para.35). The Senior Costs Judge had no hesitation in holding that the deed was ineffective by reason of the statement of principle set out in *Kellar*.

Master Hurst was also impressed by the fact that the deed 'was only entered into when it was realised that the original CFA had a potentially fatal defect' (para.50). The fact that the client was in agreement 'is of no assistance' since:

> If the position were otherwise, it would be open to solicitors and their successful client to, for example, alter the level of success fee late in the day.

Given the decision in *Garrett & Myatt* which dismisses the relevance of the outcome of the case and which requires enforceability to be determined when the CFA was made, it is difficult to see any court permitting a deed of variation to be used even if the deed is entered into prior to the date of the costs order. A receiving party who is alive to the difficulties of a CFA and who is willing to enter into an alternative agreement would be better advised to try his luck by entering into a fresh agreement in which the costs already incurred have been backdated.

Severance

The possibility of severing an unlawful aspect of a CFA from the remainder of an agreement was canvassed in *Oyston* (see above) without success. Severance was an argument which had been advanced in *Aratra Potato Co Ltd* v. *Taylor Joynson Garrett* [1995] 4 All ER 695, and it does not look any more attractive when applied to CFAs. In *Oyston* Master Hurst was quite satisfied that 'it would be contrary to public policy to permit severance' (para.59).

Master Hurst's decision in *Oyston* was ultimately one directed by public policy (see para.59):

> If either a Deed of Variation or severance were permitted late in the day, this would have the effect of enabling virtually all defective CFAs to be put right late in the day, even if this was only after the paying party had pointed out the alleged defects.

To date there has been no challenge to this assertion, notwithstanding its ostensible origin in the special practices applicable in *Kellar* (see above).

Rectification

Rectification applies in different circumstances, namely where an instrument does not correctly record what has been agreed between the parties. It has been said that rectification will be granted not if the written agreement does not represent the true intention of the parties, but if the agreement is *contrary* to their true intentions. There must be 'very strong', 'convincing' or 'irrefragable' evidence (*Costidi* v. *Ralli* [1935] Ch 427) that the CFA 'does not truly record the terms of the transaction' (see *Snell's Equity* (31st edn) at 14–09). At the same time the Court of Appeal has stated this means examining the evidence as to what the contracts were, not analysing the 'inner minds' of the parties (*Rose* v. *William Pim* [1953] 2 QB 450, 461).

Rectification will be permitted by a court on the basis that the court is rectifying the instrument which records an agreement, rather than the agreement itself (*Meagher* 26–010). Denning LJ said that it had to be demonstrated that the parties were in complete agreement on the terms of the contract, but by an error wrote them down wrongly under a common mistake (*Rose* v. *William Pim* [1953] 2 QB 450, 461). The need for rectification arises when the court can see from the instrument that something has gone wrong which cannot be cured by the rules of construction.

There can thus be no rectification if the omission of a term was deliberate (*Whiteside* v. *Whiteside* [1950] Ch 65), or, as *Snell* records, even if the omission was due to an erroneous belief that the relevant term's inclusion was unnecessary. Rectification may be granted if the term is one which is always taken for granted (that is not the case in respect of a breach of reg.3(1)(b)), or if the parties were agreed as to the substance of the term to be included even if they had not formulated the precise words. Snell's *Equity* notes at 43–08 (2) that what is important is 'the intention of the parties at the time when the deed was executed, and not what would have been their intent if, when they executed it, the result of what they did had been present to their minds'. In cases of unilateral mistakes, the general rule is that there can be no rectification where the mistake is unilateral, for instance where one party had never heard of the term to be inserted.

The effectiveness of a claim to rectification is uncertain. Where there is no dispute between the client and his legal representative, the best (and only) course is to enter into a deed of rectification. The effect of rectification is as follows (Lord Sterndale MR in *Craddock Bros* v. *Hunt* [1923] 2 Ch 136 approving *Johnson* v. *Bragge* [1901] 1 Ch 28, 37):

> After rectification the written agreement . . . is to be read as if it had been originally drawn in its rectified form.

The regulations must surely therefore apply to the document as rectified, so that any assessment as to whether the second CFA satisfied the conditions applicable to it at the time at which it was made must be determined by reference to the rectified agreement.

Draft deeds of rectification are to be found at **Appendix 17**. As to the evidence which must be available to support rectification, this is likely to consist of the contents of contemporaneous letters, file and attendance notes, and also the witness evidence of the fee earner and possibly the client.

CHAPTER 5

Specific CFA issues

5.1 INTRODUCTION

In this chapter consideration is given to some specific issues of concern common to all types of CFAs and CFA-funded litigation. The chapter is organised into three sections. The first deals mainly with CFAs entered into in order to accommodate the proceedings of children or protected parties, the problem of clients who become protected parties during the course of proceedings being particularly difficult. The second looks briefly at different aspects of the law of contract so far as it concerns the assignment and termination of CFAs, in particular the questions whether a CFA (or indeed a whole raft of CFAs) can be assigned to a new firm, and whether a CFA can be terminated on other grounds which are generally not expressly provided for in a CFA retainer (typically termination by mutual consent). The third section is concerned with two issues of costs, namely interest on costs under Civil Procedure Rules (CPR) Part 36 and the potential liability of solicitors who work on CFA terms.

5.2 CHILDREN AND PROTECTED PARTIES

Introduction

In order to understand the position concerning CFAs entered into for the benefit of protected parties and children it is useful to understand the wider law relating to capacity, including the legislative framework (which has changed substantially with the coming into force of the Mental Capacity Act 2005). There is a particular problem in relation to claimants who become protected parties during the course of proceedings and this needs particular attention. It is also hoped that some assistance can be given in this section to the practical question whether or not it is necessary to involve the Court of Protection when entering into a CFA.

The need for a litigation friend

The relevant legislation is now contained in the Mental Capacity Act 2005. Until 1 October 2007 it was set out in the Mental Health Act 1983. The position in respect of legal proceedings is covered largely by CPR Part 21. A 'protected party' must have a litigation friend in order for proceedings to be conducted on his behalf (CPR rule 21.2(1)), and indeed if a party becomes a protected party (formerly a 'patient') during proceedings, then by rule 21.3(3) 'no party may take any step in the proceedings without the permission of the Court until the protected party has a litigation friend'.

'Protected party' (formerly 'patient')

This of course begs the question who is a 'protected party', or indeed a 'patient' under the 1983 Act regime. A new CPR Part 21 was substituted with effect from 1 October 2007 to reflect the new law under the 2005 Act. Under the old law, 'patient' was 'a person who by reason of *mental disorder*' within the meaning of the Mental Health Act 1983 was 'incapable of managing and administering his own affairs'. 'Mental disorder' was defined by s.1(2) of the Act. It is important, however, to remember the conclusion of the Court of Appeal in *Masterman-Lister* v. *Brutton & Co* [2003] 1 WLR 1511. Rule 21.1(2)(b) was never a 'one size fits all' test:

> What . . . does seem to me to be of some importance is the issue-specific nature of the test; that is to say the requirement to consider the question of capacity in relation to the particular transaction (its nature and complexity) in respect of which the decisions as to capacity fall to be made.

The legal representative (and the court) had to be astute to ensure that the client was a 'patient' for the purposes of the particular proceedings. There is a presumption of capacity, and it has always been a gross invasion of a person's civil rights to take away his ability to conduct proceedings on his own behalf.

The presumption of capacity is the mainstay of the Mental Capacity Act 2005, enshrined as it is in s.1(1) of that Act, and what is meant by capacity (and also 'people who lack capacity') is further set out in Part I of the Act. The new Act expressly recognises that the question whether or not a party 'lacks capacity' is a question to be determined by reference to the particular matter in question. CPR rule 21.1(2)(d), therefore, describes a 'protected party' as a person who 'lacks capacity to conduct the proceedings', and rule 21.1(2)(c) defines 'lacks capacity' to mean 'lacks capacity within the meaning of the 2005 Act'.

The Court of Protection

Part 2 of the Mental Capacity Act 2005 ('The Court of Protection and the Public Guardian') has established a new Court Protection. It is governed by the Court of Protection Rules 2007, SI 2007/1744. Under the new legislative regime a 'deputy' will take the place of the former receiver and may be appointed as the protected party's agent to make decisions on his behalf. Section 18 of the 2005 Act expressly extends a deputy's power to include the conduct of legal proceedings in the protected party's name or on his behalf. If a deputy under the 2005 Act does not have a power under the terms of his appointment to conduct litigation, then he would be acting prudently in writing to the Court of Protection (in the shape of the Public Guardianship Office) to ensure that the court is content for any litigation in favour of the client to be conducted, but this is not necessary (see below).

The deputy does not need to be the litigation friend

CPR rule 21.6 tells us 'How a person becomes a litigation friend by Court Order'. If there is no court order, then rule 21.4(2) tells us that a deputy *is entitled* to be the litigation friend. By rule 21.5 either the deputy or 'any other person' who wishes to act as a litigation friend (so long as he can pass the test in rule 21.4(3)) without court order can become the litigation friend by filing a certificate of suitability which must be served on the parties.

Contracting with children

In the case of a child who has permission to conduct proceedings under rule 21.2(3), it is unlikely that a lawyer should agree to work under CFA (or possibly indeed any terms) since only contracts which are 'contracts for necessaries' are binding on children and the burden is on the supplier of services to demonstrate that the services required are 'necessaries'. It is unlikely that the provision of litigation services will constitute 'necessaries' (the conclusion for instance in *Steeden* v. *Naden* [1910] 2 Ch 393; cf. *Helps* v. *Clayton* 17 CB (NS) 553).

The litigation friend as a party to a CFA

Where a protected party or child has a litigation friend, then it is important that the legal representative contracts directly with the litigation friend. The litigation friend is a principal to the contract and in this context at least is not an agent for the child or protected party. He is probably best considered a funder. Contracts with both children and protected parties are unenforceable (save for the proviso above in respect of the former in the case of a contract for 'necessaries'), and in the case of a protected party at least, the protected party will inevitably be deemed incapable of giving instructions and cannot appoint a solicitor to be his agent at all. A receiver under the old legislative regime has been described as the 'statutory agent' of the protected party and in his capacity as receiver has no personal liability for the costs of the solicitor who acts on the protected party's behalf (*In re EG (A Person of Unsound Mind Not So Found by Inquisition)* [1914] 1 Ch 927). Furthermore, a solicitor who acts for a protected party who is incapable of giving instructions is at risk of paying the costs personally (*Yonge* v. *Toynbee* [1910] 1 KB 215).

It is necessary, then, to contract with the litigation friend, whether he is the deputy or some other person. In relation to the child or protected party, the litigation friend is entitled at common law to an indemnity for his costs and expenses. The policy reasons for this go back to eighteenth-century cases and show that the courts are concerned to ensure that 'No discouragement ought to be thrown in the way of persons bona fide suing as next friends' (*Nalder* v. *Hawkins* (1833) 2 My & K 243, 247), and that it must not be permitted to become 'very dangerous to attempt the management of infants' estates' (*Taner* v. *Ivie* 2 Ves Sen 466). According to this latter judgment, the litigation friend will or will not get his costs met by the child or protected party depending on the answer to the question whether or not the action was 'brought and carried on in a reasonable manner', and this rule must apply today.

Where a child becomes 18, or where a protected party obtains capacity, then the CFA should either be ratified or a new CFA entered into. If the prospects of success have become worse and the uplift is likely to be higher with a new CFA then of course this should be spelled out.

The deputy's consent to a CFA is not necessary

So, a legal representative contracting with a child or litigation friend who is a child or protected party at the beginning of proceedings must contract with the litigation friend, whether or not the litigation friend is the deputy. Whether the deputy should be asked to give his express consent is really a matter of protection for the litigation friend, but the litigation friend will get this in any event by reason of the approval settlement under rule 21.10. Assuming the court gives its approval to the compromise then a deputy can hardly refuse to authorise payment of the costs. Rule 21.11 provides added protection (control of money recovered by or on behalf of a child or protected party), the High Court having an inherent supervisory jurisdiction over solicitors as well as these express rules governing children and protected parties.

Further protections come in the form of rule 48.5 (costs where money is payable by or to a child or protected party) and accompanying Practice Direction (CPD, s.51) and rule 21.11A. These rules protect both the litigation friend and also the child or protected party, since ultimately they limit and restrict the amounts which are to be paid out of the monies due to the child or protected party by court order. CFAs are no different from any other retainers in this respect, so that it is not strictly necessary to get approval via the Court of Protection.

Clients who become protected parties during the course of proceedings

But what happens when a client becomes a protected party during the course of proceedings?

When a client becomes incapable, the effect is that the retainer is frustrated (see the commentary on *Yonge*'s case in *Halsbury's Laws* and *Cordery on Solicitors*). This probably depends on the nature of the illness and whether or not it is likely to be permanent or temporary, but in practical terms frustration is the likely consequence.

At common law, where a contract is frustrated the agreement comes to an end 'forthwith, without more and automatically' and the losses ordinarily lie where they fall (see *Chitty* (29th edn) at paras.23–069 and 23–070). In the context of most CFAs (including the Law Society model) there is no express provision on developing incapacity. In the case of death, on the other hand, the agreement reads:

> This agreement automatically ends if you die before your claim for damages is concluded. We will be entitled to recover our basic charges and disbursements up to the date of your death from your estate.

The editors of *Cordery on Solicitors* (see para.E447) take the view that the rights and liabilities of the parties to a retainer prior to a frustrating event are unaffected, so that notwithstanding the absence of a provision to similar effect on a client becoming a protected party, it is more likely than not that the right to payment continues to exist pending the outcome of the win event provided for in the CFA.

One option for solicitors to take with a view to rendering the position more certain is to amend their CFA terms. This could be done by introducing a clause similar to that applicable on death (see above). Another possibility is expressly to accommodate the terms set out in Law Reform (Frustrated Contracts) Act 1943, s.2(3), (4):

> (3)   Where any contract to which this Act applies contains any provision which, upon the true construction of the contract, is intended to have effect in the event of circumstances arising which operate, or would but for the said provision operate, to frustrate the contract, or is intended to have effect whether such circumstances arise or not, the court shall give effect to the said provision and shall only give effect to the foregoing section of this Act to such extent, if any, as appears to the court to be consistent with the said provision.

(4) Where it appears to the court that a part of any contract to which this Act applies can properly be severed from the remainder of the contract, being a part wholly performed before the time of discharge, or so performed except for the payment in respect of that part of the contract of sums which are or can be ascertained under the contract, the court shall treat that part of the contract as if it were a separate contract and had not been frustrated and shall treat the foregoing section of this Act as only applicable to the remainder of that contract.

Without a clause on these lines, the position in respect of the costs of a client who becomes a protected party during proceedings is likely to cause confusion and may be in jeopardy.

5.3 DEATH

A standard CFA provides in the event of death that a new agreement will be offered to the deceased's executors. The new agreement should require the executors expressly to assume all the liabilities of the previous agreement, including any success fee. See also the standard clause set out above which expressly reserves a right to payment of costs on a client's demise.

5.4 CONTRACTUAL ISSUES

Assignment

It is possible to assign a CFA, indeed a whole CFA practice, although there are several ostensibly serious difficulties. Assignment is necessary where one firm takes over the conduct of proceedings, where firms merge, or where a firm becomes an LLP. In these circumstances the assignor is unlikely to want the burden of having to obtain the consent of the clients whose retainers are being assigned to the new entity, and this in itself gives rise to the question whether their consent is needed. Whether or not there was an assignment of a CFA agreement was particularly important before the CFA Regulations 2000 were abolished, since if it were possible to prove that there had not been an assignment of the CFA then it was likely to follow that there had not been compliance with the client care provisions of the Regulations when the new solicitors took over the case.

One difficulty is the question whether it is possible to assign a retainer with a solicitor without the client's consent because the retainer constitutes a personal contract and is otherwise incapable of assignment (see *Tolhurst* v. *Associated Portland Cement Manufacturers Ltd* [1902] 2 KB 660, 668–9). In that case Collins MR pointed out that in the case of a personal contract:

> the assignor [cannot] rely upon the act of another as performance by himself . . .
> He cannot vouch the capacity of another to perform that which the other party to
> the contract might, however unreasonably, insist was what alone he undertook to
> pay for – namely, work to be executed by the party himself. If, for instance, he had
> ordered a painting from some unknown artist of his own choice, he could not be
> compelled to accept instead of it the work of another artist, however eminent.

In 'factory' low-value personal injury litigation it is unlikely that the retainer
is really one where the client requires the services of a specific solicitor, but in
a high-value claim where the client has sought out the individual practitioner
the position is likely to be very different.

Another significant problem is the question whether the burden of an
agreement (in the case of a CFA the obligation to provide legal services) can
be assigned at all. In *Jenkins* v. *Young Bros Transport Limited* [2006] 1 WLR
3189 Rafferty J decided that the assignment of such a burden falls within the
exception to the general rule that the burden of a contract cannot be
assigned. This exception was explained by Megarry VC in *Tito* v. *Waddell
(No.2)* [1977] 1 Ch 106, 302B: a burden can be assigned so long as the burden
is conditional on the benefit, which is to say that 'the condition must be relevant to the exercise of the right' (Lord Upjohn in *Halsall* v. *Brizell* [1957] Ch
169). In the case of a CFA, the taking of the benefit (the payment of fees) was
said to be conditional on performing the obligation to provide legal services.

In these circumstances a CFA can be assigned by the operation of the Law
of Property Act 1925, s.136. The relevant minimal requirements are that the
assignment must be in the assignor's writing and notice must be given to the
client.

Where the assignment is valid then the effect of Raffery J's decision in
Jenkins is that there was no need to go through the regulatory client care
requirements of the CFA Regulations 2000. In that case the individual solicitor moved twice during the conduct of the client's proceedings and on each
case a set of terms of business was sent to the client purporting to continue
the pre-existing CFA (subject to some significant variations). Rafferty J
decided that even if the court was wrong that there had been an effective variation of the CFA, then the letters and the failure to provide more detailed
information or to enter into new written agreements were not to be considered material breaches. In other words, the court strove hard to support the
validity of the CFA against the technical challenge made by the paying party.

Termination outside the express terms of the CFA

Assignment between firms, then, is permissible. What happens if a client
wishes to move solicitor but the new firm does not wish to entertain an
assignment of the agreement?

Here there would appear to be two options depending on the terms of the agreement. Either the client may terminate the retainer, since a client is normally entitled to terminate without cause, or the solicitor in the old firm may terminate under the usual provision that the client has not complied with his responsibilities, namely his obligation to cooperate and to provide instructions. There must be agreement, however, between the parties as to the consequences of termination and this must be recorded in writing. Under both termination provisions the options tend to be the same and the solicitor is likely to agree to await the outcome of proceedings when he can claim his success fee as well as his other costs and expenses.

Similar difficulties can exist where one CFA is replaced for another. This may happen in a variety of situations. One is where there has been an original 'investigative' CFA. The other is where the parties have simply agreed to new terms incorporating the provision for a new (generally improved) uplift.

In these circumstances either the first or second CFA must make it clear that both CFAs are intended to be kept alive for the recovery of costs in the event of an overall 'win'. Termination by mutual agreement is not provided for in a CFA and such a termination is occasionally challenged by paying parties.

5.5 COSTS

Interest on costs where a Part 36 offer is beaten by a successful claimant

An award of interest on costs where a Part 36 offer has not been beaten (now under CPR rule 36.14) is intended to be compensatory in nature and not punitive (*McPhilemy* v. *Times Newspapers Ltd & Others* (2001) EWCA Civ 933, (2001) EMLR 858). This has led to different judgments as to whether interest is payable where the client has the benefit of a CFA. In *Montlake* v. *Lambert Smith Hampton Group Ltd* [2004] EWHC 1503 (Comm) Langley J held that the fact that there was a recoverable success fee of 100 per cent meant that it was unjust to allow an award of interest on the costs. In *Nedlloyd Lines UK Ltd* v. *CEL Group Ltd* [2004] 1 Lloyd's Rep 382 and in *Anthony* v. *Coal Authority* (28 July 2005, Pitchford J) it was held that the fact that CFA retainer was deployed to fund the client's costs and expenses had no effect on the Part 36 costs.

The position of a solicitor working on CFA terms

In an early CFA case in the pre-Access to Justice Act 1999 regime, Lord Woolf considered the position of a lawyer working on CFA terms. *Hodgson* v. *Imperial Tobacco* [1998] 1 WLR 1056 concerned a group action aiming to recover damages for those who contracted lung disease as a result of smoking. Legal aid had been refused and the lawyers were all engaged on CFAs. There was no ATE at all. The defendants made it clear that they intended making applications for costs to be paid personally by the claimant lawyers and the claimants issued an application aiming to debar the defendants from making such an application. Lord Woolf MR stated:

> There is no reason why the circumstances in which a lawyer, acting under a CFA, can be made personally liable for the costs of a party other than his client should differ from those in which a lawyer who is not acting under a CFA would be so liable. Any suggestion by the defendants' lawyers, and any concern of the plaintiffs' lawyers, that the position of the plaintiffs' lawyers is different from that of any other legal adviser is misconceived. The existence of a CFA should make a legal advisers' position as a matter of law no worse, so far as being ordered to pay costs is concerned, than it would be if there was no CFA.

The promise of immunity by the courts has been thrown into doubt by the judgment of the Court of Appeal in *Myatt* v. *NCB* [2007] 1 WLR 1559, which concerned the costs incurred by the successful respondent in the conjoined appeals of *Garrett* v. *Halton B.C.*; *Myatt* v. *NCB* [2007] 1 WLR 554. This was the case which considered the question whether a CFA is enforceable by reference to the relevant circumstances which existed at the date of the agreement or alternatively at the time of the costs assessment.

Following *Garrett & Myatt*, the National Coal Board went on to seek its costs from the appellants' solicitors, asserting that it would have been content to obtain its costs against the ATE providers if it were not for the fact that there was a clause in the ATE policy which expressly made it 'a condition precedent to the liability of the insurers under the claimants' ATE policies that enforceable CFAs were in place'. Nevertheless it is a curiosity that if the NCB had obtained its orders against the claimants and threatened to enforce them, the solicitors would surely have been compelled to have met the costs personally since the unenforceability was the result of their own default.

Dyson LJ felt able to conclude (by inference) that it was very unlikely that the four claimants themselves would have pursued their appeals to the Court of Appeal in order to obtain reimbursement for their disbursements (of about £2,500 each). The fact was that the solicitors' profit costs were by far the larger part of the costs which were subject to the appeal. They ranged from about £5,000 to £7,100 in each case. Moreover, the four cases before the court were in reality test cases since there were about 60 other cases where clients had entered into CFAs with the solicitors in very similar circumstances. On the basis that the solicitors' average profit costs in all of the cases were in the range of about £3,000 to £4,000, what was at stake in the appeals was about £200,000 of profit costs. The judge decided that even if the solicitors had been warned that there might have been a costs application against them personally, they would not have abandoned the appeal.

The Court of Appeal decided that Supreme Court Act 1981, s.51 was sufficiently wide in its jurisdiction to enable an order to be made against the solicitors as the true parties to the appeals. Since there was no ATE in force, the appeal was brought really so that the solicitors could recover their costs. Applying the criteria by which a funder may be exposed to an order for costs in *Dymocks* v. *Todd* [2004] 1 WLR 2807 (see **12.3**) the court in *Myatt* v. *NCB* [2007] 1 WLR 1559 concluded that 'there is jurisdiction to make an order under s.51(3) against a solicitor where litigation is pursued by the client for the benefit or to a substantial degree for the benefit of the solicitor'. According to Lloyd LJ the principle as enunciated by the court was limited to cases where the litigation is funded by a CFA.

Myatt should give any solicitor some cause for concern where the case is being prosecuted without any ATE policy in place or alternatively without an ATE policy which is likely to become void depending on the findings of the trial judge. It is quite possible that costs orders could become a more common armoury in the hands of receiving parties, but the extent to which this will become permissible must, at the time of writing, be a matter of speculation. The consequences in particular on claimant lawyers in media proceedings in particular will need careful consideration (see **Chapter 6**).

In *Myatt* the court stated that a solicitor should be warned if there was an intention to make a costs order against him. The solicitors in *Myatt* were only made to pay half the costs because there had been no such warning.

CHAPTER 6

Media proceedings

Introduction

Media defendants face particular difficulties when confronted with claimants working on CFA terms. This is by reason of the special position of the media and the exercise by the media of their right of comment and of free speech. The courts have sought to put in place some (not particularly helpful) means to try to ameliorate the problems occasioned by aggressive CFA litigation. The courts appear to have felt unable to assist to any greater extent by reason of the perceived legislative intention of Parliament in encouraging access to the courts by the use of risk-free litigation and by the general effect of the Access to Justice Act 1999 which has been to shift the burden of funding all cases onto unsuccessful defendants.

The Civil Justice Council has been trying to find some consensus since about July 2004 and organised a forum to discuss the CFA issues arising between claimant and defendant parties. This took place in October 2006. Since then, some representatives are reported to have agreed bilateral arrangements, and at the time of writing a process of consultation is under way in the form of the paper entitled 'Conditional Fee Agreements in Publication Proceedings' (August 2007). The consultation paper 'seeks views on proposals to implement recommendations from the Civil Justice Council on fixed recoverable success fees and After the Event insurance premiums in publication proceedings funded under conditional fee agreements'. The consultation finished at the end of October 2007.

Special considerations

A salutary example is the case of Naomi Campbell in her litigation with the *Daily Mirror* for breach of confidence. The trial judge awarded her £2,500 damages. The trial judge's decision was reversed on appeal to the Court of Appeal but then restored by the House of Lords (see [2005] 1 WLR 3394). Naomi Campbell's legal costs were in excess of £1 million. An even more acute example of the special form of the problems faced by media defendants occurs when the particular claimant (who is likely to recover very modest damages) is impecunious and does not have ATE insurance. Libel lawyers' standard hourly rates tend to be very high, and when a 100 per cent success fee is added on top, the effect is like putting a gun to the defendant's temple. It would be cheaper to pay the matter off at the very beginning than to take the matter anywhere near trial, especially since it has been characteristic of these cases that there is a substantial amount of front-loading of costs.

The reason why special considerations are necessary in these cases is because of the wider public consequences for the freedom of the press and other media interests. In the Naomi Campbell case Lord Hoffmann summarised matters in the following paragraphs (after an initial approval of the judgment of Eady J in *Turcu* v. *News Group Newspapers Ltd* [2005] EWHC 799 (QB) (4 May 2005, unreported):

> 7. Faced with these circumstances, there must be a significant temptation for media defendants to pay up something, to be rid of litigation for purely commercial reasons, and without regard to the true merits of any pleaded defence. This is the so-called 'chilling effect' or 'ransom factor' inherent in the conditional fee system, which was discussed by the Court of Appeal in *King v Telegraph Group Ltd* . . . This is a situation which could not have arisen in the past and is very much a modern development.
>
> . . .
>
> 31. The blackmailing effect of such litigation appears to arise from two factors. First, the use of CFAs by impecunious claimants who do not take out ATE insurance. That, of course, is not a feature of the present case. If MGN are right about Ms Campbell's means, she would have been able to pay their costs if she had lost. The second factor is the conduct of the case by the claimant's solicitors in a way which not only runs up substantial costs but requires the defendants to do so as well. Faced with a free-spending claimant's solicitor and being at risk not only as to liability but also as to twice the claimant's costs, the defendant is faced with an arms race which makes it particularly unfair for the claimant afterwards to justify his conduct of the litigation on the ground that the defendant's own costs were equally high. That was particularly evident in *King v Telegraph Group Ltd (Practice Note)* [2005] 1 WLR 2282, to which Eady J. referred. In that case also, the claimant was without means and had no ATE insurance. Nevertheless, as Brooke LJ observed:
>
> > 58. There were no pre-action costs other than those associated with preparing the original letter before action, yet the claimant's solicitors revealed that by the time the original statements of case had been exchanged they had already incurred costs in excess of £32,000 (a sum equivalent to a potential liability of £64,000 for the other side on the basis of a 100% success fee). Over 54 hours of a partner's time had already been charged out at just over £20,000 and over 48 hours of a trainee solicitor's time at over £7,000 . . .
> >
> > 64. . . . the claimant's solicitors served a substantial request for further information concerning the defence, to which the defendant responded in detail . . .
> >
> > 65. [In reply, the claimant's solicitors] dispatched a ten-page letter . . . which was settled by junior counsel in as aggressive a style as their letter before

> action . . . the preparation of this letter, to which the defendant's solicitors were put to the expense of preparing a courteous and concise three-page [reply] . . . would be charged out at £750 per hour (assuming a 100% mark-up), not including counsel's fees.
>
> 73.   . . . the claimant's witness statement contained 114 pages . . .

Unfortunately there is little the courts have been able to do to provide comfort for media interests. The attempt to obtain security for costs because of the combination of the claim to a success fee and the absence of ATE insurance failed in *Musa King* v. *Telegraph Group Limited* for the reasons summarised at para.100:

> It is not for this court to thwart the wish of Parliament that litigants should be able to bring actions to vindicate their reputations under a CFA, and that they should not be obliged to obtain ATE cover before they do so. Nor do we have any power to override the express provisions of CPD para 19.1(1) and require a litigant supported by a CFA to disclose the level of the success fee to the other side in advance of any costs assessment proceedings.

The courts in both *Musa King* and *Campbell* decided that notwithstanding the special position of the media the CFA regime did not offend either Art.6 or Art.10 of the European Convention on Human Rights since 'in principle it is open to the legislature to fund access to justice' by shifting the burden of the funding of claimants' cases to losing defendants, the deliberate policy of the Access to Justice Act 1999 being 'to impose the cost of all CFA litigation, successful or unsuccessful, upon unsuccessful defendants as a class'. Losing defendants are 'required to contribute to the funds which would enable lawyers to take on other cases which might not be successful but would provide access to justice for people who could not otherwise have afforded to sue'. This was a 'choice open to the legislature'.

Lord Hoffmann decided that the solution lay with Parliament, and indeed by s.58A(3) the Lord Chancellor may prescribe different requirements 'for different descriptions of conditional fee agreements'.

Cost-capping

All that the courts have been able to do to date is to require a system of cost-capping in media proceedings. The place of cost-capping orders is discussed at **13.3**, but in the context of media proceedings, the Court of Appeal in *Musa King* has recommended the employment of specific procedural measures to achieve this:

> 93. In my judgment, the court possesses pursuant to CPR r 3.1(2)(m) similar powers in relation to the conduct of litigation which it may exercise without the parties having any opportunity to agree otherwise. If defamation proceedings are initiated under a CFA without ATE cover, the master should at the allocation stage

make an order analogous to an order under section 65(1) of the 1996 Act. In the ordinary course of things this order would cover the normal costs of the litigation. The master may consider it desirable to make the order subject to a condition along the following lines:

> 'that if either party wishes to make any application to the court that may significantly increase the costs in this action, it must first apply to the court in writing for a direction varying this order and serve notice of its application on all the other relevant parties; all relevant parties must file and serve up to date estimates of costs pursuant to section 6 of the Costs Practice Direction within . . . days of such notice being given; the court will then decide whether and to what extent it will vary this direction before it permits the application to be issued.'

94. It would be helpful if the senior master were to assign a particular master to handle case management applications in this specialist field of law because they demand a degree of practical experience that will not become available if they are distributed generally among the masters. If the master considers that a budget or cap is required he should refer the issue of imposing a cap to a costs judge. The costs judge should determine what sum is reasonable and proportionate to fix as the recoverable costs of the action. Similar arrangements should be made, if and when necessary, in district registries of the High Court outside London.

See also *Henry* v. *British Broadcasting Corporation* [2006] 1 All ER 154 in which a cost-capping order was not made by the court because the application itself had been made so near to trial.

Disclosure of the ATE policy

What the courts have achieved in media cases is some ease on the part of a defendant in obtaining a copy of the claimant's ATE insurance policy (see *Al-Koronky* v. *Time Life* [2005] EWHC 1688 and *Henry* (above)). This is because the standard terms of such a policy are likely to contain provisions which allow a policy to be voided in the event that a plea of justification succeeds. A media defendant is entitled to know the extent of the cover available in order 'to assess its financial exposure in the action and to consider whether to apply for a cost capping order' (*Henry* para.24). An ATE policy is not privileged (*Henry* para.26). This is consistent with the non-media cost capping case of *Hobson* v. *ASM* (Turner J, 18 May 2006).

The 'well-off' claimant on CFA terms

The House of Lords in *Campbell* could not find a reason to interfere arising from the receiving party's submission that Naomi Campbell could afford to meet fees without the use of a CFA. See Lord Hoffmann at para.24 of *Campbell*:

There is in my opinion nothing in the relevant legislation or practice directions which suggests that a solicitor, before entering into a CFA, must inquire into his client's means and satisfy himself that he could not fund the litigation himself.

The claimant's solicitor's exposure to costs

A more recent possibility is the threat of a costs order against a solicitor personally in a case where no ATE has been obtained. This is the consequence of *Myatt* v. *NCB* [2007] 1 WLR 1559 in which the Court of Appeal decided that the appellants' solicitors should pay the costs of the appeal personally since they stood to benefit significantly from the outcome of the appeal (for which their clients had no ATE). Whether this case will help media defendants where the facts are similar to those of *Musa King* (above) will need observation. *Myatt* is considered further at **5.5**.

CHAPTER 7

Commercial litigation funding

7.1 INTRODUCTION

This chapter provides some observations about the use of CFAs and CCFAs in the context of commercial litigation. However, it is not just the possibilities of individual CFAs and collective CFAs (CCFAs) to which the prudent commercial solicitor will have an eye, but also other non-CFA forms of litigation funding. These include ATE insurance products, the possibility of funding by maintainers (including 'pure' funders), and, critically, in today's marketplace, litigation funding support. To date this latter funding vehicle is restricted to a means by which an expert agrees to provide litigation support facilities on a contingency basis to other court experts and solicitors. The work and costs of these funders will often include extensive accountancy information connected with claims for damages and an active input in settlement. Their workload may easily exceed those of the lawyers and court experts and they are rewarded by a share of the damages recovered. These are not considered champertous arrangements so long as there are safeguards in place which prohibit the funder from having too much of an influence in the day-to-day conduct of the litigation. This is a strong growth area and it likely that the courts will become more and more accommodating towards these funders so that they are not restricted to the role of back-up experts. A fuller, but nevertheless brief, account of litigation funding support will be found in **Chapter 12** at **12.2** (see 'Litigation support funding'). An introduction to the use of maintainers and other funders will also be found at **12.2**. Pointers to forms of ATE insurance are contained in a few introductory paragraphs below.

Commercial litigators will note that in its paper 'Improved Access to Justice – Funding Options & Proportionate Costs' dated June 2007, the Civil Justice Council made two recommendations that should be monitored. One was that Rules of Court be developed to validate and regulate litigation funding support vehicles, and the other that in limited circumstances contingency fees should be permissible.

This chapter is intended to be discursive in nature since it focuses on the use of CCFAs both as a means of funding litigation and as a means of attracting clients. These are highly attractive products with benefits for both claimant and defendant lawyers and for their clients. Only a little will be said about individual CFAs since the decision to use a CFA on a one-off basis is one which is very fact-specific and entails few considerations unique to commercial litigation. The other chapters in this book, while written mainly in the context of personal injury litigation, can be readily adapted to commercial work.

7.2 INSURANCE PRODUCTS

Access to Justice Act 1999, s.29 allows the recovery of any insurance premium in respect of any 'insurance policy [taken out] against the risk of incurring a liability in those proceedings'. This not only means after-the-event (ATE) insurance to support a CFA, but also cover obtained to support an ordinary private retainer. It might or might not stretch to disbursements and even to own side's as well as other side's costs. Insurers see their profitable future in providing ATE products to commercial (and other 'big ticket') litigators rather than to personal injury lawyers. **Chapters 2** and **3** consider the legal bases for ATE insurance products (see **2.11** and **3.9**) and **Chapter 11** considers the practical position of the ATE market.

7.3 CFAs

Individual CFAs

Whether or not to work on CFA terms is a difficult matter for a practice to determine. The advantages and disadvantages do not need spelling out: certainty and regular fees on the one hand, or an element of risk with the possibility of additional gain on the other. It is the case that courts are generous with success fees in litigation which is not run on a portfolio of winners and losers and where it can also be said that the use of a CFA is an entirely speculative venture. Perhaps the best way to think of a CFA as a speculative venture is by thinking of the effect on hourly rates. A solicitor ordinarily charging £400 per hour recovers £800 per hour if he is expecting a 100 per cent uplift. CFAs are generally becoming more attractive to clients, and some firms will think them useful marketing tools in their own right. The section on CCFAs (see below), it is hoped, will assist in making some determination about the use and advisability of bulk arrangements designed to attract clients.

The principal difficulty in the use of a commercial CFA is thought to be in defining 'success'. This difficulty is, we suggest, overstated. It is not difficult to define 'success' – what is problematic is defining success so that it strikes an appropriate balance between the interest of the solicitor and the client. A CFA which is too advantageous to the lawyer is likely to earn the client's distrust. Moreover, where 'win' is easy to achieve, the success fee is unlikely to be suitably rewarding. The more risk the solicitor takes and the more of the funding burden he takes on (for instance in paying for disbursements), the greater the success fee. Defining 'success' is not difficult where it is defined by reference to the likely remedies. Some CFAs even suggest that a success is achieved where there some 'advantage' has been gained by the client from the proceedings. 'Success' as achieved by reference to the recovery of money, whether by way of court order or compromise, will be sufficient in many cases. The cautious lawyer might perhaps list a series of alternatives based on possible outcomes, for instance 'an order for the payment of compensation and/or an injunction and/or an order for costs and/or some other relief for the benefit of the client'. This definition will attract a modest uplift even thought the client may be left to enforce the order which he succeeds in obtaining: that will depend on the clause in the CFA which defines the scope of the retainer. A good commercial lawyer capable of drafting complicated commercial instruments or documents required under the CPR should not have difficulty in drafting a definition of 'success' to be read in conjunction with a definition of the action covered by the agreement.

It will be recalled that CFAs are available not just in litigation in court but in all types of 'proceedings for resolving disputes' (Courts and Legal Services Act 1990, s.58A(4)), whether by way of arbitrations, mediations or tribunals. While the definition of 'success' is indeed important in these cases, it is just as important to ensure that the agreement can be clearly understood by the client and that the provisions of the Solicitors' Code of Conduct 2007 have been observed.

A lawyer who is not accustomed to working on CFA terms must remember that he should make a careful and reasoned assessment why his uplift is to be set at the level stated in the CFA and record that assessment so that it can be produced to justify his uplift, if necessary, at a later date, typically at a detailed assessment.

Insolvency

Special considerations are relevant to CFAs which are used to fund insolvency litigation.

The ability to undertake insolvency proceedings on CFA terms has existed since the inception of the original pre-Access to Justice Act 1999 reforms. Even under the CFA Order 1995, proceedings which could be run on CFA terms included winding-up proceedings, administration proceedings, proceedings on behalf of liquidators and trustees in bankruptcy. Now, of course, there are no limitations save for those set out in Courts and Legal

Services Act, s.58A (as inserted by the Access to Justice Act 1999), and none of those will apply.

The main difficulty for insolvency proceedings, which deserves separate mention in this chapter, is the need to be able to fend off an application for security for costs under CPR Part 25 rule 25 (see rule 25.13(1), (2)(c)). In such circumstances an ATE policy (subject of course to its conditions) will constitute suitable security. It is usual practice to disclose the schedule to the policy, although an ATE policy is not covered by privilege. Unlike the problems faced by a potentially successful plea of justification in the case of media proceedings when the policy is likely to become void, it is very unlikely that there will be any other clause in an ATE policy covering insolvency proceedings which could make it of interest to an opponent.

Insolvency practitioners therefore need a good and reliable ATE provider on board, and it will help enormously for the legal representative to have delegated powers. As in other areas of litigation, a broad caseload and a good track record will make it easier for the insurer to swallow the pill and pay up on demand when necessary. Insolvency lawyers otherwise face the same difficulties as other commercial practitioners. In particular it is important to strike the right balance when defining 'success', and there is now the increasing risk of having to meet a personal costs order following *Myatt* v. *NCB* [2007] 1 WLR 1559 (see **5.5**). Ironically, the more access-to-justice friendly the arrangements with the ultimate client, the more likely that such an order might be made. It is reported that 100 per cent uplifts are the norm with practitioners who take on a reasonable share of risk.

7.4 COLLECTIVE CONDITIONAL FEE AGREEMENTS (CCFAs)

What are CCFAs?

CCFAs are vehicles for the bulk purchase of legal services which provide for payment of the legal representative's fees by a funder (such as trade union or insurance company) only in the event of success or other contractually specified circumstances (i.e. on conditional terms). As the CCFA 2000 Regulations used to state (before their revocation), a CCFA is an agreement which 'does not refer to specific proceedings, but provides for fees to be payable on a common basis in relation to each class of proceedings covered by the agreement'. A CCFA may or may not include the funder as a client, and it need not name any specific clients in the agreement. Some CCFAs, therefore, will define those payment terms which have been agreed between a firm of solicitors and a particular client (for instance a bank or utility). Others will set out the arrangements by which a funder who has agreed to supply legal advice and representation to its members (for instance, a trade union or even an insurer) engages solicitors to fulfil that obligation.

CCFAs are extremely flexible instruments which offer significant advantages to both funders and their legal representatives, as well as to individual clients.

Trade unions and other prescribed organisations

Collective agreements were seized on enthusiastically by the trade union movement when they first came into being, and indeed the consultation papers produced prior to the introduction of the new CFA Scheme show that the former Lord Chancellor's Department specifically had trade union funders in mind when the CCFA Regulations were drafted. From the point of view of a funder such as a trade union, CCFA terms are extremely attractive, apart from the obvious advantage of being relieved of the burden of having to pay costs in the event of failure, because of the possibility of being able to tie CCFA terms in with the recovery of membership organisation 'premiums' payable from an opponent by virtue of Access to Justice Act 1999, s.30 (considered in more detail below). These are amounts awarded as costs which are intended to represent the sum which an organisation (which has been recognised under arrangements made by the Ministry of Justice) would have had to have set aside to meet the risk of having to pay the costs of specific proceedings. They are the equivalent of ATE insurance premiums, and indeed they are assessed by the courts by reference to the amount which would be necessary to buy an ATE premium on the open market. Given that these bodies are likely to be self-insuring, the additional revenue from membership organisation premiums will be very welcome. How an organisation becomes 'prescribed' is a somewhat dark mystery which cannot be understood from any transparent legislative or other provision. See **2.12**.

CCFAs in the commercial world

It perhaps seems strange with the benefit of hindsight that the commercial world has not been quicker to adopt CCFAs as a means of funding the provision of legal services since they offer significant advantages to funders and their legal representatives (as well as to clients). One explanation may be the initial uncertainty which surrounded their enforceability. The main driving force has probably been the realisation by bulk purchasers of legal services, in particular by insurers, that CCFA terms will reduce their costs. But at the same time legal representatives have appreciated that CCFAs may in fact be a better option than an ordinary retainer if they are receiving instructions in significant quantities.

A CCFA is likely to be attractive to a funder which is a bulk purchaser of legal services and wishes to offer a legal representative favoured status by way of one agreement in respect of a certain class or type of proceedings. A CCFA in such circumstances is a convenient way of entering into a discounted fee arrangement (if not a straight 'no win, no fee' arrangement). Thus, the agreement in *Aratra Potato Co. Ltd* v. *Taylor Joynson Garrett* [1995] 4 All ER 695 in which the solicitors agreed to waive 20 per cent of their fees in unsuccessful cases would have been lawful if it could have been contained within a CCFA rendered lawful by the Access to Justice Act 1999. See also *Gloucestershire CC* v. *Evans* [2008] EWCA Civ 21, 31 January 2008.

As a result of the possibility of entering into 'simplified' terms, a funder can be assured that it will not have to pay more in costs to its lawyers than the lawyers are able to obtain from the opposing party. Some negotiation will inevitably be necessary between legal representatives and funders over the grey areas. What happens, for instance, if the opposing party has the benefit of a public funding certificate and a charge has been obtained over his house after a successful application for costs? Does this represent a 'success', and can it be said at this stage that the costs have been 'recovered' on behalf of the defendant?

Advantages to legal representatives

Agreements made under CCFA terms are also of significant advantage to the legal representative. Apart from being a means of obtaining an uplift in the event of success, the client care obligations which have to be met for individual clients within a tripartite arrangement are not as onerous as those required of a CFA. During the lifetime of the CFA Regulations 2000 when a challenge based on an error in the client care conditions of reg.4 might have resulted in a declaration that the costs were not recoverable, this was obviously a very significant advantage. Moreover, the lower standard of individual client care which is required in the case of a CCFA means that the legal representative does not have to spend the same amount of unrecoverable time in embarking on providing information and explanation which an individual will need under an individual CFA.

To explain the advantages of a CCFA to legal representatives, it must be recalled that conditional fee terms do not permit only 'no win, no fee' arrangements. It is quite lawful to enter into a conditional agreement, for instance, to be paid £normal in the event of failure but also an enhanced rate in the event of success, together with an uplift (see *Jones* v. *Wrexham B.C.* [2007] EWCA 1356, 11 December 2007).

In all, collective conditional arrangements offer many permutations in the way in which profit costs can be calculated. As well as the 'no win, no fee' model and the '£normal, £enhanced' varieties referred to above, another possibility includes the provision for fixed fees for different categories of case.

A CCFA with carefully prepared terms can represent a successful marketing tool for lawyers confident in their ability to make substantial profits where the bulk of their cases results in successful actions. It was not intended when success fees were permitted that every case should result in a premium for the lawyers, the original scheme having contemplated that uplifts in successful cases would compensate for the losers. The advantages of undertaking bulk services for one client should outweigh the disadvantages of losing some cases, especially since a well drawn up agreement will make it clear that the legal representative has complete control over which cases continue to court.

For those lawyers who are concerned about the risks of working on differential terms, they should note that the costs rules can be used to ensure that they recover the agreed uplifts from the clients and not just those recovered from losing parties. In commercial cases the success fees and ATE premiums which are awarded by costs judges can be very high and there are good reasons why a commercial client might be required to pay a success fee which the court has disallowed on the ground that it was unreasonable (under the procedure set out at CPR rule 44.16).

CCFAs and defence interests

Lawyers who for years have worked in the highly competitive defence market where insurers are used to driving costs well below the amounts awarded on assessments to claimant lawyers, have discovered that their insurer clients are not averse to agreeing CCFA terms where the lawyers get paid an enhanced rate on achieving success.

A further indication that CCFAs are likely to get into wide circulation is the fact that the providers of some common household insurance policies have understood that wide savings on costs may be made if the legal representatives can be required to work on conditional fee terms.

If a service agreement between the legal representative and funder places an obligation on the legal representative to insist on CFA terms with an individual client, there is the risk that this might breach the terms of the underlying BTE insurance between the insurer and client. If a client who has purchased ordinary BTE cover finds when he goes to a recommended solicitor that the legal representative requires him to enter into a CFA, but his household insurance agreement has not made this clear, then this could constitute a breach of the policy. More seriously, perhaps, there is likely to be a loss of overall confidence in the original policy. That is to say nothing of any regulatory implications.

At least one relatively longstanding BTE policy does in fact tell policy holders that if they need to take legal proceedings then they will have to enter into a CFA with the solicitors. So long as the insured has been told that he will have to enter into a CFA, then there is no reason in principle why the legal representative cannot recover his success fee.

As well as offering apparent costs benefits, a CCFA can also be attractive to a client by offering additional incentives, typically the agreement to handle fast track or small claims track cases for small fixed amounts.

This has become easier since the amendment to the CCFA Regulations brought about by the CFA (Miscellaneous Amendments) Regulations 2003. These Amendment Regulations have given statutory effect to the 'simplified' CFA or CCFA (called the CFA or CCFA 'Lite' by some commentators). They permit a funder to agree with a legal representative that costs and expenses are only payable to the extent that they are 'recovered' in the proceedings 'whether by way of costs or otherwise'.

The future of CCFAs

The possibilities in the commercial world which are offered by CCFA terms are considerable. Clients are beginning to understand their advantages, and for those who properly understand the way in which profit costs are earned by their litigation departments, they can be a very suitable means of attracting volume clients.

Even this sort of CFA, however, should be seen as only one step on the road towards the full evolution of the CCFA. As has been argued above, where a legal representative is in receipt of large numbers of instructions, a CCFA can be a profitable arrangement, allowing the lawyers to recover higher fees than they might otherwise obtain from a BTE insurer. Further, a CCFA is also to be preferred to any arrangement whereby the legal representatives is required to enter into separate CFAs for each individual client because of the significant client care costs required by such schemes.

CHAPTER 8

Litigation practice management

Robert Rose

8.1 INTRODUCTION

The aim of this chapter is primarily to assist with the wider mechanics of how to ensure a profitable CFA practice. The focus is unashamedly that of the busy personal litigation practice, since it is still predominantly in the personal injury field that a full litigation practice is run on mainly CFA lines. It examines the wider marketplace and the profitability of personal injury departments generally before looking at the tools which a good CFA practice needs to ensure profitability and control risk. Ultimately any law firm, or indeed any department within a law firm that is acting on a predominantly 'no win, no fee' basis must remember that its fortunes are built entirely on risk. It is the management of that 'risk' which will determine the success or otherwise of the firm/department. This chapter also seeks to discuss the principles of good financial management in this area, a solicitor being expected more and more to fund every aspect of its clients' CFA litigation. Standardisation and efficiency are the keys to profitability to a department or firm working primarily on CFA terms. **Chapter 9**, associated with this chapter, is concerned with the running of an individual CFA case and that chapter is more likely to be of assistance with non-CFA work. Primarily **Chapter 9** examines the obligations to give advice as to the client's funding options under the Solicitors' Code of Conduct 2007 (now that the CFA Regulations 2000 have been revoked) and also how best to risk-assess a claim when it is presented to the solicitor.

8.2 THE WIDER PICTURE: ENSURING PROFITABILITY

Are firms who conduct their litigation on a CFA basis profitable? There is considerable debate about what are the key benchmarks and acceptable levels of profit for a modern personal injury (PI) practice. The Law Society's Law Management Section (LMS) indicates that median fees for small practices (two to four solicitors) appear low at just under £58,000 per equity partner.

Profits increase for the two to four and five to 10 solicitors group who make median gross profits of approximately £65,000 per equity partner.

Size, however, is not an indicator that a firm is necessarily going to make better profits. Many larger PI firms have found they have become less profitable as their overheads spiral out of control and they fail to put in place proper credit controls.

How to measure profitability

The 'rule of thumb' is that firms adopted a 30 per cent rule for margins simply taking the net profit available and dividing this into the total fees of the firm. A more accurate way of calculating profitability is to look at two other benchmarks, namely fees per equity partner and gearing/leverage (ratio of fee earners who are not equity partners to equity partners). The '30 per cent rule' does not take into account the notional salaries for equity partners and therefore is somewhat flawed.

Key indicators

The key to profitability is provided by a variety of factors, for instance by the way in which the work is conducted, whether a practice is making the best use of its staff and whether a practice is making best use of its IT. Good-quality work may become extremely unprofitable because of poor management, for example if there is no proper analysis of the duration of any one case, no proper analysis of a fee earner's recovery rate and no proper analysis of the type of cases that any one fee earner is working on at any time.

The following key indicators should be considered by any practice which bases its work on conditional fees.

Management information

The partners of any firm must have up-to-date and relevant financial information. Monthly/quarterly management accounts must be made available, and those accounts should focus upon fees and the profitability of those fees. Those accounts should disclose the amount of money that a personal injury department is 'contributing' to the firm as a whole. If the overheads are extraordinarily high, if work in progress (WIP) is out of control, and you are losing cases, what, frankly, is the point of being involved in PI litigation? The partners must have information relating not only to how the department is functioning, but also how teams of fee earners are operating. Fees and time-recording must be assessed on a monthly basis. However, the information must be used carefully. Complex high-value PI work and clinical negligence work tends to take a lot longer to process. As long as the partners accept that, fee earners must be motivated and must be provided with reports and to have those reports explained to them in a suitable context.

Fees and gearing

The LMS report of 2002 reveals that a small number of PI/clinical negligence firms are extremely profitable, with figures such as gross fee income per partner of £768,960. This may not only be due to good financial control but could be due to the gearing or leverage of the practices concerned. By limiting the number of partners and charging non-partner staff out to clients, high profits will be achieved rather than doing the work themselves. The top-performing firms appear to have 7.19 fee earners per equity partner. The bottom-performing firms appear to have only 2.54 fee earners per equity partner.

However, these figures must be treated with some caution. Expensive fee earners such as salaried partners, legal executives, and so on, need to be taken into account. Nevertheless, PI departments enjoy a unique position in respect of improvements in 'gearing', particularly in relation to the standardisation of some legal work and the impact that IT can have in respect of the way that firms can carry out such work.

Cost of doing the work: overheads

The principal overheads of a PI practice are twofold:

- staff salary costs (the Law Society survey suggests that the most profitable firms have staff salaries at about 50–55 per cent of gross fees);
- the costs of 'purchasing' the work, whether it be through claims management companies, a venture with other solicitors or simply referral fees.

The challenge of any litigation practice is to keep overall running costs under control and to focus on the generation of fee income. Firms should, however, invest in their future – simply reducing support staff on the basis of a mathematical ratio without looking at what role they fulfil could cause huge difficulties in the generation of fee income.

'Lock up': work in progress, unpaid bills and unbilled disbursements

Without proper management PI practices can easily be extinguished because of the long period of 'lock up' of this type of work. The LMS surveys indicate that smaller firms tend to be better at billing and collecting cash than larger firms. This must be treated with some caution, however, as some of the larger firms are dealing with high value work which is less profitable because of the long period from the date of instruction to the date of settlement. Moreover, highly specialised and expensive staff must be employed.

For some PI firms the period of lock up is as high as 589 days; the better performers are down to approximately 250 days.

The difficulty PI departments have is that as they expand and as fee earners take on new cases (and on the face of it, profitable work), then this translates into a loss for a given period until fee earners are producing fees. The benefits of the new work are often not seen for a couple of years.

Therefore most practices which are engaged in personal injury CFAs will have to convince their funders (i.e. the bank manager) that they are going to manage their working capital and they will try and improve their cash flow and any consequential borrowing. They must also show that their work in progress will be realised and managed effectively.

A useful set of management accounts will include how the department is progressing in relation to its WIP days: are they going up or down? If they are going up it is likely the department is experiencing expansion. If it is, this needs to be carefully managed and the firm's other partners will need convincing that there is profit waiting just around the corner!

As discussed earlier, management of disbursements needs careful consideration. Where disbursements are capable of being deferred, they should be. Fee earners must understand the importance of cash flow and the impact the disbursements have on the practice's finances cannot be overstated.

A poor accounts system will lead to disbursements being missed at the end of a case and should be treated with the utmost seriousness.

The individual practice

The team

More important than marketing, and more important than a business plan or IT, is the team of fee earners and support staff who will determine a firm's success in running a risk-based litigation department. It is vital to create the right 'team' of fee earners and support staff who are going to assist in managing the risk.

Supervision

In relation to fee earners there are different levels of expertise available and these are discussed further below.

One particular debate which remains unsettled, however, is whether a firm's PI team should consist largely of paralegals or whether it should consist largely of qualified staff. Likewise, administrative support staff have increasingly taken on a new role – in particular, recording and tracking insurance policies on the firm's preferred ATE provider; and recording work that is coming in and the amount of work that is being converted into fee earning cases. Despite the evolution of IT, the key to any successful team is good supervision; without this, the firm will not be able to manage its risk adequately.

Paralegals

The combination of an increasing number of law graduates/LPC students and diminishing training contracts has led to a huge number of bright, young graduates currently on the market. Well educated, they are often keen, enthusiastic and adaptable. They are particularly attracted to the PI field and are now beginning to form the core of some of the larger PI practices. From their point of view, the growth in the PI market provides them with the access to a legal firm which otherwise they would be denied, while, from the firm's point of view, salary expectations tend to be far lower than qualified staff and there are less pressures in terms of aspirations.

Ultimately the majority of paralegals will wish to qualify and unless a firm is able to offer them a training contract, a relatively high turnover of staff is to be expected. This does have considerable implications for any practice – not just because they will need careful supervision but also the firm must weigh that against the probability that the firm is not going to have them for very long. Their length of time with a practice can be lengthened if you make their work interesting but this can be a challenge, particularly as paralegals tend to be used for the more routine, fast turnaround type of work.

Legal executives

Legal executives can be extremely knowledgeable and can contribute much to a practice. Those with many years' experience, however, can be resistant to any changes and there may be some difficulties involved in persuading them to embrace a new culture. Their expertise, however, can be crucial, particularly as they tend to want to have long-term futures within their present practices.

Solicitors

Young solicitors need to have a development plan, in other words they need to have confidence that a practice is going to assist them in developing their careers so that they can have a major input into the work of the firm both in terms of substantive law and to assist in supervising the non-qualified staff. Without such a plan, it will be extremely difficult to hold on to bright, young solicitors for more than two years post-qualification.

Partners

PI practice partners tend to head up departments with a considerable number of fee earners below them. This has meant the role of the partner has changed considerably. If a partner is still the major fee earner in the department, then that partner is probably not doing his or her job properly. A partner must be responsible for the business plan, for supervision, delegation of work, marketing and for embracing some form of case management system. They must understand what is good for the department and must be prepared to deal with the business challenges as and when they occur.

Support staff

There has been much talk in recent years as to the way in which case management systems, digital dictation/voice recognition IT has reduced the need for each fee earner to have a secretary. That, to a certain extent, is true, but the role of the secretary has changed considerably. It is fair to say that the new generation of paralegals do not require secretarial support. They are usually extremely computer literate and have access to reasonable case management systems which have taken away the burden of 'volume typing'. However, other factors which have enhanced the role of secretarial support include the approved commitment to client care in most law firms, increased administrative burdens (usually as a result of practice management standards, e.g. ISO 9001) which have required the need for a dedicated and experienced core of secretaries which can assist fee earners in some of these tasks. Secretaries are still often the first point of contact with clients and can assist greatly in respect of 'turning over the work'.

Training and motivating the staff

By having in place an appraisal system which not only formally appraises fee earners/members of support staff once a year, but also builds into it 'one-to-one sessions' on a quarterly basis, provides management with a tool to motivate staff by finding out what they know, by building on that knowledge, and by sharing that knowledge throughout the team.

In relation to fee earners, training is of paramount importance. In-house training has the benefit of using other more experienced fee earners to train those below them. 'Outside training' can provide a department with a refreshing view of the changes in practice.

Also, support staff must be trained, not only within the role that they undertake on a day-to-day basis, but also in the law and procedure. Most support staff are extremely interested in what fee earners are doing and if they have a better understanding of it they will often be able to deal with the client enquiries in a far more confident and appropriate way.

Other ways of motivating staff are through bonus systems (preferably on a team basis), regular appraising of staff and providing staff with a comfortable and modern working environment.

IT systems

In order for the firm's team to work efficiently, it will have to institute a high-quality IT system and will almost certainly require the services of in-house IT support staff.

Litigation practices, particularly PI departments cannot operate without the proper IT systems to ensure repeated file reviews, the monitoring of key dates and the production of work in the most cost-effective way possible. Any such system should be easy to use, provide fee earners with the case management capabilities of running a file load, and enable their managers to monitor the nature of their work. Indeed it is difficult to imagine how any practice can function properly and effectively without a significant investment in IT. Without an efficient case management system, operating such a department will be almost impossible.

There are an increasing number of case management systems available on the market which can be bought off the shelf, however most systems cannot be invented overnight and before purchasing a system the department must understand that it will take a significant amount of work for that system to assist the practice. A system which has been bought off the shelf must provide for a document management system (to assist in the use of precedent letters), must identify key dates (such as limitation), and prompt fee earners in relation to different work type flows (in order to assist in the progression of the case).

The system must be flexible and must be adapted to the needs of the practice. Standard letters should be produced with a couple of keystrokes, and progress logs should be readily available so that supervisors can assess what their teams are doing.

The system should involve case management. It should not only assist the fee earner in reminding them what the 'key dates' are, but should also encourage the fee earner to become proactive. For example, there should be a procedure whereby once the pre-action protocol period has expired and no response has been achieved, then an application for pre-action disclosure should be 'flagged'.

Firms will have to devise specific work types so that PI cases can be subcategorised (e.g. road traffic accident, public liability, occupiers' liability, slip and trip, clinical negligence). From those different work types, it should be possible to monitor fee income levels, success fees, disbursements and profitability. Monitoring the firm's WIP is crucial to the success or otherwise of a risk-based department, in the sense that a fast turnaround of work must be achieved and that WIP is a form of 'lock up' which, if left to get out of control, will have serious implications for the cash flow of the business.

Such systems should also be used to assess the progress and costs exposure of individual cases. This should assist management in assessing how long cases are going on for (preferably by work types), the level of disbursements, the level of success fees, and whether a particular fee earner is dealing with cases in an appropriate way to stop them stagnating. Data on the outcome of cases will have to be put back into the system so that assessments can be made as to the type of work the practice wants to carry on and the type of work which has too high a risk profile so as to make it uneconomic.

Financial information and management

PI practices have now been put in the same position as the Legal Services Commission – they are expected to provide access to justice. Unlike the Legal Services Commission, they must replace state funding in all monetary claims but will also have to make a profit out of it at the same time. This means that there are no payments on account and that firms have to fund not only work in progress, but also disbursements and sometimes insurance premiums. This is all in addition to assuming the risk of not being paid at the conclusion of the case.

In order to decide whether a practice can run the risk of embarking on this kind of work, the partners need to have detailed knowledge of the firm's cash flow.

In relation to a PI practice, such financial information should be readily available in relation to all the different work types. Success fees, disbursements and costs should be capable of being monitored in relation to road traffic accident work, employers' liability work, industrial disease work, and so on. It is only from building up that bank of information that one can properly assess the risk of each and every type of work and the likely costs involved in losing such cases.

The days of a client funding such cases appear to be over. The firm therefore is going to have to pay for disbursements, in particular for medical reports. This means that it is imperative that a firm has arrangements with either medical experts personally or with experts generally in relation to the deferment of such payment. There are also a number of schemes available whereby a disbursement loan is taken out by a client. Unfortunately the rates of interest tend to be prohibitive and as a result the firm has to fund these itself.

ATE insurance also needs funding. Since many premiums are now deferred until the end of the case some pressure at least has been taken off many litigation practices.

8.3   MANAGING RISK

Transparent and consistent risk assessment procedures

The key to managing risk is the risk assessment process. The 'risk' itself must be managed properly. The firm must have open and transparent risk assessment procedures which should not be capable of being overridden, e.g. an established private client of the firm insists you act for him on a 'no win, no fee' basis. Fee earners need to understand what they can and cannot do in relation to commencing claims and they need to understand the way in which they have to prepare cases for consideration by risk assessment committees.

Risk assessment committee

A CFA committee should sit regularly and frequently – in the writer's view at least once a week. Such a committee will deal with requests from fee earners to enter into 'no win, no fee' agreements. Such a committee should consist of at least one senior fee earner who is able to take a global view of the type of cases that are being pursued.

Any risk assessment process should provide some consistency (so for example, a risk assessment committee should consist of at least one senior fee earner/partner). Further, all fee earners must receive training in risk assessment and the best type of training is to risk assess cases themselves by sitting on a CFA committee. Whatever the case, the decision as to whether a case should proceed on a CFA should not be taken by one person.

The volume of new instructions will determine how often the committee meets. The decisions of the committee should be recorded in writing and the practice will have to produce its own 'risk assessment' forms for that purpose. **Chapter 9** considers in greater detail the issue of risk assessment, but what should be remembered is that risk should not only be assessed at the beginning of a CFA case, but also during the case itself. Proper supervision will enable the risk assessment to be checked not just for the decision as to whether a case should be taken on, but also to assist the fee earner in assessing whether the case should proceed to issue and ultimately to trial.

Self-insurance

In order to deal with the difficulties of the before-the-event (BTE) panels taking work from a firm, it may be necessary to 'self-insure' certain cases. This in turn creates greater risks for the firm and arguably a separate committee, consisting of at least one partner, should deal with those cases because a loss at trial would actually mean that the firm would not only take on its own losses, but also those of the other side.

Partnerships: establishing a wider team

Experts

A practice's relationship with experts, and in particular its ability to pick the right expert will be vital to the success of a risk-based department.

In relation to PI work the most vital expert is the medical expert. It should be remembered that in fast-track trials the judge will only have one report in front of him. Those experts who are credible in the local courts, who provide a fast turnaround in relation to reports, and who can provide a definitive opinion on a case are to be treasured. A list of experts must be kept, and constantly updated. Those experts who are slow, unable to provide a definitive opinion on a particular case, or are held in low esteem by the local judiciary are of no use to a risk-based department.

The expert must receive a proper letter of instruction. The expert must consider all the matters that the firm wants him to and the firm must ensure that its medical expert reads all the notes and records before providing his report. Likewise, so should the fee earner: weak claims are often weeded out at this stage in the case.

The expert is going to have to be ready to deal with questions on his report and should provide his responses quickly. The expert should also try to indicate when something is outside his area of expertise, so that, for instance, orthopaedic surgeons should not be commenting on psychiatric injuries.

If a firm's workload tends to be based around its locality, then it is often sensible to instruct experts directly.

Medico-legal agencies

In recent years there has been considerable growth in the number of medico-legal agencies. These provide a 'one-stop service', so that solicitors can instruct an agency to find them a suitable expert and even to obtain the notes themselves. For those firms that are dealing with clients on a national basis, it is probably sensible to consider using such an agency. However, practices must be very careful not to divest themselves of control in this respect – they should liaise very carefully with the medico-legal agency concerning the quality of medical experts and their suitability. They should also obtain the medical records themselves. Many PI cases have been lost because of errors in relation to limitation or causation issues which are not apparent until consideration has been given to the notes themselves.

There have also been many difficulties in obtaining payment of all of the agency's fees. Prior to the predictable costs regime, those fees were recovered on an agency basis. Following *Woollard* v. *Fowler*, there have been many challenges to the recoverability of 'agency' fees in predictable costs regime cases.

As a result of an appeal, followed by a prolonged mediation process, an agreement has been reached with a number of insurers which will, it is hoped, bring an end to disputes over the recoverability of those fees. A group of set fees has now been agreed between the parties.

Investigators

Investigators can be a valuable resource, particularly in relation to obtaining statements. There are various organisations, predominantly employing ex-policemen, who can provide a useful role in this respect. These can be useful, particularly in relation to taking the pressure off a fee earner. Many firms traditionally have employed an outdoor clerk or have started using agencies consisting of ex-policemen and others who take statements.

Statement-taking, however, is vital both in relation to the initial risk assessment process and fully understanding the claimant's case. A poorly drafted statement at the onset of a case can be disastrous, since it can 'frame a case' in a negligent way.

A disadvantage perhaps of using an outdoor clerk will be that the fee earner will not be in a position to form an impression of the witness's/claimant's reliability.

Counsel

The Bar's reluctance to take on work on a conditional fee basis is legendary and regrettably still continues. Strong relationships with the Bar are, however, essential, particularly in enabling firms to obtain competent counsel to deal with fast-track cases (where necessary) and experienced counsel to deal with the more complex multi-track work. A barrister who understands costs is also an added bonus.

A good working relationship with a number of chambers is vital to the success of a risk-based department. A firm must find a chambers that is happy dealing with CFA cases and the firm can rely both on them providing good juniors and more senior counsel when necessary.

Counsel must be specialists in the work they do and must be available.

Counsel, as they are fond of reminding solicitors, face a different risk in respect of CFA cases. Counsel tends to see cases at a later stage than the solicitors and invariably they are exposed to the 'riskier cases'.

There is therefore, some would say, an understandable reluctance on the part of counsel to accept instructions with regards to those high-risk cases. Counsel will argue that he is more exposed in relation to those cases than instructing solicitors.

There will be cases therefore when a practice may have to consider briefing or instructing counsel on a traditional fee-paying basis.

There are alternative methods of financing counsel. Many chambers will agree to deferment of payment until the conclusion of the claim. Counsel may be persuaded to take a case under a straightforward CFA or he may be prepared to accept the case on the basis that a firm will waive all or part of its fees if the claimant loses. Alternatively, some ATE insurance providers treat counsel's fees as a disbursement, so counsel will be paid win or lose. Those policies are actually shrinking in popularity.

ATE insurer

A practice's relationship with the ATE insurance policy holder is absolutely crucial. That insurer is in a powerful position since they can decide whether or not to back the cases that a firm has risk-assessed. On the other hand, the firm is providing that insurer with a steady stream of work and the relationship should be one of equals, working together to achieve the best possible result for the client. A practice should ensure that it has delegated authority to do the work on which the practice specialises. A practice will need to be satisfied that the policy provides a suitable financial limit.

A practice will have to ensure that the cost of the premium is recoverable. Cash flow problems can be eased through a deferred premium policy. The policy will be self-insured and will not have to paid if the claim fails. The policy should cover the claimant's disbursements whether or not proceedings have been issued and counsel instructed.

It is hoped that with a good track record the ATE provider will have the confidence in the firm to back its judgement on cases.

There are instances where a practice may wish to self-insure its cases. This may become more prevalent particularly as the predictable costs scheme is extended further. It is also a way around losing work to BTE insurance companies who instruct their own panels of solicitors. Nevertheless the practice has to be very careful, since there are risks and a case which is lost will have to be paid for by the firm.

8.4   CAN YOU MAKE A PROFIT? GOOD FINANCIAL MANAGEMENT

Conditional fee work has not only now transferred the risk of losing a case from the client/Legal Services Commission to the solicitor, but has also transferred the burden of funding a case firmly and squarely upon the shoulders of the lawyer.

Since the abolition of legal aid, firms have had to get used to the fact that they were no longer going to receive payments on account and their cash flow has become a serious problem.

Any firm in this field of work must undertake a critical analysis of the type of work that it is going to do on a CFA, how long those cases will take to complete, how many losses on what types of cases, the level of losses and what the winning and losing cases have been worth.

The results of such analysis are bound to trouble the managing partner. All lawyers would like to see road traffic accident claims completed within six to eight months, but the reality is that they often take 12 to 14 months. Employers' liability cases invariably take two years, while other losses incurred in what lawyers thought were simple 'slip and trip cases' will add to the concerns of the profession (from the claimant's point of view, the defendant's statutory defence is defeating many of those traditionally straightforward trip claims).

Once the critical analysis has been undertaken, cash flow strategies will then be utilised.

Disbursements

Experts

A firm cannot instruct experts on a 'no win, no fee' basis. The Civil Justice Council issued a protocol for the instruction of experts to give evidence in civil claims in June of 2005. Paragraph 7.6 explicitly states that any payments contingent upon the outcome of a case must not be offered or accepted. This would contravene an expert's overriding duty to the court and compromise his duty of independence. However, a firm can enter into agreements with them to be paid at the end of the case, as long at the amount of the fee does not depend on the outcome of the case itself. It is worthwhile firms approaching their own experts to agree a period of deferment, for example that the expert gets paid for his report at the end of 12 months or when the case settles, whichever is sooner. Many experts, troubled by the recent changes in taxation will probably want to charge a small uplift for deferring their fees. If a firm has experts that it does not use on a repeat basis, then certainly it is worth trying to come to some agreement. The growth in medico-legal agencies over recent years has assisted practices in terms of funding experts' fees. The service they provide however can be erratic. The recent confusion following the *Woollard* v. *Fowler* case has made the agencies less attractive, although as indicated earlier a mediation process appears to be forcing the medico-legal reporting industry to adopt fixed costs.

Insurance premiums

When ATE premiums were first made available on the market, payment was required upfront. Increasingly now premiums can be deferred. Other companies offer a loan. This means that the premium is paid immediately to the insurer/claims management company and the client has to repay the loan out of damages recovered. Solicitors have a duty to read and understand

153

the agreements and particularly to draw the client's attention to the amount of interest that runs against the amounts drawn down – which typically range from 12 per cent to 19 per cent. The client should also be told that the defendants will not be required to pay that interest element. This makes loans an increasingly unattractively way of funding either ATE premiums or disbursements. Costs Judges are increasingly hostile to them and are sceptical as to the arrangements surrounding them.

Deferred premiums

In relation to deferred premiums, subject to the terms and conditions of the agreement, this is likely to be a form of credit and therefore regulated by the Consumer Credit Act 1974. A Consumer Credit Agreement will have to be entered into with the client, otherwise the loan is unenforceable against the client and therefore (because of the indemnity principle) would probably be unrecoverable from the defendant. In *Tilby* v. *Perfect Pizza* the court found against the challenge to the concept of using Consumer Credit Agreements for deferred premiums. Here, the Temple Legal Protection policy had a deferred premium of £350. Senior Cost Judge Hurst found that there was no normal insurance business practice which required that the ATE premium should be paid at the inception of the policy. He also found that there was no deferment of the payment of the premium unless it was deferred beyond the conclusion of the case for a 'significant period'. Arguably, therefore, deferred premium arrangements are not credit arrangements requiring Consumer Credit Agreement. However, other companies, such as Allianz Cornhill, continue to require their solicitors and clients to enter into such agreements.

Ideally an ATE policy will be low-cost, self-insured (in other words if a client loses the case, he does not have to pay the premium) and will be deferred. By this means, it eases the burden both on the firm and the client. Many firms are now 'self-insuring' their cases to avoid difficulties with premium recovery. This has the advantage of 'turning over the work' a little quicker but risks the fact that if a claim is lost the firm will have to bear not only the loss of its own profit costs but also its own disbursements. If the case is issued, those losses will extend to the defendant's profit costs and disbursements.

Referral fees

Lawyers have always been able to 'purchase' cases from one another, but since March 2004 solicitors are now allowed to pay such fees to non-lawyers introducing work. In the PI field many firms are now 'paying for their work' and invariably those payments occur at the beginning rather than the end of the case. This has serious consequences on all litigation practices and every effort must be made to try to transfer those costs to the end of a case.

Following the Law Society's referrals warning and guidance (issued in February 2007) and the Solicitors' Code of Conduct 2007 (commencing 1 July 2007), solicitors have to be very careful to ensure that they do not engage in improper referral arrangements. Solicitors must make sure that if they are using any claims management services, that those services have been regulated in accordance with the regulatory regime established by the Compensation Act 2006. The guidance stresses that when making or receiving referrals to or from third parties, solicitors must do nothing which would compromise their independence or their ability to act and advise in the best interests of their clients. The Solicitors' Code of Conduct 2007 strictly prohibits entering into an arrangement for the referral of clients in relation to PI work with a company which is receiving contingency fees in respect of such claims. In particular, the solicitor must give to the client all relevant information concerning the referror, in particular confirming that the referror has a financial arrangement with your firm and the amount of any payment that the firm has made to the claims management company. All of this must be confirmed in the client care letter.

Counsel

Counsel should agree to defer fees until the end of a case, otherwise solicitors are not using their bargaining power with barristers in the way that they should.

Charge the client?

Lawyers have the ability, if they are using the Law Society's standard model CFA, still to charge a success fee which is payable by the client. This uplift relates to the delay in the firm being paid and is not recoverable from the defendant. This is sometimes known as the 'subsidiary element'. This can relate to profit costs and/or disbursements.

Where the firm is paying for the disbursements, an uplift for the latter element arguably may be recovered from the opponent as the court can consider this when looking at recoverability. If the disbursements are insured then this is a 'subsidiary'. If they are not, then it may be possible surely not only to charge the client a subsidiary uplift but also the defendant a risk-based uplift.

Court fees

Court fees are imposing an ever-increasing burden on practices. The claimant's solicitor generally has to bear these himself, although the somewhat forgotten form EX160 still applies if the client is on state benefits and in those circumstances court fees can be waived.

Other upfront costs

The costs that a firm cannot avoid include the obvious, namely staff salaries, accommodation and other general overhead expenses such as postage, telephones and general office expense. Performance-related salaries can assist.

8.5 ENSURING EFFICIENCY

Firms should be vigilant in measuring their WIP days.

One of the most important matters relating to a manager analysing his fee earners' work is addressing the central issue of how to turn cases over quickly and efficiently.

A manager must have the ability to measure WIP days. In other words, he should have IT support which can measure, for specific work types, the length of time it has taken for the file to be opened and the final bill being submitted.

Individual fee earners can be assessed. The higher the WIP days, may indicate that a fee earner is overburdened with work, or, alternatively, that the fee earner has a complex caseload which may indicate that he requires some assistance.

The longer a case takes, the longer it will be before the practice is paid. This should be considered in relation to the type of work that a practice wishes to undertake.

Measuring your WIP days is not enough. Specific action must be taken to address those fee earners or those aspects of the claim which cause the department as a whole difficulty.

Standardisation

In relation to cases in general, specific steps such as ensuring that a firm nominates a medical expert in its letter of claim will shave off a number of days, possibly even weeks for the amount of time it takes for a claim to be completed.

Standardising procedures is crucial to the success or otherwise of a PI department. A bank of precedent letters and/or a case management system will ensure some uniformity.

Training staff in this respect is vital. Many qualified solicitors have in the past shown hostility to the idea of some of their work being standardised. It must be explained to them that this is absolutely vital from the point of view of providing both access to justice to the claimant and ensuring that the solicitor in question earns a decent living.

The issue of costs has slowed cases considerably over the last few years. The advent of fixed costs in road traffic accidents, and the imminent arrival of fixed costs in other areas of work, such as public liability and employers' liability will, it is hoped, assist in respect of some of those delays.

Costs

Cost recovery

In the meantime, fee earners once again must be trained in respect of the issue of cost recovery. Alternatively, one or two in-house cost specialists may be the short-term answer, or a long-term option for the larger practice.

There are many firms of costs draftsmen who offer their services in relation to taking a file away from a fee earner and pursuing costs thereafter.

Having a good debt collection department can also be of great assistance. Insurance companies in PI work can be notoriously slow at paying bills and PI practices must show that they mean business. In respect of getting paid quickly, a firm may wish to consider forwarding an interim bill to the client once his damages have been received. This could cut down on the significant delay that firms are facing actually getting paid for completed cases. However, it may lead to antagonism with the client, particularly as most PI clients feel their cases have gone on for far too long in any event.

Obtaining costs on account

In respect of the larger issued cases, CPR rule 44.3(8) can provide some assistance. The rule states:

> Where the Court has ordered a party to pay costs, it may order an amount to be paid on account before the costs are assessed.

CPD 44.2, para.8.6 states:

> Where, under Rule 44.3(8) the Court orders an amount to be paid before costs are assessed: –
>
> (i)   The order will state that amount, and
> (ii) If no other date for payment is specified in the order Rule 44.8 (time for complying with an order for costs) will apply.

157

Further, CPD 44.6, para.12.3 states:

> Whenever the Court awards costs to be assessed by way of detailed assessment, it should consider whether to exercise the power in Rule 44.3(8) (Court's discretion as to costs) to order the paying party to pay such sum of money it thinks just on account of those costs.

For the court to consider ordering a payment on account of costs it would not expect to see a properly drawn bill of costs at the time that the payment on account is ordered. It is going to take some months after the order or judgment for such a bill to be drafted and lodged. The court must of course have some information available upon which to base an order for payment on account and it appears from the case law that a statement of costs modelled on form N260 will be sufficient.

Paying parties are entitled to see approximate details of the receiving party's solicitors' fees and information in order to prove disbursements.

If the paying party insists on the sight of a properly drawn bill, then arguably this conduct is unreasonable and the matter should be taken back to the court.

Interim costs certificates

The other method that should not be overlooked is in relation to interim cost certificates. CPR provisions on detailed assessment, CPR rule 47.15 means that a request for a payment on account can be made on the agreed bill. A further request for the undisputed part on receipt of points of dispute can be made and an application for an interim certificate for the undisputed part refused can also be made.

Costs agreed

In any event under CPR rule 47.10 you can apply for a cost certificate for the amount agreed and then you can enforce.

8.6 GETTING PROFITABLE WORK

The Compensation Act 2006 now provides a statutory framework for the regulation of claims management activities which can apply for authorisation from 30 November 2006. Indeed it has been an offence to provide claims management services without authorisation or exemption when the Act came into force on 23 April 2007. This follows very considerable bad publicity in relation to TAG/Claims Direct. In particular it is hoped that the legislation will stop claims management companies taking a percentage of the claimant's compensation.

Alternatively you may be involved in an organisation where PI referrals are generated by firms sharing their marketing budget but employing a company that knows something about marketing. A disadvantage of such schemes is that the fees are payable up front. This will affect cash flow. Whatever the case, a firm needs to consider the quality of claims that are being referred to it. A firm needs to understand the exact costs of the case before it commences any business agreement. The predictable costs regime is having an important impact on 'the justifiable costs' of purchasing those cases.

Usually, the most profitable work is the 'free' work, which usually arrives by way of client recommendation.

8.7   SUMMARY: THE FUTURE IS BRIGHT

There are five distinct processes in respect of running of a CFA case:

(a)   risk assessment;
(b)   case handling;
(c)   supervision/quality;
(d)   the litigation process itself; and
(e)   costs.

Most practices have now learned that it is essential to delegate work to the cheapest competent individual in the team, or outsource that work. The team needs to focus on the areas in which they are trained in, namely analysis of legal issues. Their single most important role is deciding on the legal and business merits of a potential action.

It is important to ensure that the processes must be to take away a lot of the routine, dull administrative tasks from fee earners, so that they can focus on the important aspects of the claim.

A firm will run into difficulties if its responsibility is fragmented. If a firm creates processes where no one has overall control, the firm could be heading for disaster.

Instead, firms should be empowering fee earners by providing adequate training, education and support rather than having them become slaves to an IT case management system.

Fee earners focus on clients, not manuals or procedures and a reward is not for the time they record but for the value they create. In turn, the partners' role must not only be to analyse the financial information mentioned in the previous chapter, but must act as motivators, moving closer to the clients and the staff, educating and empowering the staff throughout the business.

Change is inevitable, in all areas of litigation, none more so than in PI. The Data Monitor Report 2001 indicated that the PI market is worth approximately £3 billion per annum and is rising by about 7 per cent each year. 'Time' is being called in a number of areas – the office-based lawyer may soon be replaced by the home-based lawyer working with a laptop and linked with his manager and accounts department at the central office.

CHAPTER 9

Running a CFA case

Robert Rose

9.1 INTRODUCTION

This chapter looks at the obligations solicitors have when giving costs information and dealing with clients. First, it will set out the background to the
changes which have taken place during the past few years. These include those
specific changes which have had an impact on the way in which a CFA case is
run, and also those changes which have affected professional conduct generally. Secondly, we will seek to put these changes into context by highlighting
the most relevant aspects and then by examining the way in which cases can
be funded and the risks assessed. The importance of an ongoing risk assessment during a case will be emphasised throughout: no lawyer wants to be in
charge of a department which is operating something like a spread bet on the
horses. Instead, he will need to have a team which is focused on assessing risk,
not only at the outset of a case, but also while events occur which could have
a dramatic effect on the prospects of winning the claim.

9.2 NEW REGULATIONS

There have been three recent developments which have had an impact on the
way a conditional fee case is run. On 1 November 2005 the new regime for
CFAs and collective CFAs (CCFAs) came into force and the CFA Regulations
2000 and the CCFA Regulations 2000 were revoked. At the same time,
primary responsibility for client care, contractual and guidance matters were
moved to the Law Society's Costs Information and Client Care Code 1999
('the 1999 Code') under the auspices of the Solicitors Regulation Authority.
On 1 July 2007 the new Solicitors' Code of Conduct 2007 ('the 2007 Code')
replaced the Guide to the Professional Conduct of Solicitors 1999 ('1999
Guide'), moving the governance of client care, contractual and guidance
matters to the 2007 Code.

The aim of the 2005 change was to simplify how CFAs and CCFAs were
governed. In effect, the 2005 Regulations 'moved' the detailed requirements

to the 1999 Guide. It was anticipated that failures fully to comply would not result in disproportionate sanctions.

The Law Society requirements in the 1999 Guide repeated previous regulations as to the information about costs which must be given to clients. The one critical amendment that was made (under the Solicitors' Practice (Client Care) Amendment Rule 2005) was that where clients are represented under a CFA or a CCFA, the solicitors must explain the circumstances in which the client may be liable for their own costs and for the other party's costs, the client's right to assessment of costs wherever the solicitor intends to seek payment of any or all of their costs from a client, and any interest a solicitor may have in recommending a particular policy or other funding. These obligations remain in force under the new 2007 Code (see especially 2007 Code subrules 1.04 'Best interests of clients', 2.02 'Client care', 2.03 'Information about the cost' and the Guidance to rule 2 generally and specifically at para.17). Further, it remains the case that solicitors must always be very careful to ensure that they do declare an 'interest' where it is relevant – i.e. if a solicitor receives work from a particular claims management company and is obliged to recommend a particular after-the-event (ATE) insurance policy, then this must be declared because this is a very real interest to the firm of solicitors. (**Appendix 10** contains many of the most significant rules.)

The obligations in the 1999 Guide, then, have largely been replicated in the 2007 Code, but a number of new requirements have also been put in place. One of the most significant aspects relates to rule 2 (Client relations) of the 2007 Code. Included are rules for taking on clients, client care, information about costs, contingency fees, complaints handling, commissions and limiting civil liability in contract. Also of particular relevance to this chapter are the provisions contained in rule 9 (Referrals of business), governing the financial arrangements between a solicitor and an introducer or claims-handling company.

What have remained the same during this period of change have been the requirements made under the Courts and Legal Services Act 1990, s.58 (as substituted). The agreements still have to be in writing, not relate to criminal or family proceedings, and in the case of a success fee, must specify the percentage increase which must not exceed 100 per cent. If the s.58 requirements are not met, then the agreement is unenforceable and, by virtue of the indemnity principle, the losing party is not liable for the winning party's costs (see **Chapter 4**).

The Law Society has prepared a model CFA which should be used. While the one-page agreement is refreshingly short (and contains all the statutory and basic requirements) the attached leaflet 'What You Need to Know About a CFA' is unfortunately, from the client's point of view, depressingly long (see **Appendices 7** and **8**).

9.3   THE SOLICITOR'S OBLIGATIONS

Client care

The Solicitors' Code of Conduct 2007 concentrates on solicitors' conduct obligations. It introduces a number of core duties which will remind the legal profession that it must adopt the highest standards of integrity and professionalism. These core duties are set out in rule 1 (Core duties) and deal with: justice and the rule of law; integrity; independence; best interest of clients; standards of service; and public confidence. They form an overarching framework, within which the other more detailed and context-specific rules can be understood, and fill the gaps where the other rules appear silent. The relevant rules are set out in **Appendix 10** below.

The rules setting out the information solicitors should give clients about costs and client care have been set out in rule 2 (Client relations) of the Code. There are two subrules: client care (2.02) and costs (2.03). It is important that solicitors consider the costs requirements in the light of the client care requirements.

By rule 2, solicitors must ensure that clients are given the information necessary to enable them to make appropriate decisions about, if and how their matter should proceed. This largely replays what solicitors remember as the old Law Society Practice rule 15. Subrule 2.02 of the 2007 Code, however, puts more detail to this requirement as well as emphasis on agreeing service levels with the client and explaining what responsibility falls on the solicitor and what on the client.

Under subrule 2.02, solicitors must, at the outset, and when appropriate thereafter:

(a)   identify the client's objectives;
(b)   give the client a clear explanation of the issues involved and the options available;
(c)   agree the next steps;
(d)   keep the client informed of progress;
(e)   agree an appropriate level of service;
(f)   explain mutual responsibilities;
(g)   give the client in writing the name and status of both the person dealing with the matter on a day-to-day basis and the person supervising; and
(h)   explain constraints created by funder, introducer or fee sharer.

It is also worth noting that subrule 2.02 repeats the provision in the 1999 Guide allowing solicitors to avoid some or all of its requirement if they can demonstrate it would be inappropriate to do so.

Costs

When using a CFA it is important that solicitors have regard to their client's individual circumstances: advice must be given as to the question of costs. The former CFA Regulations 2000 may have been revoked, but the Solicitors' Code of Conduct 2007 is just as onerous in the duties which it imposes on solicitors. Subrule 2.03 of the 2007 Code sets out very clearly what solicitors must do specifically in relation to a CFA, as well as generally, and replicates many of the requirements contained in the 1999 Guide.

At the outset of the retainer, and 'when appropriate, as the matter progresses', the solicitor 'must' provide the client with 'the best information possible about the likely overall cost of a matter'. In particular, subrule 2.03(1) requires that a solicitor must:

- advise the client of the basis and terms of his charges;
- advise the client if charging rates are to be increased (and this is vitally important even in conditional fee work where failure to do so may be in breach of the indemnity principle);
- advise the client of likely payments which the solicitor or the client may need to make to others;
- discuss with the client how the client will pay, in particular whether the client may be eligible and should apply for public funding;
- discuss whether the client's own costs are covered by insurance or may be paid by someone else such as an employer or trade union;
- advise the client that there are circumstances where the solicitor may be entitled to exercise a lien (if the client is not pre warned then a solicitor will not be able to exercise his right to a lien – it is therefore essential to ensure that client care letters and or terms of business cover this);
- advise the client of his potential liability for any other party's costs; and
- discuss with the client whether the client's liability for another party's costs may be covered by existing insurance or whether specially purchased insurance may be obtained.

Subrule 2.03(2) of the 2007 Code requires solicitors to explain, at the outset, and when appropriate as the matter progresses:

- the circumstances in which the client may be liable for the solicitor's costs and whether the solicitor will seek payment of these from the client, if entitled to do so;
- if the solicitor intends to seek payment of any or all of his costs from the client, he must advise the client of their right to an assessment of those costs; and
- where applicable, the fact that the solicitor is obliged under a fee sharing agreement to pay to a charity any fees which he receives by way of costs from the client's opponent or third party.

Whether acting under a CFA or not, solicitors must also discuss with the client the cost–benefit of the claim. The client needs to know whether the likely outcome in a matter will justify the expense or risk involved including the risk of having to bear an opponent's cost. This obligation is clearly set out in the 2007 Code at 2.03(6).

Any information about costs must be clear and confirmed in writing. This was the case under the 1999 Guide and again it is set out clearly in subrule 2.03(5). Solicitors must also ensure that the information given about costs is worded in a way that is appropriate for the client.

It is possible to use the 'let out' rule contained in 2.03(7), which states that if solicitors can demonstrate that it was inappropriate in the circumstances to meet some of the requirements in 2.03(1) and (5) there will be no breach of 2.03. It may be useful to rely on this 'let out' where a solicitor is conducting repeat work for an existing client on agreed terms (see Guidance to 2.03 at para.28). However, this 'let out' does not apply to the provisions contained in 2.03(2) concerning CFAs. Therefore solicitors must *always* give information to CFA-funded clients about the circumstances in which they may be liable for our costs, the solicitor's intention to seek payment for his costs, the right for these to be assessed and if applicable any fee-sharing agreements with a charity.

While solicitors must ensure that information about costs is given in writing and regularly updated, there is no requirement in the 2007 Code to update the client at least every six months, as there was in the 1999 Guide. The 2007 Code simply requires that advice should be given to the client about costs 'when appropriate as the matter progresses' (see PLC Practice Note, dated 12 June 2007: 'Informing the Client about Costs: at Outset of Retainer and Beyond', p.8). As a matter of best practice, however, solicitors should continue to tell their client at least every six months what level the costs have reached. In appropriate cases, interim bills should be delivered, explaining to the client any circumstances which affect the amount of the costs, the degree of risk involved and the cost benefit to the client of continuing with the matter. The client should also be informed in writing as soon as it appears that a costs estimate or agreed upper limit may be exceeded and the client's eligibility for legal aid should be considered if there is a material change in the client's means.

Solicitors also remain under a duty to have in place a written complaints procedure and to notify clients of this. This is dealt with in subrule 2.05 of the 2007 Code. While the guidance to this rule makes clear that the content of the procedure is a matter for firms themselves, it does reiterate that the procedure must be in writing, clear and unambiguous. Clients need to be told in writing: their entitlement to complain; and that following a complaint the complainant must be told in writing how the complaint will be handled, and be given a timescale within which they will be given an initial and/or substantive response.

Finally, before moving on to deal with other obligations under the 2007 Code, it is worth stressing two further subrules of rule 2: namely 2.04 (Contingency fees) and 2.06 (Commissions). Subrule 2.04, as in the 1999 Guide, makes clear that contingency fees are not permitted in contentious business except as required by statute or the common law. Subrule 2.06 maintains a requirement that a solicitor must pay commission sums over £20 to the client unless the client, having been told the amount, or, if the amount is not known, an approximate amount or how the amount is to be calculated, has agreed he may keep it. This is overridden if the commission is attributed to activities regulated by the Financial Services Authority (including insurance mediation activities).

9.4 GENERAL OBLIGATIONS

As well as the rules in relation to costs and client relations, the 2007 Code introduced a number of other rules which have an impact on the profession's work generally and specifically in relation to CFAs. Again, many of the provisions replicate the previous rules. The rules mentioned in this chapter are set out in full in **Appendix 10**.

Referral fees

Changes made in 2004 to permit the payment of referral fees subject to conditions have been carried over into the 2007 Code. There has been some rationalisation of the disparate requirements attaching to the different types of referral arrangement. It is therefore imperative that any arrangement a solicitor has complies with rule 9.

Subrule 9.01 reiterates the requirement that when making or receiving referrals of clients, solicitors must do nothing which would compromise their independence. Introducers must be alerted to the rules regarding publicity in rule 7. Further, in any personal injury (PI) claim, solicitors must not enter into an arrangement for referrals or act in association with any person whose business is to make, support or prosecute claims involving PI or death who has received or solicited a contingency fee in respect of such claims.

One common situation for many firms involves the agreement of financial arrangements with introducers and claims-handling companies. If a firm is involved in such an arrangement, it must also comply with 9.02 (Financial arrangements with introducers). This provides that:

- the agreement must be in writing and available for inspection by the Solicitors Regulation Authority (SRA);
- the introducer must undertake, as part of the agreement, to comply with the provisions of this rule;

- the solicitor must be satisfied that clients referred by the introducer have not been acquired as a result of marketing or publicity or other activities which, if done by a person regulated by the SRA, would be in breach of any of these rules;
- the agreement must not include any provision which would compromise, infringe or impair any of the duties set out in these rules or allow the introducer to influence or constrain a solicitor's professional judgement;
- the agreement must provide that before making a referral the introducer must give the client all relevant information concerning the referral (this includes the fact that the introducer has a financial arrangement with a solicitor and the amount of any payment to the introducer which is calculated by reference to that referral);
- if the solicitor has reason to believe that the introducer is breaching any of the terms of the agreement required by this rule, they must take all reasonable steps to ensure that the breach is remedied; and
- if the introducer continues to breach any terms of the agreement required by rule 9 the solicitor must terminate the agreement.

It is also important to remember that *before* accepting instructions to act for a client referred under 9.02, in addition to the requirements contained in 2.02 (Client care), 2.03 (Information about the cost) and 2.05 (Complaints handling) the client must be given, in writing:

- all relevant information concerning the referral (including the details of the financial arrangement with the introducer and the amount of any payment to the introducer which is calculated by reference to that referral);
- a statement that any advice given will be independent and that the client is free to raise questions on all aspects of the transaction; and
- confirmation that information disclosed to the solicitor by the client will not be disclosed to the introducer unless the client consents; that that where the solicitor is also acting for the introducer in the same matter and a conflict of interest arises, the solicitor might be obliged to cease acting.

While rule 9 permits solicitors to pay for referrals, it also reminds them not to allow the requirements of the introducer to affect the advice a solicitor may have given to a client. A solicitor must not become so reliant on an introducer as a source of work that it affects the advice that is given to a client (see Guidance to rule 9 at paras.1 and 2).

On a practical note, it is important to agree in advance with the introducer the nature of the information it will be giving to clients. Solicitors also need to be confident that they are not breaching any of the requirements of rule 7 (Publicity), for example by 'cold calling', or indeed any of the requirements in rule 9 itself. It is therefore best practice to set up a system to review and keep reviewing any agreements with introducers to ensure full compliance with the provisions in the Code (see Guidance to rule 9 at paras.9 and 10).

Fee sharing

Rule 8 of the Code deals with fee sharing and when this is, and is not, permitted. Changes made in 2004 widened the categories of persons with whom solicitors could share their professional fees and in 2006 further changes were made to permit fee sharing with charities. Both are incorporated into the Code (see 'Unravelling the Code', [2007] *Gazette*, 14 June, 23). Subrule 8.01 covers situations where a CFA is used and there is agreement to pay to a charity fees received by way of costs from the client's opponent or other third party. Guidance to the rule makes clear that if a solicitor acts in accordance with a pro bono CFA and disbursements are advanced on behalf of a client, and these disbursements are received by way of costs from a client's opponent or from another third party, a solicitor may retain from the costs which are received the element which covers such disbursements. The terms of this arrangement will need to be set out in the CFA (see Guidance to rule 8 at para.5).

In-house practice

In-house practice is covered specifically in the 2007 Code by rule 13. The basic rule here generally limits in-house solicitors to acting for their employee. However, it does provide exceptions, and one involves acting under a CFA. Subrule 13.04 provides that an in-house lawyer may, in the course of his employment, conduct work on a pro bono basis for a client other than his employer, provided the work is covered by sufficient indemnity insurance and either no fees are charged or a CFA is used and the only fees charged are those which are received by way of costs from a client's opponent or other third party and paid to a charity under a fee-sharing agreement.

Publicity

Rule 7 (Publicity) largely carries over the requirements of the Solicitors' Publicity Code 2001, but in a clearer form and accompanied by guidance on issues such as websites and emails (see 'Unravelling the Code', [2007] *Gazette*, 14 June, 23). Rule 7 applies to publicity in connection with practice from any office, whether in England and Wales or overseas, although subrule 15.07 amends the provisions for an overseas practice. However, it does not apply to websites and electronic communication from any practice conducted from an office in an EU state other than the UK. There are also different provisions regarding a firm's letterhead if the practice is conducted from outside England and Wales (see Guidance to rule 7 at para.1).

Rule 15 is specific to overseas practice and in effect it applies or disapplies the provisions of the rules in the Code to overseas practice, and in some cases substitutes alternative provisions. As well as dealing with provisions such as publicity referred to above, the rule substitutes the client care provisions contained in rule 2. In relation to a CFA case, subrule 15.02(4)(a) and (b) are relevant. They prohibit entering into a contingency fee in contentious proceedings, except as permitted by statute or common law; determine the information a solicitor must give a client if he has entered into a CFA; and prohibit entering into contingency fee agreements for contentious work overseas unless it would be permitted in that jurisdiction.

The final rule which has a particular impact on CFA work is that contained in subrule 19.01(4)(b). Rule 19 generally deals with financial services and aims to ensure solicitors' independence. By 19.01(4)(b) a 'general insurance contract' is defined as any contract of insurance within Part 1 to Schedule 12 of the Financial Services and Markets Act 2000 (Regulated Activities) Order 2001, SI 2001/544. This is important to remember as insurance contracts are a key part of the CFA process.

9.5   FUNDING OPTIONS

Private clients

In areas of work where success fees and insurance premiums are now recoverable it is perhaps difficult to envisage why a client would wish to instruct the firm on a private basis, at least if the client is not willing to undertake the risk of having to meet any success fee or ATE premiums. In areas of litigation where CFAs are routinely used, for instance where a 'book' of such cases is maintained by a fee earner such as in PI work, there cannot be many such clients left. If there are, then careful consideration will have to be given to providing all the information set out in the 2007 Code.

Legal expense insurance (LEI)

Rule 2 of the 2007 Code, provides that the solicitor must inform the client whether other methods of financing the case are available and how they could be used. LEI is the most common alternative to CFAs.

A complication has arisen concerning whether solicitors who are not on the 'insurers' panel' can act. In 1990 the EC directive on legal expense insurance (87/344) was incorporated into the law of England and Wales in the Insurance Companies (Legal Expenses Insurance) Regulations 1990, SI 1990/1159. It adopted the wording of the directive in its entirety in reg.6:

> Where under a LEI contract recourse is had to a lawyer . . . to defend, represent or service the interest of the insured in any enquiry or proceedings, the insured shall be free to chose that lawyer (or other person).

The then Insurance Ombudsman felt that the consumer could only have freedom to chose their lawyer when proceedings were issued. Because claimant lawyers now have a duty to consider alternative non-CFA funding by the liability insurers when faced with the demand for payment of the success fee and ATE premium, this matter has now become a contentious issue.

After *Sarwar* v. *Allam* [2002] 1 WLR 125, claimant lawyers had to face the fact that if the client had 'satisfactory' before-the-event (BTE) insurance it should be used in preference to a CFA with additional liabilities (success fee and/or ATE premium). The bad news is that in many cases a solicitor will lose that client to the BTE's firm's panel solicitor.

The present Insurance Ombudsman believes that if the policy does restrict the choice of solicitor, then it must be looked at to see if there are special circumstances which dictate that the client's first choice of solicitor should be instructed. Even if the language is unclear, then unless there is prejudice to the policyholder in claims such as road accident ones, 'minor personal injury' and routine consumer claims should stay with the panel firm.

The Ombudsman would expect the policyholder's preferred solicitors to act in cases involving large PI matters and complex cases such as medical negligence, significant boundary or employment disputes. This means clients who have LEI, and who are involved in the run-of-the-mill PI actions, will probably be forced to instruct their insurance panel solicitor.

It is open to the privately instructed solicitor to decide to waive his success fee in a pre-issue CFA and wait until proceedings are issued and then attempt to invoke the LEI as a right. Some LEI providers take the view that unless a solicitor from one of their panel firms has reviewed the case pre-issue, then a free choice of solicitor when proceedings are issued is not available. That does appear contrary to the 1990 Regulations. Others will argue that the lawyer/insured person may have prejudiced the company's right and the claim refused to indemnify.

It should be noted that the LEI simply provides an indemnity for the client's liability to their solicitor and their opponent. There must be a retainer between the solicitor and the client. Many LEI providers will only pay a reduced hourly rate if a claim is made on the policy, as well as seeking to obtain the full hourly rate recovery from the opponent but to limit the charges for losing the claim to the indemnity amount then a discounted CFA may be the way to proceed. Even risking only recovering the lower rate rather than the full rate is a risk for the solicitor and entitles the solicitor to charge an uplift for risk (success fee) although this would not be the full rate that would have been charged in a 'no win, no fee' situation.

It must be remembered that if a solicitor signs a client up on a CFA when he had available LEI, they are unlikely to recover the success fee and any ATE insurance premium.

Trade unions

Most trade unions are now dealing with PI work under CCFAs, thereby seeking to recover both the success fee and a notional premium. If a solicitor receives instructions from a union member but does not act for the union, then they will have to justify to the client that his best interests are served in agreeing to enter into a CFA. Those firms that bear the premium costs upfront may actually have a chance of recovering this from the defendant – if the union would have dealt with the case under a CCFA and then sought to recover both the success fee and the notional premium, then the firm may be able to argue that the defendant is in the same position and, therefore, that additional liabilities are recoverable. Where a client has been refused assistance from union-funded lawyers, the solicitor may well justify not only a CFA and ATE but also impose a high success fee.

In any event, as a result of *Sarwar*, trade union panel firms now have to check whether the union member has 'satisfactory' BTE insurance which should be used in preference to a CCFA with additional liabilities.

Public funding

Public funding is available now for special categories including:

- clinical negligence (subject to a merits and means test but only available to firms on the AVMA/Law Society panels);
- housing claims where injury has been caused;
- assault/abuse – potentially available;
- abuse of public office – potentially available for police actions;
- solicitors' negligence – although this will almost always be refused on the grounds that a CFA could be signed;
- legal aid also remains for 'proceedings which have a significant wider public interest' – if a CFA might be signed up instead, then public funding will not normally be granted;
- family and claims involving children – funding is potentially available.

Public funding is available in some cases for investigative help, in particular to investigate whether to enter into a CFA. This will only be granted if the prospects of success are uncertain and substantial work (six hours or more) will be required before those prospects can be determined. In clinical negligence actions, investigative help may be refused if the NHS complaints procedure has not been pursued. Even now that the CFA Regulations 2000 have been revoked, it is very important to explore whether public funding might be appropriate.

This is to ensure both compliance with the Solicitors' Code of Conduct 2007 and also the recovery of the firm's fees and additional liabilities (see *David Truex (A Firm)* v. *Simone Kitchin* [2007] PNLR 33). However, it should be pointed out that some firms run CFA systems which they maintain offer a better funding package than legal aid (with the risk of the statutory charge). It must be remembered that a successful defendant may be able to enforce his costs against a publicly-funded client, whereas in a Simplified CFA scheme where an ATE premium has been deferred and is self-insured (and the policy paid for by the firm), the client may not be at risk at all.

9.6 RISK ASSESSMENTS

Determining the risks

One of the most important parts of managing risk will be to determine what the risk factors are, the risk that one or other of those factors will become a reality and what can be done to reduce some of those risks during the course of a case. The correct recording of risk factors in an individual case is a critical part of ensuring the recovery of a very considerable part of a practice's revenue.

There are general risk factors which will apply to almost all cases being litigated. These include:

- The fact that the outcome of the litigation is always uncertain. The firm will need to spread the risk of losses in individual cases across the working caseload of the firm.
- Although a case may appear strong in relation to liability, greater risk often arises in relation to dealing with Part 36 offers and payments, which cannot be predicted in advance (although a CFA which does not expressly state that basic fees are irrecoverable if a Part 36 offer is not beaten at trial does not carry any real risk at all).
- The fact that there is a delay until payment of the firm's costs (known as the funding only risk).
- The extra cost of CFA work (non-payment for risk assessment calculations; non-recovery of part or all of these; additional administrative work) – once again this relates to the funding only difficulties.

Firms generally enter into CFAs with clients at an early stage because clients are unable to pay the investigation costs and because it is important to have a retainer in place as a vehicle for recovering the cost. The risks of that investigation will rest squarely with the firm. The costs of investigating cases which do not eventually proceed is part of the risk assessment procedure which is reflected in the firm's success fees. An alternative possibility may be the type of initial letter considered in *Gaynor* [2007] 1 WLR 1045.

The process of risk assessment varies from firm to firm. Some firms consider that it should be carried out by the fee earner involved in the case, but that the analysis of that assessment and the decision of whether to take a case needs to be taken by someone else, for instance a partner. Other practices have established a risk assessment committee which might meet on a regular (for instance a weekly) basis to consider whether to accept a case on a CFA and to validate a fee earner's risk assessment. Such a committee is likely to consist of at least two fee earners, one of whom is a senior member of the PI department. In other practices a partner will carry out the risk assessment based on information provided by individual fee earners.

Whoever undertakes the final risk-assessment will do so on a on a case-by-case basis and have sufficient information to decide whether the risk of losing a case should be transferred from the client to the firm. Initially they will have to identify the case-specific risk factors:

(1) *The facts of the case:* Are there any witnesses to the accident? Are they reliable? Is the client's version of events supported by any documentation? Has an accident like this happened before?

(2) *Liability:* Can the firm in law establish that the defendant breached his duty of care to the claimant? Did the claimant in any way contribute to his own accident?

(3) *Limitation:* Has the client notified the firm about the accident within a reasonable period of time? If it is very near the end of the limitation period, what extra risks does this create for this particular case?

(4) *The opponent:* The key issue here is whether the opponent is insured? Alternatively, can the firm establish the identity of the opponent?

(5) *Causation:* What pre-existing medical condition is 'lurking in the background'? Is this a case where it would be advisable to see the general practitioner notes before proceeding further?

(6) *Quantum:* Is the case sufficiently serious to justify an assessment of quantum in excess of the small claims limit? Are there particular issues with regards to the loss of earnings claim or is there a private heath scheme which has paid medical fees and which will have to be added into the claim itself? What risks are there in respect of a Part 36 offer? In assessing the quantum, how many different medical experts will be required?

(7) *The client:* Is the client credible? Can the client be trusted? Is the client prone to exaggeration? Is the client a poor historian?

After assessing these risks, the same person or committee will make a decision as to whether the case should be supported or not. In completing the risk assessment, a note is likely to be prepared setting out what the fee earner is to do next.

In respect of some cases there will be significant reservations about the case and the fee earner will be authorised to proceed only up to and including the stage of the pre-action protocol. Alternatively, there may be some significant reservations with regards to the claimant's, say, back injury, which will necessitate an investigation of the claimant's medical history prior to the claim being commenced.

Risk assessment however is not a static concept. Risks change and evolve throughout the course of a case. Any firm that has a risk-based PI practice must have in place procedures whereby changes in risk can be assessed. Therefore, for example, there should be a procedure whereby no fee earner is able to issue proceedings without a case being reassessed for the purposes of risk analysis. In addition, or alternatively, every CFA case would have to undergo a 12-month assessment in order once again to identify any changes in risk.

The 12-monthly reviews can be made more sophisticated – a separate review can take place for those cases where liability is in dispute, and where cases only have quantum as an outstanding issue. Where liability is disputed, the fee earner would have to list the main issues which are in dispute, estimate the percentage of the prospects of success, note what expert reports have been obtained, and so on. If no expert reports have been obtained, the fee earner would have to provide reasons why this was the case and would indicate what further expert reports would be required. The CFA risk assessment committee (or other assessing machinery) would need to know whether the claim was issued or whether limitation was less than four months away, and would need to understand what Part 36 offers have been made in respect of either liability or quantum. The fee earner would have to indicate whether proceedings should now be issued. The person reviewing risk or the risk assessment committee would provide its comments, noting what action was to be taken, and might put in a re-review date if less than the usual 12 months.

Whether conducting a risk assessment at the outset of the case or later, then it must be noted that all records should be placed in a suitable form. A written risk assessment will be used to justify and recover any uplift being sought. If the matter goes before a judge, then the solicitor must explain his thinking behind the assessment in order to recover the success fee and possibly the insurance premium. Judges want to see a reasoned analysis of the risk factors to the case in hand before allowing these additional items to be recovered. The solicitor will have to show that he has considered the merits of a particular case as well as taking into account the general risk factors as mentioned earlier. The Costs Practice Direction requires details of any additional liabilities to be provided when detailed assessment proceedings are commenced.

Assessing the success fee is becoming a more straightforward exercise. The predictable costs regime is now beginning to impose success fees in different areas of work. It is anticipated that, within a year, there will be standard success fees for a wide range of PI cases within an extended fast-track system.

For the time being, those areas not affected by set success fees do deserve very detailed consideration. The recovery of success fees is vital to the success or otherwise of a risk-based practice – success fees are the 'icing on the cake' in the sense of each individual case in relation to the recovery of costs, for the firm as a whole, however, they pay for those cases that are lost or are abandoned at whatever stage they have reached. Success fees should at least pay for the firm's losses – if they do not, the practice will not survive.

The vast majority of success fees will be recovered when cases settle, relatively early, and as a result most success fees will be low. These success fees need to be collected to compensate for the ones that are lost at trial. Success fees overall should be subject to review.

It is vital to properly assess the risks in each individual case. Success fees should reflect those risk assessment levels as there is not going to be a second chance to increase the proposed uplift if the case does not settle. There is, however, every opportunity to accept a reduced uplift.

As to the correct form to be used for assessing risk, these will vary from practice to practice. Most firms probably operate a standard matrix listing the usual relevant factors, for instance the existence of witnesses, the possibility of an early Part 36 offer or the need for complicated evidence. Some firms require a percentage of the overall risk to be attributed to each factor. Others prefer a general weighting to be allocated to each factor (for instance low, medium or high risk). Some examples of real but anonymised risk assessment documents are set out in the Appendices (see **Appendix 15**).

CHAPTER 10

CFAs and the Bar

10.1 INTRODUCTION

This chapter seeks to set out by way of background the overall approach to CFAs which has been adopted by, and is relevant to, barristers. The Bar has available to it two model agreements, one being the joint APIL/PIBA (Association of Personal Injury Lawyers/Personal Injuries Bar Association) agreement for use in personal injury (PI)/clinical negligence cases, and the other the Chancery Bar Association model. The Chancery Bar model is extremely flexible and is suitable in a wide variety of circumstances. This chapter ultimately seeks to direct barristers towards the two model agreements (which are self-explanatory) and the very extensive and helpful guidance documents made available by the Bar Council. Save for seeking to provide solicitors with some understanding of how barristers view CFA practice, to attempt more than to offer some signposting to barristers as to what is available would be entirely otiose.

Chapter 3 gives general guidance on the principles applicable to the recovery of success fees.

10.2 CHALLENGES FOR THE BAR

CFAs present particularly acute challenges of a practical nature to the Bar as an independent referral profession, all the more evidence now that barristers can undertake work direct from the public.

It must be said that the Bar, especially its senior members, has not responded enthusiastically to CFAs. This is probably, in part, because barristers would simply rather not share the risks of the litigation, the attendant perils being more acute when the fees are high, the caseload relatively low and the bulk of the barrister's fees are incurred towards the end of the case once key strategic decisions have been taken. It is also because barristers tend to be particularly nervous about the effect of CFAs on their relationship with the judges, and about any imputation that their independence is compromised by the nature of the funding. Some barristers see CFAs as a direct

176

affront to their status as providers of independent, objective advice. This reaction may or may not be understandable, but it has led to wider concerns, especially among the solicitor's profession, about the Bar's willingness to play fully its part in providing advocacy services under CFA terms.

The Bar Council's preferred position indeed is that barristers should be engaged as disbursements in the usual way, and a solicitor should certainly ask himself whether the client would be better or worse off by the instruction of counsel on a CFA basis. Appropriate use of a barrister under an ordinary retainer allows the client and solicitor to ensure that no conflicts can arise as a direct result of the CFA. This may be particularly valuable, for instance, where a settlement is proposed or a Part 36 offer is made, the acceptance of which guarantees the payment of the lawyers' fees. If the client can afford to do so, the use of a barrister as a disbursement in the ordinary way may assist the solicitor in relieving the client of any residual doubts which the client may have over the independence and objectivity of any advice to settle. The sophistication of combined loan and after-the-event (ATE) insurance products can enable clients effectively to make use of the Bar's services on a referral basis (see **Chapter 7**), and this method of funding is likely to represent the most attractive way forward to many members of the Bar. Some ATE insurers insist that barristers are retained on non-CFA terms.

From a purely commercial point of view, CFAs are not always attractive to the Bar. In the PI market they are the industry-accepted model. In commercial cases, 'differential' or 'mixed' fee agreements are likely to be more attractive to the Bar, and they do not carry all the risks usually associated with failure. Under the terms of such agreements, the barrister agrees to receive his normal fees if the case succeeds (with or without a percentage uplift) and a reduction of his normal fees in the event of failure.

The risks to which barristers are particularly exposed when working under CFA terms arise first, because each member of chambers carries his own losses (as well as successes) and secondly, because counsel cannot scrutinise what is happening on a day-to-day basis with the proceedings. Both individual barristers and their practices as a whole must be alert to the need to minimise the financial risks to which they are likely to be exposed as a result of entering into CFAs. Procedures need to be put in place to ensure that these risks are controlled and that the outcomes are monitored. This will require the resolution of difficult questions within chambers as to how (if at all) such procedures are to be enforced against individuals.

10.3 THE LEGISLATIVE FRAMEWORK

The legal framework which permits the engagement of barristers on a conditional fee basis after 1 November 2005 (when the Revocation Regulations 2005 brought an end to the CFA Regulations 2000) is no different from that which governs the relationship of solicitor and lay client and barristers must ensure that the basic requirements are met.

In outline, a solicitor/barrister CFA is only enforceable if it is caught by the provisions of the Courts and Legal Services Act, ss.58, 58A (as substituted and inserted by the Access to Justice Act 1999, Part II) (see **Chapter 2**). This means that the agreement must be in writing (s.58(3)(a)), and it must 'not relate to proceedings which cannot be the subject of an enforceable conditional fee agreement' (s.58(3)(b)). Further, any CFA between a solicitor and counsel must comply with any relevant regulations prescribed by the Lord Chancellor (s.58(3)(c)). The effect of ss.58, 58A, is that there must be strict compliance with both the Act and any regulations for a CFA to be enforceable (see **Chapter 4** for the consequences of unenforceability). **Chapter 2** contains an account of the operation and historic development of the relevant legislative provisions.

10.4 TERMS OF WORK

The ordinary relationship between solicitor and barrister is not affected by the use of CFA terms. Either a CFA does or does not have contractual force, and depending on this question, the terms of work on which barristers offer their services in either annexes G1 or G2 of the Code of Conduct of the Bar of England and Wales will apply (see the Bar Standards Board website: **www.barstandardsboard.org.uk**). Should a solicitor–client arrangement be declared unenforceable, that does not affect the solicitor's liability to pay counsel's fees.

Can a barrister turn down a CFA case?

Paragraph 604 of the Code of Conduct of the Bar of England and Wales provides an exception to that part of the Code which appears under the heading 'acceptance of instructions and the "cab-rank rule"':

> a barrister in independent practice is not obliged to accept instructions . . . (c) to do any work under a conditional fee agreement.

In other words, a barrister can turn down any case offered to him which is to be funded by way of a CFA. If a barrister refuses to take on a case on a CFA basis, then he must take this decision speedily, since not to do so is to run the risk of falling foul of para.701 of the Code of Conduct of the Bar of England and Wales (requiring instructions to be read expeditiously and to be returned promptly).

Direct professional access

A difficulty has arisen by the failure of the parliamentary draftsman to acknowledge that since July 2004 the Bar is available to offer direct access work to the public. Members of the public do not have the protection of the client care provisions of the Solicitors' Code of Conduct 2007, the Solicitors Act 1974 or the relevant provisions of the costs rules in the Civil Procedure Rules (CPR). The Bar Council has provided guidance entitled: 'Conditional Fee Agreement Work on Public Access' (see **Appendix 11**). Any barrister intending to enter into a CFA on such terms may well think that the underlying recommendation is not to do so but rather to redirect the client to a solicitor.

10.5 BMIF

Rule 10.1.1 of the rules of BMIF, the Bar's mutual insurer, states that:

> BMIF shall indemnify the Insured against claims by a solicitor for payment of all or part of the solicitor's fees under a conditional fee agreement between the Insured Barrister and that solicitor, only if and to the extent that:
>
> > the conditional fee agreement entered into by the Barrister and the solicitor is in a form previously approved in writing by the Directors.

Privately, senior figures at BMIF have expressed concern that the wording of this rule might lead to an influx of divergent CFAs being sent to BMIF for formal approval. BMIF is not concerned with the general provisions of CFA agreements and does not want to be seen to have given approval to anything other than the express indemnity clause usually prevalent in a CFA. In the normal way, if an error or omission on the part of a barrister leads to the failure of a claim, the solicitor would recover his fees as part of the damages sought by the client. Since carelessness on the part of a barrister where the solicitor represents his client under CFA terms makes the recovery of fees more difficult to assess (the solicitor having to demonstrate the extent to which it was likely that success would have been achieved), an express indemnity on the part of the barrister is a standard part of a barrister–solicitor CFA. In turn, the solicitor can also expect to have provided such an express indemnity in the agreement. Such mutual obligations are to be found for instance in APIL/PIBA 6 at para.17.

In practice BMIF has not been overwhelmed with applications for the approval of CFA agreements. This is probably because barristers have preferred to work on the standard models drawn up by those professional bodies which have received BMIF approval (see below). Barristers need, at the very least, to ensure that where there is an express indemnity that this is capped at £25,000, since it is the extent of the cap which is of concern to BMIF; £25,000 is the maximum liability to which, at the time of writing, BMIF is willing to expose itself.

Model agreements and clauses

As has been said above, there are currently only two model agreements available which have BMIF approval. One is the joint APIL/PIBA agreement (APIL/PIBA 6), and the other is the Chancery Bar Association terms of engagement (see **Appendix 15**). The first represents a compromise reached between PI solicitors and barristers. In certain critical areas it contains alternative provisions, and counsel should be careful to ensure that any agreement entered into is entered into on the appropriate clauses. APIL/PIBA 6 was drafted specifically with PI and clinical negligence proceedings in mind where the solicitor is also working under CFA terms with his client (on the Law Society model agreement, see **Appendix 7**). It is an industry-wide agreement and there is little prospect of a prudent PI solicitor departing from its key clauses. The Chancery Bar Association agreement is a much more flexible instrument and is more effective at protecting the interests of barristers. In particular it contains express provision allowing the CFA to be treated as a contractual retainer, and it allows for fees to be agreed on a differential basis (reduced fees rather than no fees in the event of failure). The Chancery Bar Association terms of engagement can be easily adapted to cover a very wide range of circumstances.

As the Bar Council explains in its guidance at para.60, the following aspects of CFAs are likely to merit closer consideration:

Potentially problematic clauses in CFAs

60. It may be helpful to identify certain clauses to which particular attention might usefully be paid, as they may be potentially problematic. This is not to say that other clauses may not also give problems.

(1) Clauses defining 'success'. Success is particularly difficult to define in cases where there are more than one party or various forms of relief sought.
(2) Clauses dealing with the rights of the parties where a payment into court has been made.
(3) Clauses dealing with unavailability of counsel. For example, who is to provide or arrange for alternative counsel and who is to pay for the services of such alternative counsel? Counsel should be extremely cautious about adopting responsibility for 'successor' counsel's fees.
(4) Clauses defining when there is a right to terminate the CFA and the consequences of termination. Counsel must ensure that they cannot be obliged to continue in the face of proper advice to settle or withdraw the claim.

(5) Clauses dealing with the impact of Part 20 proceedings. For example, will the 'after the event' insurance cover an order that an unsuccessful claimant pay a third party's costs.
(6) Clauses dealing with the impact of actual or possible set-off or counterclaim.
(7) Clauses dealing with the effect of a finding of contributory negligence.
(8) Clauses which purport to give a right to increase the uplift in certain circumstances. These will be unlawful if the fees or uplift are contingent upon the size of the compensation or other award to the lay client. However, the parties can agree to define 'success' in terms, for example, of 'beating a Part 36 payment' and provide for normal fees and a success fee if it is beaten, but only for normal fees (with no success fee) if it is not beaten.

10.6 THE 'PROCEEDINGS' TO BE COVERED BY A CFA

It is important for a CFA to specify clearly the particular proceedings or parts of them to which the agreement relates, an aspect of the Chancery Bar Association model which needs careful attention. Defining the action or the proceedings covered by the CFA requires some careful thought on the part of both solicitor and barrister. While most agreements are entered into at the commencement of instructions and are intended to run to the conclusion of the action, there is no reason why a barrister cannot be brought into a complex case as and when required under new agreements for limited purposes on each occasion. Such a procedure requires the barrister to embark on a new risk assessment on each occasion when he or she is presented with a new CFA. At the same time it confers benefits on the barrister as well as on the solicitor and client. On the part of the solicitor and client, a CFA restricted to part of the proceedings allows use to be made of a barrister under an ordinary retainer where appropriate (for instance advice as to settlement), but it also gives the barrister the power to limit his or her commitment to the CFA. What may appear an attractive commercial risk when first taken on may become less so some years down the line once the matter is booked in for trial. In a complex case counsel should have reservations about entering into an open-ended CFA, especially where it may be prudent to revisit the appropriate percentage uplift at a later date. The current legislation does not provide a mechanism for a revision of the measure of the success fee after the original agreement, save that the court has power to reduce an unreasonably high percentage uplift down, having regard to the factors known to the legal representative at the time at which the CFA was made.

Consideration needs to be given to the extent to which the proceedings specified in the CFA are to include any appeal or enforcement or any interlocutory proceedings. The agreement should state whether the proceedings include any appeal, counterclaim or proceedings to enforce a judgment or order or any costs proceedings.

10.7 SPECIFYING THE CIRCUMSTANCES IN WHICH FEES ARE PAYABLE: 'SUCCESS'

The definition of 'success' as defined in most CFAs may well overlap with the way in which 'proceedings' are defined, and counsel must decide the appropriate standard by which success is to be determined. The easiest method, it is suggested, is to determine success by reference to the relief granted by the court (or as set out in any compromise agreement). Another method could be to determine success by reference to the question whether any costs are awarded by the court, although this is somewhat unsatisfactory, for instance where an opposing party was content to compromise an action, but to limit its exposure to any costs order. In cases where the relief sought was equitable in nature it is more likely that the description of success would have to have some reference to the facts in issue. The default position under APIL/PIBA 6 is that 'success' is to be determined by reference to the definition of 'win' under the solicitor–client CFA.

Amending a CFA or entering into a new agreement

The question is often posed whether a CFA should be amended or whether a new one needs to be entered into when circumstances change, for instance where a second defendant has been joined. This will depend on the circumstances and possibly on the risk. It is quite legitimate to amend the CFA. Regulation 6 of the former CFA Regulations 2000 expressly envisaged that amendments would take place. When there is an amendment there must be a new assessment of risk (see Costs PD, para.11.7), so that if the risks have decreased then arguably a new CFA would be preferable to cover the new circumstances alone. The former agreement will still allow a higher uplift on the matters covered by the previous agreement.

10.8 MANAGING CFAs IN CHAMBERS

Neither individual barristers nor their chambers should allow themselves to run a significant CFA caseload without adopting procedures which allow them to control the potential risks of losing income. This means that barristers should do the best they can to make prudent decisions about whether to accept instructions under CFA terms. It also requires careful monitoring of cases which have already been commenced under CFAs, although there are thought to be a limited number of chambers which put this into practice. The Bar Council Guidance at paras.70–88 ('Chambers' Approach to CFAs' provides useful and comprehensive guidance). Some of the most material issues are touched on below.

Screening procedures and providing alternative cover

Individual barristers need to ensure, if possible, that there are colleagues in chambers with whom they can screen cases prior to taking them on. The nature of the arrangements made between individual members will vary from chambers to chambers. In a busy set where a great deal of CFA work is undertaken in PI cases, chambers may need to set up regular procedures, and a panel which is required to examine the potential risks of each case. It is more likely that individual members will want to form themselves into smaller groups, and they may only discuss those cases where the prospects of success are considered by the individual who has received a particular brief to be below a particular percentage. Small groups are more likely to be the norm since different members of chambers will be more likely to trust the judgement of like-minded individuals, and there will be collections of barristers who are agreed about those solicitors from whom they will, and from whom they will not, accept CFA work. On the other hand, individuals will need to adopt close working relationships with a reasonable number of colleagues at the screening stage in order to ensure that there is sufficient cover available in the event that a brief has to be returned. It is not conducive to good commercial relationships either with solicitors, or within a set of chambers, to discover that when a brief has to be returned there is no one available who is willing to take on the case. Some chambers do, and some do not, strictly enforce both a rule that a CFA must be approved by other member(s) of chambers before it is agreed and also a rule that other members of chambers must be willing to provide cover where the first choice is unavailable.

Monitoring outcomes

Monitoring the outcome of a CFA caseload is important to gauge the accuracy of barristers' decisions when agreeing to undertake CFA work. Proper monitoring ensures that screening practices are working correctly, that barristers are making the right decisions about the firms from which it is safe to accept CFA instructions, that they are making accurate assessments of risk, and that chambers is not overexposed to the possibility of losing an unacceptably large number of CFA cases.

The Bar's Guidance document sets out a variety of steps which chambers can take to facilitate effective monitoring. These include establishing a log of CFA cases, a contemporaneous record for production in the event of assessment, an individual log for each member of chambers, and both chambers' and individuals' records of CFA cases. Barristers are advised to maintain a file in respect of each case which should become available to barristers to whom a case has to be returned.

Many of the suggestions made in the guidance perhaps constitute something of a counsel of perfection, and they require intensive labour on the part either of barristers or of administrative staff. They also add to the financial burdens of chambers, and in a highly competitive market-place, the increased fees required to ensure the adoption and maintenance of such systems run the risk of making chambers commercially unattractive. Good monitoring records on the other hand are vital, and those chambers which are most likely to accommodate such records are those which are most IT minded. In chambers where members have access to a shared hard drive, whether from home or at work, joint access to data files in CFA cases will assist in sharing, and in assessing, CFA information. The costs of running a CFA practice can be incorporated in counsel's basic fees, but can play no part in determining the success fee.

Returns of work

Both the APIL/PIBA 6 terms and conditions and those of the Chancery Bar Association require a barrister who is obliged to return work to 'endeavour' to find an acceptable replacement, but if such a barrister cannot be found then this does not constitute a breach of the agreement.

Chambers will have to find solutions where possible to the problem of organising alternative counsel. In areas where chambers rely on bulk suppliers of similar work, notably PI, it is unsatisfactory for instructing solicitors not to be able to rely on the one chambers to be able to offer alternative representation. There is no doubt that the system of returns is highly unpopular with solicitors, and they are particularly concerned about difficulties which may arise in the case of CFA cases. This is one issue where chambers need to devise effective policies to enable returned cases to be covered and where chambers need to take decisions how these procedures can be enforced.

Enforcement of chambers' policies

Practical measures which might be taken on a chambers or group basis to ensure uniformity of approach are set out in the Bar's Guidance document. They include consideration of the extent to which screening procedures need to be adopted throughout chambers, and whether chambers' policies (such as that relating to the return of work) should be published. What is likely to be much more difficult in practice is for chambers to be able to 'police' such agreed policies internally. What happens, for instance, if barrister X simply refuses to take any returns from barrister Y because he does not trust Y's judgement about screening, or if barrister Z refuses, against chambers' published criteria, to accept any returns from a certain firm of solicitors because he believes that that particular firm does not always make proper disclosure of the materials necessary adequately to screen the risks? The answers to such questions are generally being worked out on an ad hoc basis, but chambers needs to consider whether rules of conduct in relation to CFA work need to be incorporated within their constitutions and what steps can legitimately be taken to enforce such rules.

10.9 RECOVERABILITY OF COUNSEL'S FEES AND ASSESSMENTS

Notwithstanding that when working under CFA terms the solicitor remains liable in the ordinary way to pay counsel's fees (save for the question of payment of a disallowed percentage uplift), barristers should be familiar with those parts of the CPR and Costs PD which are relevant to CFAs (see **Chapter 2** and the comprehensive account set out in the Bar Council's guidance).

Providing information

Notwithstanding that a barrister looks to his fees from the solicitor whatever a solicitor's errors and omissions, counsel should perhaps ensure that some notice of funding has been given to an opponent where a barrister is engaged on CFA terms which provides for a success fee. Only one notice needs to be given where one of the team is engaged under a CFA, so that so long as a form N251 has been given if the solicitor is engaged under a CFA, then a separate notice does not have to be provided where the barrister is working on a CFA. Without notice (or relief from sanction) a success fee is not recoverable from an opponent (see **3.4**).

'Disallowed' uplifts in the barrister–solicitor relationship

Regulation 3(2)(b) of the CFA Regulations 2000 expressly provides that where part of a percentage uplift is disallowed on the basis that the level at which the increase was set was unreasonable in the light of the facts known to the lawyer at the time at which the increase was set, then that amount is 'not payable under the agreement'. A similar provision applied where there is a compromise of an action. CPR rule 44.16 allows for the legal representative to apply to the court that the full amount should 'continue to be payable by his client', and the detailed procedure is set out at s.20 of the Costs PD (including steps to be taken by counsel, for instance at paras.20.4 and 20.7(2)). As the Bar Council notes at para.43 of its guidance document, 'it is ... necessary for counsel and counsel's clerk to set up and implement a system to respond rapidly to any challenge to a success fee'.

Charging for the initial advice

The risk assessment process faced by a barrister presents him with special difficulties which are unlikely to be faced by the solicitor who first receives the case. Solicitors in firms where conditional fee work is the norm, that is to say those which have busy PI departments, are used to taking an informed view about the likely success and complexity of a matter at an early stage. They may well have a brief statement from the client, some details of what witnesses are going to say and some photographs of the scene of the accident. All of this material may even have been prepared by an agent and not by the solicitor, who will have to make a speedy assessment of the merits prior to embarking on further expensive investigative costs and the expense of embarking on pre-action protocols.

In the case of a barrister, a full set of papers is more likely to be received with instructions perhaps to advise on merits, evidence and quantum. The decision whether to accept a case on CFA terms may well require hours of preparation. The Chancery Bar Association proposed a solution by the drafting of 'Terms of Engagement for Preliminary Work where Retainer on a Conditional Fee Basis Is Contemplated', which terms allow for payment of fees in a variety of circumstances once the preliminary work has been completed. For instance, fees may be required to be paid on an ordinary hourly basis if a CFA is subsequently not entered into, alternatively fees might be added to the fees due under the full CFA.

Foreign proceedings

The Code itself contains no other express reference which specifically refers to barristers and the use of CFAs, save that it must be remembered that in relation to work falling within certain criteria set out in Annex D, a barrister is permitted to work for a 'conditional or contingent fee where this is permissible under the laws or rules of the place where the services are to be provided'.

10.10   ETHICAL CONSIDERATIONS

The Bar's CFA guidance document contains an extensive discussion of the ethical considerations perceived by the Bar Council to apply to instructions accepted on CFA terms. These are important considerations and are to be found at **Appendix 11**. The separate guidance note 'Conditional Fee Agreement Work on Public Access' provides further ethical assistance in respect of direct professional access (see **Appendix 12**).

PART III

ATE insurance and other forms of funding

CHAPTER 11

Litigation insurance

Matthew Amey

The focus of this chapter is practical advice intended to help the busy solicitor understand what insurance may be available, how the market works, and how best to enter into the right insurance arrangements for their clients. After some initial general observations, this chapter goes on to set out the nature of the ATE (after-the-event) market (see **11.2**) and then seeks to set out the best means of finding and entering into appropriate insurance contracts (see **11.3**).

Section **11.2** ('Understanding the ATE market') is intended to enable a legal representative to comprehend how the insurance market is made up and gives a brief description of the some of the different types of policy which a solicitor might be contemplating acquiring for the client (for instance, hybrid policies or both sides' cover). The focus is on the difference and similarities as they currently exist between the 'non-injury' and 'injury' market sectors. There is a word of caution expressed in this section about coverholders and their role.

Section **11.3** ('Making insurance arrangements') includes a detailed consideration of the delegated authority market and is intended to assist a solicitor in determining whether or not a delegated arrangement is preferable when compared with individual policies. Then there is a detailed account of 'increasing' premiums, by which are meant stepped, staged, rebated and similar products, which have recently obtained a certain amount of judicial sanction. The essence of such products will include some element of block rating although this may only apply to the early stages of a case, with a formula for ascertaining a specific premium for the final trial period. As this final premium is invariably expensive (as the case is at its riskiest stage), this may make a defendant consider carefully his options in deciding whether or not to go to trial. Top-up cover is considered in some detail, this being an increasingly important issue for solicitors seeking to tread a fine line between not incurring too much initial cover whilst also ensuring that their clients are adequately covered. The section ends with some specific comments about the use of ATE insurance with commercial and then defence clients, and with a section designed to set out some best-practice guidance when applying for ATE insurance.

11.1 INTRODUCTION

Is litigation insurance necessary?

First, something must be said about the initial decision which a firm must make in those cases in which the client does not wish to assume the burden of the risk of having to meet the opponent's costs, namely the question whether or not to insure at all. Choosing not to insure a case is becoming an increasingly risky business. After all, the premiums, if set correctly and accepted following a search of the market, are recoverable from the losing party. Why risk the consequences of not trying to insure early on?

Anecdotally, professional negligence cases are now surfacing where the client is suing his solicitors for failing either to present ATE insurance/ litigation funding as an option or failing to investigate what may be available for the case in question. Solicitors also face the problems now thrown up by *Myatt* v. *NCB* [2007] 1 WLR 1559 (see **5.5**). In some circumstances a solicitor whose client is not insured runs the risk of being made to pay some or all of the costs personally.

The vast majority of ATE policies now have a deferred premium which is only payable if the case is successful (because the premium is self-insured). It is at least arguable that failing to advise about these unusual features of ATE insurance is negligence in itself even where the possibility of ATE insurance is raised with the client. It is surely one thing to explain that ATE insurance exists but quite another to explain that it may pay a claim without the insured ever having to pay any money to the insurer for the benefit.

Given that the premium is recoverable from the opponent under the Access to Justice Act 1999, s.29 one might be forgiven for thinking that there is no risk to any individual claimant at all in taking out such insurance and as a result, a solicitor who has decided that they will recommend an ATE insurance policy may feel that it is unnecessary to understand the ATE market as a whole. Why grapple with this complex area, which is utterly incidental to the job of running litigation when the client has nothing to lose once the policy is in place? Why bother to research other products in the market when the policy in front of you does enough? Of course, this is not the case. Beyond failing to advise on the existence of ATE, there are yet more risks for solicitors who do not advise their clients properly on the coverage that they need for their case. There is still much to consider and very good reasons to search the market for the best policy available. Indeed, ATE policies are not like your run-of-the-mill standard motor policy where most policies are harmonious. It is just as important to consider the scope of the cover being provided as it is the payment terms of the premium. For example, the definition of success is of paramount importance to the insured. What use is an insurance policy, which defines success as 'any offer made by the opponent'?

For the insured, even with a deferred and self-insured policy in place, there are still some risks to be aware of, such as the following:

(a) Shortfall on premium recovery where the premium is not fully recoverable inter-partes on detailed assessment.

(b) Policy voidance. The policy can be voided due to a breach of a condition precedent of the policy made by either the insured themselves or their legal representatives. This could lead to the insured having no cover.

(c) A situation arising where the insured is liable to pay their opponent's costs despite having themselves received an award of costs/damages in their favour, where the policy only provides an indemnity for the liability over and above any sums the insured has received. Such situations may arise in multi-defendant cases, with issue based costs orders and where an opponent's Part 36 offer is not beaten at trial.

Beyond this, it must be remembered that the ATE insurance is simply insurance, so that where funding is required for disbursements or own fees, the ATE policy alone will not solve the problem. The policy does not fund these costs for the insured, it merely reimburses the client in the event that the case is lost. Most policies will not even pay an interim claim where an interim hearing is lost (albeit they will indemnify these costs at the conclusion of the substantive action). It may not be enough to simply understand the ATE market; it may well be necessary to consider the funding market as well.

Tactical reasons for obtaining insurance

Whether or not the litigant is impecunious, there are positive tactical advantages in obtaining ATE insurance. In particular, stepped premiums can offer a tactical advantage as they put the pressure on the opponent to settle the case before incurring any liability to pay a bigger premium. Moreover, opponents may be prevented from using their greater financial muscle to bleed their opponent's resources dry by stringing the proceedings out or by notifying their opponent of very high costs estimates. The insured has the backing of an ATE insurer who has invested in the case and can assist the insured in seeing it through. What is more, by implication, the merits of the case must have been assessed as reasonable or higher for insurers to have made this investment in the first place. The pendulum will have swung in the insured litigant's favour.

ATE insurance as a marketing tool in commercial litigation

Some commercial litigation departments may already be coming under increasing pressure from institutional clients to look at new and innovative litigation funding solutions for their business clients because of their increasing awareness of CFAs and ATE insurance. It is likely that the more aggressive firms, hungry to win new clients will look to ATE insurance, CFAs (or differential rate CFAs) as a way of going one better than the competition. Good-quality funding options will have the greatest impact on serial litigants, who have the most to gain from the certainty and cash flow benefits provided by CFAs and ATE insurance packages. Of course, it is these key clients that are mostly likely to shape the future thinking of the law firms that service them.

11.2 UNDERSTANDING THE ATE MARKET

Differences between market sectors

There is more than one ATE market. There are in fact two principal ATE markets – or perhaps they are better described as 'market segments'. To know one well does not mean you can transfer what you know to the other automatically. Both are supported by different organisations and subjected to different pressures. Although in more recent times uniform standards across the whole industry have replaced some of the historical differences, the health and long-term future of each market segment is very different. The two market segments are generally classed by those in the industry as 'injury litigation' and 'non-injury litigation'.

In addition to these two market segments there are the sub-categories relating to small/medium-sized litigation on the one hand, and larger or 'big ticket' litigation on the other. At the moment, the cut-off point between what is thought of as 'small/medium' and 'big ticket' litigation for the purposes of applying for ATE insurance is approximately £200,000 of cover. If the need for cover goes above this, the case is going beyond what most ATE providers are prepared to underwrite on their own. The companies that support the larger cases are invariably well-known established insurers as opposed to companies who are better known as 'coverholders'. Understanding the differences between these organisations is the key to understanding how the market is structured, and more is said about 'coverholders' below.

The different options for the payment of premiums now available in both non-injury litigation and injury litigation is one example of where the differences between the two markets has converged. For example, the concept of the self-insured premium policy (which means that the insured does not pay the premium in the event the case is lost) is now commonly available for commercial litigants. It is a feature that developed in the personal injury (PI) market which has now spread to other areas of law. The popular deferred payment option is also now available in a growing number of non-injury cases.

Setting aside the difference between small/medium-sized litigation and 'big ticket' litigation, so long as things continue the way they are, then the long-term future for non-injury ATE insurance is far brighter than for the PI segment. This is for a number of reasons. There are several pressures and threats that plague PI insurers to which commercial ATE insurers are immune. For example, every year the pool of insurable CFA/ATE cases reduces in the injury litigation world. The saturation of before-the-event (BTE) insurance policies is considered to be the biggest obstacle, due to the fact that additional liabilities, such as ATE premiums, are only recoverable where there are no alternative funding options. The problem of BTE insurance does not and is not likely in the future to pose the same problems to commercial ATE providers. BTE cover is expensive for businesses and is limited in terms of cover. In the commercial arena it is difficult to see ATE insurers being starved of suitable cases due to alternative funding options.

In addition to the BTE hurdle, there are threats such as an increase in the small claims track limit and calls from liability insurers for fixed premiums. The Department of Constitutional Affairs (now the Ministry of Justice) has released a consultation paper on the future of PI claims which recommends changes that could dramatically reduce the number of PI cases that ATE insurers can offer cover on. The paper is entitled 'Case Track Limits and the Claims Process for Personal Injury Claims' and was released on 20 April 2007.

The exact impact on the sustainability of the industry is unclear if both or either of these become reality, but it is clear that both would affect the profitability of ATE insurance in fast-track PI litigation.

Delegated authority schemes

The PI market is dominated by delegated authority schemes and a firm can now obtain an insurance scheme without committing to insure anything but a nominal amount of cases per year. On the other hand, delegated authority schemes for non-injury litigation remain rare. This is an area that is expected to change over time. For the time being, however, the vast majority of commercial and civil litigation cases will be assessed individually and the decision to offer terms rests with underwriters. Even this process varies between injury and non-injury litigation though, with ATE providers relying on in-house underwriters to assess PI risks while decisions on the merits of commercial litigation are often outsourced to specialists. More is said about the advantages of delegated insurance schemes as opposed to individual arrangements at **11.3**.

Non-CFA insurance in the non-injury sector

A stark and certainly less well-known difference between the injury and non-injury markets is the availability of cover for non-CFA cases in the non-PI market. After all, Access to Justice Act 1999, s.29 allows premiums to be recoverable not just in cases which are run on CFAs.

It seems that commercial lawyers are not being compelled by clients to act on CFA terms, contrary to what is happening in the PI sector. This is not to say that pure 'both sides' costs' cover is being offered to commercial clients. Policies are still generally restricted to adverse costs and own disbursements, but ATE insurers do offer terms on cases where the legal representative is acting under a normal private fee paying retainer or perhaps a hybrid CFA (where the solicitor is taking a partial risk on their own fees). This should be a welcome development for those who are serious about opening up the commercial market. ATE insurance needs to be as attractive as possible to survive in the non-PI segment and flexibility in relation to the retainer is vital.

Hybrid BTE/ATE policies

In recent times various organisations have sought to offer a hybrid BTE policy that converts to an ATE policy when the BTE indemnity is exhausted. Unless there is an obvious benefit to the insured or to the opponent in such a policy it is hard to see what the point of such an arrangement is. Attempts to create such products have failed on several occasions in recent years. The difficulty with such products is that they often have a very limited BTE indemnity and in effect the product is a client capture tool which attempts to put in place an obligation upon the insured to use their product because the BTE funding should be used ahead of any ATE policy. Thereafter, the client will need more cover and will have to purchase an ATE policy. The effect is to increase the number of cases where opponents have to pay an additional liability for the ATE premium.

Both sides' costs cover

This is still very rare. Historically, a number of providers offered both sides' costs cover but underwriting results were not good. This may have been partly because neither the client nor the solicitor retained a stake in the risks attached to the litigation. The insurer assumed all of the risk. Funding arrangements in the future, however attractive, are likely to retain risk for the client, the solicitor or both in addition to the ATE insurer. Where both sides' costs cover is offered, it is usually at a prohibitively high cost and is only likely to be available where the case has very good prospects of success. It is perhaps these cases that are best suited for CFAs in any event.

Coverholders: a word of caution

The term 'ATE providers' is used throughout this chapter, since not all the companies in the market are insurers notwithstanding the fact that they provide ATE insurance. Some companies look like insurers by providing risk assessment services, policy administration and claims-handling services but they are not insurance companies. Such companies are called 'coverholders'. What is the difference? The answer is simple. Coverholders do not take any risk. They operate under a binding authority on behalf of an insurer or insurers who ultimately carry the risk. A binding authority means that the coverholder is authorised by the insurer to issue certificates on its behalf, in doing so 'binding' the insurer.

Why is this important? Well, it may not be. Some coverholders have been in the market longer than some insurers but it must be borne in mind that coverholders are separate companies from the insurer. They are much smaller companies. The propensity to struggle to meet service standards or perhaps to disappear entirely is much greater with coverholders. Indeed, it has been known for coverholders to switch between different insurers at awesome speed so that one day the insurance is with 'X' insurer which has a strong financial rating (A rating) to 'Y' insurer which has a weak financial rating (B rating). Again, this may not pose a problem but it is fundamentally important that every solicitor knows who their client is insured with and whether that insurer is adequately regulated and secure. When we make choices about who to bank with, or insure our lives with, reputation and security are of paramount importance. The same should surely be true when advising clients on the purchase of ATE insurance.

Lastly, coverholders are not independent insurance brokers. Whether or not they have a binder with two, three or even four insurers, they are still only recommending the policies to which they have access – a thin slice of the market. A solicitor should not assume a coverholder is adequately searching the market on your behalf to meet the client's obligation to select a policy reasonably.

Security for costs

Is an ATE policy adequate security for costs? ATE insurance has generally not been viewed as adequate security for costs because of the ability of the ATE insurer to void the policy in certain circumstances, leaving the opponent without security (cf. 'Insolvency' in **7.3**). There are always going to be legitimate reasons to void a policy. This is the nature of insurance policies. For instance, ATE policies do rely on the solicitor complying with court timetables and the client's full disclosure of all material facts. Nonetheless, some insurers will agree to offer a policy to a litigant that faces the prospect of a security for costs order in the near future on the basis that the policy is voided *ab initio* if an order is subsequently made which cannot be satisfied by the ATE policy on its own.

11.3 MAKING INSURANCE ARRANGEMENTS

Delegated authority v. individual applications: pros and cons

What is delegated authority?

Some ATE providers are prepared to offer certain firms the authority to issue policies on their behalf. They are able to bind the insurer to a risk that falls within specific underwriting criteria. For such an arrangement to be viable and worthwhile, it is fundamental that the firms run a volume of cases and can demonstrate a certain level of expertise/track record in the field of law in question. Most delegated authority policies involve block-rated premiums.

Why would a firm want to consider delegated authority?

A short answer is 'certainty'. A solicitor can be certain that his client will be offered cover if he has authority to bind the insurer to a risk. Another reason is that that delegated authority saves time. There is no need to await a decision from the insurers as to whether they are prepared to issue a policy.

It must also be remembered that it is easier to insure the more difficult cases if a solicitor has delegated powers. Insurers may more readily accept more difficult cases when they know that they are insuring the run-of-the-mill actions as well. Marketing opportunities are also available where there is dele-gated authority. The comfort of being certain that cover will be available to clients allows a firm to advertise its approach to protection for the client against litigation costs. Furthermore, a good track record which has been established with an ATE provider could one day form the basis for an improved deal in an increasingly competitive market.

Exclusivity in a delegated scheme

Delegated authority schemes and indeed block-rated premiums generally work on the basis that a firm signs up to insure all their cases with that ATE provider. While there may not be an insistence on absolute exclusivity, having an obligation of this kind can make some firms feel uncomfortable.

Are delegated scheme premiums cheaper?

If a solicitor can demonstrate a bespoke search of the market in every case, he can ensure that the premium is appropriate to the actual case in question. Indeed on average, block-rated premiums should be cheaper, but whether or not this is the case will depend very much on the profile of cases a firm runs. If the majority of cases are high value clinical negligence cases, then a block-rated premium on a dental negligence case may prove to be far more expensive than an individually assessed premium.

Cases falling outside the binding authority of a delegated scheme

Some cases will fall outside the binding authority of a delegated scheme. While most insurers will say that they will do their best to accommodate these cases by assessing them individually, a great many cases are simply rejected. This leaves the individually assessed market as the client's only recourse. Crucially, a rejection from a scheme insurer would need to be disclosed: not a good start. Some firms/cases will never be suitable for delegated authority and ATE providers will simply not offer it. In these circumstances the firm will have no choice but to insure on an individual basis.

Choosing between using a delegated scheme and individual assessments

Ultimately, whether or not to enter into a binding delegated scheme will depend on the expertise of the firm, its fee earners, the profile of its cases, the insurers who can offer a package, the business model of the firm and internal administration systems. The key is that every firm who chooses to insure a case continues to search the market for competitive terms for its clients. In the context of delegated schemes, it is fundamentally important that the market is reviewed regularly to ensure that the scheme remains competitive and appropriate. It is suggested that a record of the searches and enquiries should be kept on file as evidence.

11.4   ADVERSE SELECTION

There are two types of adverse selection. First, adverse selection occurs when a firm only chooses to insure its difficult actions and does not bother to insure the easier cases. Secondly, adverse selection occurs to the detriment of a specific provider under a delegated authority policy when the solicitor only insures the riskier cases under the scheme. The practice of adverse selection is an industry-wide problem mostly affecting the individually assessed market. ATE insurers are naturally cautious that they are only being asked to consider cases because they are risky. Firms who send a high volume of individual cases often receive a much higher quotation rate in percentage terms as insurers will grow more confident that they are seeing the majority of risks.

If there is adverse selection under a delegated authority policy, the insurer will not receive the premium income it anticipates and which is necessary to cover its expected losses. Insurers need to be able to calculate premiums for delegated authority policies on the basis that the majority of the early winners will pay for the costly (and often late) losers.

Increasing premiums

Whether the insurance is arranged on an individual basis or through a block-rated delegated authority scheme the premium is often subject to increase throughout the life of the litigation. Such premiums are designed to be an incentive for the opponent to settle as well as a mechanism for insurers to tailor the premium to the size of the insurer's exposure. There is no doubt that increasing premiums are seen as a good thing for both individual policies and scheme arrangements and insurers have been encouraged to adopt such structures following comments made in recent case law. (In *Rogers* v. *Merthyr Tydfil* [2007] 1 WLR 808, stepped premiums found favour with the court and in the RSA Pursuit Test Cases (SCCO) Master Hurst found a multiplier premium model to be reasonable if adjusted to actual costs in the context of the six test cases.) However, notwithstanding a background of apparent judicial approval, to date, the reasonableness of any premium calculation methodology will depend on how the increases are calculated.

The methodologies available are varied and their suitability to a particular type of litigation depends on what effect the methodology has on the average cost of the premium for that area of litigation.

Different models for increasing premiums

(a) *Stepped premiums*

The amount of premium due to the insurer and then in turn recoverable from the opponent will depend on how far the litigation progresses. The premium increases in steps at various 'trigger points' in the litigation process. For example, the premium will increase from £5,000 (step 1) to £15,000 (step 2) once proceedings have been issued.

Usually there are three steps but the timing of the third step varies greatly between providers. Some will say the final premium is due once trial starts, while others will state the tertiary step occurs after 45 days post-exchange of expert evidence, for example.

Some providers will charge very low initial steps with much higher final steps while others will prefer the reverse.

Throughout the duration of the case, the maximum amount that the insurer will pay (the limit of indemnity) remains static no matter what step the premium has risen to. This is different to what some providers call a 'staged premium'.

(b) *Staged premiums*

The amount of the premium increases in the same way that the stepped premium does and very often at the same trigger points in the litigation (e.g. issue of proceedings) but unlike a stepped premium structure, the limit of indemnity also increases with each trigger point. For example, at stage 1, the premium is £5,000 but the maximum amount that the insurer would pay under a claim is capped at £50,000 should the case discontinue. At stage 2, the premium increases to £15,000 and at the same time the cap is elevated to £100,000 of cover.

One might argue that staged premiums are more proportionate than stepped premiums as the insured is only buying more cover as and when they need it. However, solicitors must be very careful with staged premiums as they can lead to difficulties if, for whatever reason, the insurer refuses to accept the additional premium and increase the cover accordingly. This can happen where the prospects of success diminish and notwithstanding the insurer's initial intention to honour the staged increases in cover, the insurer decides under the terms of the policy to refuse to top-up the cover. Finding alternative cover at a later stage may then prove impossible or expensive.

(c)   *Rebated premiums*
Rebated premiums may take precisely the same form as stepped premiums in the sense that the trigger points of one provider's rebate will match another's steps. The net effect to the paying party may not be affected by whether the premium is stepped or rebated but rebates are perceived as a discount on the premium due which may be why this terminology is preferred. The limit of indemnity under a rebated premium model is always static, as with stepped.

(d)   *Incremental premiums*
The insurer sets a 'base' premium which acts as the minimum premium payable. After an agreed period (which may be a month, a quarter or a year), the premium will increase by a certain amount, 'the increment'.

This is a time-based premium which may well prove cost-effective in comparison to another structure but it is not based on the actual litigation process and in cases where the litigation drags on, the premiums can become disproportionate. To counter this, the insurer may agree to put the increments on hold (where quantum is being investigated by the insured after an admission of liability, for example) or put a cap on the maximum premium.

(e)   *Multipliers of exposure*
The premium is expressed as a percentage of the of the insurer's exposure. This means the premium is 'floating' (upwards) until the conclusion of the case.

Following the RSA Pursuit Test Cases (SCCO), Master Hurst made it clear that the percentage would need to be applied to the actual exposure the insurer faces and not an estimated exposure.

This process requires disclosure of the actual costs incurred by the opponent up until the claim is successfully concluded in the insured's favour, in order to calculate the premium due. A process made slightly easier by rules in relation to the provision of cost estimates.

This is not an exhaustive list and new structures are constantly being developed in an effort to differentiate one provider from another. Every insurer wants to offer a demonstrably more reasonable premium structure than their nearest rival and preferably on an exclusive basis. However, more recently some providers have been combining elements of two or more of the above structures to offer the benefits of each. For example, one scheme may adopt stepped premiums for low value cases but a multiplier of exposure where the cases are much bigger and the costs are more unpredictable.

Are increasing premiums always available?

Some insurers employ increasing premiums in some areas of law and not others. For example, one insurer offers an increasing premium for commercial cases while preferring to offer single stage (of flat) premiums in low-value PI cases. For another insurer, the reverse is true.

Where two insurers agree that a particular subset of litigation requires an increasing premium structure they may decide to use entirely different approaches. For example, one insurer uses a stepped premium model for PI cases and another uses an incremental premium model. Further still, even where insurers share the view that a premium should be, for instance, stepped, the timing of the steps will usually be different.

The suitability of the increasing premium structure

One might reasonably ask the question whether it matters which methodology from those listed above is used. After all, there is clearly no consensus in the ATE insurance industry. There is no one methodology all insurers agree is most appropriate for any area of law or type of case so how can a solicitor without underwriting experience be expected to make the right choice?

This sounds logical but solicitors should be aware that it does matter. Solicitors need to consider carefully each methodology available to them so that they can evaluate the impact their choice will have on the likely cost of the premium. Simply put, one type of premium may well be, on average, more expensive than another when considered in the context of the solicitor's own caseload. One day, it may be open to the opponents to argue that the selection was unreasonable and the solicitor should have adopted a more suitable methodology for their caseload to keep the average cost to the opponent down. If the solicitor cannot demonstrate that they made an appropriate evaluation of their choices at the time, based on statistical analysis, they may not be able to justify their choice.

This is particularly important where the increasing premium is adopted for a block-rated delegated authority scheme (as opposed to a one-off case), as an adverse decision by the court on the premium methodology chosen would affect every case that a solicitor places with an insurer under the scheme. The solicitor will need to feel comfortable with the premium calculation methodology, as it is in those cases that are most out of kilter with the methodology employed, that the solicitor will be called upon to justify their choice of block-rated scheme at detailed assessment.

Tertiary steps subject to individual assessment

The *Rogers* judgment supported stepped premiums which was not surprising. However, it is of some interest that the policy in question was not assessed by means of a fully block-rated methodology, and it is perhaps worth noting that the final step in that policy was 'individually assessed' at the final trigger point, close to trial.

It is dangerous to infer that merely because the premium in *Rogers* was allowed in full on that occasion, the Court of Appeal was endorsing all individually assessed premiums generated by such a model. That is to say one should not assume that that tertiary step assessment will be automatically reasonable in every case, merely because of the preceding steps.

It is natural to assume that an individually assessed tertiary step premium will be more expensive than a predetermined tertiary step premium because the premium is only individually assessed once it is known for certain that the case is heading to trial. It must surely remain open to challenge an individual assessed tertiary premium if it can be shown to be unreasonably high in comparison to fully block-rated stepped policies available at the time.

The problem this generates for the solicitor, with an individually assessed tertiary step, is uncertainty. The insured does not know what their ultimate premium liability will be so how does the solicitor know that the third step is going to be a reasonable (and recoverable) premium if he/she does not know what it is? At the stage that they find out what the premium is going to be, it is too late to then search for competitive alternatives. Put another way, if the premium was not recoverable, would the solicitor still feel comfortable advising their client to enter into an insurance contract with a premium that they cannot know or indeed calculate.

Informing opponents of stepped premiums

In the *Rogers* case, all sides agreed that the opponent should be informed that the premium will be subject to increase(s) at certain trigger points. This disclosure was recognised as a sensible approach from the perspective of the insured, the opponent and the ATE underwriters – necessarily implying that there is a tactical advantage to be gained by insuring in this way.

Challenging premiums

Following the decisions in *Callery* v. *Gray* [2002] UKHL 28 and *Rogers* v. *Merthyr Tydfil*, times are tough for defendants wishing to challenge ATE premiums. The courts have demonstrated reluctance to interfere with the pricing of ATE policies, preferring to state that the premium must be reasonable. This is sensible from one perspective as ATE insurers are few and far between and the market, crucial for access to justice, could be mortally wounded by any judgment that significantly reduces the attractiveness of servicing this class of insurance. On the other hand, it necessarily means that every premium needs to be considered in the context of the case, particularly the original estimate of the likelihood of a claim being made and the costs exposure faced by the insurer. This means that defendants will need to be able to challenge the information given to the insurer to rate the risk in question and challenge this in the courts on each case, rather than rely on a judgment that says all premiums should be 'X'. Because it is impossible to create a uniform premium rate for all areas of litigation, defendants have the onus upon them to demonstrate why the premium is unreasonable. In reality, defendants have little information available to them to understand how the risk premium was calculated and what is more, the courts do not want to entertain endless satellite litigation. A challenge is only worth making, therefore, where some damaging information is available because of the costs consequences.

However, there are areas that defendants might seek to exploit in the future. One such area is the premium indemnity guarantee or 'shortfall cover'. It has long been the practice of most ATE insurers to take a commercial view on the recovery of their premium, leading, on some occasions to an acceptance of a smaller premium than had been originally envisaged. This is more often than not a cost and time-saving device to avoid a protracted argument over the premium recovery. However, some policies promise that the client need not worry about any liability for a shortfall arising from a detailed assessment, sometimes in the policy or accompanying literature. Some will give a contractual undertaking to waive any shortfall so that the client has no uncertainty at all over their risk on the premium recovery. If such a practice is allowed to continue unabated, it potentially leaves very little incentive for the ATE insurance industry to be price competitive. There is no risk to the insured and therefore no incentive for their legal representative to shop around for cheaper comparator quotes. There is a need for some uncertainty over the issue of recovery for the insured to have any concern whatsoever over what they are buying and in turn asking someone else to pay for.

The practice of contractually waiving any shortfall has itself not yet been fully tested in the courts and if it is deemed that such a practice is not lawful, surely this begs the question, who would pay the premium if any element attributable to this guarantee is not recoverable? Could it be that the recovery of the entire premium is disallowed? It is easy to see why defendants may wish to challenge such a guarantee given the potential this has for fixing premiums at a higher level than a fully price competitive market would afford, not to mention the issue of the indemnity principle.

Top-up cover

The potential need for top-up cover needs to be considered throughout the duration of a case. The question of when to apply for ATE insurance is even more important where the applicant is applying for additional top-up cover because their BTE insurance cover is not sufficient to reach the conclusion of the case. Many solicitors have made such applications far too late to have a reasonable chance of securing the additional cover that their client needs. This is because some solicitors are simply not sure when to start thinking about applications for top-up cover. Mistakes have been made in the past where some solicitors have not considered ATE top-up cover early enough. For example, a solicitor may feel obliged to wait until every penny of the BTE indemnity has been spent before making an application for top-up cover. An application may then be submitted with only weeks remaining before the start of trial. As stated above, the further down the litigation time-line the case has travelled, the less likely it is that an ATE insurer will offer terms. Some clients have simply not been able to secure top-up insurance, resulting in the case discontinuing for want of funding purely because the application was made too late.

It is important to be alive to the issue from the start and make an application to insurers as soon as there is a distinct possibility that the indemnity could run out without enough cover for a fully contested trial. It must be remembered that a reasonable proportion of the BTE indemnity is supposed to be for opponent's costs and it is therefore very unwise simply to exhaust the BTE indemnity with own side's costs without reserving any of the indemnity for adverse costs – this could leave your client exposed if ATE top-up is not available.

It is submitted that the better approach is to work out when the projected costs to conclude a fully contested trial (including adverse costs) are likely to exceed the BTE policy's limit of indemnity. If more cover is likely to be required to conclude the case at a contested trial, the solicitor will need to apply for the extra cover required. When doing so, it may be advisable to request that the BTE insurer allocate any unused indemnity to fund own disbursements (and to allocate any further remainder to the first £X amount of adverse costs that may be awarded at the conclusion of the case). If the BTE insurer provides their consent to this allocation approach, it will allow the ATE top-up application to take place at an earlier stage when it is much more likely to be successful, because the allocation has meant the costs have been incurred under the policy and this source of funding has been exhausted. At this point an ATE insurance policy will be required adequately to protect the client if the case is fully contested: it should be seen as the actions of a reasonable solicitor to incur the additional liability, even at an early stage. The alternative is to risk no top-up cover being available or to incur a much higher ATE premium. In that sense, early consideration of a client's top-up insurance needs may save the opponent's money.

ATE top-up cover

ATE top-up cover may also be required whether there is already an ATE policy in place but the maximum sum payable under that policy (the limit of indemnity) is no longer sufficient to see the case through to the end. In this instance, it is wise to approach the same insurer who provided the initial policy to request that they top-up their policy. They will usually require an additional premium for agreeing to do so.

However, while it may seem expedient to approach the same insurer, not least because they already have a stake in the litigation by reason of the original policy, it should be remembered that the additional premium charged will still need to be reasonable and proportionate if it is to be recovered in full. The trouble is that top-up premiums can be very expensive, often due to the fact that applications are made late in the litigation process due to unexpected high costs estimates provided by the opponent. It may be advisable to search the market for competitive quotes at the point of making an application with the original insurer. That way, there is evidence to demonstrate that the top-up policy chosen was a reasonable choice. Exactly the same issue is relevant to stepped premium policies where the latter stages are 'individually assessed'. Stepped premiums are discussed earlier in this chapter.

It should be noted that some ATE insurers will refuse to consider top-up insurance on top of some existing ATE policies because of who the existing insurer is. If the original insurer is not perceived to be a good quality insurer with a solid reputation and excellent security, other insurers may not wish to provide an additional layer of cover. This is the case even though top-up policies will exclude the first £X amount of an adverse costs award incurred on the basis that such sums are necessarily covered by the original policy. It is usually a reputation issue rather than any concern that they will be exposed to an increased claim.

11.5   ATE AND COMMERCIAL CLIENTS

Undoubtedly, ATE insurers are showing increasing interest in commercial litigation. The question is whether insurers are pushing on an open door or whether they will face an uphill struggle to create demand. After all, to date, ATE has made very little penetration into the commercial litigation world.

There are some valid reasons for this, and some reasons are probably more myth than reality. One reason commonly cited is that commercial clients have no appetite for it and do not see any benefits in taking out the insurance, particularly as they are often bolstered by positive advice on the merits of their case. It is also often said that commercial clients have deep pockets and that they are not concerned by adverse costs exposure to the same degree as individuals. Although such statements may be true, it makes little business sense, even leaving aside the obvious risks of not insuring, namely that it can be expensive to lose. There are sound commercial and tactical reasons to insure beyond merely transferring or sharing the exposure through insurance.

Reasons to insure: cash flow and financial certainty

Large businesses may well be setting aside a financial reserve for funding a piece or pieces of litigation. ATE insurance can render this process unnecessary for little or no cost and beyond this ATE insurance can give the litigants much needed certainty with regard to their exposure. By illustration, take a situation where company A decides not to obtain insurance for their claim in comparison to the decision of company B who does take out insurance for their claim. Both companies have instructed a commercial solicitor on a private fee paying basis. As their litigation continues, neither companies A nor B will not know exactly how much they will ultimately have to pay for their own solicitor's fees to conclusion of the case, but at least company B will know that it is insured for adverse costs and own disbursements to the conclusion of the case. It can remove this cost from its balance sheet and/or reserve.

To go a step further, let us suppose that company C has insured like B, but it has a self-insured premium policy. This means that it can also remove the cost of the premium from the balance sheet, since, win or lose, it will recover the premium whether by way of a claim to the ATE provider itself or from the opponent as part of the costs recovery process. Moreover, if company D takes out a policy similar to that taken out by C but also enters into an agreement with the solicitor that they will act on a CFA, company D can remove the cost of its own solicitor's fees off the balance sheet as well. Company D has considerably more certainty in relation to the cost of its litigation than company A. While company D may well been able to afford to run the case without the insurance, it makes far more sense to free this money up so that it can be applied for other matters rather than sit in a stagnant reserve. Company A is left with its money tied up in its reserve, and more importantly, it is left with a considerable degree of uncertainty as to whether it has set the reserve correctly.

Now consider company E which has taken the same approach as company D but has a deferred as well as a self-insured premium. In this case the premium is not payable until the end of the case and is only payable if the case is successful, and usually only payable when the costs are recovered from the opponent. Company E has all the benefits of company D without tying up any money in the premium itself. In such circumstances, company E is only required to fund disbursements upfront and is safe in the knowledge that even this outlay is covered by the insurance.

Defendant applications

ATE insurance is available for defendant cases, but the chances of securing cover are generally much lower than in claimant cases. The difficulty that underwriters face with defendant cases is defining success under the terms of the policy. Many defendants may take a commercial decision to settle a case, even though their defence is strong, perhaps because of the nuisance value of the litigation. The ATE insurer will understandably not agree to cover adverse costs in such circumstances.

If a suitable definition of success can be agreed between the client, the solicitor and the ATE insurer then it is possible to arrange cover with some ATE insurers. Whether a suitable definition can be agreed between the parties depends on the nature of the case and the time the insurer is willing to commit to exploring the possibilities. Such cases can lead to a drain on resources and many insurers will simply decline to consider such applications. A solicitor should consider how they might structure success under a CFA (whether such a retainer is being used or not) to try and pre-empt the questions that an ATE insurer might have about how to define a 'win'. It is also possible to arrange cover for counter-claims but again, only a small number of insurers will commit the resource to tailor the cover to such situations.

Best practice in applying for ATE insurance

If an insurer declines a case, this needs then to be declared to the next insurer, automatically tainting the application and your chances of receiving competitive terms. With this in mind, there are a few guidelines to follow if you are seeking insurance for an individual case. Although the ATE market has seen many changes in the last five years, these guidelines have stood the test of time and are just as relevant today.

Contacting the right insurer

Do not send an intellectual property case (for example) to an insurer just because they regularly provide cover for your firm's PI work without checking that they will agree to consider the type of risk in question. Many ATE providers in the PI segment will never consider a non-PI risk and vice versa. Do not take what an insurer's sales literature says as gospel as the practical reality is often very different. Consider seeking assistance from an expert or someone who has insured a similar case with that insurer before. Some providers will invite you to send them everything but in reality they are limited to a specific indemnity level, or types of risk. Months of to-ing and fro-ing can be fruitless. This problem is especially apparent among insurers or coverholders which have sales staff and whose knowledge of litigation and ATE is sometimes extremely limited.

Simultaneous proposals

Send the case to several insurers simultaneously either on your own account or via an independent broker. This gets over the problem of insurers rejecting cases and tainting the proposal before consideration by other insurers. In addition, it will provide invaluable assistance when it comes to premium recoverability.

When to apply

Apply early. There are exceptions, for instance, where the merits of a case are not known until after investigative expert reports are available to support the case (for instance, some clinical negligence cases), but the general rule is that it is harder to insure cases the less time the case has to run. Once proceedings have been issued some insurers may be less inclined to offer insurance, and once a trial date has been set the available insurance market is extremely small indeed. This is because ATE insurers like to know that the parties have plenty of time left to settle and may be less entrenched in their positions at an earlier stage.

Guidance on applying for the right amount of cover

Preparing a proposal for ATE insurance for a provider(s) can take up valuable time and a lot of effort, particularly for cases that are more complicated than the norm or outside the insurer's usual area of expertise. Save yourself wasted time and money before starting the process by taking the following actions.

The correct amount of cover

First, state clearly how much cover you require for adverse costs and disbursements to the conclusion of a fully contested trial (the insurer's worst case scenario). Insurers are used to dealing with estimates and they appreciate that it is not an exact science. However, if you buy a lot more cover than necessary then the premium may well be the subject of a challenge at detailed assessment. On the other hand, more trouble can arise from failing to insure sufficiently. Cases have discontinued through failure to obtain top-up ATE cover late in proceedings. If the solicitor should or could have purchased an increased amount of cover at the outset, this could possibly give rise to a professional negligence claim against the solicitor.

Retrospective cover

Secondly, remember to ask for retrospective cover if this is required. Some insurers do not automatically offer it but it is often possible to obtain.

Counsel

Thirdly, state clearly whether you require cover for counsel's fees or whether counsel is on a CFA.

Commission

Some firms of solicitors receive financial rewards for using a specific ATE provider – although regard must be had to recent authority and the FSA rules on receiving direct or indirect rewards for recommending a particular policy. Excellent guidance on this point is provided by the Law Society in its publication 'A Guidance Note for Firms Wanting to Make Financial Services Introductions and Receive Commissions' – available on its website. Of particular note is the section on commissions (see para.5 of the guidance), where it is made clear that any commission received belongs to the client, and requires the client's informed consent for the solicitor to keep it. Furthermore, the FSA does not consider that seeking agreement with the client by means of standard terms and conditions is acceptable, so if solicitors do receive commission from ATE insurers, great care must be taken.

Keeping abreast of developments in the ATE market

It is difficult for busy solicitors to keep up-to-date with developments in the market, not least because the immaturity of the market has led to very quick changes. Indeed, new case law and legislation is forcing the market to change all the time to meet the needs of litigants and the solicitor community that services them. Sources of information are available albeit relatively scarce. *Litigation Funding*, published by the Law Society, is a well-known guide to which companies operate in the market and what products they are seeking to offer. A variety of CPD-accredited courses on litigation funding are also available from various training centres and these should always touch upon developments in the market. The important thing for a solicitor to consider is that whatever source they prefer, that the source is independent as many companies have exploited their client's lack of knowledge on this area to the detriment of the firm's own reputation.

11.6 CONCLUSIONS

The ATE market represents an excellent opportunity for good-quality firms and a threat to those who are unwilling or incapable of adapting to the new litigation funding world. Firms stand to win clients and lose them as a result of their interaction, or lack of, with ATE insurance. Indeed, there will be circumstances where a failure to grasp the importance of ATE and some of its unique facets may lead to professional negligence allegations.

ATE insurance should not be treated as a sub-paragraph in a client care letter, but as an integral part of how a firm markets for clients and retains their loyalty for future instructions. Lessons can be drawn from PI litigation, in that those firms who have embraced ATE seem to be prospering. However, a firm should not stop at gaining access to ATE with one insurer. Not every policy available now or in the future will be the same. Forward-thinking firms should search for the best deal possible now, whether or not they themselves are willing to look at CFAs, so that they have the optimum package that the market has to offer every year, whatever that may be.

The ATE market is too fast-moving and bespoke to assume that a certain subset of cases will not receive offers at all, since each case will be considered on its own merits. Moreover, if insurance is not originally available from the market, this may well not be the case six months later. Many cases that seem destined to win are left uninsured only for circumstances to change and for the solicitor to be left with a frantic and often fruitless scramble for insurance at the last minute. Experience shows that insurers show very little sympathy to solicitors when this happens.

The most ambitious firms should talk to an expert about creating their own bespoke delegated authority facility, as there can be no greater certainty for the client or for the firm than a decision process led by the solicitor running the case. So, despite understandable scepticism from some quarters, the ATE 'experiment' is succeeding, and now that firms are adopting it across the litigation spectrum, it certainly looks as though it is here to stay.

CHAPTER 12

Non-CFA litigation funding

12.1 INTRODUCTION

The effect of Parliament's call for 'access to justice' in the Courts and Legal Services Act 1990 has been felt in other non-CFA areas relevant to the contemporary funding of litigation. While this is primarily a book about CFAs, it is not useful to examine them in pure isolation. In this chapter, therefore, there will be a small excursus into other forms of litigation funding (but not the ordinary private retainer or public funding), and some observations about related costs.

As to cost liabilities, in the world of commercial litigation, the question whether a person is willing to fund another's litigation cannot be sensibly separated from a consideration of the circumstances in which that person might end up with a liability to meet the other side's costs. This is for two reasons. It is necessary, therefore, to trespass to some small degree into this territory, and we make little apology for citing extensively from the relatively recent authority of *Dymocks Franchise Systems (NSW) Pty Ltd* v. *Todd and ors* [2004] 1 WLR 2807, which sets out a series of key propositions as to the exercise of the power under the Supreme Court Act 1981, s.51 to award costs against non-parties.

Something will also be said briefly about the risks which solicitors face of having to meet orders for costs, especially since in *Myatt (No.2)* the court has opened up the possibility that solicitors handling CFA cases may have a special vulnerability (contrary, perhaps, to previous authorities) (see **5.5**).

The wider possibilities for non-CFA funding machineries are likely to result in steady, if not rapid, growth over the next decade. Indeed, the Civil Justice Council has made recommendations as to the regulation of litigation support funding by way of Court Rules, and has also recommended that research should be undertaken into the use of contingency fees in group actions as a means of obtaining access to justice (see 'Improved Access to Justice – Funding Options & Proportionate Costs' (June 2007)).

210

12.2   CONTRIBUTING TO A LITIGANT'S FUNDING

Introduction

The extent to which disapproval as to the funding of litigation will be expressed by the courts has changed significantly during roughly the last 10 years. This change in approach has been felt significantly in the courts' approach to arrangements ostensibly tainted by maintenance and champerty (see **Chapter 1**). The courts' position today is that it will not take a blanket approach where there is a finding of maintenance or champerty, but will analyse the facts to see whether there is any real risk of prejudice to justice. Two significant examples of this approach are *Stocnia Gdanska* v. *Latreefers Inc* [2001] 2 BCLC 116 and *Faryab* v. *Smyth* (unreported, 28 August 1998) (but see also *Abraham* v. *Thompson* [1997] 4 All ER 362).

In *Faryab* an impecunious appellant had been ordered to find £40,000 as security for costs in the Court of Appeal. In order to obtain the money he had offered a 'pyramid package' under the terms of which 'the higher the total investment from any individual member of the consortium the higher the return exponentially'. See Simon Brown LJ:

> The point at which any particular funding agreement, even assuming it is technically champertous, could be said to constitute an abuse of process is itself very far from clear. Many factors are likely to be in play. Amongst them will be these: (1) the terms of the funding agreement between the litigant and his funder; (2) their relationship quite apart from that agreement; (3) whether or not (and if so how and in what circumstances) the litigant proposes to repay the funder; (4) the relationship between the fund provided, the sum (if any) to be repaid and the sum at issue in the action; (5) the precise purpose within the proceedings for which the fund was provided.

Chadwick LJ said:

> It was accepted by this Court in *Abraham v Thompson* that, although the court retains the power to stay proceedings if satisfied that they constitute an abuse of process, the mere fact that the proceedings are being financed by a third party with no interest in the outcome – other than in relation to the prospects of repayment – is not of itself sufficient abuse to invoke the jurisdiction of the court. The court is entitled to protect its own procedures; see *Roache v News Group Newspapers, The Times*, November 23, 1992; but it should be careful not to use that power so as to deny access to justice to a party who has sought to fund his proceedings in a way which may itself become contrary to public policy, unless that which has been done can be seen to amount to an abuse of the court's own process.

The court held that it was 'required to consider in the light of the facts in each case whether its process is affected or threatened by the agreement for the division of spoils', holding that although there might well be cases where the court could see that there is 'some element of trafficking in litigation'.

In the *Stocnia Gdanska* case, shipbrokers agreed to fund litigation by a shipyard against purchasers who failed to make instalment payments for three vessels. In exchange for providing the funding, the brokers agreed to accept 55 per cent of the proceeds of the litigation. Morritt LJ held that:

> the fact that a funding agreement may be against public policy and therefore unenforceable as between the parties to it is by itself no reason for regarding the proceedings to which it relates or their conduct as an abuse.

See also the judgment of Judge Seymour QC in *Dal-Sterling Group plc* v. *WSP South & West Ltd* (18 July 2001, unreported) in which he stated:

> It is no longer the case that the mere fact that a stranger to litigation provides financial or material support to a party in return for a share in the proceeds of the action means that inevitably the agreement under which this is done must be champertous.

See further *Stuart James Mansell* v. *Robert Owen Robinson* [2007] EWHC 101 (QB) (30 January 2007, Underhill J). These cases all show that the courts are willing to be increasingly creative as to the methods of funding employed to fund litigation.

Pure funders

In *Hamilton* v. *Fayed (No. 2)* [2003] QB 1175 the Court of Appeal held that the successful defendant in a libel action could not recover his costs from funders who had no interest in the outcome of proceedings but who were content to provide a 'fighting fund'. This was on the grounds of 'of a trend in public policy towards funding access to justice to the courts' (Hale LJ at para.81 commenting that 'I would not be so presumptuous as to assume that access to the courts and access to justice were synonymous, although of course it is always the courts' aim to achieve both procedural and substantive justice'). (Costs issues as against pure funders are considered below at **12.3.**)

Litigation support funding

A very significant vehicle providing litigation funding is achieved by contractual arrangements whereby experts pay for and provide advice to independent experts in exchange for a share of the damages (see *Regina (Factortame Ltd and others)* v. *Secretary of State for Transport, Local Government and the Regions (No.8)* [2002] 3 WLR 1104 and *Arkin* v. *Bochard Lines Ltd* 1 WLR

3055 and the wider principles set out in the Australian cases of *Campbells Cash and Carry Pty Ltd* v. *Fostif Pty Ltd* [2006] HCA 41 and *Mobil Oil Australia Pty Ltd* v. *Trendlen Pty Ltd* [2006] HCA 42). In exchange for the services rendered by the funder (who also bears the costs of the experts to be engaged), the funder takes a proportion of the damages. The percentage which constitutes profit is relatively modest, much of the percentage agreed being required to fund the expenses. The amounts at stake, however, have been very considerable and the overall expert costs are well in excess of the costs of the lawyers.

The contracts in these two cases share common themes. The first is the provision by the funder of back-up services for use by experts who are going to be relied on at trial. By providing these services as back-up arrangements, the experts who are going to be called are able to avoid the allegation that their expert status has been compromised by any contingent funding arrangement.

Secondly, while the funder is entitled to be fully informed as to the nature of the conduct of the litigation and all the decisions to be taken up to trial, the actual decisions which are taken are contractually ring-fenced so that the funder does not have a part in the final say as to what is going to be done. That is typically left to leading counsel, who in effect is required to adjudicate on the competing options.

Thirdly, the amount of the proceeds on success are limited.

The courts have not objected to these funding arrangements on grounds of champerty. What they have now done is to hold that if a funding arrangement like this is in place, then the funder must expect to have to meet some part of the losing party's costs if the litigation is unsuccessful. The overall cost is reported to have been some £6 million, but the funder was only ordered to pay the value of its own stake, being some £1.3 million. As a result of the costs order the Court of Appeal recognised that commercial funders may seek to increase their share of the damages in order to cover the risks that they may have to pay a losing party's costs. To what extent a higher rate of return puts the litigation at risk of complaints remains to be seen in other cases.

In *The Eurasian Dream* [2002] 2 Lloyd's Rep 692, charges for very extensive litigation support services went beyond mere expert support. The provider of the services committed itself, for instance, to 'attending conference with counsel . . . reviewing fire experts' further comments and request for further information in relation to the Defence and the response to the request for further information'. The provider agreed to render its services in exchange for a cut of the damages, but the percentage fee it earned was recoverable in costs from the paying party without being tainted by champerty.

What all of these cases show is that we are getting nearer to a position where a commercial funder may be able to take on an assignment of a pure cause of action (see below). It might initially take a brave funder, but there are reasons to suppose that in a properly drafted funding arrangement, a pure assignee who is paying for the litigation in exchange for a reasonable and proportionate share of any damages may be able to find a niche in the funding market.

In June 2007 the Civil Justice Council published a paper 'The Future Funding of Litigation – Alternative Funding Strategies' which included as recommendation 3 the recommendation that Rules of Court be established to provide a proper framework for these type of funding arrangements. The CJC was particularly concerned with the usefulness of such arrangements in the context of group actions.

Assigning the right to litigate

There is a serious practical difficulty about the application of the law of champerty outside the area of solicitors' retainers, and that is the question when it is possible to assign the fruits of litigation or the right to litigate. This book is certainly not the forum for a detailed account of such circumstances, but it represents an important qualification to the rule against champerty, and in future years this may represent an avenue where a funder who has no interest in the particular litigation may ultimately be able to acquire the litigation itself and risk being paid by way of a share of any damages. As with litigation support funders (see above) there would have to be adequate safeguards to protect the course and conduct of any litigation itself. If a right to litigate can be assigned under current rules, however, then it may be possible to assign the matter to someone who can afford to pursue the proceedings.

The best starting point for those needing advice in this area as currently interpreted and as currently applied is perhaps the judgment of Lloyd LJ in *Brownton Ltd and others* v. *Edward Moore Inbucon Ltd* [1985] 3 All ER 499, and it seems churlish, having ventured even a little way into the law concerning maintenance and champerty (see **Chapter 1**), not to set out this key decision. If a right to litigate can be assigned then it can be assigned to a party with the means to fund an action.

At 505–6 Lloyd LJ summarised the difficulty in assigning a right to litigate and the manner in which it has come to be faced by more modern courts:

> In his judgment in the Court of Appeal in *Trendtex Trading Corp v Crédit Suisse* [1980] 3 All ER 721 at 749, 754, [1980] QB 629 at 664, 670 Oliver LJ referred to the 'maze of contradictory cases and oversubtle distinctions' which have bedevilled this branch of the law, and to the confusion which has sometimes resulted. No single phrase has given rise to greater confusion than the rule, described by Lord Roskill in the House of Lords as still being a fundamental principle of our law, that you cannot assign a 'bare right to litigate' (see [1981] 3 All ER 520 at 531, [1982] AC 697 at 703).
>
> What is meant by a bare right to litigate? In origin it meant no more and no less than a right to claim damages divorced from any transfer of property. In *Glegg v Bromley* [1912] 3 KB 474 at 490, [1911–13] All ER Rep 1138 at 1146 Parker J. said:

The question was whether the subject-matter of the assignment was, in the view of the court, property with an incidental remedy for its recovery, or was a bare right to bring an action either at law or in equity.

The reason why equity refused to give effect to the assignment of such a right was always said to be that it savoured of maintenance. But, as the boundaries of unlawful maintenance have been pushed back, starting with *Plating Co v Farquharson* (1881) 17 Ch D 49 ... in the nineteenth century, continuing through *British Cash and Parcel Conveyors Ltd v Lamson Store Service Co Ltd* [1908] 1 KB 1006 ... at the beginning of this century and culminating in the judgment of Danckwerts J and the Court of Appeal in *Martell v Consett Iron Co Ltd* ... [1955] Ch 363; *affd* [1955] 1 All ER 481, [1955] Ch 363, CA, to which I would add the decision of the Court of Appeal, and in particular the judgment of Danckwerts LJ, in *Hill v Archbold* ... [1968] 1 QB 686, so, it seems to me, the prohibition on the assignment of a bare right to litigate has become more strictly confined. It is still a fundamental principle of our law, as stated by Lord Roskill; but within much narrower limits.

The judge went on to offer this summary as to the correct approach to be followed (at 508):

I now attempt to summarise in my own words the principles established by the House of Lords in *Trendtex*, as follows. (i) Maintenance is justified, inter alia, if the maintainer has a genuine commercial interest in the result of the litigation. (ii) There is no difference between the interest required to justify maintenance of an action and the interest required to justify the taking of a share in the proceeds, or the interest required to support an out-and-out assignment. (iii) A bare right to litigate, the assignment of which is still prohibited, is a cause of action, whether in tort or contract, in the outcome of which the assignee has no genuine commercial interest. (iv) In judging whether the assignee has a genuine commercial interest for the purpose of (i) to (iii) above, you must look at the transaction as a whole. (v) If an assignee has a genuine commercial interest in enforcing the cause of action it is not fatal that the assignee may make a profit out of the assignment. (vi) It is an open question whether, if the assignee does make such a profit, he is answerable to the assignor for the difference.

12.3 NON-PARTY COSTS ORDERS

The Supreme Court Act 1981, s.51(1) simply states:

(1) Subject to the provisions of this or any other Act and to rules of court, the costs of and incidental to all proceedings in the civil division of the Court of Appeal and in the High Court, including the administration of estates and trusts, shall be in the discretion of the court, and the court shall have full power to determine by whom and to what extent the costs are to be paid.

Ever since *Aiden Shipping* v. *Interbulk (No.2)* [1986] AC 965 the courts have been flexing their muscles more and more when exercising the wide jurisdiction under this subsection. The Court of Appeal in that case had allowed an appeal in which they held that they were bound by previous decisions of the court to hold that an order for costs could only be made against a party to the proceedings in question. The House of Lords held that:

> the discretionary power to award costs in section 51(1) of the Supreme Court Act 1981 was expressed in wide terms, leaving it to the rule-making authority, if it saw fit to do so, to control its exercise by rules of court and to the appellate courts to establish principles for its exercise; and that there was no justification for implying a limitation to the effect that costs could only be ordered to be paid by parties to the proceedings.

In *Dymocks Franchise Systems (NSW) Pty Ltd* v. *Todd & ors* [2004] 1 WLR 2807 the Privy Council asked itself the question (at para.24): 'What, then, are the principles by which the discretion to order costs to be paid by a non-party is to be exercised'. The answer provided is as follows (para.25):

(1) Although costs orders against non-parties are to be regarded as 'exceptional', exceptional in this context means no more than outside the ordinary run of cases where parties pursue or defend claims for their own benefit and at their own expense. The ultimate question in any such 'exceptional' case is whether in all the circumstances it is just to make the order. It must be recognised that this is inevitably to some extent a fact-specific jurisdiction and that there will often be a number of different considerations in play, some militating in favour of an order, some against.

(2) Generally speaking the discretion will not be exercised against 'pure funders', described in para 40 of *Hamilton v Al Fayed (No 2)* [2003] QB 1175, 1194 as 'those with no personal interest in the litigation, who do not stand to benefit from it, are not funding it as a matter of business, and in no way seek to control its course'. In their case the court's usual approach is to give priority to the public interest in the funded party getting access to justice over that of the successful unfunded party recovering his costs and so not having to bear the expense of vindicating his rights.

(3) Where, however, the non-party not merely funds the proceedings but substantially also controls or at any rate is to benefit from them, justice will ordinarily require that, if the proceedings fail, he will pay the successful party's costs. The non-party in these cases is not so much facilitating access to justice by the party funded as himself gaining access to justice for his own purposes. He himself is 'the real party' to the litigation, a concept repeatedly invoked throughout the jurisprudence-see, for example, the judgments of the High Court of Australia in the *Knight* case 174 CLR 178 and Millett LJ's judgment in *Metalloy Supplies Ltd v MA (UK) Ltd* [1997] 1 WLR 1613. Consistently with this approach, Phillips LJ described the non-party underwriters in *T G A Chapman Ltd v Christopher* [1998] 1 WLR 12, 22 as 'the defendants in all but name'. Nor, indeed, is it necessary that the non-party be 'the only real party' to the litigation in the sense explained in the *Knight* case, provided that he is 'a real party in . . . very important and critical respects': see *Arundel Chiropractic Centre Pty Ltd v Deputy Comr of Taxation* (2001) 179 ALR 406, 414, referred to in the *Kebaro* case [2003] FCAFC 5, at [96], [103] and [111]. Some reflection of this concept of 'the real party' is to be found in CPR

216

r 25.13(2)(f) which allows a security for costs order to be made where 'the claimant is acting as a nominal claimant'.

(4) Perhaps the most difficult cases are those in which non-parties fund receivers or liquidators (or, indeed, financially insecure companies generally) in litigation designed to advance the funder's own financial interests. . . . Generally speaking, where a non-party promotes and funds proceedings by an insolvent company solely or substantially for his own financial benefit, he should be liable for the costs if his claim or defence or appeal fails. . . . That is not to say that orders will invariably be made in such cases, particularly, say, where the non-party is himself a director or liquidator who can realistically be regarded as acting rather in the interests of the company (and more especially its shareholders and creditors) than in his own interests.

See also the guidance given in *Chapman* v. *Christopher* [1998] 1 WLR 12 (at 20) and the wider observations by Morritt LJ in *Globe Equities Ltd* v. *Globe Legal Services Ltd* [1999] BLR 232.

Practice

The following costs rule in the Civil Procedure Rules (CPR) applies in respect of s.51 applications:

48.2 (1) Where the court is considering whether to exercise its power under section 51 of the Supreme Court Act 1981 (costs are in the discretion of the court) to make a costs order in favour of or against a person who is not a party to proceedings –

(a) that person must be added as a party to the proceedings for the purposes of costs only; and
(b) he must be given a reasonable opportunity to attend a hearing at which the court will consider the matter further.

Insurers

In the case of insurance-backed litigation the courts have considered both the principles of access and of motive and conduct in determining whether an insurer should meet the successful party's costs beyond the limits of the insurer's indemnity. Thus in *Murphy* v. *Young's Brewery* [1997] 1 WLR 1591 such an application failed, the Court of Appeal deciding that legal expense insurance was in the public interest and that the insurer had not had a direct commercial interest in the outcome. In *Chapman Ltd* v. *Christopher* [1998] 1 WLR 12, on the other hand, the insurers were ordered to pay the successful party's costs since they had funded and conducted the unsuccessful litigation for their own interest. See also *Citibank* v. *Excess Insurance Co Ltd* [1999] CLC 120.

Company directors

In *Secretary of State for Trade & Industry v. Aurum Marketing* 20 July 2002 the criteria set out in (4) of *Dymocks* were satisfied in the case of a company director who had perpetrated a swindle through his company. He had prolonged the company's litigation solely because he considered that it was in his interest to do so. He was not able to escape the costs of the action and was bound by the findings of fact which had been made against the company.

12.4 COSTS ORDERS AGAINST SOLICITORS

A s.51 order may be made against solicitors if the criteria in *Dymocks* are satisfied. A recent example (at the time of writing) is the case of *Myatt* v. *NCB* [2007] 1 WLR 1559 which was an appeal to the Court of Appeal prosecuted by solicitors who had represented clients whose CFAs had been declared unenforceable. For the purposes of the appeal the clients did not have ATE insurance (see **5.5**). *Globe Equities Limited* v. *Globe Legal Services Limited* [1999] BLR 232 should also be noted, in which the firm of solicitors had known that it was unlikely that the client was unlikely to be able to pay either its own or the other side's costs.

A more common basis is the jurisdiction to make a wasted costs order under Courts and Legal Services Act 1990, s.51(6), (7). The procedure to be followed is set out in CPR rule 48.7 and section 53 of the Costs Practice Direction. Section 51(7)(b) requires a judge to be satisfied that it would be 'unreasonable to expect [the aggrieved] party to pay' the wasted costs, while s.53.4(3) states that 'it [must be] just in all the circumstances to order him to compensate that party for the whole or part of those costs'.

These ingredients were examined in *Ridehalgh's* case:

> 'Improper' means what it has been understood to mean in this context for at least half a century. The adjective covers, but is not confined to, conduct which would ordinarily be held to justify disbarment, striking off, suspension from practice or other serious professional penalty. It covers any significant breach of a substantial duty imposed by a relevant code of professional conduct. But it is not in our judgment limited to that. Conduct which would be regarded as improper according to the consensus of professional (including judicial) opinion can be fairly stigmatised as such whether or not it violates the letter of a professional code.
>
> 'Unreasonable' also means what it has been understood to mean in this context for at least half a century. The expression aptly describes conduct which is vexatious, designed to harass the other side rather than advance the resolution of the case, and it makes no difference that the conduct is the product of excessive zeal and not improper motive. But conduct cannot be described as unreasonable simply because it leads in the event to an unsuccessful result or because other more cautious legal representatives would have acted differently. The acid test is whether the conduct permits of a reasonable explanation. If so, the course adopted may be

regarded as optimistic and as reflecting on a practitioner's judgment, but it is not unreasonable.

'Negligent' . . . should be understood in an untechnical way to denote failure to act with the competence reasonably to be expected of ordinary members of the profession.

In adopting an untechnical approach to the meaning of negligence in this context, we would however wish firmly to discountenance any suggestion that an applicant for a wasted costs order under this head need prove anything less than he would have to prove in an action for negligence: 'advice, acts or omissions in the course of their professional work which no member of the profession who was reasonably well-informed and competent would have given or done or omitted to do;' an error 'such as no reasonably well-informed and competent member of that profession could have made:' see *Saif Ali v Sydney Mitchell & Co.* [1980] A.C. 198, 218, 220, per Lord Diplock.

. . . We do not think any sharp differentiation between these expressions is useful or necessary or intended.

Finally, it should be said that the judges in the Supreme Court retain a disciplinary jurisdiction in relation to solicitors where there has been some misconduct. In the exercise of this jurisdiction they have the power to make discretionary orders of compensation. See Lord Atkin in *Myers* v. *Elman* [1940] AC 282, 303: 'the Court is not concerning itself with a breach of duty to the other litigant but with a breach of duty to itself'.

CHAPTER 13

Group litigation orders and cost-capping

13.1 INTRODUCTION

This chapter will briefly refer to some of the rules governing group litigation and the way in which it is funded, and then in a little more detail to cost-capping orders. A short account of the provisions applicable to group litigation orders (GLOs) has been included because multi-party actions are often supported by CFA retainers. They tend to be conducted on behalf of personal injury, travel litigation, consumer or environmental claimants whose claims are individually relatively low in value but which, when put together, can be worth a great deal. CFAs, especially on simplified terms (see **2.8**), enable clients to take proceedings together with relatively little risk. They can be left in the hands of a steering group which is able to liaise directly with the solicitors acting on their behalf. These are currently the type of proceedings we have which are contingency fee-funded 'class actions'.

As to cost-capping orders, these can be made in single actions, so that the heading of this chapter is not intended to suggest that cost-capping is limited to group litigation. At the same time, however, it is acknowledged that some judges have said that cost-capping orders should be the norm in group litigation, notwithstanding it is the handling of the individual cases which tends to cause most expense, and individual cases are normally stayed pending determination of the generic issues. It is because cost-capping orders are customary in group litigation that they have been discussed in this section.

13.2 GROUP LITIGATION

Part III of Civil Procedure Rules (CPR) Part 19 has been in force since 2 May 2000. It was the hope of the Woolf Inquiry that this Part would encourage access to the courts, make the means of pursuing cases 'expeditious, effective and proportionate' and 'achieve a balance between the normal rights of claimants and defendants, to pursue and defend cases individually, and the interests of a group of parties to litigate the action as a whole in an effective manner'. There is a useful editorial introduction on the background to GLOs in the White Book.

GLOs have been prevalent in financial and tax cases, in environmental actions and in PI cases, indeed in any case in which 'common or related issues of fact or law' can be identified (rule 19.10 – a 'group litigation issue'), the effect of a GLO being to bind all of the parties to the litigation (rule 19.12). At the same time it is important to contemplate whether or not other procedures can be adopted to take litigation forward. Sir Michael Turner's decision in *Hobson* v. *AMS Solicitors* (18 May 2006) is a resounding attack against an inappropriate application for a GLO. His criticisms include findings that there were alternative means of adjudicating the claims; no group litigation issue had been properly identified; claims were not common; parties should have been joined who had not been; and further that there was a lack of certainty about any ATE protection said to be afforded to the defendants.

The procedures relevant to the making of GLOs are clearly set out in CPR Part 19, Part III and 19BPD, and will not be repeated in detail here. An application for a GLO should make it clear that the Law Society MPA panel has been consulted to make sure there are no similar cases, the application should be made to the right level of judge (depending on whether the matter is in the county or High Court), it should identify the managing judge at the local court and describe the register of which the claimant becomes a part. It is a disagreeable feature of the rules in their amended form that each claimant is effectively required to pay an issue fee in order to join the register, although sensible parties will attempt to bypass this requirement if possible (see para.6.1A of 19BPD introduced in October 2002). The requirement adds nothing to the attempt to save expense, and simply adds to costs. The register is generally kept by the claimants' solicitor, and it might have been thought better to require one fee for the GLO application. Some solicitors, where possible, use one claim form to name all the claimants, rounding up the total amount of any compensation thought to be recoverable as the basis for paying one level of fee. There is a question whether this section of the Practice Direction is lawful since it arguably seeks to legislate in a highly contentious area which is otherwise governed by statute (see s.92ff., Courts Act 2003). The observation of Hale LJ in: *Re C: Legal Aid – Preparation of Bill of Costs* Hale LJ are relevant when she says of Practice Directions:

> They are not laid before Parliament or subject to either the negative or positive resolution procedures in Parliament. They go through no democratic process at all, although if approved by the Lord Chancellor he will bear ministerial responsibility for them to Parliament. But there is a difference in principle between delegated legislation which may be scrutinised by Parliament and ministerial executive action. There is no ministerial responsibility for Practice Directions made for the Supreme Court by the Heads of Division. As Professor Jolowicz says, *loc cit*, p.61, 'It is right that the court should retain its power to regulate its own procedure

within the limits set by statutory rules, and to fill in gaps left by those rules; it is wrong that it should have power actually to legislate.'

Section 92 of the 2003 Act contains the provision that 'When including any provision in an order under this section, the Lord Chancellor must have regard to the principle that access to the courts must not be denied' (as well as extensive provisions about consultation) and there must be question whether or not Art.6 of the European Convention is breached by para.6.1A.

Importantly, the Practice Direction (para.11) allows the claimant's representative to publicise the making of a GLO and the relevant cut-off date. Publicity is likely to mean a combination of leafleting within a certain area and advertising in national, local or trade publications. Take-up is anecdotally low. A cut-off date is likely to be about three to six months. Before making the application it is helpful to get the defendant's consent. Indeed a practical defendant will seek to work with the claimants to agree the class and to ensure that those within it are given the opportunity to join to reduce the likelihood of a second wave of claims.

At the core of the GLO is a cost-sharing provision which is now in standard terms. This provides for early leavers and discontinuers and generally enables all the claimants to share their costs.

While the effect of a GLO is to bind the parties, what is the position for a latecomer who misses a cut-off date? Can he commence proceedings? This was the question raised in *Taylor* v. *Nugent Care Society* [2004] 1 WLR 1129. The Court of Appeal decided that a latecomer could indeed commence separate proceedings, but the court hedged this around with so many case management caveats that the latecomer would be unlikely to do anything other than await the outcome of the group litigation. It is worth quoting the headnote:

Held . . . that it was essential for the court to have wide powers to manage litigation involving a substantial number of claimants, in order to deal with that litigation more efficiently and economically than would otherwise be possible; that, therefore, if there was a group litigation order, it was of the greatest importance to support that order appropriately; but that CPR Pt 19, which dealt with group litigation orders, did not give the court power to require a claimant to join a group action and a claimant was perfectly entitled to choose to bring his own individual action instead; that the court could, however, manage the proceedings of such a claimant in a way that took account of the position of those litigants, whether claimants or defendants, who were part of the group action; that those litigants were entitled to have their interests given a higher priority since they were likely to be a numerically large group and they were co-operating with the proper management of the proceedings; that it would not have been possible to bring the claimant's proceedings to an end on the grounds of delay alone and it had been disproportionate to strike out the claim when the court could have taken other steps fairly to protect the defendant's position, in particular, by staying the claim until after completion of the group action, or part of it, and by requiring that the claimant be bound by the generic decisions in the group action; that the court could also have ordered that the defendant, in the event that a costs order was made against it, should not pay costs additional to those that it would have had to pay if the claimant had been part of the group action; and that, accordingly, the claim would be restored but would be stayed until the judge in charge of the group action had considered an application for directions as to its future management.

As to funding, larger firms can afford to run a certain number of these cases on CFA terms since they can afford to fund initial investigations and disbursements, and can wait until the end of proceedings to collect fees (assuming they succeed, that is). LSC Support Funding may be available in the investigative stages. Nevertheless, client funding in such cases is fraught, and the Civil Justice Council's papers 'Improved Access to Justice – Funding Options & Proportionate Costs' (June 2007) includes several recommendations designed to assist. These include a 'SLAS' (Supplementary Legal Aid Scheme) and the possibility of contingency fee arrangements in multi-party actions.

13.3 COST-CAPPING

Background

Although this book will be published significantly after the decision of the Court of Appeal in *Willis* v. *Nicolson* [2007] EWCA Civ 199 (13 March 2007), the bulk of this particular section was written well before that decision became available. It will be apparent from the following paragraphs that the editors have reservations about cost-capping orders in the form in which they are made as of the time of writing. They are entirely judge-made and built on general case-management powers. It is something of an oddity that after extensive industry-wide mediations a way forward was slowly found to fix the costs in the lowest value cases (now in CPR Part 45), but that judges have been content to impose fixed costs limits on cases which were likely to be very expensive without any input from either claimants or defendants, Parliament or the Civil Justice Council. This section of the book reflects the editors' personal view of the merits of cost-capping orders, although we hope that the authorities referred to will be a starting point for a further examination of the extent to which judges have made these orders.

Why have cost-capping applications been popular with judges? This is in part because they are not at all content with the ability of lawyers to do what CPR Part 19 and the access-to-justice agenda expects, which is to bring forward very many low value cases collectively to court at the same time. It is also because, in the early stages, there was very little opposition to these applications. It must further be admitted, however, that there have been some examples where costs have been grossly inflated or incurred, or where parties have no apparent control over their expenditure.

In some cases there may well be a good argument that the making of a costs capping order represents a failure in the ability of a court to manage a case properly. With effective case management at stages of proceedings it should be possible to leave detailed assessment as the safe means of policing unreasonable costs.

To a limited extent the editors feel somewhat vindicated by the Court of Appeal's first foray into cost-capping orders in *Willis*. Whilst the jurisdiction was acknowledged by the court it expressed understanding at the difficulties and delicacies involved in making such orders, and refused to issue guidelines pending deliberation by the Rules Committee.

In these circumstances we have maintained most of our text as it was before *Willis* was decided, although we commence this section with an account of what the Court of Appeal tells us that the law is.

Willis v. *Nicolson* and cost-capping orders

The judgment of the court in *Willis* commences with a succinct statement of the circumstances in which a cost-capping order might be made and the nature and effect of such orders. It is appropriate to reproduce this in full:

> 7. In cases where a Group Litigation Order has been made it is well recognised, first, that excessive costs may be a significant problem; and second that the court must for that reason, amongst others, exercise direct and continuing control over the proceedings. Costs capping, or something equivalent to it, is therefore a familiar exercise in that context. And after some uncertainty as to the exact basis for such an order in an individual case, such as the present, it is now settled that the various weapons of the Civil Procedure Rules give the court ample powers to make an order at any stage of the proceedings: *King v Telegraph Group Ltd* [2005] 1 WLR 2282[85]. The effect of a costs capping order is to advance the process of assessment and limitation of costs from the assessment after trial to an earlier point in the process; and to limit the amount of recoverable costs prospectively and not merely by an exercise conducted after the costs have been incurred. Unless a successful application is made to increase the cap, the party against whom an order has been made cannot recover on final assessment more than the amount of the order. That does not prevent the paying party from attempting on final assessment to reduce that amount, but the Senior Costs Judge indicated to us that his colleagues, having assessed the costs once, would look for good reasons, usually founded in a change of circumstances, before they intervened further.
> 8. Such orders are essentially case-management decisions, depending heavily on the judge's perception of the needs of his case, and general statements about when and in what circumstances a costs capping order should be made can only be general statements.

As to the court's reservations these come in later paragraphs:

> 10. But however attractive costs capping orders may be in theory, in practice they present some formidable problems. . . .

22. To limit the way in which the professionals intend to conduct the case is a delicate matter. As Lindsay J put it at §28 of his judgment in *Weir v Secretary of State for Transport* If there is to be a cap in any case, the party capped is likely to be required to alter its conduct in relation to costs, if that were not part of the intent behind the cap then there would probably be no point in having a cap. The court will be careful before imposing such a restriction, particularly when those restricted are, as in the present case, acting for a claimant who has suffered catastrophic injuries. To conduct the exercise properly the court will need reliable information about, and understanding of, the nature of the particular case and the general demands of that type of litigation.

In the view of the editors, even after *Willis*, the best statement as to the circumstances in which a cost-capping order should be made is that of Keith J in *Sayers* v. *Smithkline Beecham plc* [2004] EWCA 1899, discussed below.

Judicial and legislative discussion relevant to cost-capping: a historical account

When Lord Woolf prepared his Interim Access to Justice Report he hoped that there would be scope for prospective budget setting and fixed recoverable costs. The purpose of a separate paper by Professor Zuckerman entitled 'Devices for Controlling the Cost of Litigation through Costs Taxation' JILT (1996) (1) was to generate a debate on these possibilities.

In the Final Access to Justice Report the Inquiry noted of the Zuckerman paper that it 'occasioned a general outcry from the legal profession' and that its suggested restrictions were 'artificial and unworkable' (para.17).

Chapter 7 of the Final Report reflects the importance of costs as seen by the Inquiry. The Inquiry intended by its Recommendations to achieve the following (para.5):

(a) reduce the scale of costs by controlling what is required of the parties in the conduct of proceedings;
(b) make the amount of costs more predictable;
(c) make costs more proportionate to the nature of the dispute;
(d) make the courts' powers to make orders as to costs a more effective incentive for responsible behaviour and a more compelling deterrent against unreasonable behaviour;
(e) provide litigants with more information as to costs so that they can exercise greater control of the expenses which are incurred by their lawyers on their behalf.

So far as any direct impact on costs was concerned, the inquiry considered its objectives achieved by the creation of the small claims and fast tracks (para.6). It was in the lowest value claims that costs were most disproportionate (para.13). Subsequently, the Rules Committee has sanctioned further developments in the rules governing fixed predictable costs (CPR Part 45), the CPR being introduced by way of statutory instrument and therefore by Parliament.

In the multi-track, however, the inquiry made no recommendations which aimed directly at controlling or fettering recoverable costs. It is clear that it considered that its objectives were to be achieved by the use of procedural directions by judges, allied to the use of costs estimates (paras.7, 20–2, 32–4). Para.33 is important:

> Estimates need not go into detail and would therefore not disclose confidential information which might be of tactical value to an opponent. They would fall short of the radical proposals set out by Adrian Zuckerman in the issues paper. The estimates would be indications to help the procedural judge decide the best course of action rather than budgets which limited what parties could recover. My other recommendations need to be 'bedded down' before proceeding further in this direction on costs.

In *Solutia* v. *Griffiths* [2001] EWCA Civ 736, [2001] Costs LR 247 (26 April 2001) Staughton LJ and Mance LJ made brief *obiter* comments in what were apparently *ex tempore* judgments about the need to control costs so that they were proportionate by the exercise of case management powers and by the scrutiny of costs estimates.

AB v. *Leeds Teaching Hospitals NHS Trust* [2003] 3 Costs LR 405 ('NOGL') was decided by Gage J on 9 May 2003 and *Various Ledward Claimants* v. *Kent & Medway HA* [2004] 1 Costs LR 101 by Hallett J on 3 November 2003. In these cases the claimants concurred, or at least they did not resist, the making of the costs-capping orders. They could be argued to be of somewhat limited assistance in determining the circumstances in which cost-capping orders should be made and why they should be made, although they have gained widespread acceptance.

Smart v. *East Cheshire NHS Trust* [2004] 1 Costs LR 124 ('Smart') was decided by Gage J on 26 November 2003. This concerned an application for a cost-capping order in an individual case.

In *Leigh* v. *Michelin Tyre plc* [2004] 1 WLR 846 (8 December 2003) the Court of Appeal emphasised the importance of accurate costs estimates as a means (1) of keeping the parties informed about their potential liabilities and (2) enabling the court to decide what orders to make about case management directions (paras.15, 17, 28).

Sayers v. *Smithkline Beecham plc* [2004] EWCA 1899, a contested application for a cost-capping order (albeit a small part of the issues before the court), was decided by Keith J on 30 July 2004. He held, in dismissing the application, that (para.22):

> The power to make cost-capping orders is now recognised, despite the absence in the Civil Procedure Rules of an express power to do so. The exercise of that power

in group litigation was considered by Gage J. in *A B v Leeds Teaching Hospitals NHS Trust* [2003] EWHC 1034. Without wishing to lay down a hard and fast rule, it seems to me that a prospective order limiting the amount of costs which one party to group litigation may recover from another party should only be contemplated where there are grounds for believing that a party may incur excessive legal costs, i.e. costs which are not justified by the scale of the litigation or the complexity of the issues which it raises, or which are disproportionate to the sums of money at stake, and where the risk that excessive legal costs are being incurred unnecessarily will not be picked up by the court when exercising case management functions or when conducting a detailed assessment of the costs after the trial. . . . Cost-capping is a relatively dramatic course to take, and it will only be ordered on cogent evidence.

In January 2004 Professor Peysner published 'Predictability and Budgeting', CJQ vol.23:15, which recommended in its conclusions that budgeting 'could well be a suitable pilot project for some complex multi-track cases in one or more courts' (at 37). This was the subject of a Civil Justice Council consultation exercise in March 2004.

More recently the CJC produced its paper 'Improved Access to Justice – Funding Options and Proportionate Costs (Report and Recommendations) (August 2005)', the conclusion of a review commenced in 2001 (see pp.21–7). This made the recommendation that in multi-track cases where the value exceeds £1 million the parties should have to present budgets which should be 'supervised by the court at appropriate stages to ensure compliance with the proportionality provisions of the overriding objective of the CPR' (Recommendation 7).

There have been additional consultation documents not referred to above (see for instance the references in the CJC, August 2005, p.52).

The dangers of cost-capping; when such an order is appropriate

In *Sayers* Keith J described a cost-capping order as 'dramatic', and there are numerous dangers in making an order of the open-ended type as made in both *NOGL* and *Ledward*.

First, it is simply impossible to give costs estimates from the date of a cost-cap hearing all the way through to the end of litigation which have the same reliability as costs estimates provided to cover a relatively short period of case management. An open-ended order cannot accommodate the unpredictable.

Secondly, a costs-cap order makes no allowance for the possibility that more than proportionate costs may still be reasonable because they are necessary as a result of a defendant's action.

Thirdly, such an order does not satisfactorily accommodate the possible consequences of Part 36 in the event of success by a claimant (namely an award of indemnity costs).

Further, the process of estimation is likely to result in a defendant obtaining an unacceptable tactical advantage.

Costs-capping orders applications represent satellite litigation on a gross scale. They have become hugely expensive, distract from the substantive litigation to the detriment of the parties and take up court resources.

There are some dangers for a defendant. If a global cap is reached and the solicitor's costs turn out to be lower than the cap, it is possible that the defendant will not reap the benefit of the saving.

A cap on both parties

Where a defendant is not offering to have his costs capped a court should be very slow to make a cost-capping order. The dangers of putting the defendant at a tactical advantage are acute. He will have secured a prospective cap, and has the possibility of a retrospective attack on the level of costs at a detailed assessment. He is in a position to influence the amount of costs which the claimant may spend without fear of being subject to any limitation himself. It could be said that a review clause is not sufficient protection, but an additional hurdle with its own litigation risks (not the least of which is the highly discretionary nature of costs orders).

Cost-capping as a route to predictable or fixed costs

The courts should, in the editors' view, be reluctant to make a costs-capping order, since such an order is in reality the application of a form of predictable or fixed-cost regime, a regime which has yet to be sanctioned by Parliament or the Rules Committee despite various consultation processes over the years. Indeed from a claimant's point of view a cost-capping order is more draconian in its effect because a defendant retains a right to challenge the costs at a detailed assessment. The cap acts a ceiling on the costs.

When should a cost cap be made?

When, then, should a cost-capping order be made? The thrust of the Woolf Final Report, of *Solutia* and of *Leigh*, and also of the CJC August 2005 Report is that a court should be able to control costs by the exercise of its procedural powers in the light of effective estimates of costs provided by parties. The costs rules are themselves 'redolent of proportionality' and represent a further and well-tested method of controlling costs at the end of litigation. The process of assessment is the ordinary and preferable way of controlling disproportionate costs. At that stage the court has access to all the information and the outcome of the litigation is known.

It is suggested that an open-ended cost-capping order is a very blunt tool and can be punitive in nature. After all, it is to be employed, according to many authorities, when the evidence is that the costs are spiralling out of control. It is a legitimate sanction to be employed by the court where the court finally has no alternative but to step in and provide (with the assistance of the parties) its own estimates of likely costs when determining what procedural orders should be made. It is also a legitimate sanction where estimates of costs are misrepresented, since the failure to provide such estimates can be considered prejudicial to a defendant. The prejudice arises out of the inability of the defendant in such circumstances to judge how to react to the claim, in particular whether it should settle the matter.

The reasoning of Keith J in *Sayers* is perhaps to be preferred as the test of when a cost-capping order is appropriate. In that case the judge asked whether:

> the risk that excessive legal costs are being incurred unnecessarily will not be picked up by the court when exercising case management functions or when conducting a detailed assessment of the costs after the trial.

If effective procedural directions can be given from time to time in the light of reliable estimates and if a solicitor's figures in the material put before the court can be relied upon at a procedural hearing, then an open-ended cost-capping order is, in our view, not the correct method of case management. It is, as the authorities themselves suggest, too 'broad brush' an approach.

This suggestion is consistent with both Lord Woolf's proposals and those of the CJC in 2005. See in particular:

Woolf Inquiry Final Report, para.57:

> My general proposals for information on costs to be made available at every stage when the managing judge is involved are all the more important in relation to multi-party actions, where many claimants will be legally aided and have no direct control over costs and where costs can escalate dramatically. At every stage in the management of the MPS the judge should consider, with the help of the parties, the potential impact on costs of the directions that are contemplated, and whether these are justified in relation to what is at issue. Parties and their legal representatives, as in other cases on the multi-track, should provide information on costs already incurred and be prepared to estimate the cost of proposed further work. It has been suggested that such examination should occur at intervals of three months. That must be for the managing judge to determine in each individual case.

Woolf Inquiry Final Report, para.75:

> I am recommending generally that costs should be actively considered by the judge throughout the case and that, if appropriate, a Taxing Master should also be involved throughout. Because of this continuing involvement, they will have a store of knowledge about the case. That involvement at the taxing stage will be invaluable. Moreover, if the lawyers know that the judge and his team managing the case may have an influence on their remuneration, this is likely to act as a strong incentive to proper and reasonable behaviour on their part.

CJC August 2005, Recommendation 7:

> In multi track cases where the value exceeds £1 million, in all group actions and in other complex proceedings there should be a rebuttable presumption requiring the parties to present budgets, supervised by the Court at appropriate stages to ensure compliance with the proportionality provisions of the overriding objective of the CPR.

The expense of periodic case management conferences on the suggested model is small compared with a one-off cost-capping hearing and the possibility of future variations under a review clause.

A cost-capping order, we suggest, should never be made as a matter of course, even where there is a GLO in place. Sir Christopher Staughton was surely correct in *Solutia* when he stated (para.30): 'I would hope that in [group litigation] cases more control will be exercised by way of case management than apparently has been in the past'. In huge litigation, such as COPD and VWF, there are periodic CMCs every year in which the case is carefully managed.

Cost-capping and CFAs

The additional concern expressed by the Woolf Inquiry that costs must be controlled for the protection of a solicitor's own clients surely has limited relevance under a CFA arrangement where the client is at no exposure as to costs. (This is the target of what is, it is respectfully submitted, Master Hurst's inappropriate comment at para.51 of the Beach Club litigation (*Various Claimants* v. *TUI UK Ltd & Ors* (11 August 2005, unreported)) when he said that the litigation was 'being used to generate excessive and unreasonable costs'. The comment was inappropriate because it runs counter to Parliament's aims in promoting the right to litigate under the access-to-justice banner.)

Cost-capping where public bodies are involved in the litigation

Both the *NOGL* and *Ledward* cases were claims made against publicly funded organisations, namely NHS Trusts, a particularly important factor for a court to take into consideration when deciding whether or not to make a cost-capping order.

Is s.51 a sufficient vehicle to justify a cost-capping order?

It could be argued that the courts should be slow to use the breadth of Supreme Court Act 1981, s.51 and its wide case management powers to fill any perceived lacunas which need to be examined either by the CJC or Parliament.

The consultation/academic papers referred to above show that there is doubt and debate about what rules should be made to govern predictability in costs. CPR Part 45 has gradually resulted in some new rules after discussion with industry representatives at CJC 'big tent' mediations. The CJC August 2005 paper shows that further consultation and consideration is contemplated. The CJC has considered budgeting so long as it applies to both parties and so long as it allows the budget to be set incrementally. See at 27 (top):

> Budgets, which should apply to both parties to an action, could be agreed by stages as the proceedings progress or imposed by the court if no agreement is possible, with liberty to the parties to apply should there be a change in the circumstances on which the budget was based. The budget should set a cap for each step of the litigation and thus the budget may develop as the action proceeds.

The CJC's proposals are currently no more than proposals and recommendations.

Courts should perhaps also take cognisance of the fact that MPAs of this nature are considered by Parliament to be a positive benefit of the Access to Justice Act 1999 regime. See para.2(a), Woolf Inquiry Final Report (reproduced verbatim in the White Book). However, procedures for the effective management of MPAs, especially where the size of some individual claims are small, still faces considerable difficulties, and there are likely to be developments (see the CJC August 2005 paper) which are best made through the CJC or Parliament after wide consultation between interested parties.

In the absence of a legislative or rules committee solution to any current lacunas, courts might surely think that they should be slow to try to take it upon themselves to fill what it may perceive to be gaps. This was the view of the Court of Appeal in *Willis* v. *Nicholson* [2007] EWCA Civ 199.

A review clause

A review clause is generally introduced into a cost-capping order to allow the expenditure limit to be reconsidered. However, there is a question whether or not it is a sufficiently mitigating factor which can relieve the potential injustices brought about by the imposition of a costs cap. It will certainly result in extra expenditure if it has to be used. It can be argued that the proper inference to be drawn from the perceived need for a review clause (which must be included into any order) is that the court would be managing the case better by periodic case management meetings at intervals considered appropriate by the judge. By this course the litigation can be justly accommodated and managed in accordance with the overriding objective as it develops.

Retrospective capping

A retrospective cost cap has never been made, although some judges have suggested obiter that it might be possible. In *Henry* v. *BBC* the judge held that there is 'ample authority that cost-capping orders should invariably operate prospectively, not retrospectively' (para.39), and in *Willis* it was said (para.22) that:

> both for reasons of fairness and for reasons of practicality a cap cannot be imposed retrospectively.

It seems unlikely that s.51 or the case management powers available under the CPR should entitle a court to make a retrospective order.

13.4   ATE

It should be noted that it is in cost-capping circumstances that courts have permitted inquiries into the adequacy of ATE insurance. See the decisions in *Hobson* and *Henry*.

Appendices

1   STATUTES (EXTRACTS)

Courts and Legal Services Act 1990, ss.17(1), 58, 58A, 58B, 119(1)
Access to Justice Act 1999, ss.29–31

2   STATUTORY INSTRUMENTS (EXTRACTS)

Conditional Fee Agreements Order 1995, SI 1995/1674 [revoked]
Conditional Fee Agreements Regulations 1995, SI 1995/1675 [revoked]
Conditional Fee Agreements Order 1998, SI 1998/1860 [revoked]
Conditional Fee Agreements Regulations 2000, SI 2000/692 [revoked]
Access to Justice (Membership Organisations) Regulations 2000, SI 2000/693
[revoked]
Conditional Fee Agreements Order 2000, SI 2000/823
Collective Conditional Fee Agreements Regulations 2000, SI 2000/2988 [revoked]
Conditional Fee Agreements (Revocation) Regulations 2005, SI 2005/2305

3   CIVIL PROCEDURE RULES 1998, SI 1998/3132 (EXTRACTS)

CPR Part 43: rules 43.2(1)(a), (k), (l), (m), (n), (o), 43.2(3)
CPR Part 44: rules 44.3(8), 44.3A, 44.3B, 44.5, 44.7, 44.12A, 44.15, 44.16
CPR Part 47: 47.1, 47.10

4   COSTS PRACTICE DIRECTION (EXTRACTS)

Section 2, paras.8.6, 11.4, 11.5, 11.7–11.11, section 12, para.13.2, paras.14.1, 14.2, section 17, section 19, section 20, para.27.3, paras.32.3–32.7, para.35.7, section 36, paras.40.10, 40.12, 40.14, para.41.1, paras.57.8(1) and 57.9(1)

5   PRACTICE DIRECTION ON PROTOCOLS (EXTRACTS)

Paras.4A.1, 4A.2

6   PRESCRIBED FORMS

N251
N260

Statutes (extracts)

COURTS AND LEGAL SERVICES ACT 1990

*****

17 The statutory objective and the general principle

(1) The general objective of this Part is the development of legal services in England and Wales (and in particular the development of advocacy, litigation, conveyancing and probate services) by making provision for new or better ways of providing such services and a wider choice of persons providing them, while maintaining the proper and efficient administration of justice.

*****

58 Conditional fee agreements

(1) A conditional fee agreement which satisfies all of the conditions applicable to it by virtue of this section shall not be unenforceable by reason only of its being a conditional fee agreement; but (subject to subsection (5)) any other conditional fee agreement shall be unenforceable.

(2) For the purposes of this section and section 58A –

    (a) a conditional fee agreement is an agreement with a person providing advocacy or litigation services which provides for his fees and expenses, or any part of them, to be payable only in specified circumstances; and

    (b) a conditional fee agreement provides for a success fee if it provides for the amount of any fees to which it applies to be increased, in specified circumstances, above the amount which would be payable if it were not payable only in specified circumstances.

(3) The following conditions are applicable to every conditional fee agreement –

    (a) it must be in writing;

    (b) it must not relate to proceedings which cannot be the subject of an enforceable conditional fee agreement; and

    (c) it must comply with such requirements (if any) as may be prescribed by the Lord Chancellor.

(4) The following further conditions are applicable to a conditional fee agreement which provides for a success fee –

(a) it must relate to proceedings of a description specified by order made by the Lord Chancellor;

(b) it must state the percentage by which the amount of the fees which would be payable if it were not a conditional fee agreement is to be increased; and

(c) that percentage must not exceed the percentage specified in relation to the description of proceedings to which the agreement relates by order made by the Lord Chancellor.

(5) If a conditional fee agreement is an agreement to which section 57 of the Solicitors Act 1974 (non-contentious business agreements between solicitor and client) applies, subsection (1) shall not make it unenforceable.

[Section 58 was substituted by the Access to Justice Act 1999, and is in force from 1 April 2000.]

58A   Conditional fee agreements: supplementary

(1) The proceedings which cannot be the subject of an enforceable conditional fee agreement are –

(a) criminal proceedings, apart from proceedings under section 82 of the Environmental Protection Act 1990; and

(b) family proceedings.

(2) In subsection (1) 'family proceedings' means proceedings under any one or more of the following –

(a) the Matrimonial Causes Act 1973;

(b) the Adoption and Children Act 2002;

(c) the Domestic Proceedings and Magistrates' Courts Act 1978;

(d) Part III of the Matrimonial and Family Proceedings Act 1984;

(e) Parts I, II and IV of the Children Act 1989;

(f) Part IV of the Family Law Act 1996;

(fa) Chapter 2 of Part 2 of the Civil Partnership Act 2004 (proceedings for dissolution etc of civil partnership);

(fb) Schedule 5 to the 2004 Act (financial relief in the High Court or a county court etc);

(fc) Schedule 6 to the 2004 Act (financial relief in magistrates' courts etc);

(fd) Schedule 7 to the 2004 Act (financial relief in England and Wales after overseas dissolution etc of a civil partnership); and

(g) the inherent jurisdiction of the High Court in relation to children.

(3) The requirements which the Lord Chancellor may prescribe under section 58(3)(c) –

(a) include requirements for the person providing advocacy or litigation services to have provided prescribed information before the agreement is made; and

(b) may be different for different descriptions of conditional fee agreements (and, in particular, may be different for those which provide for a success fee and those which do not).

(4) In section 58 and this section (and in the definitions of 'advocacy services' and 'litigation services' as they apply for their purposes) 'proceedings' includes any sort of proceedings for resolving disputes (and not just proceedings in a court), whether commenced or contemplated.

(5)   Before making an order under section 58(4), the Lord Chancellor shall consult –

(a)   the designated judges;
(b)   the General Council of the Bar;
(c)   the Law Society; and
(d)   such other bodies as he considers appropriate.

(6)   A costs order made in any proceedings may, subject in the case of court proceedings to rules of court, include provision requiring the payment of any fees payable under a conditional fee agreement which provides for a success fee.

(7)   Rules of court may make provision with respect to the assessment of any costs which include fees payable under a conditional fee agreement (including one which provides for a success fee).

[*Section 58A was inserted by the Access to Justice Act 1999, and is in force from 1 April 2000.*]

58B   Litigation funding agreements

(1)   A litigation funding agreement which satisfies all of the conditions applicable to it by virtue of this section shall not be unenforceable by reason only of its being a litigation funding agreement.

(2)   For the purposes of this section a litigation funding agreement is an agreement under which –

(a)   a person ('the funder') agrees to fund (in whole or in part) the provision of advocacy or litigation services (by someone other than the funder) to another person ('the litigant'); and
(b)   the litigant agrees to pay a sum to the funder in specified circumstances.

(3)   The following conditions are applicable to a litigation funding agreement –

(a)   the funder must be a person, or person of a description, prescribed by the Lord Chancellor;
(b)   the agreement must be in writing;
(c)   the agreement must not relate to proceedings which by virtue of section 58A(1) and (2) cannot be the subject of an enforceable conditional fee agreement or to proceedings of any such description as may be prescribed by the Lord Chancellor;
(d)   the agreement must comply with such requirements (if any) as may be so prescribed;
(e)   the sum to be paid by the litigant must consist of any costs payable to him in respect of the proceedings to which the agreement relates together with an amount calculated by reference to the funder's anticipated expenditure in funding the provision of the services; and
(f)   that amount must not exceed such percentage of that anticipated expenditure as may be prescribed by the Lord Chancellor in relation to proceedings of the description to which the agreement relates.

(4)   Regulations under subsection (3)(a) may require a person to be approved by the Lord Chancellor or by a prescribed person.

(5)   The requirements which the Lord Chancellor may prescribe under subsection (3)(d) –

(a)   include requirements for the funder to have provided prescribed information to the litigant before the agreement is made; and
(b)   may be different for different descriptions of litigation funding agreements.

(6) In this section (and in the definitions of 'advocacy services' and 'litigation services' as they apply for its purposes) 'proceedings' includes any sort of proceedings for resolving disputes (and not just proceedings in a court), whether commenced or contemplated.

(7) Before making regulations under this section, the Lord Chancellor shall consult –

(a) the designated judges;
(b) the General Council of the Bar;
(c) the Law Society; and
(d) such other bodies as he considers appropriate.

(8) A costs order made in any proceedings may, subject in the case of court proceedings to rules of court, include provision requiring the payment of any amount payable under a litigation funding agreement.

(9) Rules of court may make provision with respect to the assessment of any costs which include fees payable under a litigation funding agreement.

[*Section 58B was inserted by the Access to Justice Act 1999 and is not yet in force.*]

*****

119 Interpretation

(1) In this Act –

*****

'advocacy services' means any services which it would be reasonable to expect a person who is exercising, or contemplating exercising, a right of audience in relation to any proceedings, or contemplated proceedings, to provide;

*****

'litigation services' means any services which it would be reasonable to expect a person who is exercising, or contemplating exercising, a right to conduct litigation in relation to any proceedings, or contemplated proceedings, to provide;

*****

'proceedings' means proceedings in any court;

*****

'right of audience' means the right to appear before and address a court including the right to call and examine witnesses;

'right to conduct litigation' means the right –

(a) to issue proceedings before any court; and
(b) to perform any ancillary functions in relation to proceedings (such as entering appearances to actions);

*****

ACCESS TO JUSTICE ACT 1999

*****

Costs

29 Recovery of insurance premiums by way of costs

Where in any proceedings a costs order is made in favour of any party who has taken out an insurance policy against the risk of incurring a liability in those proceedings, the costs payable to him may, subject in the case of court proceedings to rules of court, include costs in respect of the premium of the policy.

30 Recovery where body undertakes to meet costs liabilities

(1) This section applies where a body of a prescribed description undertakes to meet (in accordance with arrangements satisfying prescribed conditions) liabilities which members of the body or other persons who are parties to proceedings may incur to pay the costs of other parties to the proceedings.

(2) If in any of the proceedings a costs order is made in favour of any of the members or other persons, the costs payable to him may, subject to subsection (3) and (in the case of court proceedings) to rules of court, include an additional amount in respect of any provision made by or on behalf of the body in connection with the proceedings against the risk of having to meet such liabilities.

(3) But the additional amount shall not exceed a sum determined in a prescribed manner; and there may, in particular, be prescribed as a manner of determination one which takes into account the likely cost to the member or other person of the premium of an insurance policy against the risk of incurring a liability to pay the costs of other parties to the proceedings.

(4) In this section 'prescribed' means prescribed by regulations made by the Lord Chancellor by statutory instrument; and a statutory instrument containing such regulations shall be subject to annulment in pursuance of a resolution of either House of Parliament.

(5) Regulations under subsection (1) may, in particular, prescribe as a description of body one which is for the time being approved by the Lord Chancellor or by a prescribed person.

31 Rules as to costs

In section 51 of the Supreme Court Act 1981 (costs), in subsection (2) (rules regulating matters relating to costs), insert at the end 'or for securing that the amount awarded to a party in respect of the costs to be paid by him to such representatives is not limited to what would have been payable by him to them if he had not been awarded costs.'

*****

APPENDIX 2

Statutory instruments (extracts)

CONDITIONAL FEE AGREEMENTS ORDER 1995, SI 1995/1674

[This order has been revoked by SI 1998/1860 as from 30 July 1998.]

Whereas a draft of the above Order has been laid before and approved by resolution of each House of Parliament:

Now, therefore, the Lord Chancellor, in exercise of the powers conferred on him by sections 58(4) and (5) and 120 of the Courts and Legal Services Act 1990, having consulted in accordance with section 58(7) of that Act, hereby makes the following Order: –

1 Citation and commencement

This Order may be cited as the Conditional Fee Agreements Order 1995 and shall come into force on the day after the day on which it was made.

2 Specified proceedings

(1) The proceedings specified for the purpose of section 58(4) of the Courts and Legal Services Act 1990 (conditional fee agreements in respect of specified proceedings not to be unenforceable) are the following: –

    (a) proceedings in which there is a claim for damages in respect of personal injuries or in respect of a person's death, and 'personal injuries' includes any disease and any impairment of a person's physical or mental condition;

    (b) proceedings in England and Wales by a company which is being wound up in England and Wales or Scotland;

    (c) proceedings by a company in respect of which an administration order made under Part II of the Insolvency Act 1986 is in force;

    (d) proceedings in England and Wales by a person acting in the capacity of –

        (i) liquidator of a company which is being wound up in England and Wales or Scotland; or

        (iii) trustee of a bankrupt's estate;

    (e) proceedings by a person acting in the capacity of an administrator appointed pursuant to the provisions of Part II of the Insolvency Act 1986;

    (f) proceedings before the European Commission of Human Rights and the European Court of Human Rights established under article 19 of the Convention for the Protection of Human Rights and Fundamental Freedoms opened for signature at Rome on 4th November 1950, ratified by the United Kingdom on 8th March 1951, which came into force on 3rd August 1953,

provided that the client does not have legal aid in respect of the proceedings.

(2) Proceedings specified in paragraph (1) shall be specified proceedings notwithstanding that they are concluded without the commencement of court proceedings.

(3) In paragraphs (1)(b) and (1)(d) 'company' means a company within the meaning of section 735(1) of the Companies Act 1985or a company which may be wound up under Part V of the Insolvency Act 1986.

(4) Where legal aid in respect of the proceedings to which a conditional fee agreement relates is granted after that agreement is entered into the proceedings shall cease to be specified from the date of the grant.

(5) In this article, 'legal aid' means representation under Part IV of the Legal Aid Act 1988·

3 Maximum permitted percentage increase on fees

For the purpose of section 58(5) of the Courts and Legal Services Act 1990 the maximum permitted percentage by which fees may be increased in respect of each description of proceedings specified in article 2 is 100.

CONDITIONAL FEE AGREEMENTS REGULATIONS 1995, SI 1995/1675

[This regulation has been revoked by SI 2000/692 as from 1 April 2000.]

Whereas a draft of the above Regulations has been laid before and approved by resolution of each House of Parliament:

Now, therefore, the Lord Chancellor, in exercise of the powers conferred on him by sections 58(1) and 119 of the Courts and Legal Services Act 1990, hereby makes the following Regulations: –

1 Citation, commencement and interpretation

(1) These Regulations may be cited as the Conditional Fee Agreements Regulations 1995 and shall come into force on the day after the day on which they are made.

(2) In these Regulations –

'agreement', in relation to an agreement between a legal representative and an additional legal representative, includes a retainer;

'legal aid' means representation under Part IV of the Legal Aid Act 1988;

'legal representative' means a person providing advocacy or litigation services.

2 Agreements to comply with prescribed requirements

An agreement shall not be a conditional fee agreement unless it complies with the requirements of the following regulations.

3 Requirements of an agreement

An agreement shall state –

(a) the particular proceedings or parts of them to which it relates (including whether it relates to any counterclaim, appeal or proceedings to enforce a judgment or order);

   (b) the circumstances in which the legal representative's fees and expenses or part of them are payable;

   (c) what, if any, payment is due –

      (i) upon partial failure of the specified circumstances to occur;

      (ii) irrespective of the specified circumstances occurring; and

      (iii) upon termination of the agreement for any reason;

   (d) the amount payable in accordance with sub-paragraphs (b) or (c) above or the method to be used to calculate the amount payable; and in particular whether or not the amount payable is limited by reference to the amount of any damages which may be recovered on behalf of the client.

4 Additional requirements

(1) The agreement shall also state that, immediately before it was entered into, the legal representative drew the client's attention to the matters specified in paragraph (2).

(2) The matters are –

   (a) whether the client might be entitled to legal aid in respect of the proceedings to which the agreement relates, the conditions upon which legal aid is available and the application of those conditions to the client in respect of the proceedings;

   (b) the circumstances in which the client may be liable to pay the fees and expenses of the legal representative in accordance with the agreement;

   (c) the circumstances in which the client may be liable to pay the costs of any other party to the proceedings; and

   (d) the circumstances in which the client may seek taxation of the fees and expenses of the legal representative and the procedure for so doing.

5 Application of regulation 4

Regulation 4 shall not apply to an agreement between a legal representative and an additional legal representative.

6 Form of agreement

An agreement shall be in writing and, except in the case of an agreement between a legal representative and an additional legal representative, shall be signed by the client and the legal representative.

7 Amendment of agreement

Where it is proposed to extend the agreement to cover further proceedings or parts of them regulations 3 to 6 shall apply to the agreement as extended.

CONDITIONAL FEE AGREEMENTS ORDER 1998, SI 1998/1860

[This order has been revoked by SI 2000/823 as from 1 April 2000.]

The Lord Chancellor, in exercise of the powers conferred on him by sections 58(4) and (5) of the Courts and Legal Services Act 1990, having consulted in accordance with section 58(7) of that Act, makes the following Order, a draft of which has been laid before and approved by resolution of each House of Parliament:

1 Citation, commencement and interpretation

(1) This Order may be cited as the Conditional Fee Agreements Order 1998 and shall come into force on the day after the day on which it is made.
(2) In this Order 'the Act' means the Courts and Legal Services Act 1990.

2 Revocation of 1995 Order

The Conditional Fee Agreements Order 1995 is revoked.

3 Specified proceedings

(1) All proceedings are proceedings specified for the purposes of section 58(3) of the Act (conditional fee agreements in respect of specified proceedings not to be unenforceable).
(2) Proceedings specified in paragraph (1) shall be specified proceedings notwithstanding that they are concluded without the commencement of court proceedings.

4 Maximum permitted percentage increase on fees

For the purposes of section 58(5) of the Act the maximum permitted percentage by which fees may be increased in respect of any proceedings designated by article 3 as proceedings specified for the purposes of section 58(3) of the Act is 100%.

CONDITIONAL FEE AGREEMENTS REGULATIONS 2000, SI 2000/692

[*This regulation has been revoked by SI 2005/2305 as from 1 November 2005 except in relation to conditional fee agreements entered into before that date.*]

The Lord Chancellor, in exercise of the powers conferred on him by sections 58(3)(c), 58A(3) and 119 of the Courts and Legal Services Act 1990 and all other powers enabling him hereby makes the following Regulations:

1 Citation, commencement and interpretation

(1) These Regulations may be cited as the Conditional Fee Agreements Regulations 2000.
(2) These Regulations come into force on 1st April 2000.
(3) In these Regulations –

'client' includes, except where the context otherwise requires, a person who

(a) has instructed the legal representative to provide the advocacy or litigation services to which the conditional fee agreement relates, or
(b) is liable to pay the legal representative's fees in respect of those services; and

'legal representative' means the person providing the advocacy or litigation services to which the conditional fee agreement relates.

2 Requirements for contents of conditional fee agreements: general

(1) A conditional fee agreement must specify –

    (a) the particular proceedings or parts of them to which it relates (including whether it relates to any appeal, counterclaim or proceedings to enforce a judgement or order),

    (b) the circumstances in which the legal representative's fees and expenses, or part of them, are payable,

    (c) what payment, if any, is due –

        (i) if those circumstances only partly occur,

        (ii) irrespective of whether those circumstances occur, and

        (iii) on the termination of the agreement for any reason, and

    (d) the amounts which are payable in all the circumstances and cases specified or the method to be used to calculate them and, in particular, whether the amounts are limited by reference to the damages which may be recovered on behalf of the client.

(2) A conditional fee agreement to which regulation 4 applies must contain a statement that the requirements of that regulation which apply in the case of that agreement have been complied with.

3 Requirements for contents of conditional fee agreements providing for success fees

(1) A conditional fee agreement which provides for a success fee –

    (a) must briefly specify the reasons for setting the percentage increase at the level stated in the agreement, and

    (b) must specify how much of the percentage increase, if any, relates to the cost to the legal representative of the postponement of the payment of his fees and expenses.

(2) If the agreement relates to court proceedings, it must provide that where the percentage increase becomes payable as a result of those proceedings, then –

    (a) if –

        (i) any fees subject to the increase are assessed, and

        (ii) the legal representative or the client is required by the court to disclose to the court or any other person the reasons for setting the percentage increase at the level stated in the agreement,

    he may do so,

    (b) if –

        (i) any such fees are assessed, and

        (ii) any amount in respect of the percentage increase is disallowed on the assessment on the ground that the level at which the increase was set was unreasonable in view of facts which were or should have been known to the legal representative at the time it was set,

    that amount ceases to be payable under the agreement, unless the court is satisfied that it should continue to be so payable, and

    (c) if –

        (i) sub-paragraph (b) does not apply, and

        (ii) the legal representative agrees with any person liable as a result of the proceedings to pay fees subject to the percentage increase that a lower amount than the amount payable in accordance with the conditional fee agreement is to be paid instead, the amount payable under the conditional fee agreement in respect of those fees shall be reduced accordingly, unless the court is satisfied that the full amount should continue to be payable under it.

(3) In this regulation 'percentage increase' means the percentage by which the amount of the fees which would be payable if the agreement were not a conditional fee agreement is to be increased under the agreement.

3A Requirements where the client's liability is limited to sums recovered

(1) This regulation applies to a conditional fee agreement under which, except in the circumstances set out in paragraphs (5) and (5A), the client is liable to pay his legal representative's fees and expenses only to the extent that sums are recovered in respect of the relevant proceedings, whether by way of costs or otherwise.

(2) In determining for the purposes of paragraph (1) the circumstances in which a client is liable to pay his legal representative's fees and expenses, no account is to be taken of any obligation to pay costs in respect of the premium of a policy taken out to insure against the risk of incurring a liability in the relevant proceedings.

(3) Regulations 2, 3 and 4 do not apply to a conditional fee agreement to which this regulation applies.

(4) A conditional fee agreement to which this regulation applies must –

  (a) specify –
    (i) the particular proceedings or parts of them to which it relates (including whether it relates to any appeal, counterclaim or proceedings to enforce a judgment or order); and
    (ii) the circumstances in which the legal representative's fees and expenses, or part of them, are payable; and

  (b) if it provides for a success fee –
    (i) briefly specify the reasons for setting the percentage increase at the level stated in the agreement; and
    (ii) provide that if, in court proceedings, the percentage increase becomes payable as a result of those proceedings and the legal representative or the client is ordered to disclose to the court or any other person the reasons for setting the percentage increase at the level stated in the agreement, he may do so.

(5) A conditional fee agreement to which this regulation applies may specify that the client will be liable to pay the legal representative's fees and expenses whether or not sums are recovered in respect of the relevant proceedings, if the client –

  (a) fails to co-operate with the legal representative;
  (b) fails to attend any medical or expert examination or court hearing which the legal representative reasonably requests him to attend;
  (c) fails to give necessary instructions to the legal representative;
  (d) withdraws instructions from the legal representative;
  (e) is an individual who is adjudged bankrupt or enters into an arrangement or a composition with his creditors, or against whom an administration order is made; or
  (f) is a company for which a receiver, administrative receiver or liquidator is appointed.

(5A) A conditional fee agreement to which this regulation applies may specify that, in the event of the client dying in the course of the relevant proceedings, his estate will be liable for the legal representative's fees and expenses, whether or not sums are recovered in respect of those proceedings.

(6) Before a conditional fee agreement to which this regulation applies is made, the legal representative must inform the client as to the circumstances in which the client or his estate may be liable to pay the legal representative's fees and expenses, and provide such further explanation, advice or other information as to those circumstances as the client may reasonably require.

4 Information to be given before conditional fee agreements made

(1) Before a conditional fee agreement is made the legal representative must –

    (a) inform the client about the following matters, and

    (b) if the client requires any further explanation, advice or other information about any of those matters, provide such further explanation, advice or other information about them as the client may reasonably require.

(2) Those matters are –

    (a) the circumstances in which the client may be liable to pay the costs of the legal representative in accordance with the agreement,

    (b) the circumstances in which the client may seek assessment of the fees and expenses of the legal representative and the procedure for doing so,

    (c) whether the legal representative considers that the client's risk of incurring liability for costs in respect of the proceedings to which agreement relates is insured against under an existing contract of insurance,

    (d) whether other methods of financing those costs are available, and, if so, how they apply to the client and the proceedings in question,

    (e) whether the legal representative considers that any particular method or methods of financing any or all of those costs is appropriate and, if he considers that a contract of insurance is appropriate or recommends a particular such contract –

        (i) his reasons for doing so, and

        (ii) whether he has an interest in doing so.

(3) Before a conditional fee agreement is made the legal representative must explain its effect to the client.

(4) In the case of an agreement where –

    (a) the legal representative is a body to which section 30 of the Access to Justice Act 1999 (recovery where body undertakes to meet costs liabilities) applies, and

    (b) there are no circumstances in which the client may be liable to pay any costs in respect of the proceedings,

paragraph (1) does not apply.

(5) Information required to be given under paragraph (1) about the matters in paragraph (2)(a) to

    (d) must be given orally (whether or not it is also given in writing), but information required to be so given about the matters in paragraph (2)(e) and the explanation required by paragraph (3) must be given both orally and in writing.

(6) This regulation does not apply in the case of an agreement between a legal representative and an additional legal representative.

5 Form of agreement

(1) A conditional fee agreement must be signed by the client and the legal representative.

(2) This regulation does not apply in the case of an agreement between a legal representative and an additional legal representative.

6 Amendment of agreement

Where an agreement is amended to cover further proceedings or parts of them –

(a) regulations 2, 3, 3A and 5 apply to the amended agreement as if it were a fresh agreement made at the time of the amendment, and

(b) the obligations under regulation 4 apply in relation to the amendments in so far as they affect the matters mentioned in that regulation.

7 Revocation of 1995 Regulations

The Conditional Fee Agreements Regulations 1995 are revoked.

8 Exclusion of collective conditional fee agreements

These Regulations shall not apply to collective conditional fee agreements within the meaning of regulation 3 of the Collective Conditional Fee Agreements Regulations 2000.

ACCESS TO JUSTICE (MEMBERSHIP ORGANISATIONS) REGULATIONS 2000, SI 2000/693

[*This regulation has been revoked by SI 2005/2306 as from 1 November 2005 except in relation to a conditional fee agreement entered into before that date.*]

The Lord Chancellor, in exercise of the powers conferred on him by section 30(1) and (3) to (5) of the Access to Justice Act 1999 and all other powers enabling him hereby makes the following Regulations:

1 Citation, commencement and interpretation

(1) These Regulations may be cited as the Access to Justice (Membership Organisations) Regulations 2000.

(2) These Regulations come into force on 1st April 2000.

2 Bodies of a prescribed description

The bodies which are prescribed for the purpose of section 30 of the Access to Justice Act 1999 (recovery where body undertakes to meet costs liabilities) are those bodies which are for the time being approved by the Lord Chancellor for that purpose.

3 Requirements for arrangements to meet costs liabilities

(1) Section 30(1) of the Access to Justice Act 1999 applies to arrangements which satisfy the following conditions.

(2) The arrangements must be in writing.

(3) The arrangements must contain a statement specifying –

    (a)   the circumstances in which the member or other party may be liable to pay costs of the proceedings,

    (b)   whether such a liability arises –

        (i)   if those circumstances only partly occur,

        (ii)   irrespective of whether those circumstances occur, and

        (iii) on the termination of the arrangements for any reason,

    (c)   the basis on which the amount of the liability is calculated, and

    (d)   the procedure for seeking assessment of costs.

(4)   A copy of the part of the arrangements containing the statement must be given to the member or other party to the proceedings whose liabilities the body is undertaking to meet as soon as possible after the undertaking is given.

4 Recovery of additional amount for insurance costs

(1)   Where an additional amount is included in costs by virtue of section 30(2) of the Access to Justice Act 1999 (costs payable to a member of a body or other person party to the proceedings to include an additional amount in respect of provision made by the body against the risk of having to meet the member's or other person's liabilities to pay other parties' costs), that additional amount must not exceed the following sum.

(2)   That sum is the likely cost to the member of the body or, as the case may be, the other person who is a party to the proceedings in which the costs order is made of the premium of an insurance policy against the risk of incurring a liability to pay the costs of other parties to the proceedings.

CONDITIONAL FEE AGREEMENTS ORDER 2000, SI 2000/823

The Lord Chancellor, in exercise of the powers conferred upon him by section 58(4)(a) and (c) of the Courts and Legal Services Act 1990, and all other powers enabling him in that behalf, having consulted in accordance with section 58A(5) of that Act, makes the following Order, a draft of which has been laid before and approved by resolution of each House of Parliament:

1 Citation, commencement and interpretation

(1)   This Order may be cited as the Conditional Fee Agreements Order 2000 and shall come into force on 1st April 2000.

(2)   In this Order 'the Act' means the Courts and Legal Services Act 1990.

2 Revocation of 1998 Order

The Conditional Fee Agreements Order 1998 is revoked.

3 Agreements providing for success fees

All proceedings which, under section 58 of the Act, can be the subject of an enforceable conditional fee agreement, except proceedings under section 82 of the Environmental Protection Act 1990, are proceedings specified for the purposes of section 58(4)(a) of the Act.

4 Amount of for success fees

In relation to all proceedings specified in article 3, the percentage specified for the purposes of section 58(4)(c) of the Act shall be 100%.

COLLECTIVE CONDITIONAL FEE AGREEMENTS REGULATIONS 2000, SI 2000/2988

[*This regulation has been revoked by SI 2005/2305 as from 1 November 2005 except in relation to a conditional fee agreement entered into before that date.*]

The Lord Chancellor, in exercise of the powers conferred upon him by sections 58(3)(c), 58A(3) and 119 of the Courts and Legal Services Act 1990 hereby makes the following Regulations:

1 Citation, commencement and interpretation

(1) These regulations may be cited as the Collective Conditional Fee Agreements Regulations 2000, and shall come into force on 30th November 2000.
(2) In these Regulations, except where the context requires otherwise –

'client' means a person who will receive advocacy or litigation services to which the agreement relates;

'collective conditional fee agreement' has the meaning given in regulation 3;

'conditional fee agreement' has the same meaning as in section 58 of the Courts and Legal Services Act 1990;

'funder' means the party to a collective conditional fee agreement who, under that agreement, is liable to pay the legal representative's fees;

'legal representative' means the person providing the advocacy or litigation services to which the agreement relates.

2 Transitional provisions

These Regulations shall apply to agreements entered into on or after 30th November 2000, and agreements entered into before that date shall be treated as if these Regulations had not come into force.

3 Definition of 'collective conditional fee agreement'

(1) Subject to paragraph (2) of this regulation, a collective conditional fee agreement is an agreement which –

(a) disregarding section 58(3)(c) of the Courts and Legal Services Act 1990, would be a conditional fee agreement; and
(b) does not refer to specific proceedings, but provides for fees to be payable on a common basis in relation to a class of proceedings, or, if it refers to more than one class of proceedings, on a common basis in relation to each class.

(2) An agreement may be a collective conditional fee agreement whether or not –

(a) the funder is a client; or
(b) any clients are named in the agreement.

4 Requirements for contents of collective conditional fee agreements: general

(1) A collective conditional fee agreement must specify the circumstances in which the legal representative's fees and expenses, or part of them, are payable.

(1A) The circumstances referred to in paragraph (1) may include the fact that the legal representative's fees and expenses are payable only to the extent that sums are recovered in respect of the proceedings, whether by way of costs or otherwise.

(2) A collective conditional fee agreement must provide that, when accepting instructions in relation to any specific proceedings the legal representative must –

    (a) inform the client as to the circumstances in which the client or his estate may be liable to pay the costs of the legal representative; and

    (b) if the client requires any further explanation, advice or other information about the matter referred to in sub-paragraph (a), provide such further explanation, advice or other information about it as the client may reasonably require.

(3) Paragraph (2) does not apply in the case of an agreement between a legal representative and an additional legal representative.

(4) A collective conditional fee agreement must provide that, after accepting instructions in relation to any specific proceedings, the legal representative must confirm his acceptance of instructions in writing to the client.

5 Requirements for contents of collective conditional fee agreements providing for success fees

(1) Where a collective conditional fee agreement provides for a success fee the agreement must provide that, when accepting instructions in relation to any specific proceedings the legal representative must prepare and retain a written statement containing –

    (a) his assessment of the probability of the circumstances arising in which the percentage increase will become payable in relation to those proceedings ('the risk assessment');

    (b) his assessment of the amount of the percentage increase in relation to those proceedings, having regard to the risk assessment; and

    (c) the reasons, by reference to the risk assessment, for setting the percentage increase at that level.

(2) If the agreement relates to court proceedings it must provide that where the success fee becomes payable as a result of those proceedings, then –

    (a) if –

        (i) any fees subject to the increase are assessed, and

        (ii) the legal representative or the client is required by the court to disclose to the court or any other person the reasons for setting the percentage increase at the level assessed by the legal representative,

    he may do so,

    (b) if –

        (i) any such fees are assessed by the court, and

        (ii) any amount in respect of the percentage increase is disallowed on the assessment on the ground that the level at which the increase was set was unreasonable in view of facts which were or should have been known to the legal representative at the time it was set that amount ceases to be payable under the agreement, unless the court is satisfied that it should continue to be so payable, and

    (c)   if –
        (i)   sub-paragraph (b) does not apply, and
        (ii)   the legal representative agrees with any person liable as a result of the proceedings to pay fees subject to the percentage increase that a lower amount than the amount payable in accordance with the conditional fee agreement is to be paid instead,
        the amount payable under the collective conditional fee agreement in respect of those fees shall be reduced accordingly, unless the court is satisfied that the full amount should continue to be payable under it.

(3)   In this regulation 'percentage increase' means the percentage by which the amount of the fees which would have been payable if the agreement were not a conditional fee agreement is to be increased under the agreement.

(4)   Sub-paragraphs (b) and (c) of paragraph (2) do not apply to a collective conditional fee agreement under which, except in the circumstances set out in paragraphs (6) and (7), the client is liable to pay his legal representative's fees and expenses only to the extent that sums are recovered in respect of the proceedings, whether by way of costs or otherwise.

(5)   In determining for the purposes of paragraph (4) the circumstances in which a client is liable to pay his legal representative's fees and expenses, no account is to be taken of any obligation to pay costs in respect of the premium of a policy taken out to insure against the risk of incurring a liability in the relevant proceedings.

(6)   A collective conditional fee agreement to which paragraph (4) applies may specify that the client will be liable to pay his legal representative's fees and expenses whether or not sums are recovered in respect of the relevant proceedings, if the client –

    (a)   fails to co-operate with the legal representative;
    (b)   fails to attend any medical or expert examination or court hearing which the legal representative reasonably requests him to attend;
    (c)   fails to give necessary instructions to the legal representative;
    (d)   withdraws instructions from the legal representative;
    (e)   is an individual who is adjudged bankrupt or enters into an arrangement or a composition with his creditors, or against whom an administration order is made; or
    (f)   is a company for which a receiver, administrative receiver or liquidator is appointed.

(7)   A collective conditional fee agreement to which paragraph (4) applies may specify that, in the event of the client dying in the course of the relevant proceedings, his estate will be liable for the legal representative's fees and expenses, whether or not sums are recovered in respect of those proceedings.

6   Form and amendment of collective conditional fee agreement

(1)   Subject to paragraph (2), a collective conditional fee agreement must be signed by the funder, and by the legal representative.

(2)   Paragraph (1) does not apply in the case of an agreement between a legal representative and an additional legal representative.

(3)   Where a collective conditional fee agreement is amended, regulations 4 and 5 apply to the amended agreement as if it were a fresh agreement made at the time of the amendment.

7 Amendment to the Conditional Fee Agreements Regulations 2000

After regulation 7 of the Conditional Fee Agreements Regulations 2000 there shall be inserted the following new regulation: –

'8 Exclusion of collective conditional fee agreements

These Regulations shall not apply to collective conditional fee agreements within the meaning of regulation 3 of the Collective Conditional Fee Agreements Regulations 2000.'

CONDITIONAL FEE AGREEMENTS (REVOCATION) REGULATIONS 2005, SI 2005/2305

[*This regulation revokes SI 2000/692, SI 2000/2988, SI 2003/1240, SI 2003/3344 in respect of conditional fee agreements and collective conditional fee agreements entered into on or after 1 November 2005.*]

The Secretary of State, in exercise of the powers conferred upon the Lord Chancellor by sections 58(3)(c), 58A(3), 119 and 120(3) of the Courts and Legal Services Act 1990 and now vested in him makes the following Regulations:

1 Citation and commencement

These Regulations may be cited as the Conditional Fee Agreements (Revocation) Regulations 2005 and shall come into force on 1st November 2005.

2 Revocation

Subject to regulation 3, the Conditional Fee Agreements Regulations 2000 (the 'CFA Regulations'), the Collective Conditional Fee Agreements Regulations 2000 (the 'CCFA Regulations'), the Conditional Fee Agreements (Miscellaneous Amendments) Regulations 2003, and the Conditional Fee Agreements (Miscellaneous Amendments) (No. 2) Regulations 2003 are revoked.

3 Savings and transitional provisions

(1) The CFA Regulations shall continue to have effect for the purposes of a conditional fee agreement entered into before 1st November 2005.
(2) Paragraph (1) shall apply in relation to a collective conditional fee agreement as if there were substituted for a reference to the CFA Regulations a reference to the CCFA Regulations.

APPENDIX 3

Civil Procedure Rules 1998, SI 1998/3132 (extracts)

*****

PART 43

SCOPE OF LOST RULES AND DEFINITIONS

*****

43.2 Definitions and application

(1) In Parts 44 to 48, unless the context otherwise requires –

(a) 'costs' includes fees, charges, disbursements, expenses, remuneration, reimbursement allowed to a litigant in person under rule 48.6, any additional liability incurred under a funding arrangement and any fee or reward charged by a lay representative for acting on behalf of a party in proceedings allocated to the small claims track;

*****

(k) 'funding arrangement' means an arrangement where a person has –
  (i)   entered into a conditional fee agreement or a collective conditional fee agreement which provides for a success fee within the meaning of section 58(2) of the Courts and Legal Services Act 1990(1);
  (ii) taken out an insurance policy to which section 29 of the Access to Justice Act 1999 (recovery of insurance premiums by way of costs) applies; or
  (iii) made an agreement with a membership organisation to meet his legal costs;

(l) 'percentage increase' means the percentage by which the amount of a legal representative's fee can be increased in accordance with a conditional fee agreement which provides for a success fee;

(m) 'insurance premium' means a sum of money paid or payable for insurance against the risk of incurring a costs liability in the proceedings, taken out after the event that is the subject matter of the claim;

(n) 'membership organisation' means a body prescribed for the purposes of section 30 of the Access to Justice Act 1999 (recovery where body undertakes to meet costs liabilities); and

(o) 'additional liability' means the percentage increase, the insurance premium, or the additional amount in respect of provision made by a membership organisation, as the case may be.

[*In force 3 July 2000. For transitional provisions see SI 2000/1317, r.39.*]

*****

(3) Where advocacy or litigation services are provided to a client under a conditional fee agreement, costs are recoverable under Parts 44 to 48 notwithstanding that

the client is liable to pay his legal representative's fees and expenses only to the extent that sums are recovered in respect of the proceedings, whether by way of costs or otherwise.

[*In force 2 June 2003. For agreements entered into on or after this date see SI 2003/1242, r.6.*]

*****

PART 44

GENERAL RULES ABOUT COSTS

****

44.3(8)   Where the court has ordered a party to pay costs, it may order an amount to be paid on account before the costs are assessed.

*****

44.3A   Costs orders relating to funding arrangements

(1)   The court will not assess any additional liability until the conclusion of the proceedings, or the part of the proceedings, to which the funding arrangement relates.

('Funding arrangement' and 'additional liability' are defined in rule 43.2)

(2)   At the conclusion of the proceedings, or the part of the proceedings, to which the funding arrangement relates the court may –

   (a)   make a summary assessment of all the costs, including any additional liability;

   (b)   make an order for detailed assessment of the additional liability but make a summary assessment of the other costs; or

   (c)   make an order for detailed assessment of all the costs.

(Part 47 sets out the procedure for the detailed assessment of costs)

[*In force 3 July 2000. For transitional provisions see SI 2000/1317, r.39.*]

44.3B   Limits on recovery under funding arrangements

(1)   A party may not recover as an additional liability –

   (a)   any proportion of the percentage increase relating to the cost to the legal representative of the postponement of the payment of his fees and expenses;

   (b)   any provision made by a membership organisation which exceeds the likely cost to that party of the premium of an insurance policy against the risk of incurring a liability to pay the costs of other parties to the proceedings;

   (c)   any additional liability for any period in the proceedings during which he failed to provide information about a funding arrangement in accordance with a rule, practice direction or court order;

   (d)   any percentage increase where a party has failed to comply with –

      (i)   a requirement in the costs practice direction; or

      (ii)   a court order,

to disclose in any assessment proceedings the reasons for setting the percentage increase at the level stated in the conditional fee agreement.

(2) This rule does not apply in an assessment under rule 48.9 (assessment of a solicitor's bill to his client).

(Rule 3.9 sets out the circumstances the court will consider on an application for relief from a sanction for failure to comply with any rule, practice direction or court order)

[*In force 3 July 2000. For transitional provisions see SI 2000/1317, r.39.*]

44.5 Factors to be taken into account in deciding the amount of costs

(1) The court is to have regard to all the circumstances in deciding whether costs were –

    (a) if it is assessing costs on the standard basis –
        (i) proportionately and reasonably incurred; or
        (ii) were proportionate and reasonable in amount, or
    (b) if it is assessing costs on the indemnity basis –
        (i) unreasonably incurred; or
        (ii) unreasonable in amount.

(2) In particular the court must give effect to any orders which have already been made.

(3) The court must also have regard to –

    (a) the conduct of all the parties, including in particular –
        (i) conduct before, as well as during, the proceedings; and
        (ii) the efforts made, if any, before and during the proceedings in order to try to resolve the dispute;
    (b) the amount or value of any money or property involved;
    (c) the importance of the matter to all the parties;
    (d) the particular complexity of the matter or the difficulty or novelty of the questions raised;
    (e) the skill, effort, specialised knowledge and responsibility involved;
    (f) the time spent on the case; and
    (g) the place where and the circumstances in which work or any part of it was done.

(Rule 35.4(4) gives the court power to limit the amount that a party may recover with regard to the fees and expenses of an expert)

*****

44.7 Procedure for assessing costs

Where the court orders a party to pay costs to another party (other than fixed costs) it may either –

    (a) make a summary assessment of the costs; or
    (b) order detailed assessment of the costs by a costs officer,

unless any rule, practice direction or other enactment provides otherwise.

(The costs practice direction sets out the factors which will affect the court's decision under this rule.)

*****

44.12A Costs-only proceedings

(1) This rule sets out a procedure which may be followed where –

    (a) the parties to a dispute have reached an agreement on all issues (including which party is to pay the costs) which is made or confirmed in writing; but

    (b) they have failed to agree the amount of those costs; and

    (c) no proceedings have been started.

(2) Either party to the agreement may start proceedings under this rule by issuing a claim form in accordance with Part 8.

(3) The claim form must contain or be accompanied by the agreement or confirmation.

(4) Except as provided in paragraph (4A), in proceedings to which this rule applies the court –

    (a) may

        (i) make an order for costs to be determined by detailed assessment; or

        (ii) dismiss the claim; and

    (b) must dismiss the claim if it is opposed.

(4A) In proceedings to which Section II of Part 45 applies, the court shall assess the costs in the manner set out in that Section.

(5) Rule 48.3 (amount of costs where costs are payable pursuant to a contract) does not apply to claims started under the procedure in this rule. (Rule 7.2 provides that proceedings are started when the court issues a claim form at the request of the claimant)

(Rule 8.1(6) provides that a practice direction may modify the Part 8 procedure)

[In force 3 July 2000. For transitional provisions see SI 2000/1317, r.39.]

*****

44.15 Providing information about funding arrangements

(1) A party who seeks to recover an additional liability must provide information about the funding arrangement to the court and to other parties as required by a rule, practice direction or court order.

(2) Where the funding arrangement has changed, and the information a party has previously provided in accordance with paragraph (1) is no longer accurate, that party must file notice of the change and serve it on all other parties within 7 days.

(3) Where paragraph (2) applies, and a party has already filed –

    (a) an allocation questionnaire; or

    (b) a pre-trial check list (listing questionnaire)

he must file and serve a new estimate of costs with the notice.

(The costs practice direction sets out –

  • the information to be provided when a party issues or responds to a claim form, files an allocation questionnaire, a pre-trial check list, and a claim for costs;

  • the meaning of estimate of costs and the information required in it)

(Rule 44.3B sets out situations where a party will not recover a sum representing any additional liability)

[In force 3 July 2000. For transitional provisions see SI 2000/1317, r.39.]

44.16 Adjournment where legal representative seeks to challenge disallowance of any amount of percentage increase

(1) This rule applies where the Conditional Fee Agreements Regulations 2000 or the Collective Conditional Fee Agreements Regulations 2000 continues to apply to an agreement which provides for a success fee.

(2) Where –

(a) the court disallows any amount of a legal representative's percentage increase in summary or detailed assessment proceedings; and

(b) the legal representative applies for an order that the disallowed amount should continue to be payable by his client,

the court may adjourn the hearing to allow the client to be –

(i) notified of the order sought; and

(ii) separately represented.

(Regulation 3(2)(b) of the Conditional Fee Agreements Regulations 2000, which applies to Conditional Fee Agreements entered into before 1st November 2005, provides that a conditional fee agreement which provides for a success fee must state that any amount of a percentage increase disallowed on assessment ceases to be payable unless the court is satisfied that it should continue to be so payable. Regulation 5(2)(b) of the Collective Conditional Fee Agreements Regulations 2000, which applies to Collective Conditional Fee Agreements entered into before 1st November 2005, makes similar provision in relation to collective conditional fee agreements.)

*****

PART 47

PROCEDURE FOR DETAILED ASSESSMENT OF COSTS AND DEFAULT PROVISIONS

*****

47.1 Time when detailed assessment may be carried out

The general rule is that the costs of any proceedings or any part of the proceedings are not to be assessed by the detailed procedure until the conclusion of the proceedings but the court may order them to be assessed immediately.

(The costs practice direction gives further guidance about when proceedings are concluded for the purpose of this rule.)

*****

47.10 Procedure where costs are agreed

(1) If the paying party and the receiving party agree the amount of costs, either party may apply for a costs certificate (either interim or final) in the amount agreed.

(Rule 47.15 and rule 47.16 contain further provisions about interim and final costs certificates respectively.)

(2) An application for a certificate under paragraph (1) must be made to the court which would be the venue for detailed assessment proceedings under rule 47.4.

[*Paragraph (2) in force 3 July 2000. For transitional provisions see SI 2000/1317, r.39.*]

*****

APPENDIX 4

Costs Practice Direction (extracts)

*****

SECTION 2 SCOPE OF COSTS RULES AND DEFINITIONS

RULE 43.2 Definitions and applications

2.1 Where the court makes an order for costs and the receiving party has entered into a funding arrangement as defined in rule 43.2, the costs payable by the paying party include any additional liability (also defined in rule 43.2) unless the court orders otherwise.

2.2 In the following paragraphs –

'funding arrangement', 'percentage increase', 'insurance premium', 'membership organisation' and 'additional liability' have the meanings given to them by rule 43.2.

'conditional fee agreement' is an agreement with a person providing advocacy or litigation services which provides for his fees and expenses, or part of them, to be payable only in specified circumstances, whether or not it provides for a success fee as mentioned in section 58(2)(b) of the Courts and Legal Services Act 1990.

'base costs' means costs other than the amount of any additional liability.

2.3 Rule 44.3A(1) provides that the court will not assess any additional liability until the conclusion of the proceedings or the part of the proceedings to which the funding arrangement relates. (As to the time when detailed assessment may be carried out see paragraph 27.1 below).

2.4 For the purposes of the following paragraphs of this practice direction and rule 44.3A proceedings are concluded when the court has finally determined the matters in issue in the claim, whether or not there is an appeal. The making of an award of provisional damages under Part 41 will also be treated as a final determination of the matters in issue.

2.5 The court may order or the parties may agree in writing that, although the proceedings are continuing, they will nevertheless be treated as concluded.

*****

SECTION 8 COURT'S DISCRETION AND CIRCUMSTANCES TO BE TAKEN INTO ACCOUNT WHEN EXERCISING ITS DISCRETION AS TO COSTS: RULE 44.3

*****

8.6 Where, under rule 44.3(8), the court orders an amount to be paid before costs are assessed –

(1)   the order will state that amount, and
(2)   if no other date for payment is specified in the order, rule 44.8 (Time for complying with an order for costs) will apply.

*****

SECTION 11   FACTORS TO BE TAKEN INTO ACCOUNT IN DECIDING THE AMOUNT OF COSTS: RULE 44.5

*****

11.4   Where a party has entered into a funding arrangement the costs claimed may, subject to rule 44.3B include an additional liability.

11.5   In deciding whether the costs claimed are reasonable and (on a standard basis assessment) proportionate, the court will consider the amount of any additional liability separately from the base costs.

*****

11.7   Subject to paragraph 17.8(2), when the court is considering the factors to be taken into account in assessing an additional liability, it will have regard to the facts and circumstances as they reasonably appeared to the solicitor or counsel when the funding arrangement was entered into and at the time of any variation of the arrangement.

11.8   (1)   In deciding whether a percentage increase is reasonable relevant factors to be taken into account may include:
         (a)   the risk that the circumstances in which the costs, fees or expenses would be payable might or might not occur;
         (b)   the legal representative's liability for any disbursements;
         (c)   what other methods of financing the costs were available to the receiving party.
        (2)   Omitted.

11.9   A percentage increase will not be reduced simply on the ground that, when added to base costs which are reasonable and (where relevant) proportionate, the total appears disproportionate.

11.10 In deciding whether the cost of insurance cover is reasonable, relevant factors to be taken into account include:

         (1)   where the insurance cover is not purchased in support of a conditional fee agreement with a success fee, how its cost compares with the likely cost of funding the case with a conditional fee agreement with a success fee and supporting insurance cover;
         (2)   the level and extent of the cover provided;
         (3)   the availability of any pre-existing insurance cover;
         (4)   whether any part of the premium would be rebated in the event of early settlement;
         (5)   the amount of commission payable to the receiving party or his legal representatives or other agents.

11.11 Where the court is considering a provision made by a membership organisation, rule 44.3B(1) (b) provides that any such provision which exceeds the likely cost to the receiving party of the premium of an insurance policy against the risk of incurring a liability to pay the costs of other parties to the proceedings is not recoverable. In such circumstances the court will, when assessing the additional liability, have regard to the factors set out in paragraph 11.10 above, in addition to the factors set out in rule 44.5.

*****

SECTION 12 PROCEDURE FOR ASSESSING COSTS: RULE 44.7

12.1 Where the court does not order fixed costs (or no fixed costs are provided for) the amount of costs payable will be assessed by the court. This rule allows the court making an order about costs either

(a) to make a summary assessment of the amount of the costs, or
(b) to order the amount to be decided in accordance with Part 47 (a detailed assessment).

12.2 An order for costs will be treated as an order for the amount of costs to be decided by a detailed assessment unless the order otherwise provides.

12.3 Whenever the court awards costs to be assessed by way of detailed assessment it should consider whether to exercise the power in rule 44.3(8) (Courts Discretion as to Costs) to order the paying party to pay such sum of money as it thinks just on account of those costs.

SECTION 13 SUMMARY ASSESSMENT: GENERAL PROVISIONS

*****

13.2 The general rule is that the court should make a summary assessment of the costs:

(1) at the conclusion of the trial of a case which has been dealt with on the fast track, in which case the order will deal with the costs of the whole claim, and
(2) at the conclusion of any other hearing, which has lasted not more than one day, in which case the order will deal with the costs of the application or matter to which the hearing related. If this hearing disposes of the claim, the order may deal with the costs of the whole claim;
(3) in hearings in the Court of Appeal to which Paragraph 14 of the Practice Direction supplementing Part 52 (Appeals) applies;

unless there is good reason not to do so e.g. where the paying party shows substantial grounds for disputing the sum claimed for costs that cannot be dealt with summarily or there is insufficient time to carry out a summary assessment.

*****

SECTION 14 SUMMARY ASSESSMENT WHERE COSTS CLAIMED INCLUDE AN ADDITIONAL LIABILITY

Orders made before the conclusion of the proceedings

14.1 The existence of a conditional fee agreement or other funding arrangement within the meaning of rule 43.2 is not by itself a sufficient reason for not carrying out a summary assessment.

14.2 Where a legal representative acting for the receiving party has entered into a conditional fee agreement the court may summarily assess all the costs (other than any additional liability).

*****

SECTION 17   COSTS-ONLY PROCEEDINGS: RULE 44.12A

17.1 A claim form under this rule should not be issued in the High Court unless the dispute to which the agreement relates was of such a value or type that had proceedings been begun they would have been commenced in the High Court.

17.2 A claim form which is to be issued in the High Court at the Royal Courts of Justice will be issued in the Supreme Court Costs Office.

17.3 Attention is drawn to rule 8.2 (in particular to paragraph (b)(ii)) and to rule 44.12A(3). The claim form must:

(1) identify the claim or dispute to which the agreement to pay costs relates;
(2) state the date and terms of the agreement on which the claimant relies;
(3) set out or have attached to it a draft of the order which the claimant seeks;
(4) state the amount of the costs claimed; and,
(5) state whether the costs are claimed on the standard or indemnity basis. If no basis is specified the costs will be treated as being claimed on the standard basis.

17.4 The evidence to be filed and served with the claim form under Rule 8.5 must include copies of the documents on which the claimant relies to prove the defendant's agreement to pay costs.

17.5 A costs judge or a district judge has jurisdiction to hear and decide any issue which may arise in a claim issued under this rule irrespective of the amount of the costs claimed or of the value of the claim to which the agreement to pay costs relates. A costs officer may make an order by consent under paragraph 17.7, or an order dismissing a claim under paragraph 17.9 below.

17.6 When the time for filing the defendant's acknowledgement of service has expired, the claimant may by letter request the court to make an order in the terms of his claim, unless the defendant has filed an acknowledgement of service stating that he intends to contest the claim or to seek a different order.

17.7 Rule 40.6 applies where an order is to be made by consent. An order may be made by consent in terms which differ from those set out in the claim form.

17.8 (1) An order for costs made under this rule will be treated as an order for the amount of costs to be decided by a detailed assessment to which Part 47 and the practice directions relating to it apply. Rule 44.4(4) (determination of basis of assessment) also applies to the order.

(2) In cases in which an additional liability is claimed, the costs judge or district judge should have regard to the time when and the extent to which the claim has been settled and to the fact that the claim has been settled without the need to commence proceedings.

17.9 (1) For the purposes of rule 44.12A(4)(b) –

(a) a claim will be treated as opposed if the defendant files an acknowledgment of service stating that he intends to contest the making of an order for costs or to seek a different remedy; and

(b) a claim will not be treated as opposed if the defendant files an acknowledgment of service stating that he disputes the amount of the claim for costs.

(2) An order dismissing the claim will be made as soon as an acknowledgment of service opposing the claim is filed. The dismissal of a claim under rule 44.12A(4) does not prevent the claimant from issuing another claim form under Part 7 or Part 8 based on the agreement or alleged agreement to which the proceedings under this rule related.

17.10 (1) Rule 8.9 (which provides that claims issued under Part 8 shall be treated as allocated to the multi-track) shall not apply to claims issued under this rule. A claim issued under this rule may be dealt with without being allocated to a track.

(2) Rule 8.1(3) and Part 24 do not apply to proceedings brought under rule 44.12A.

17.11 Nothing in this rule prevents a person from issuing a claim form under Part 7 or Part 8 to sue on an agreement made in settlement of a dispute where that agreement makes provision for costs, nor from claiming in that case an order for costs or a specified sum in respect of costs.

*****

SECTION 19   PROVIDING INFORMATION ABOUT FUNDING ARRANGEMENTS: RULE 44.15

19.1 (1) A party who wishes to claim an additional liability in respect of a funding arrangement must give any other party information about that claim if he is to recover the additional liability. There is no requirement to specify the amount of the additional liability separately nor to state how it is calculated until it falls to be assessed. That principle is reflected in rules 44.3A and 44.15, in the following paragraphs and in Sections 6, 13, 14 and 31 of this Practice Direction. Section 6 deals with estimates of costs, Sections 13 and 14 deal with summary assessment and Section 31 deals with detailed assessment.

(2) In the following paragraphs a party who has entered into a funding arrangement is treated as a person who intends to recover a sum representing an additional liability by way of costs.

(3) Attention is drawn to paragraph 57.9 of this Practice Direction which sets out time limits for the provision of information where a funding arrangement is entered into between 31 March and 2 July 2000 and proceedings relevant to that arrangement are commenced before 3 July 2000.

Method of giving information

19.2 (1) In this paragraph, 'claim form' includes petition and application notice, and the notice of funding to be filed or served is a notice containing the information set out in Form N251.

(2) (a) A claimant who has entered into a funding arrangement before starting the proceedings to which it relates must provide information to the court by filing the notice when he issues the claim form.

(b) He must provide information to every other party by serving the notice. If he serves the claim form himself he must serve the notice with the claim form. If the court is to serve the claim form, the court will also serve the notice if the claimant provides it with sufficient copies for service.

(3) A defendant who has entered into a funding arrangement before filing any document

> (a) must provide information to the court by filing notice with his first document. A 'first document' may be an acknowledgement of service, a defence, or any other document, such as an application to set aside a default judgment.
>
> (b) must provide information to every party by serving notice. If he serves his first document himself he must serve the notice with that document. If the court is to serve his first document the court will also serve the notice if the defendant provides it with sufficient copies for service.

(4) In all other circumstances a party must file and serve notice within 7 days of entering into the funding arrangement concerned.

(5) There is no requirement in this Practice Direction for the provision of information about funding arrangements before the commencement of proceedings. Such provision is however recommended and may be required by a pre-action protocol.

Notice of change of information

19.3 (1) Rule 44.15 imposes a duty on a party to give notice of change if the information he has previously provided is no longer accurate. To comply he must file and serve notice containing the information set out in Form N251. Rule 44.15(3) may impose other duties in relation to new estimates of costs.

(2) Further notification need not be provided where a party has already given notice:

> (a) that he has entered into a conditional fee agreement with a legal representative and during the currency of that agreement either of them enters into another such agreement with an additional legal representative; or
>
> (b) of some insurance cover, unless that cover is cancelled or unless new cover is taken out with a different insurer.

(3) Part 6 applies to the service of notices.

(4) The notice must be signed by the party or by his legal representative.

Information which must be provided

19.4 (1) Unless the court otherwise orders, a party who is required to supply information about a funding arrangement must state whether he has –

entered into a conditional fee agreement which provides for a success fee within the meaning of section 58(2) of the Courts and Legal Services Act 1990;

taken out an insurance policy to which section 29 of the Access to Justice Act 1999 applies;

made an arrangement with a body which is prescribed for the purpose of section 30 of that Act;

or more than one of these.

(2) Where the funding arrangement is a conditional fee agreement, the party must state the date of the agreement and identify the claim or claims to which it relates (including Part 20 claims if any).

(3) Where the funding arrangement is an insurance policy, the party must state the name and address of the insurer, the policy number and the date of the policy, and must identify the claim or claims to which it relates (including Part 20 claims if any).

(4)   Where the funding arrangement is by way of an arrangement with a relevant body the party must state the name of the body and set out the date and terms of the undertaking it has given and must identify the claim or claims to which it relates (including Part 20 claims if any).

(5)   Where a party has entered into more than one funding arrangement in respect of a claim, for example a conditional fee agreement and an insurance policy, a single notice containing the information set out in Form N251 may contain the required information about both or all of them.

19.5   Where the court makes a Group Litigation Order, the court may give directions as to the extent to which individual parties should provide information in accordance with rule 44.15. (Part 19 deals with Group Litigation Orders.)

SECTION 20   PROCEDURE WHERE LEGAL REPRESENTATIVE WISHES TO RECOVER FROM HIS CLIENT AN AGREED PERCENTAGE INCREASE WHICH HAS BEEN DISALLOWED OR REDUCED ON ASSESSMENT: RULE 44.16

20.1   (1)   Attention is drawn to Regulation 3(2)(b) of the Conditional Fee Agreements Regulations 2000 and to Regulation 5(2)(b) of the Collective Conditional Fee Agreements Regulations 2000, which provide that some or all of a success fee ceases to be payable in certain circumstances. [Both sets of regulations were revoked by the Conditional Fee Agreements (Revocation) Regulations 2005 but continue to have effect in relation to conditional fee agreements and collective conditional fee agreements entered into before 1 November 2005.]

(2)   Rule 44.16 allows the court to adjourn a hearing at which the legal representative acting for the receiving party applies for an order that a disallowed amount should continue to be payable under the agreement.

20.2   In the following paragraphs 'counsel' means counsel who has acted in the case under a conditional fee agreement which provides for a success fee. A reference to counsel includes a reference to any person who appeared as an advocate in the case and who is not a partner or employee of the solicitor or firm which is conducting the claim or defence (as the case may be) on behalf of the receiving party.

Procedure following Summary Assessment

20.3   (1)   If the court disallows any amount of a legal representative's percentage increase, the court will, unless sub-paragraph (2) applies, give directions to enable an application to be made by the legal representative for the disallowed amount to be payable by his client, including, if appropriate, a direction that the application will be determined by a costs judge or district judge of the court dealing with the case.

(2)   The court that has made the summary assessment may then and there decide the issue whether the disallowed amount should continue to be payable, if:

(a)   the receiving party and all parties to the relevant agreement consent to the court doing so;

(b)   the receiving party (or, if corporate, an officer) is present in court; and

(c)   the court is satisfied that the issue can be fairly decided then and there.

Procedure following Detailed Assessment

20.4 (1) Where detailed assessment proceedings have been commenced, and the paying party serves points of dispute (as to which see Section 34 of this Practice Direction), which show that he is seeking a reduction in any percentage increase charged by counsel on his fees, the solicitor acting for the receiving party must within 3 days of service deliver to counsel a copy of the relevant points of dispute and the bill of costs or the relevant parts of the bill.

(2) Counsel must within 10 days thereafter inform the solicitor in writing whether or not he will accept the reduction sought or some other reduction. Counsel may state any points he wishes to have made in a reply to the points of dispute, and the solicitor must serve them on the paying party as or as part of a reply.

(3) Counsel who fails to inform the solicitor within the time limits set out above will be taken to accept the reduction unless the court otherwise orders.

20.5 Where the paying party serves points of dispute seeking a reduction in any percentage increase charged by a legal representative acting for the receiving party, and that legal representative intends, if necessary, to apply for an order that any amount of the percentage disallowed as against the paying party shall continue to be payable by his client, the solicitor acting for the receiving party must, within 14 days of service of the points of dispute, give to his client a clear written explanation of the nature of the relevant point of dispute and the effect it will have if it is upheld in whole or in part by the court, and of the client's right to attend any subsequent hearings at court when the matter is raised.

20.6 Where the solicitor acting for a receiving party files a request for a detailed assessment hearing it must if appropriate, be accompanied by a certificate signed by him stating:

(1) that the amount of the percentage increase in respect of counsel's fees or solicitor's charges is disputed;

(2) whether an application will be made for an order that any amount of that increase which is disallowed should continue to be payable by his client;

(3) that he has given his client an explanation in accordance with paragraph 20.5; and,

(4) whether his client wishes to attend court when the amount of any relevant percentage increase may be decided.

20.7 (1) The solicitor acting for the receiving party must within 7 days of receiving from the court notice of the date of the assessment hearing, notify his client, and if appropriate, counsel in writing of the date, time and place of the hearing.

(2) Counsel may attend or be represented at the detailed assessment hearing and may make oral or written submissions.

20.8 (1) At the detailed assessment hearing, the court will deal with the assessment of the costs payable by one party to another, including the amount of the percentage increase, and give a certificate accordingly.

(2) The court may decide the issue whether the disallowed amount should continue to be payable under the relevant conditional fee agreement without an adjournment if:

       (a)   the receiving party and all parties to the relevant agreement consent to the court deciding the issue without an adjournment,

       (b)   the receiving party (or, if corporate, an officer or employee who has authority to consent on behalf of the receiving party) is present in court, and

       (c)   the court is satisfied that the issue can be fairly decided without an adjournment.

(3)   In any other case the court will give directions and fix a date for the hearing of the application.

*****

SECTION 27   POWER TO AWARD MORE OR LESS THAN THE AMOUNT OF FAST TRACK TRIAL COSTS: RULE 46.3

*****

27.3   The court has the power, when considering whether a percentage increase is reasonable, to allow different percentages for different items of costs or for different periods during which costs were incurred.

*****

SECTION 32   COMMENCEMENT OF DETAILED ASSESSMENT PROCEEDINGS: RULE 47.6

*****

32.3   If the detailed assessment is in respect of costs without any additional liability, the receiving party must serve on the paying party and all the other relevant persons the following documents:

       (a)   a notice of commencement;

       (b)   a copy of the bill of costs;

       (c)   copies of the fee notes of counsel and of any expert in respect of fees claimed in the bill;

       (d)   written evidence as to any other disbursement which is claimed and which exceeds £250;

       (e)   a statement giving the name and address for service of any person upon whom the receiving party intends to serve the notice of commencement.

32.4   If the detailed assessment is in respect of an additional liability only, the receiving party must serve on the paying party and all other relevant persons the following documents:

       (a)   a notice of commencement;

       (b)   a copy of the bill of costs;

       (c)   the relevant details of the additional liability;

       (d)   a statement giving the name and address of any person upon whom the receiving party intends to serve the notice of commencement.

32.5   The relevant details of an additional liability are as follows:

       (1)   In the case of a conditional fee agreement with a success fee:

           (a)   a statement showing the amount of costs which have been summarily assessed or agreed, and the percentage increase which has been claimed in respect of those costs;

    (b)   a statement of the reasons for the percentage increase given in accordance with Regulation 3(1)(a) of the Conditional Fee Agreements Regulations or Regulation 5(1)(c) of the Collective Conditional Fee Agreements Regulations 2000. [Both sets of regulations were revoked by the Conditional Fee Agreements (Revocation) Regulations 2005 but continue to have effect in relation to conditional fee agreements and collective conditional fee agreements entered into before 1 November 2005.]

  (2)   If the additional liability is an insurance premium: a copy of the insurance certificate showing whether the policy covers the receiving party's own costs; his opponents costs; or his own costs and his opponent's costs; and the maximum extent of that cover, and the amount of the premium paid or payable.

  (3)   If the receiving party claims an additional amount under Section 30 of the Access of Justice Act 1999: a statement setting out the basis upon which the receiving party's liability for the additional amount is calculated.

32.6   Attention is drawn to the fact that the additional amount recoverable pursuant to section 30 of the Access to Justice Act 1999 in respect of a membership organisation must not exceed the likely cost of the premium of an insurance policy against the risk of incurring a liability to pay the costs of other parties to the proceedings as provided by the Access to Justice (Membership Organisation) Regulations 2000 Regulation 4 (for the purposes of arrangements entered into before 1st November 2005) and The Access to Justice (Membership Organisation) Regulations 2005 Regulation 5 (for the purposes of arrangements entered into on or after 1st November 2005).

32.7   If a detailed assessment is in respect of both base costs and an additional liability, the receiving party must serve on the paying party and all other relevant persons the documents listed in paragraph 32.3 and the documents giving relevant details of an additional liability listed in paragraph 32.5.

SECTION 35 POINTS OF DISPUTE AND CONSEQUENCES OF NOT SERVING: RULE 47.9

*****

35.7   (1)   Where the receiving party claims an additional liability, a party who serves points of dispute on the receiving party may include a request for information about other methods of financing costs which were available to the receiving party.

  (2)   Part 18 (further information) and the Practice Direction Supplementing that part apply to such a request

SECTION 36 PROCEDURE WHERE COSTS ARE AGREED: RULE 47.10

36.1   Where the parties have agreed terms as to the issue of a costs certificate (either interim or final) they should apply under rule 40.6 (Consent judgments and orders) for an order that a certificate be issued in terms set out in the application. Such an application may be dealt with by a court officer, who may issue the certificate.

36.2   Where in the course of proceedings the receiving party claims that the paying party has agreed to pay costs but that he will neither pay those costs nor join in a consent application under paragraph 36.1, the receiving party may apply under Part 23 (General Rules about Applications for Court Orders) for a certificate either interim or final to be issued.

36.3 An application under paragraph 36.2 must be supported by evidence and will be heard by a costs judge or a district judge. The respondent to the application must file and serve any evidence he relies on at least two days before the hearing date.

36.4 Nothing in rule 47.10 prevents parties who seek a judgment or order by consent from including in the draft a term that a party shall pay to another party a specified sum in respect of costs.

36.5 (1) The receiving party may discontinue the detailed assessment proceedings in accordance with Part 38 (Discontinuance).

(2) Where the receiving party discontinues the detailed assessment proceedings before a detailed assessment hearing has been requested, the paying party may apply to the appropriate office for an order about the costs of the detailed assessment proceedings.

(3) Where a detailed assessment hearing has been requested the receiving party may not discontinue unless the court gives permission.

(4) A bill of costs may be withdrawn by consent whether or not a detailed assessment hearing has been requested.

*****

SECTION 40 DETAILED ASSESSMENT HEARING: RULE 47.14
*****

40.10 (1) If a party wishes to vary his bill of costs, points of dispute or a reply, an amended or supplementary document must be filed with the court and copies of it must be served on all other relevant parties.

(2) Permission is not required to vary a bill of costs, points of dispute or a reply but the court may disallow the variation or permit it only upon conditions, including conditions as to the payment of any costs caused or wasted by the variation.

*****

40.12 The following provisions apply in respect of the papers to be filed in support of the bill;

(a) If the claim is for costs only without any additional liability the papers to be filed, and the order in which they are to be arranged are as follows:

(i) instructions and briefs to counsel arranged in chronological order together with all advices, opinions and drafts received and response to such instructions;

(ii) reports and opinions of medical and other experts;

(iii) any other relevant papers;

(iv) a full set of any relevant pleadings to the extent that they have not already been filed in court.

(v) correspondence, files and attendance notes;

(b) where the claim is in respect of an additional liability only, such of the papers listed at (a) above, as are relevant to the issues raised by the claim for additional liability;

(c) where the claim is for both base costs and an additional liability, the papers listed at (a) above, together with any papers relevant to the issues raised by the claim for additional liability.

*****

40.14   The court may direct the receiving party to produce any document which in the opinion of the court is necessary to enable it to reach its decision. These documents will in the first instance be produced to the court, but the court may ask the receiving party to elect whether to disclose the particular document to the paying party in order to rely on the contents of the document, or whether to decline disclosure and instead rely on other evidence.

*****

SECTION 41   POWER TO ISSUE AN INTERIM CERTIFICATE: RULE 47.15

41.1   (1)   A party wishing to apply for an interim certificate may do so by making an application in accordance with Part 23 (General Rules about Applications for Court Orders).

(2)   Attention is drawn to the fact that the court's power to issue an interim certificate arises only after the receiving party has filed a request for a detailed assessment hearing.

SECTION 57   TRANSITIONAL ARRANGEMENTS

*****

Transitional provisions concerning the Access to Justice Act 1999 sections 28 to 31

57.8   (1)   Sections 28 to 31 of the Access to Justice Act 1999, the Conditional Fee Agreements Regulations 2000, the Access to Justice (Membership Organisations) Regulations 2000, and the Access to Justice Act 1999 (Transitional Provisions) Order 2000 came into force on 1 April 2000. The Civil Procedure (Amendment No.3) Rules came into force on 3 July 2000. [The Conditional Fee Agreements Regulations 2000 were revoked by the Conditional Fee Agreements (Revocation) Regulations 2005 but continue to have effect in relation to conditional fee agreements entered into before 1 November 2005. The Access to Justice (Membership Organisation) Regulations 2000 were revoked by the Access to Justice (Membership Organisation) Regulations 2005 but continue to have effect in relation to arrangements entered into before 1 November 2005.]

*****

57.9   (1)   Rule 39 of the Civil Procedure (Amendment No 3) Rules 2000 applies where between 1 April and 2 July 2000 (including both dates) –

a funding arrangement is entered into, and proceedings are started in respect of a claim which is the subject of that agreement.

Practice Direction on protocols (extracts)

INFORMATION ABOUT FUNDING ARRANGEMENTS

4A.1 Where a person enters into a funding arrangement within the meaning of rule 43.2(1)(k) he should inform other potential parties to the claim that he has done so.

4A.2 Paragraph 4A.1 applies to all proceedings whether proceedings to which a pre-action protocol applies or otherwise.

(Rule 44.3B(1)(c) provides that a party may not recover any additional liability for any period in the proceedings during which he failed to provide information about a funding arrangement in accordance with a rule, practice direction or court order).

APPENDIX 6

Prescribed forms

FORM N251

Notice of funding of case or claim

Notice of funding by means of a conditional fee agreement, insurance policy or undertaking given by a prescribed body should be given to the court and all other parties to the case:
- on commencement of proceedings
- on filing an acknowledgment of service, defence or other first document; and
- at any later time that such an arrangement is entered into, changed or terminated.

In the	
The court office is open between 10 am and 4 pm Monday to Friday. When writing to the court, please address forms or letters to the Court Manager and quote the claim number.	
Claim No.	
Claimant (include Ref.)	
Defendant (include Ref.)	

Take notice that in respect of

☐ all claims herein

☐ the following claims

☐ the case of *(specify name of party)*

[is now][was] being funded by:

(Please tick those boxes which apply)

☐ a conditional fee agreement
Dated

which provides for a success fee

☐ an insurance policy issued on
Date   Policy no.

Name and address of insurer

☐ an undertaking given on
Date

by
Name of prescribed body

in the following terms

The funding of the case has now changed:

☐ the above funding has now ceased

☐ the conditional fee agreement has been terminated

☐ a conditional fee agreement
Dated

which provides for a success fee has been entered into;

☐ an insurance policy
Date

has been cancelled

☐ an insurance policy has been issued on
Date   Policy no.

Name and address of insurer

☐ an undertaking given on
Date

has been terminated

☐ an undertaking has been given on
Date

Name of prescribed body

in the following terms

Signed

Dated

Solicitor for the (claimant) (defendant)
(Part 20 defendant) (respondent) (appellant)

APPENDIX 6

FORM N260

Statement of Costs
(summary assessment)

In the	
	Court
Judge/Master	
Case Reference	

Case Title

[Party]'s Statement of Costs for the hearing on *(date)*   **(interim application/fast track trial)**

Description of fee earners*
   (a) *(name) (grade) (hourly rate claimed)*
   (b) *(name) (grade) (hourly rate claimed)*

Attendances on   *(party)*
   (a) *(number)*   hours at £   £
   (b) *(number)*   hours at £   £

Attendances on opponents
   (a) *(number)*   hours at £   £
   (b) *(number)*   hours at £   £

Attendance on others
   (a) *(number)*   hours at £   £
   (b) *(number)*   hours at £   £

Site inspections etc
   (a) *(number)*   hours at £   £
   (b) *(number)*   hours at £   £

Work done on negotiations
   (a) *(number)*   hours at £   £
   (b) *(number)*   hours at £   £

Other work, not covered above
   (a) *(number)*   hours at £   £
   (b) *(number)*   hours at £   £

Work done on documents
   (a) *(number)*   hours at £   £
   (b) *(number)*   hours at £   £

Attendance at hearing
   (a) *(number)*   hours at £   £
   (b) *(number)*   hours at £   £
   (a) *(number)*   hours travel and waiting at £   £
   (b) *(number)*   hours travel and waiting at £   £

                                                                 Sub Total £

Brought forward £ [ ]

Counsel's fees *(name) (year of call)* [ ]
      Fee for [advice/conference/documents] £ [ ]
      Fee for hearing £ [ ]

Other expenses
      [court fees] £ [ ]
      Others £ [ ]
      (give brief description) [ ]

Total £ [ ]
Amount of VAT claimed
      on solicitors and counsel's fees £ [ ]
      on other expenses £ [ ]
Grand Total £ [ ]

The costs estimated above do not exceed the costs which the *(party)* [ ]
is liable to pay in respect of the work which this estimate covers.

Dated [ ]   Signed [ ]

               Name of firm of solicitors
               [partner] for the *(party)* [ ]

---

* 4 grades of fee earner are suggested:

(A) Solicitors with over eight years post qualification experience including at least eight years litigation experience.

(B) Solicitors and legal executives with over four years post qualification experience including at least four years litigation experience.

(C) Other solicitors and legal executives and fee earners of equivalent experience.

(D) Trainee solicitors, para legals and other fee earners.

"Legal Executive" means a Fellow of the Institute of Legal Executives. Those who are not Fellows of the Institute are not entitled to call themselves legal executives and in principle are therefore not entitled to the same hourly rate as a legal executive.

In respect of each fee earner communications should be treated as attendances and routine communications should be claimed at one tenth of the hourly rate.

Law Society model CFA for personal injury cases

[*The Law Society has produced a CFA model agreement, for use from 1 November 2005. It is to assist solicitors using CFAs for providing personal injury and clinical negligence legal services to their clients.*

The Law Society does not place copyright restrictions on solicitors who use the model for this purpose. If changes are made to the model it cannot be represented as the Law Society's model. Solicitors wishing to adapt it for other types of legal services may do so, providing they do not refer to their agreement as the Law Society's model.

This CFA applies to conduct issues occurring before 1 July 2007. For rules governing conduct after 1 July 2007, see www.rules.sra.org.uk.

To be read in conjunction with 'Law Society model CFA – information for clients', contained in Appendix 8.]

CFA

For use in personal injury and clinical negligence cases only.

This agreement is a binding legal contract between you and your solicitor/s. Before you sign, please read everything carefully. This agreement must be read in conjunction with the Law Society document 'What you need to know about a CFA'.

Agreement date
[. . . . .]

I/We, the solicitor/s [. . . . .]

You, the client [. . . . .]

What is covered by this agreement

- Your claim against [. . . . .] for damages for personal injury suffered on [. . . . .] *(if either the name of the opponent or the date of the incident are unclear then set out here in as much detail as possible to give sufficient information for the client and solicitor to understand the basis of the claim being pursued)*
- Any appeal by your opponent.
- Any appeal you make against an interim order.
- Any proceedings you take to enforce a judgment, order or agreement.
- Negotiations about and/or a court assessment of the costs of this claim.

What is not covered by this agreement

- Any counterclaim against you.
- Any appeal you make against the final judgment order.

Paying us

If you win your claim, you pay our basic charges, our disbursements and a success fee. You are entitled to seek recovery from your opponent of part or all of our basic charges, our disbursements, a success fee and insurance premium as set out in the document 'What you need to know about a CFA.'

It may be that your opponent makes a Part 36 offer or payment which you reject on our advice, and your claim for damages goes ahead to trial where you recover damages that are less than that offer or payment. If this happens, we will *[not add our success fee to the basic charges] [not claim any costs]* for the work done after we received notice of the offer or payment.

If you receive interim damages, we may require you to pay our disbursements at that point and a reasonable amount for our future disbursements.

If you receive provisional damages, we are entitled to payment of our basic charges our disbursements and success fee at that point.

If you lose you remain liable for the other sides costs.

The Success Fee

The success fee is set at [. . . . . .]% of basic charges, where the claim concludes at trial; or [. . . . . .]% where the claim concludes before a trial has commenced. In addition [. . . . . .]% relates to the postponement of payment of our fees and expenses and can not be recovered from your opponent. The Success fee inclusive of any additional percentage relating to postponement cannot be more than 100% of the basic charges in total.

Other points

The parties acknowledge and agree that this agreement is not a Contentious Business Agreement within the terms of the Solicitors Act 1974.

Signatures

Signed by the solicitor(s):   . . . .

Signed by the client:. . . . .

APPENDIX 8

Law Society model CFA – information for clients

[*To be read in conjunction with 'Law Society model CFA for personal injury cases', contained in Appendix 7.*]

CONDITIONAL FEE AGREEMENTS: WHAT YOU NEED TO KNOW

Definitions of words used in this document and the accompanying CFA are explained at the end of this document.

What do I pay if I win?

If you win your claim, you pay our basic charges, our disbursements and a success fee. The amount of these is not based on or limited by the damages. You can claim from your opponent part or all of our basic charges, our disbursements, a success fee and insurance premium.

It may be that your opponent makes a Part 36 offer or payment which you reject on our advice, and your claim for damages goes ahead to trial where you recover damages that are less than that offer or payment. Refer to the 'Paying Us' section in the CFA document to establish costs we will be seeking for the work done after we received notice of the offer or payment.

If you receive interim damages, we may require you to pay our disbursements at that point as well as a reasonable amount for our future disbursements.

If you receive provisional damages, we are entitled to payment of our basic charges, our disbursements and success fee at that point.

If you win overall but on the way lose an interim hearing, you may be required to pay your opponent's charges of that hearing.

If on the way to winning or losing you are awarded any costs, by agreement or court order, then we are entitled to payment of those costs, together with a success fee on those charges if you win overall.

What do I pay if I lose?

If you lose, you pay your opponent's charges and disbursements. You may be able to take out an insurance policy against this risk. If you lose, you do not pay our charges but we may require you to pay our disbursements.

Ending this agreement

If you end this agreement before you win or lose, you pay our basic charges and disbursements. If you go on to win, you also pay a success fee.

We may end this agreement before you win or lose.

Basic charges

These are for work done from now until this agreement ends. These are subject to review.

How we calculate our basic charges

These are calculated for each hour engaged on your matter. Routine letters and telephone calls will be charged as units of one tenth of an hour. Other letters and telephone calls will be charged on a time basis. The hourly rates are:

Grade of Fee Earner	Hourly Rate
1 Solicitors with over eight years post qualification experience including at least eight years litigation experience.	
2 Solicitors and legal executives with over four years post qualification experience including at least four years litigation experience.	
3 Other solicitors and legal executives and fee earners of equivalent experience	
4 Trainee solicitors, paralegals and other fee earners.	

We review the hourly rate on [review date] and we will notify you of any change in the rate in writing.

Road Traffic Accidents

[If your claim is settled before proceedings are issued, for less than £10,000, our basic costs will be £800; plus 20% of the damages agreed up to £5,000; and 15% of the damages agreed between £5,000 and £10,000.] [If you live in London, these costs will be increased by 12.5%]. These costs are fixed by the Civil Procedure Rules.

Success fee

The success fee percentage set out in the agreement reflects the following:

(a) the fact that if you lose, we will not earn anything;
(b) our assessment of the risks of your case;
(c) any other appropriate matters;
(d) the fact that if you win we will not be paid our basic charges until the end of the claim;
(e) our arrangements with you about paying disbursements.

277

Value added tax (VAT)

We add VAT, at the rate (now [. . . . . . .]%) that applies when the work is done, to the total of the basic charges and success fee.

The Insurance Policy

In all the circumstances and on the information currently available to us, we believe, that a contract of insurance with [. . . . .] is appropriate to cover your opponent's charges and disbursements in case you lose.
   This is because

You do not have an existing or satisfactory insurance that would cover the costs of making this claim. The policy we recommend will pay:

(a) *the costs of the other party in the event that the claim fails, to a maximum of £X;*
(b) *all your disbursements if your claim fails.*
(c) *[add other key features where necessary such as, our costs and the other side's costs (without deduction from your damages) if you fail to beat an (Part 36) Offer to Settle your claim, which you rejected following our advice].*

or:
[We cannot identify a policy which meets your needs but our recommended policy is the closest that we can discover within the products that we have searched. It does not meet your needs in the following respects:

(a) *it has an excess of £Z*
(b) *the maximum cover is £ZZ*]

or:
[We cannot obtain an insurance policy at this stage but we shall continue to look for one and if we are successful in our search then we shall advise you at that stage of the benefits of the policy and purchasing it]

[NB. The italicised reasons in set out are examples only. Your solicitor must consider your individual circumstances and set out the reasons that apply.]

Law Society Conditions

The Law Society Conditions below are part of this agreement. Any amendments or additions to them will apply to you. You should read the conditions carefully and ask us about anything you find unclear.

Our responsibilities

We must:

• always act in your best interests, subject to our duty to the court;
• explain to you the risks and benefits of taking legal action;
• give you our best advice about whether to accept any offer of settlement;
• give you the best information possible about the likely costs of your claim for damages.

Your responsibilities

You must:

- give us instructions that allow us to do our work properly;
- not ask us to work in an improper or unreasonable way;
- not deliberately mislead us;
- co-operate with us;
- go to any medical or expert examination or court hearing.

Dealing with costs if you win

- You are liable to pay all our basic charges, our disbursements and success fee.
- Normally, you can claim part or all of our basic charges, our disbursements success fee and insurance premium from your opponent.
- If we and your opponent cannot agree the amount, the court will decide how much you can recover. If the amount agreed or allowed by the court does not cover all our basic charges and our disbursements, then you pay the difference.
- You will not be entitled to recover from your opponent the part of the success fee that relates to the cost to us of postponing receipt of our charges and our disbursements. This remains payable by you.
- You agree that after winning, the reasons for setting the success fee at the amount stated may be disclosed:

  (i) to the court and any other person required by the court;
  (ii) to your opponent in order to gain his or her agreement to pay the success fee.

- If the court carries out an assessment and reduces the success fee because the percentage agreed was unreasonable in view of what we knew or should have known when it was agreed, then the amount reduced ceases to be payable unless the court is satisfied that it should continue to be payable.
- If we agree with your opponent that the success fee is to be paid at a lower percentage than is set out in this agreement, then the success fee percentage will be reduced accordingly unless the court is satisfied that the full amount is payable.
- It may happen that your opponent makes an offer of one amount that includes payment of our basic charges and a success fee. If so, unless we consent, you agree not to tell us to accept the offer if it includes payment of the success fee at a lower rate than is set out in this agreement.
- If your opponent is receiving Community Legal Service funding, we are unlikely to get any money from him or her. So if this happens, you have to pay us our basic charges, disbursements and success fee.

As with the costs in general, you remain ultimately responsible for paying our success fee.

You agree to pay into a designated account any cheque received by you or by us from your opponent and made payable to you. Out of the money, you agree to let us take the balance of the basic charges; success fee; insurance premium; our remaining disbursements; and VAT.

You take the rest.

We are allowed to keep any interest your opponent pays on the charges.

If your opponent fails to pay

If your opponent does not pay any damages or charges owed to you, we have the right to take recovery action in your name to enforce a judgment, order or agreement. The charges of this action become part of the basic charges.

Payment for advocacy

The cost of advocacy and any other work by us, or by any solicitor agent on our behalf, forms part of our basic charges. We shall discuss with you the identity of any barrister instructed, and the arrangements made for payment.

Barristers who have a conditional fee agreement with us

If you win, you are normally entitled to recover their fee and success fee from your opponent. The barrister's success fee is shown in the separate conditional fee agreement we make with the barrister. We will discuss the barrister's success fee with you before we instruct him or her. If you lose, you pay the barrister nothing.

Barristers who do not have a conditional fee agreement with us

If you win, then you will normally be entitled to recover all or part of their fee from your opponent. If you lose, then you must pay their fee.

What happens when this agreement ends before your claim for damages ends?

(a) Paying us if you end this agreement

You can end the agreement at any time. We then have the right to decide whether you must:

- pay our basic charges and our disbursements including barristers' fees but not the success fee when we ask for them; or
- pay our basic charges, and our disbursements including barristers' fees and success fees if you go on to win your claim for damages.

(b) Paying us if we end this agreement

(i) We can end this agreement if you do not keep to your responsibilities. We then have the right to decide whether you must:

  - pay our basic charges and our disbursements including barristers' fees but not the success fee when we ask for them; or
  - pay our basic charges and our disbursements including barristers' fees and success fees if you go on to win your claim for damages.

(ii) We can end this agreement if we believe you are unlikely to win. If this happens, you will only have to pay our disbursements. These will include barristers' fees if the barrister does not have a conditional fee agreement with us.

(iii) We can end this agreement if you reject our opinion about making a settlement with your opponent. You must then:

  - pay the basic charges and our disbursements, including barristers' fees;
  - pay the success fee if you go on to win your claim for damages.

If you ask us to get a second opinion from a specialist solicitor outside our firm, we will do so. You pay the cost of a second opinion.

(iv) We can end this agreement if you do not pay your insurance premium when asked to do so.

(c)   Death

This agreement automatically ends if you die before your claim for damages is concluded. We will be entitled to recover our basic charges up to the date of your death from your estate.

If your personal representatives wish to continue your claim for damages, we may offer them a new conditional fee agreement, as long as they agree to pay the success fee on our basic charges from the beginning of the agreement with you.

What happens after this agreement ends

After this agreement ends, we may apply to have our name removed from the record of any court proceedings in which we are acting unless you have another form of funding and ask us to work for you.

We have the right to preserve our lien unless another solicitor working for you undertakes to pay us what we are owed including a success fee if you win.

Explanation of words used

(a)   Advocacy

Appearing for you at court hearings.

(b)   Basic charges

Our charges for the legal work we do on your claim for damages.

(c)   Claim

Your demand for damages for personal injury whether or not court proceedings are issued.

(d)   Counterclaim

A claim that your opponent makes against you in response to your claim.

(e)   Damages

Money that you win whether by a court decision or settlement.

(f)   Our disbursements

Payment we make on your behalf such as:

- court fees;
- experts' fees;
- accident report fees;
- travelling expenses.

(g)   Interim damages

Money that a court says your opponent must pay or your opponent agrees to pay while waiting for a settlement or the court's final decision.

(h)   Interim hearing

A court hearing that is not final.

(i)   Lien

Our right to keep all papers, documents, money or other property held on your behalf until all money due to us is paid. A lien may be applied after this agreement ends.

(j)   Lose

The court has dismissed your claim or you have stopped it on our advice.

(k)   Part 36 offers or payments

An offer to settle your claim made in accordance with Part 36 of the Civil Procedure Rules.

(l)   Provisional damages

Money that a court says your opponent must pay or your opponent agrees to pay, on the basis that you will be able to go back to court at a future date for further damages if:

• you develop a serious disease; or
• your condition deteriorates;

in a way that has been proved or admitted to be linked to your personal injury claim.

(m)   Success fee

The percentage of basic charges that we add to your bill if you win your claim for damages and that we will seek to recover from your opponent.

(n)   Trial

The final contested hearing or the contested hearing of any issue to be tried separately and a reference to a claim concluding at trial includes a claim settled after the trial has commenced or a judgment.

(o)   Win

Your claim for damages is finally decided in your favour, whether by a court decision or an agreement to pay you damages or in any way that you derive benefit from pursuing the claim.

'Finally' means that your opponent:

• is not allowed to appeal against the court decision; or
• has not appealed in time; or
• has lost any appeal.

APPENDIX 9

Ready reckoner

Prospects of 'Success'	% Increase
100%	0%
95%	5%
90%	11%
80%	25%
75%	33%
70%	43%
67%	50%
60%	67%
55%	82%
50%	100%

Solicitors' Code of Conduct 2007 (extracts)

RULE 1 CORE DUTIES

1.01 Justice and the rule of law

You must uphold the rule of law and the proper administration of justice.

1.02 Integrity

You must act with integrity.

1.03 Independence

You must not allow your independence to be compromised.

1.04 Best interests of clients

You must act in the best interests of each client.

1.05 Standard of service

You must provide a good standard of service to your clients.

1.06 Public confidence

You must not behave in a way that is likely to diminish the trust the public places in you or the profession.

*****

RULE 2 CLIENT RELATIONS

*****

2.01 Taking on clients

(1) You are generally free to decide whether or not to take on a particular client. However, you must refuse to act or cease acting for a client in the following circumstances:

    (a) when to act would involve you in a breach of the law or a breach of the rules of professional conduct;

    (b)   where you have insufficient resources or lack the competence to deal with the matter;

    (c)   where instructions are given by someone other than the client, or by only one client on behalf of others in a joint matter, you must not proceed without checking that all clients agree with the instructions given; or

    (d)   where you know or have reasonable grounds for believing that the instructions are affected by duress or undue influence, you must not act on those instructions until you have satisfied yourself that they represent the client's wishes.

(2)   You must not cease acting for a client except for good reason and on reasonable notice.

2.02 Client care

(1)   You must:

    (a)   identify clearly the client's objectives in relation to the work to be done for the client;

    (b)   give the client a clear explanation of the issues involved and the options available to the client;

    (c)   agree with the client the next steps to be taken; and

    (d)   keep the client informed of progress, unless otherwise agreed.

*****

2.03 Information about the cost

(1)   You must give your client the best information possible about the likely overall cost of a matter both at the outset and, when appropriate, as the matter progresses. In particular you must:

    (a)   advise the client of the basis and terms of your charges;

    (b)   advise the client if charging rates are to be increased;

    (c)   advise the client of likely payments which you or your client may need to make to others;

    (d)   discuss with the client how the client will pay, in particular:

        (i)   whether the client may be eligible and should apply for public funding; and

        (ii)   whether the client's own costs are covered by insurance or may be paid by someone else such as an employer or trade union;

    (e)   advise the client that there are circumstances where you may be entitled to exercise a lien for unpaid costs;

    (f)   advise the client of their potential liability for any other party's costs; and

    (g)   discuss with the client whether their liability for another party's costs may be covered by existing insurance or whether specially purchased insurance may be obtained.

(2)   Where you are acting for the client under a conditional fee agreement, (including a collective conditional fee agreement) in addition to complying with 2.03(1) above and 2.03(5) and (6) below, you must explain the following, both at the outset and, when appropriate, as the matter progresses:

    (a)   the circumstances in which your client may be liable for your costs and whether you will seek payment of these from the client, if entitled to do so;

(b) if you intend to seek payment of any or all of your costs from your client, you must advise your client of their right to an assessment of those costs; and

(c) where applicable, the fact that you are obliged under a fee sharing agreement to pay to a charity any fees which you receive by way of costs from the client's opponent or other third party.

*****

(5) Any information about the cost must be clear and confirmed in writing.

(6) You must discuss with your client whether the potential outcomes of any legal case will justify the expense or risk involved including, if relevant, the risk of having to pay an opponent's costs.

(7) If you can demonstrate that it was inappropriate in the circumstances to meet some or all of the requirements in 2.03(1) and (5), you will not breach 2.03.

2.04 Contingency fees

(1) You must not enter into an arrangement to receive a contingency fee for work done in prosecuting or defending any contentious proceedings before a court of England and Wales, a British court martial or an arbitrator where the seat of the arbitration is in England and Wales, except as permitted by statute or the common law.

(2) You must not enter into an arrangement to receive a contingency fee for work done in prosecuting or defending any contentious proceedings before a court of an overseas jurisdiction or an arbitrator where the seat of the arbitration is overseas except to the extent that a lawyer of that jurisdiction would be permitted to do so.

*****

2.06 Commissions

If you are a principal in a firm you must ensure that your firm pays to your client commission received over £20 unless the client, having been told the amount, or if the precise amount is not known, an approximate amount or how the amount is to be calculated, has agreed that your firm may keep it.

*****

GUIDANCE TO RULE 2 – CLIENT RELATIONS

General

1. The requirements of rule 2 do not exhaust your obligations to clients. As your client's trusted adviser, you must act in the client's best interests (see 1.04) and you must not abuse or exploit the relationship by taking advantage of a client's age, inexperience, ill health, lack of education or business experience, or emotional or other vulnerability.

2. It is not envisaged or intended that a breach of 2.02, 2.03 or 2.05 should invariably render a retainer unenforceable. As noted in the introduction to this rule, the purpose of 2.02 and 2.03 is to ensure that clients are given the information necessary to enable them to make appropriate decisions about if and how their matter should proceed. These parts of the rule together with 2.05 require you to provide certain information to your client. Subrules 2.02(3), 2.03(7) and 2.05(2) recognise that it is not always necessary to provide all this information to comply with the underlying purpose of the rule. Similarly, the information you are required to

give to your client varies in importance both inherently and in relation to the individual client and the retainer. Consequently, the rule will be enforced in a manner which is proportionate to the seriousness of the breach. For example, if you were to fail to tell your client that they would be liable to pay another party's costs in breach of 2.03(1)(f), this is likely to be treated as a more serious breach than your failure to advise your client about your right to exercise a lien for unpaid costs in breach of 2.03(1)(e).

You should note that a breach of rule 2 may provide evidence against a solicitor, an REL or a recognised body of inadequate professional services under section 37A of the Solicitors Act 1974. The powers of the Legal Complaints Service on a finding of an inadequate professional service include disallowing all or part of the solicitor's or REL's costs and directing the solicitor or REL to pay compensation to the client. Section 37A does not apply to you if you are an RFL. Solicitor and REL partners in a multi-national partnership (MNP) are subject to section 37A in respect of services provided by the MNP.

Taking on clients – 2.01

3. Subrule 2.01 identifies some situations where you must refuse to act for a client or, if already acting, must stop doing so.

    The retainer is a contractual relationship and subject to legal considerations. You should be sure of your legal position as to who is your client if you contract to provide services to a third party. For example, if you agree to provide all or part of a Home Information Pack to an estate agent or Home Information Pack provider for the benefit seller, you should ensure there is an agreed understanding as to whether the estate agent/pack provider or the seller is your client.[1]

4. Your right to decide not to accept instructions is subject to restrictions, including the following:

    (a) You must not refuse for a reason that would breach rule 6 (Equality and diversity).

    (b) Rule 11 (Litigation and advocacy), governing a solicitor or REL acting as an advocate, contains restrictions on when the solicitor or REL may refuse instructions.

    (c) Be aware of restrictions on when you can refuse to act or cease acting for a publicly funded client in a criminal matter.

5. If you are an in-house solicitor or in-house REL you are already in a contractual relationship with your employer who is, for the purpose of these rules, your client. You are not therefore necessarily as free as a solicitor or REL in a firm to refuse instructions, and will need to use your professional judgement in applying 2.01.

6. Subrule 2.01 sets out situations in which you must refuse instructions or, where appropriate, cease acting. These might include the following:

    (a) *Breach of the law or rules*
        (i) where there is a conflict of interests between you and your client or between two or more clients – see rule 3 (Conflict of interests);
        (ii) where money laundering is suspected, your freedom to cease acting is curtailed (see the Proceeds of Crime Act 2002, the Money Laundering Regulations 2003 (SI 2003/3075), other relevant law and directives, and guidance issued by the Board of the Solicitors Regulation Authority on this subject); and

---

1. This paragraph was inserted 24 July 2007. See also guidance note 8 below.

      (iii) where the client is a child or a patient (within the meaning of the Mental Health Act 1983), special circumstances apply. You cannot enter into a contract with such a person and, furthermore, if your client loses mental capacity after you have started to act, the law will automatically end the contractual relationship. However, it is important that the client, who is in a very vulnerable situation, is not left without legal representation. Consequently, you should notify an appropriate person (e.g. the Court of Protection), or you may look for someone legally entitled to provide you with instructions, such as an attorney under an enduring power of attorney, or take the appropriate steps for such a person to be appointed, such as a receiver or a litigation friend. This is a particularly complex legal issue and you should satisfy yourself as to the law before deciding on your course of action.

(b) *Insufficient resources*

Before taking on a new matter, you must consider whether your firm has the resources – including knowledge, qualifications, expertise, time, sufficient support staff and, where appropriate, access to external expertise such as agents and counsel – to provide the support required to represent the client properly. The obligation is a continuing one, and you must ensure that an appropriate or agreed level of service can be delivered even if circumstances change.

(c) *Duress or undue influence*

It is important to be satisfied that clients give their instructions freely. Some clients, such as the elderly, those with language or learning difficulties and those with disabilities are particularly vulnerable to pressure from others. If you suspect that a client's instructions are the result of undue influence you need to exercise your judgement as to whether you can proceed on the client's behalf. For example, if you suspect that a friend or relative who accompanies the client is exerting undue influence, you should arrange to see the client alone or if appropriate with an independent third party or interpreter. Where there is no actual evidence of undue influence but the client appears to want to act against their best interests, it may be sufficient simply to explain the consequences of the instructions the client has given and confirm that the client wishes to proceed. For evidential purposes, it would be sensible to get this confirmation in writing.

7.   As a matter of good practice you should not act for a client who has instructed another firm in the same matter unless the other firm agrees. If you are asked to provide a second opinion, you may do so but you should satisfy yourself that you have sufficient information to handle the matter properly.

Ceasing to act

8.   A client can end the retainer with you at any time and for any reason. You may only end the relationship with the client if there is a good reason and after giving reasonable notice.[2] Examples of good reasons include where there is a break-

---

2. On 24 July 2007 the third sentence of guidance note 8 was deleted. The sentence read as follows: 'The retainer is a contractual relationship and subject to legal considerations.' Please note the addition to guidance note 3 above.

down in confidence between you and the client, and where you are unable to obtain proper instructions.

9. If there is good reason to cease acting, you must give reasonable notice to the client. What amounts to reasonable notice will depend on the circumstances. For example, it would normally be unreasonable to stop acting for a client immediately before a court hearing where it is impossible for the client to find alternative representation. In such a case, if there is no alternative but to cease acting immediately, you should attend and explain the circumstances to the court – see rule 11 (Litigation and advocacy). There may be circumstances where it is reasonable to give no notice.

10. The relationship between you and your client can also be ended automatically by law, for example by the client's bankruptcy or mental incapacity (see note 6(a)(iii) above).

11. When you cease acting for a client, you will need to consider what should be done with the paperwork. You must hand over the client's files promptly on request subject to your right to exercise a lien in respect of outstanding costs. You should try to ensure the client's position is not prejudiced, and should also bear in mind his or her rights under the Data Protection Act 1998. Undertakings to secure the costs should be used as an alternative to the exercise of a lien if possible. There may be circumstances where it is unreasonable to exercise a lien, for example, where the amount of the outstanding costs is small and the value or importance of the matter is very great. In any dispute over the ownership of documents you should refer to the law. Further advice about the law of lien or the ownership of documents can be found in *Cordery on Solicitors* or other reference books on the subject.

Client care – 2.02

12. The purpose of 2.02 is to set out the type of information that must normally be given to a client. This information must be provided in a clear and readily accessible form.

13. Subrule 2.02 is flexible about the extent of the information to be given in each individual case. Over-complex or lengthy terms of business letters may not be helpful.

14. The 'level of service' to be provided should be agreed at the outset. For example, the client may want regular written reports. Alternatively, the client may want to provide initial instructions then to hear no more until an agreed point has been reached. This will affect the projected costs of the matter.

15. When considering the options available to the client (2.02(1)(b)), if the matter relates to a dispute between your client and a third party, you should discuss whether mediation or some other alternative dispute resolution (ADR) procedure may be more appropriate than litigation, arbitration or other formal processes. There may be costs sanctions if a party refuses ADR – see *Halsey v Milton Keynes NHS Trust and Steel and Joy* [2004] EWCA (Civ) 576. More information may be obtained from the Law Society's Practice Advice Service.

16. Subrule 2.02(2)(e) requires you to explain limitations or conditions on your acting arising from your relationship with a third party. Where such a relationship involves sharing any client information with a third party, you must inform the client and obtain their consent. Failure to do so would be a breach of client confidentiality (see rule 4 – Confidentiality and disclosure) and possibly also a breach of the Data Protection Act 1998. Some arrangements with third parties, such as introducers under rule 9 (Referrals of business) or fee sharers under rule 8 (Fee sharing), may constrain the way in which you handle clients' matters.

17. The constraints that such arrangements impose may fall into one of the following categories:

   (a) Constraints which are proper and do not require disclosure to the client. These normally relate to service standards such as dealing with client enquiries within a specified time, the use of specified computer software, telecommunications systems, a particular advertising medium, or particular training provision.

   (b) Constraints which are proper but require disclosure to the client. Some third parties may have a legitimate interest in the progress of the client's matter and the way it is dealt with – for instance, third parties who fund a client's matter, and insurers. Constraints that they impose, e.g. that you will not issue proceedings without the authority of the funder are proper provided they do not operate against the client's best interests, but should be disclosed to the client.

   (c) Constraints which are improper cannot be remedied by disclosing them to the client. These are constraints which impair your independence and ability to act in the client's best interests. You cannot accept an arrangement which involves such constraints. They might include, for instance, requirements that you do not disclose information to the client to which the client is entitled, or give advice to the client which you know is contrary to the client's best interests, or with which you disagree, or that you act towards the court in a deceitful manner or lie to a third party.

18. You must give the required information to the client as soon as possible after you have agreed to act. You must then keep the client up to date with the progress of the matter and any changes affecting the original agreement.

19. The status of the person dealing with your client must be made absolutely clear, for legal and ethical reasons. For example, a person who is not a solicitor must not be described as one, either expressly or by implication. All staff having contact with clients, including reception, switchboard and secretarial staff, should be advised accordingly.

20. All clients affected by a material alteration to the composition of the firm must be informed personally. Where the person having conduct of a matter leaves a firm, the client in question must be informed, preferably in advance, and told the name and status of the person who is to take over their matter.

21. Subrule 2.02(2)(d) refers to the person responsible for the overall supervision of a matter. Supervision requirements are dealt with in rule 5 (Business management) and guidance about who can supervise matters may be found there.

22. There may be circumstances when it would be inappropriate to provide any or all of the information required by 2.02. It will be for you to justify why compliance was not appropriate in an individual matter. For example, where you are asked for 'one-off' advice, or where you have a long-standing client who is familiar with your firm's terms of business and knows the status of the person dealing with the matter, this information may not need to be repeated. However, other aspects of 2.02 must be complied with and the client must be kept up to date and informed of changes.

23. If you are an in-house solicitor or in-house REL much of 2.02 will be inappropriate when you are acting for your employer. However, it may be necessary for you to comply with aspects of 2.02 when you are acting for someone other than your employer in accordance with rule 13 (In-house practice).

24. If you receive instructions from someone other than your client, you must still give the client the information required under 2.02. There are, however, exceptions to this. For example, where your client is represented by an attorney under

a power of attorney or where a receiver has been appointed because the client has lost mental capacity, the information required by 2.02 should be given to the attorney or receiver.

25. In order to provide evidence of compliance with 2.02, you should consider giving the information in writing even though this is not a requirement.

26. Where you are, in effect, your firm's client – for example, as an executor administering a deceased's estate or a trustee of a trust – you should consider what information, if any, should be given to interested parties. There is no requirement, for example, that beneficiaries under a will or trust should be treated as though they were clients. It may, however, be good practice to provide some information – for example, about the type of work to be carried out and approximate timescales.

Information about the cost – 2.03

27. The purpose of 2.03 is to ensure that the client is given relevant costs information and that this is clearly expressed. Information about costs must be worded in a way that is appropriate for the client. All costs information must be given in writing and regularly updated.

28. Subrule 2.03 recognises that there may be circumstances where it would be inappropriate to provide any or all of the information required. It will be for you to justify why compliance was not appropriate in an individual matter. For example, your firm may regularly do repeat work for the client on agreed terms and the client might not need the costs information repeated. However, the client should be informed, for example, of any changes in a firm's charging rates.

29. If you are an in-house solicitor or REL, much of 2.03 will be inappropriate if you are acting for your employer.

30. This guidance does not deal with the form a bill can take, final and interim bills, when they can be delivered and when and how a firm can sue on a bill. All these matters are governed by complex legal provisions, and there are many publications that provide help to firms and clients. Advice on some aspects of costs is available from the Law Society's Practice Advice Service.

31. You will usually be free to negotiate the cost and the method of payment with your clients. It will not normally be necessary for the client to be separately advised on the cost agreement. Different cost options may have different implications for the client – for example, where the choice is between a conditional fee agreement and an application for public funding. In those circumstances clients should be made aware of the implications of each option.

32. The rule requires you to advise the client of the circumstances in which you may be entitled to exercise a lien for unpaid costs. For more information see note 11 above.

33. Clients may be referred to you at a stage when they have already signed a contract for a funding arrangement – see also rule 9 (Referrals of business). You should explain the implications of any such arrangement fully including the extent to which the charges associated with such an arrangement may be recovered from another party to the proceedings.

34. There may be some unusual arrangements, however, where it should be suggested that the client considers separate advice on what is being proposed – for example, where you are to receive shares in a new company instead of costs. See also rule 3 (Conflict of interests) and 9.02(g) for details about your obligations to clients who have been referred to you.

35. Subrule 2.03 does not cover all the different charging arrangements possible or the law governing them. However, it does require that the chosen option is explained as fully as possible to the client. It also requires that if you have agreed

to pay all, or part, of your fees to a charity in accordance with rule 8 (Fee sharing) the client must be informed at the outset of the name of that charity.

36.   It is often impossible to tell at the outset what the overall cost will be. Subrule 2.03 allows for this and requires that you provide the client with as much information as possible at the start and that you keep the client updated. If a precise figure cannot be given at the outset, you should explain the reason to the client and agree a ceiling figure or review dates.

37.   Particular information will be of relevance at particular stages of a client's matter. You should, for example, ensure that clients understand the costs implications of any offers of settlement. Where offers of settlement are made, clients must be fully informed of the amount to be deducted in respect of costs and how this figure is calculated. You should advise clients of their rights to assessment of your costs in such circumstances.

38.   When a potential client contacts you with a view to giving you instructions you should always, when asked, try to be helpful in providing information on the likely costs of their matter.

Work under a conditional fee agreement or for a publicly funded client

39.   Subrule 2.03(2) and (3) set out additional information which must be explained to the client when work is done under a conditional fee agreement or on a publicly funded basis. Conditional fee agreements are subject to statutory requirements and all agreements must conform to these. Where you are acting under a conditional fee agreement and you are obliged under a fee sharing agreement to pay to a charity any fees which you receive by way of costs from the client's opponent or other third party, the client must be informed at the outset of the name of that charity.

Payments to others

40.   You must explain at the outset to your client any likely payments they will have to make. These could include court fees, search fees, experts' fees and counsel's fees. Where possible, you should give details of the probable cost and if this is not possible you should agree with the client to review these expenses and the need for them nearer the time they are likely to be incurred.

Contingency fees – 2.04

41.   A 'contingency fee' is defined in rule 24 (Interpretation) as any sum (whether fixed, or calculated either as a percentage of the proceeds or otherwise) payable only in the event of success.

42.   If you enter into an arrangement for a lawful contingency fee with a client, what amounts to 'success' should be agreed between you and your client prior to entering into the arrangement.

43.   Under rule 24 (Interpretation), 'contentious proceedings' is to be construed in accordance with the definition of 'contentious business' in section 87 of the Solicitors Act 1974.

44.   Conditional fees are a form of contingency fees. In England and Wales a conditional fee agreement for certain types of litigation is permitted by statute. See section 58 of the Courts and Legal Services Act 1990 (as amended by section 27 of the Access to Justice Act 1999) and 2.03(2) above for more information.

45.   It is acceptable to enter into a contingency fee arrangement for non-contentious matters (see section 87 of the Solicitors Act 1974 for the definition of 'non-

contentious business') but you should note that to be enforceable the arrangement must be contained in a non-contentious business agreement.

46. An otherwise contentious matter remains non-contentious up to the commencement of proceedings. Consequently, you may enter into a contingency fee arrangement for, for example, the receipt of commission for the successful collection of debts owed to a client, provided legal proceedings are not started.

Complaints handling – 2.05

47. The purpose of 2.05 is to encourage complaints to be properly and openly dealt with. There are huge benefits in terms of time, money and client satisfaction if complaints can be dealt with effectively at firm level.

48. The content of your firm's complaints handling procedure is a matter for the firm, but the procedure must be in writing, clear and unambiguous. If a complaint is made to the Legal Complaints Service (LCS) or the Solicitors Regulation Authority the firm will need to be able to demonstrate compliance. Everyone in the firm will need to know about this obligation to ensure that clients know who to contact if they have a problem, the information to give the client when a complaint is made, and the importance of recording the stages of the complaint and the final outcome. When you acknowledge the complaint, your letter should contain details of the Legal Complaints Service, with the post and web addresses of that organisation. You should also explain that the client(s) can ask the LCS to become involved at the end of the firm's own complaints procedure if they are unhappy with the outcome. It is important to advise of the time limit, which is generally 6 months from the end of the firm's procedure, and can be checked by looking at the LCS website or by telephoning the LCS.

49. Your firm's arrangements for dealing with complaints must be fair and effective. Any investigation must be handled within an agreed timescale. Any arrangements must also comply with rule 6 (Equality and diversity).

50. Subrule 2.05(3) prevents you charging your client for the cost of handling a complaint. Dealing properly with complaints is an integral part of any professional business. The associated costs are part of the firm's overheads, and complainants must not be charged separately.

51. Subrule 2.05(2) allows for situations where it may be inappropriate to give all the information required.

Commissions –2.06

52. Subrule 2.06 reflects the legal position, preventing a solicitor making a secret profit arising from the solicitor-client relationship.

53. A commission is:

(a) a financial benefit you receive by reason of and in the course of the relationship of solicitor and client; and

(b) arises in the context that you have put a third party and the client in touch with one another. (See *The Law Society v Mark Hedley Adcock and Neil Kenneth Mocroft* [2006] EWHC 3212 (Admin)).

54. Examples of what amounts to a commission include payments received from a stockbroker on the purchase of stocks and shares, from an insurance company or intermediary on the purchase or renewal of an insurance policy, and from a bank or building society on the opening of a bank account. Also, a payment made to you for introducing a client to a third party (unless the introduction was

unconnected with any particular matter which you were currently or had been handling for the client) amounts to a commission.

55. On the other hand, a discount on a product or a rebate on, for example, a search fee would not amount to a commission because it does not arise in the context of referring your client to a third party. Such payments are disbursements and the client must get the benefit of any discount or rebate.

56. A client can give informed consent only if you:

(a) provide details concerning the amount; and

(b) make it clear that they can withhold their consent and, if so, the commission will belong to them when it is received by you.

57. Commission received may be retained only if the conditions within 2.06 are complied with and the arrangement is in your client's best interests – either:

(a) it is used to offset a bill of costs; or

(b) you must be able to justify its retention – for example, the commission is retained in lieu of costs which you could have billed for work done in placing the business, but were not so billed.

58. It cannot be in the best interests of the client for you to receive the commission as a gift. There must be proper and fair legal consideration, such as your agreement to undertake legal work. In consequence, except where the commission is to be offset against a bill of costs:

(a) it is important that consent is obtained prior to the receipt of the commission (and preferably before you undertake the work leading to the paying of the commission);

(b) for the purposes of complying with 2.06 you may not obtain your client's consent to retain the commission after you have received it. If consent is not given beforehand, there can be no legal consideration and so the money belongs to the client; and

(c) if you have obtained consent but the amount actually received is materially in excess of the estimate given to your client, you cannot retrospectively obtain consent to retain the excess. The excess belongs to your client and should be handled accordingly.

59. In order to minimise possible confusion and misunderstanding, and to protect both you and your client, it is recommended that the agreement containing the details about the commission be in writing.

60. If it is your intention from the outset to use the commission to offset a bill of costs, it should be (subject to there being no specific instructions concerning the use of the commission):

(a) paid into client account as money on account of costs, if received before the bill has been submitted; or

(b) paid straight into office account if the bill has already been submitted.

61. Where you intend to retain the commission in lieu of costs and your client has provided their consent in accordance with 2.06, the money may be paid into office account as soon as it is received. Where you have requested your client's consent and it has been refused, the commission will belong to the client on receipt and must be paid into client account. It may then be paid to the client or used to offset a bill subject to note 60 above. See the Solicitors' Accounts Rules 1998 for more information.

62. Where you are a sole trustee or attorney or a joint trustee or attorney only with other solicitors, you cannot give proper consent to your retaining commission by

purporting to switch capacities. Furthermore, you are very likely to be acting contrary to your fiduciary obligations at law.

63. For further information about dealing with commission see Solicitors' Financial Services (Scope) Rules 2001.

Limitation of civil liability by contract – 2.07

64. For the qualifying insurance cover currently required see the Solicitors' Indemnity Insurance Rules.

65. The details of any limitation must be in writing and brought to the attention of the client. Because such a limitation goes to the heart of the agreement between you and your client, you should ensure that your client knows about the limitation and, in your opinion, understands its effect. Consequently, it would not be appropriate to include the limitation within a 'terms of business' letter without specifically drawing your client's attention to it.

66. Where you are preparing a trust instrument for a client and that instrument includes a term or terms which has or have the effect of excluding or limiting liability in negligence for a prospective trustee, you should take reasonable steps before the trust is created to ensure that your client is aware of the meaning and effect of the clause. Extra care will be needed if you are, or anyone in or associated with your firm is, or is likely later to become, a paid trustee of the trust.

67. Where you or another person in, or associated with, your firm is considering acting as a paid trustee you should not cause to be included a clause in a trust instrument which has the effect of excluding or limiting liability for negligence without taking reasonable steps before the trust is created to ensure that the settlor is aware of the meaning and effect of the clause.

It would be prudent to ensure both that:–

(a) there is evidence that you have taken the appropriate steps; and

(b) that evidence is retained for as long as the trust exists and for a suitable period afterwards.

68. Subrule 2.07 is subject to the position in law. The points which follow should be noted. The Solicitors Regulation Authority is entitled to expect you to undertake your own research and/or take appropriate advice as to the general law in this area. Relying upon this guidance alone may not be sufficient to ensure compliance with the law.

(a) Liability for fraud or reckless disregard of professional obligations cannot be limited.

(b) Existing legal restraints cannot be overridden. In particular, the courts will not enforce in your favour an unfair agreement with your client.

(c) Under section 60(5) of the Solicitors Act 1974 and paragraph 24 of Schedule 2 to the Administration of Justice Act 1985, a provision in a contentious business agreement that a firm shall not be liable for negligence, or shall be relieved from any responsibility which would otherwise apply is void.

(d) By section 2(2) of the Unfair Contract Terms Act 1977, a contract term which seeks to exclude liability for negligence is of no effect except in so far as it satisfies the requirement of reasonableness set out in section 11 of that Act. Section 11 specifies that the contract term must be fair and reasonable having regard to the circumstances which were or ought reasonably to have been known to, or in the contemplation of, the parties when the contract was made. Schedule 2 to the Act sets out guidelines as to the factors to be taken into account in considering whether the contract term meets the test of reasonableness.

(e)   Section 11(4) of the Unfair Contract Terms Act 1977 provides that where a contractual term seeks to restrict liability to a specified sum of money, the question of whether the requirement of reasonableness has been satisfied must also take into account the resources available to you for the purpose of meeting the liability, and the extent to which insurance is available.

(f)   The Unfair Terms in Consumer Contracts Regulations 1999 (SI 1999/2083) have a comparable effect to the Unfair Contract Terms Act 1977 as to limitation or exclusion of liability, where your client is a consumer and the term in question has not been individually negotiated. Regulation 3(1) defines a consumer as any natural person who, in contracts covered by those Regulations, is acting for purposes which are outside their trade, business or profession. Regulation 5(2) states that a term shall always be regarded as not having been individually negotiated where it has been drafted in advance and the consumer has therefore not been able to influence the substance of the term. Regulation 5(1) provides that a term is unfair if, contrary to the requirements of good faith, it causes a significant imbalance in the parties' rights and obligations. Schedule 2 to the Regulations contains an indicative, non-exhaustive list of contract terms which may be regarded as unfair. The test of fairness under these Regulations is not identical to the test of reasonableness under the Unfair Contract Terms Act 1977.

(g)   When the retainer may be affected by foreign law, such matters may need to be considered according to the law applicable to the contract.

69.   You should also note that if you want to limit your firm's liability to a figure above the minimum level for qualifying insurance but within your firm's top-up insurance cover, you will need to consider whether the top-up insurance will adequately cover a claim arising from the matter in question. For example:

(a)   If your firm agrees with a client that its liability will not exceed £4 million, and the top-up insurance is calculated on an aggregate yearly basis, there is no guarantee that the amount of the top-up cover would be sufficient where there have been multiple claims already.

(b)   Because insurance cover available to meet any particular claim is usually ascertained by reference to the year in which the claim itself is first made, or notice of circumstances which may give rise to a claim is first brought to the attention of insurers, the top-up cover when the claim is brought (or notice of circumstances given) may not be the same as it was when the contract was made.

70.   You will not breach 2.07 by agreeing with your client that liability will rest with your firm and not with any employee, director, member or shareowner who might otherwise be liable. However, any such agreement is subject to section 60(5) of the Solicitors Act 1974, the Unfair Contract Terms Act 1977 and the Unfair Terms in Consumer Contracts Regulations 1999.

71.   Subrule 2.07 does not apply in relation to your overseas practice. However, if you are a principal or a recognised body 15.02(3) prohibits you from seeking to limit your civil liability below the minimum level of cover you would need in order to comply with 15.26 (Professional indemnity).

72.   You will not breach 2.07 by a term limiting or excluding any liability to persons who are not your client under the principle in *Hedley Byrne & Co Ltd v Heller & Partners Ltd* [1964] AC 465. However, any such term will be subject to section 60(5) of the Solicitors Act 1974, the Unfair Contract Terms Act 1977 and the Unfair Terms in Consumer Contracts Regulations 1999, where appropriate.

*****

GUIDANCE TO RULE 7 – PUBLICITY

Geographical scope of the rule

1.

    (a)   Rule 7 applies to publicity in connection with practice from any office, whether in England and Wales or overseas – but the provisions are amended by 15.07 for publicity in connection with overseas practice.

    (b)   Rule 7 does not apply to the website, e-mails, text messages or similar electronic communications of any practice you conduct from an office in an EU state other than the UK (see 15.07(a)).

    (c)   Subrule 7.07 (Letterhead) does not apply to a solicitor's practice conducted from an office outside England and Wales or to an REL's practice conducted from an office in Scotland or Northern Ireland. However, you must comply with 15.07(b).

*****

GUIDANCE TO RULE 8 – FEE SHARING

*****

Fee sharing with charities and other non-lawyers

*****

5.   If you act in accordance with a pro bono conditional fee agreement and you advance disbursements on behalf of your client, and these disbursements are received by way of costs from your client's opponent or from another third party, you may retain from the costs which are received the element which covers such disbursements. The terms of this arrangement will need to be set out in the conditional fee agreement.

*****

RULE 9   REFERRALS OF BUSINESS

9.01   General

(1)   When making or receiving referrals of clients to or from third parties you must do nothing which would compromise your independence or your ability to act and advise in the best interests of your clients.

(2)   You must draw the attention of potential introducers to this rule and to the relevant provisions of rule 7 (Publicity).

(3)   This rule does not apply to referrals between lawyers.

(4)   You must not, in respect of any claim arising as a result of death or personal injury, either:

    (a)   enter into an arrangement for the referral of clients with; or

    (b)   act in association with,

any person whose business, or any part of whose business, is to make, support or prosecute (whether by action or otherwise, and whether by a solicitor or agent or otherwise) claims arising as a result of death or personal injury, and who, in the course of such business, solicits or receives contingency fees in respect of such claims.

(5) The prohibition in 9.01(4) shall not apply to an arrangement or association with a person who solicits or receives contingency fees only in respect of proceedings in a country outside England and Wales, to the extent that a local lawyer would be permitted to receive a contingency fee in respect of such proceedings.

(6) In 9.01(4) and (5) 'contingency fee' means any sum (whether fixed, or calculated either as a percentage of the proceeds or otherwise howsoever) payable only in the event of success in the prosecution or defence of any action, suit or other contentious proceedings.

9.02 Financial arrangements with introducers

The following additional requirements apply when you enter into a financial arrangement with an introducer:

(a) The agreement must be in writing and be available for inspection by the Solicitors Regulation Authority.

(b) The introducer must undertake, as part of the agreement, to comply with the provisions of this rule.

(c) You must be satisfied that clients referred by the introducer have not been acquired as a result of marketing or publicity or other activities which, if done by a person regulated by the Solicitors Regulation Authority, would be in breach of any of these rules.

(d) The agreement must not include any provision which would:

    (i) compromise, infringe or impair any of the duties set out in these rules; or

    (ii) allow the introducer to influence or constrain your professional judgement in relation to the advice given to the client.

(e) The agreement must provide that before making a referral the introducer must give the client all relevant information concerning the referral, in particular:

    (i) the fact that the introducer has a financial arrangement with you; and

    (ii) the amount of any payment to the introducer which is calculated by reference to that referral; or

    (iii) where the introducer is paying you to provide services to the introducer's customers:

        (A) the amount the introducer is paying you to provide those services; and

        (B) the amount the client is required to pay the introducer.

(f) If you have reason to believe that the introducer is breaching any of the terms of the agreement required by this rule, you must take all reasonable steps to ensure that the breach is remedied. If the introducer continues to breach it you must terminate the agreement.

(g) Before accepting instructions to act for a client referred under 9.02 you must, in addition to the requirements contained in 2.02 (Client care), 2.03 (Information about costs) or 2.05 (Complaint handling), give the client, in writing, all relevant information concerning the referral, in particular:

    (i) the fact that you have a financial arrangement with the introducer;

(ii) the amount of any payment to the introducer which is calculated by reference to that referral; or

(iii) where the introducer is paying you to provide services to the introducer's customers:

(A) the amount the introducer is paying you to provide those services; and

(B) the amount the client is required to pay the introducer;

(iv) a statement that any advice you give will be independent and that the client is free to raise questions on all aspects of the transaction; and

(v) confirmation that information disclosed to you by the client will not be disclosed to the introducer unless the client consents; but that where you are also acting for the introducer in the same matter and a conflict of interests arises, you might be obliged to cease acting.

(h) You must not enter into a financial arrangement with an introducer for the referral of clients in respect of criminal proceedings or any matter in which you will act for the client with the benefit of public funding.

(i) For the purpose of this rule:

(i) 'financial arrangement' includes:

(A) any payment to a third party in respect of referrals; and

(B) any agreement to be paid by a third party introducer to provide services to the third party's customers; and

(ii) 'payment' includes any other consideration but does not include normal hospitality, proper disbursements or normal business expenses.

9.03   Referrals to third parties

(1) If you recommend that a client use a particular firm, agency or business, you must do so in good faith, judging what is in the client's best interests.

(2) You must not enter into any agreement or association which would restrict your freedom to recommend any particular firm, agency or business.

(3) (2) above does not apply to arrangements in connection with any of the following types of contracts:

(a) regulated mortgage contracts;

(b) general insurance contracts; or

(c) pure protection contracts.

(4) The terms 'regulated mortgage contracts', 'general insurance contracts' and 'pure protection contracts' in (3) above have the meanings given in 19.01(4).

(5) Where you refer a client to a firm, agency or business that can only offer products from one source, you must notify the client in writing of this limitation.

(6) If a client is likely to need an endowment policy, or similar life insurance with an investment element, you must refer them only to an independent intermediary authorised to give investment advice.

GUIDANCE TO RULE 9 – REFERRALS OF BUSINESS

General

1. You must not allow the requirements of an introducer, nor your wish to avoid offending an introducer, to affect the advice you give to your clients. Neither must you become so reliant on an introducer as a source of work that this affects the advice you give to your client. It is therefore recommended that your firm

conducts regular reviews of your referral arrangements to ensure that this is not happening. Factors you should consider in reviewing your arrangements are:

(a) whether you have complied with the provisions of rule 9;
(b) whether you have given referred clients independent advice, which has not been affected by the interests of the introducer; and
(c) the amount and proportion of your firm's income arising as a result of each referral arrangement.

2. You should always retain control of the work you do for clients. No arrangement with an introducer should affect your duty to communicate directly with the client to obtain or confirm instructions, in the process of providing advice and at all appropriate stages of the transaction.

Financial arrangements with introducers

3. Rule 9 permits you to pay for referrals, and to be paid by an introducer to provide services to the introducer's customers, subject to conditions. These conditions apply whenever you make a payment, or give other consideration, to a third party who refers clients to you, unless you can show that the payment is wholly unconnected with the referral of any client to you. The conditions also apply regardless of how the payment (or other consideration) is described. For example, the conditions would apply to the payment of administrative or marketing fees, payments described as 'disbursements' which are not proper disbursements, and panel membership fees. Equally, you will not be able to avoid the requirements of the rule by, for example, making the payment to an intermediary who, in turn, has an arrangement with the introducer. When investigating complaints the Solicitors Regulation Authority will consider the substance of any relationship rather than the mere form.

4. 'Other consideration' might include, for example, the provision of services and secondment of staff to the introducer, or an agreement to purchase services or products from the introducer (where such a purchase is a condition of referrals being made).

Disclosure – by you

5. Where a payment is made to an introducer in relation to each client referred by the introducer, either as a fixed amount or as a proportion of the fee charged to the client, the amount of the payment must be disclosed to each client. Where a payment to an introducer is more general in nature (for example, it may be a fixed, annual or monthly fee), clients referred by the introducer should be informed that you are making a payment and of the nature of the financial arrangement (or other consideration given). If the client asks for more information about the overall amount of payments made, you should supply such information as you are able. In any case where it is reasonably possible for you to calculate how much of the payment to an introducer relates to a particular client, you must disclose the amount.

6. Where you are being paid by an introducer to provide services to the introducer's customers, both you and the introducer are required to disclose both the amount the introducer is paying you to provide services to the client and the amount the introducer is charging the client for your services. This will enable the client to ascertain whether, and if so how much, the introducer is charging for making the referral and to make an informed decision whether to accept the referral on that basis.

7. You may need to disclose to the client other information, apart from the payment, concerning the nature of the referral agreement. (See 2.02(2)(e).)

8. The requirement that you should make disclosure before accepting instructions will normally mean that you should write to the client as soon as you are asked to act for the client, rather than waiting until the first interview with the client. If time does not permit this, disclosure should be made at the beginning of the interview and confirmed in writing.

Disclosure – by the introducer

9. Subrule 9.02(e) requires the introducer to provide the client with all information concerning the referral. It will therefore be necessary for you to agree the nature of this information with the introducer. See note 5 above on disclosure of payments. It is recommended that you ask referred clients on a regular basis what information the introducer has provided about the referral arrangement. You should keep written records of checks made with clients for evidential purposes.

Publicity

10. Subrule 9.02(c) requires you to be satisfied that the introducer has not acquired the client as a consequence of marketing, publicity or other activities which, if done by a person regulated by the Solicitors Regulation Authority, would have been in breach of these rules (particularly rule 7 (Publicity)). Three requirements of rule 7 are particularly important for you to bear in mind in the context of payments for referrals:

    (a) the general ban on misleading or inaccurate publicity;
    (b) the prohibition of unsolicited visits and telephone calls to a 'member of the public' (cold calling – see 7.02); and
    (c) the requirement that you must not authorise a third party to publicise your firm in a way which would be contrary to rule 7.

Duty to monitor/terminate referral agreements

11. You will be expected to have made suitable enquiries about the way in which an introducer publicises your firm. If you become aware of possible breaches of rule 9 or rule 7 (Publicity), you must bring these to the attention of introducers, and if necessary must terminate a referral agreement.

Improper constraints

12. Subrule 9.02(d)(ii) aims to prevent the introducer from influencing or constraining your professional judgement in respect of advice given to clients. For example, the choice of an expert or the decision to instruct counsel are integral to your role in advising the client. See also notes 16 and 17 of the guidance to rule 2 (Client relations) regarding arrangements with introducers which may constrain your professional judgement.

Excepted work

13. Subrule 9.02(h) prohibits you having a financial arrangement with an introducer in respect of criminal proceedings, or in any matter in which you will act for the

client with the benefit of public funding. You would, however, not be prohibited from continuing to act for a referred client if there was a subsequent unanticipated need to obtain public funding or to represent the client in criminal proceedings. In this situation you should retain evidence as to how those circumstances had arisen.

'Normal hospitality'

14. What amounts to 'normal hospitality' (see 9.02(i)(ii)) will depend on the circumstances in every case. For example, corporate entertainment, dinners or lunches are acceptable and would not amount to payment for a referral, provided these are proportionate to the relationship with a business contact/introducer.

'Normal business expenses'

15. 'Normal business expenses' (see 9.02(i)(ii)) are payments for services provided to your firm which are totally unrelated to the referral of any client. So, for example, you would not be prevented from accepting referrals from the company with which you place your firm's indemnity or buildings insurance, or from the accountant who prepares your annual report or tax return.

Referral to third parties

16. Any referral to a third party will be subject to rule 1 (Core duties) and 9.01, as well as 9.03. You must therefore do nothing in respect of such referrals which would compromise your independence or ability to act or advise in the best interests of each of your clients. Any agreement you enter into in respect of regulated mortgage contracts, general insurance contracts (including after the event insurance contracts) or pure protection contracts will need to provide that referrals will only be made where this is in the best interests of the particular client and the contract is suitable for the needs of that client.
17. Rule 19 (Financial services) deals with referrals in relation to financial services.
18. Subrule 2.06 (Commissions) applies in relation to commission received for the introduction of clients.

European cross-border practice

19. Rule 16 (European cross-border practice) prohibits you from making payments for referrals to non-lawyers when undertaking cross-border activities (see 16.06 and notes 10 and 11 of the guidance to rule 16).

*****

RULE 13   IN-HOUSE PRACTICE

*****

13.04   Pro bono work

(1) You may, in the course of your employment, conduct work on a pro bono basis for a client other than your employer provided:

    (a) the work is covered by an indemnity reasonably equivalent to that required under the Solicitors' Indemnity Insurance Rules; and

(b) either:
  (i) no fees are charged; or
  (ii) a conditional fee agreement is used and the only fees charged are those which you receive by way of costs from your client's opponent or other third party and pay to a charity under a fee sharing agreement.

(2) (1) above does not permit you to conduct work on a pro bono basis in conjunction with services provided by your employer under 13.05 (Associations), 13.06 (Insurers), 13.07 (Commercial legal advice services) or 13.11 (Lawyers of other jurisdictions).

*****

RULE 15   OVERSEAS PRACTICE

*****

15.02   Client relations (rule 2)

(1) Rule 2 (Client relations) does not apply to your overseas practice but you must comply with (2) to (4) below.
(2) (a) You must pay to your clients any commission received, unless:
    (i) the client, having been told the amount of the commission (or an approximate amount if the precise amount is not known) has agreed that you or your firm may keep the commission; or
    (ii) in all the circumstances it is not reasonable to pay the commission to the client.
  (b) In deciding whether it is reasonable to pay a commission to your client you must have regard to all the circumstances, including the law governing the retainer and the prevailing custom of lawyers in the jurisdiction in which you are practising.

(3) If you are a principal in a firm you must not exclude or attempt to exclude by contract all liability to your clients. However, you may limit your liability, provided that such limitation:

  (a) is not below the minimum level of cover you would need in order to comply with 15.26 below;
  (b) is brought to the client's attention; and
  (c) is in writing.

(4) (a) (i) You must not enter into an arrangement to receive a contingency fee for work done in prosecuting or defending any contentious proceedings before a court of England and Wales, a British court martial or an arbitrator where the seat of the arbitration is in England and Wales, except as permitted by statute or the common law.
      (ii) If you enter into a conditional fee agreement with a client in relation to such proceedings, you must explain, both at the outset and, where appropriate, as the matter progresses:

(A) the circumstances in which your client may be liable for your costs, and whether you will seek payment of these from the client, if entitled to do so; and

(B) if you intend to seek payment of any or all of your costs from your client, you must advise your client of their right to an assessment of those costs.

(b) You must not enter into an arrangement to receive a contingency fee for work done in prosecuting or defending any contentious proceedings before a court of an overseas jurisdiction or an arbitrator where the seat of the arbitration is overseas except to the extent that a lawyer of that jurisdiction would be permitted to do so.

*****

RULE 19   FINANCIAL SERVICES

19.01   Independence

*****

(4) In this rule:

(a) 'appointed representative' has the meaning given in the Financial Services and Markets Act 2000;

(b) 'general insurance contract' is any contract of insurance within Part 1 of Schedule 1 to the Financial Services and Markets Act 2000 (Regulated Activities) Order 2001 (SI 2001/544);

(c) 'investment' means any of the investments specified in Part III of the Financial Services and Markets Act 2000 (Regulated Activities) Order 2001 (SI 2001/544) ;

(d) 'pure protection contract' has the meaning given in rule 8(1) of the Solicitors' Financial Services (Scope) Rules 2001;

(e) 'regulated activity' means an activity which is specified in the Financial Services and Markets Act 2000 (Regulated Activities) Order 2001 (SI 2001/544) ; and

(f) 'regulated mortgage contract' has the meaning given by article 61(3) of the Financial Services and Markets Act 2000 (Regulated Activities) Order 2001 (SI 2001/ 544) .

*****

Bar Council Guidance on Conditional Fee Agreements (extracts)

PART 1: ETHICAL GUIDANCE

1. Introduction

This Part is intended to provide guidance only on the ethical problems which may arise from the operation of Conditional Fee Agreements ('CFAs'). It does not form part of the Bar's Code of Conduct. However, it is strongly advised that barristers should follow the advice set out here, which is intended to ensure compliance with the Code of Conduct. Any doubts felt by a barrister after reading this ethical guidance should be referred to the Bar Standards Board. The Practical Guidance section of the Bar Council's CFA Guidance should be referred to for guidance on practical matters.

2. General

Paragraph 405 of the Code of Conduct permits a barrister in independent practice to charge for any work undertaken by her/him (whether or not it involves an appearance in court) on any basis or by any method s/he thinks fit provided that such basis or method is permitted by law; and does not involve the payment of a wage or salary. It is the responsibility of any member of the Bar who enters into a CFA to ensure that:

(1) he or she is familiar with the statutory provisions and regulations and orders made thereunder (see Practical Guidance, and note in particular the distinction between 'old' and 'new' CFAs, and the different legislative regimes applicable thereto);

(2) *he or she at all times acts in accordance with the relevant extracts of which are included in part 3 of the Guidance. For example, the barrister, before entering a CFA, must bear in mind the provisions of paragraph 603, namely, that 'A barrister must not accept any brief or instructions if to do so would cause him to be professionally embarrassed', and the subsequent sub paragraphs of the Code defining circumstances in which such professional embarrassment may arise. In particular, barristers who are asked to give CFA advice on a standard form must be satisfied that they have seen and had sufficient time to consider all relevant documents before giving the advice.*

(3) the terms of the CFA comply with the requirements of the law and the Code. Compliance with the Code will be ensured if a Bar Council approved CFA is used.

3. The 'cab rank' rule

The 'cab rank rule' does not apply to CFAs. In other words, counsel cannot be compelled to accept instructions upon a CFA basis. See § 604 (c) of the Code.

4. Internal agreements and arrangements between barristers

Some barristers and some chambers will find it appropriate to enter into standing agreements with each other, or to establish practices whereby they will work under CFAs as a chambers or in groups. The main purpose of such arrangements will be to spread the risk of CFA work. This might include the sharing of fees to the extent of, for example, the payment of a proportion of success fees into a pool which is then used to compensate members for fees not recovered, or expenses incurred, in lost cases. There may also be arrangements the sole purpose of which relates to the return of work between barristers or chambers (see section 4.5 below), or for screening (see section 5 below). However, there are some barristers and sets of chambers who will not consider it appropriate to work under CFAs at all, or who will only consider it appropriate to work under them on a one off basis agreed for each particular CFA. The considerations to be taken into account when considering such internal arrangements are as follows:

(1) *It is important to ensure that no arrangement or agreement is entered into which compromises or appears to compromise a barrister's integrity or independence, which creates or may create a partnership, or which creates or appears to create a conflict of interest (see Code §§ 104(a)(i), 301, 303, 306, 307(a), 603(e)).*

(2) The Professional Standards Committee (now the Bar Standards Board) in February 2002 gave guidance as follows in relation to fee-sharing agreements:

   (i) A simple fee sharing agreement would not of itself amount to a partnership, assuming that it does not involve sharing of responsibility for the work done.

   (ii) If fees are shared between a group of barristers, there are likely to be conflicts of interest between members of the group and their clients where members of the group are instructed for clients with opposing interests: a member of the group may have a financial interest in the success of his or her opposing fellow member. Such a conflict will arise in particular where (a) a member of the group is being paid on a conventional basis but the opponent is acting on a CFA, or (b) both are acting on a CFA, but the CFA of one is more advantageous (in terms of success fee) than the other.

   (iii) Whilst it is possible for barristers to act notwithstanding a conflict of interest provided that they have the fully informed consent of their clients, obtaining such fully informed consent will normally be fraught with difficulties, largely on grounds of confidentiality (see section 14 below): in particular, in order to give such consent, the client will need to know not only that the barrister on the opposing side is acting on a CFA, but also the terms of that agreement, including the success fee.

   (iv) It will therefore be rare for it to be acceptable for members of a fee-sharing group to accept instructions on opposite sides. Although it is possible in principle for the members of such a group to agree that any cases in which members are on opposing sides shall fall outside the scope of the agreement, such a provision is fraught with practical difficulties, not least because a member accepting instructions on a CFA basis will not at that time know whether or not a fellow member will in due course be instructed for an opposing party.

(3) *However, quite apart from the position of the Bar Council, there remains a likeli- hood that a court or arbitral institution would conclude that such an arrangement created a conflict of interest or the appearance of such a conflict, such that counsel involved should not be permitted to act against each other in any case in which a member of the group is involved, or as judge or arbitrator in any case.*

(4) Although the above guidance of the Professional Standards Committee (now the Bar Standards Board) demonstrates that fee-sharing agreements are technically possible, the practical difficulties are such that the Bar Council CFA Panel advises against any fee- or profit-sharing agreement, or any agreement which provides for a subsidy to be paid by chambers or a CFA group to members in respect of lost CFA cases. In our view, the better policy is to reduce the financial risks of CFAs by proper risk assessment and screening procedures (see Practical Guidance).

(5) *Arrangements between counsel whereby they agree to accept each others' return CFA briefs and the question whether, in those circumstances, they would be precluded from acting against each other in any action to which such arrangements applied or from appearing in front of a counsel who was a party to such arrange- ments (acting as a judge or arbitrator) are more straightforward. It is not thought that such arrangements create a potential or actual conflict of interest.*

5. Screening

If chambers operate a form of screening of CFA cases whereby one or more members of chambers read the papers in a case sent to another member with a view to deciding whether or not that case should be accepted on a CFA basis, the screener could not, in future, act on the other side, or as judge or arbitrator, in that case. Barristers acting as screeners should therefore keep records of the cases they have screened, and a record must be kept in each case of the identity of the screener. If screening would involve the disclosure of confidential information to the screener, consent to screening should be obtained in advance of the screening.

6. Forms of CFAs

There is no form of CFA *prescribed* by the Bar Council or any other body or specialist association; but see the guidance relating to insurance and the BMIF in paragraph 7 below. Under the regime which existed prior to 1st November 2005, there were approved forms of CFA for use in personal injury and clinical negligence cases, in chancery cases, and employment cases. These forms of CFA were approved by the relevant specialist bar associations. A new form of CFA for use after 1st November 2005 in personal injury and clinical negligence cases has been agreed between PIBA and APIL (APIL/PIBA 6) and it can be found on the Bar Council website. It is for the barrister entering into a CFA to be satisfied that the form of agreement used is appropriate and lawful. In any case where a barrister proposes or is asked to enter into a CFA with a solicitor upon terms which materially depart from any form of agreement approved by a specialist bar association, the barrister should ensure that such departure is lawful, fair to the lay client and reasonable in the particular circumstances of the case before agreeing to act on such terms. In particular, the barrister should ensure that no term increases or tends to increase pressure on the lay client to reach an inappropriate settlement.

There is no objection to barristers entering into contractually binding agreements. The barrister should ensure that the agreement does not contain any clause inconsistent with the Code.

307

7. Insurance

Under §§ 204(b) and 402.1 of the Code, every barrister must be covered by insurance against claims for professional negligence, and be entered as a member with BMIF. Some standard form CFAs, including the APIL/PIBA model, provide for an indemnity in favour of the solicitor in the event that counsel's breach of duty causes the solicitor to suffer a loss of fees. The BMIF has agreed (subject to financial limits) to indemnify barristers against this type of claim, provided it has approved the form of the relevant agreement. A barrister will therefore not be insured against such a claim by the solicitor if he/she has entered into an agreement on a form not approved by the BMIF. Previously, the APIL/PIBA and Chancery Bar Association agreements have been approved by the BMIF; terms of the new APIL/PIBA 6 agreement have also been approved.

8. Inducements

The payment by barristers or their chambers of commissions or inducements is strictly prohibited by the Code: see §§ 307(d) and (e). Paragraph 205 and 401(a) of the Code respectively prohibits the supply of legal services by barristers to the public through or on behalf of anyone other than solicitors, unless the Code requirements as to public access or Licensed access are complied with. Guidance was given on this topic by the Professional Standards Committee in May 2001.

Thus, for example:

(1) the payment of 'introduction' or 'administration' fees or charges to an insurer or claims organisation is not permissible;

(2) any scheme which requires barristers to pay for services provided outside chambers in order to accept work is likely to contravene § 307(e) and to involve a hidden commission contrary to § 307(e);

(3) a payment to the clerk of other chambers in return for forwarding work will be contrary to § 307(e);

(4) barristers are responsible for ensuring that their clerks do not receive or pay commission or inducements;

(5) barristers are responsible for their fee notes, which must be transparent and must not have the effect of misleading a court or any party; blank fee notes must not be sent out to be completed by third parties, nor must third parties be permitted to alter fee notes;

Barristers and their chambers should not accept or rely upon assurances from those promoting a CFA scheme that the scheme has received Bar Council approval: advice in respect of any such new scheme must be obtained from the Professional Standards Department of the Bar Council.

9. Impartiality / conflicts of interest

Having accepted instructions to act under a CFA, a barrister shall thereafter give impartial advice to the lay client at all times and take all reasonable steps to identify and declare to the lay client and to the instructing solicitor any actual or apparent conflict of interest between the barrister and the lay client.

10. Advice and interests of lay client

Advice and interests of lay client. During the currency of a CFA, the barrister should use his/her best endeavours to ensure that:

(1) any advice given by the barrister in relation to the case is communicated and fully explained to the lay client;

(2) any offer of settlement is communicated to the lay client forthwith;

(3) the consequences of particular clauses in the solicitor/lay client agreement and the solicitor/barrister agreement are explained to the client as and when they become relevant, particularly after an offer of settlement has been made.

This last obligation applies in particular to the financial consequences which may arise from the making of an offer to settle the case including consideration of (1) any increase in the offer of settlement; (2) 'conventional' costs consequences; and (3) the success fees which are or may become payable.

11.   Advising on settlement

When advising on a settlement of the action the barrister should at all times have in mind his/ her obligation under paragraph 303 (a) of the Code to

'promote and protect fearlessly and by all proper and lawful means the lay client's best interests and do so without regard to his own interests or to any consequences to himself or to any other person (including any professional client or other intermediary or another barrister)'.

The barrister's duty must be, when advising the client on a settlement or on a payment in or Part 36 offer, to advise as to the best course of action from the lay client's point of view only.

12.   Disagreement over Settlement

Difficulties may arise when the lawyers disagree about the wisdom of continuing the case or accepting an offer, whether that disagreement is:

(1) *between them on the one part and the lay client on the other; or*

(2) *between solicitor and counsel; or*

(3) *between leading and junior counsel.*

In such event careful consideration must be given to the lay client's interests. Every effort should be made to avoid unfairly putting the lay client in the position where having begun proceedings s/he is left without representation. However, where, for example, counsel has been misled about the true nature of the evidence or the lay client is refusing to accept firm advice as to the future conduct of the case, the terms of the CFA may permit counsel to withdraw. Before taking this serious step the barrister will have to check carefully whether s/he is entitled to withdraw.

13.   Withdrawal from the case

The barrister may withdraw from the casein any of the circumstances set out in the CFA agreement, but only if satisfied that s/he is permitted to withdraw pursuant to part VI of the Code. In the event that the CFA agreement does not contain a term that the barrister may withdraw from the case in particular circumstances, but the Code requires the barrister to withdraw in those circumstances, the Code takes priority over the agreement

14. Disclosure of existence and terms of CFA

Disclosure of existence and terms of CFA. The fact that the action is funded by means of a CFA, and the terms of a CFA, should not be disclosed to the other parties to the action without the express written permission of the lay client, save insofar as such disclosure is required by the court, the CPR, statute, rule, order, or Practice Direction.

*****

CHAMBERS' APPROACH TO CFAs

70. The approach of different chambers to CFAs will vary. It would be wise for all chambers to discuss the impact of CFAs and whether any chambers' policies may be appropriate regarding CFAs.
71. Queries relating to CFAs frequently arise and it is good practice for chambers to appoint one or more members with particular knowledge of the working and law of CFAs to advise members and clerks.

One-off involvement in CFAs only

72. As explained in the Ethical Guidance some chambers will consider that there should be no standing agreement or practices within chambers under which work under CFAs can be undertaken. In such chambers any CFAs which are undertaken will be agreed on a one-off basis between those involved. Even if this is the only chambers' policy regarding CFAs, the chambers may wish (subject other issues such as confidentiality) to establish a committee to monitor CFA work to see how the work done impacts on members of chambers and chambers, and to establish a pool of expertise in chambers on CFA matters. Logs and record-keeping will be appropriate even where work is accepted only on the basis of one-off CFAs.

Chambers or Group involvement in CFAs

73. Other chambers will wish to set up agreements and practices regarding the acceptance of work generally under CFAs. For such chambers the following suggestions may be helpful. It is appreciated that all of the following steps will not be appropriate for all chambers.
74. Chambers should:
    (1) consider whether it should develop standard codes of practice governing the operation of CFAs by their members.
    (2) Consider what policy ought to be adopted in respect of returned work. Chambers ought to formulate such policy in the light of the Terms of Agreement which they determine to adopt, but should be aware of the section in the current APIL/PIBA model (paragraph 20) relating to Return of Work
    (3) Be astute to avoid entering agreements which create partnerships or other prohibited relationships
75. It may be appropriate for chambers as a whole, or in a group within chambers, to agree to accept returns in CFA cases between themselves. If no policy is agreed in advance, then, depending on what term is agreed, costs repercussions and embarrassment may arise where no suitable replacement may be found to

cover a return: considerable damage could be done to relations with chambers' solicitors and the reputation of the Bar generally. A lay client may well not understand how such a situation could arise.

76. Chambers may well consider it appropriate to publish the pool of counsel who have agreed to do CFA work and to accept CFA returns.

77. Chambers should consider whether they should have a policy on whether or not tenants should seek to charge for considering whether to accept a CFA case. In a complex case, for example, in which a large amount of documentation must be read or where a conference with the client may be necessary in order to assess the prospects of success, it may be possible to agree with the instructing solicitor either to pay privately for such work, or to enter into a separate CFA for that stage of the proceedings only with provision (and written reasons) for a percentage increase based on the core documents which counsel has been able to read, in say 2 hours, for the purpose of making a risk assessment. If pleadings are needed urgently before a proper assessment of the case can be made a preliminary form of CFA can be entered into to cover that work only. There can, regrettably, be no retrospective annexation of pre-CFA work into a CFA.

Sub-Committee/monitoring/advice

78. Chambers may wish to consider appointing a permanent sub-committee charged with monitoring chambers' policy and practice on CFAs and keeping abreast of developments in the use and practice of CFA work. The Committee should include the Clerk who has primary responsibility for CFA work. If there is a substantial number of chambers' members who do not belong to the pool of those prepared to do CFA work it should be considered whether the Committee should include one tenant who does a significant amount of non-CFA work. The committee's responsibility should be to:

(1) determine whether cases should be accepted only from solicitors who are approved by the CFA team for the purposes of giving CFA briefs and instructions, and, if so, to assess which firms of solicitors are acceptable and therefore 'approved' as providers of CFA instructions for different categories of work;

(2) monitor chambers' overall CFA exposure;

(3) monitor individual tenants' CFA exposure;

(4) advise tenants upon CFA procedures and problems;

(5) advise chambers on an appropriate protocol to govern the use and practice of CFAs by chambers, and to keep such protocols, the form of the agreement, and the form of standard correspondence under review.

Logs and Record Keeping

79. Chambers should consider establishing a log of all CFA cases. Its purpose would be:

(1) to provide a record from which a picture can be built up to assist in future risk assessment;

(2) to provide a contemporaneous record for production in the event of any challenge on costs assessment or other complaint by the client, solicitor or insurer;

(3) to provide a running record of CFA cases to give a picture of chambers' current financial exposure;

(4)   to preserve confidentiality in the monitoring process each case should be given a number. There is no reason why this should not be simply ordinary numbering 1, 2, 3 etc.

80.   Proper record keeping is vital.

81.   A system should be set up whereby the clerk opens a file for each CFA case and files in it copies of the various letters of engagement and acceptances. It would be wise to date stamp all incoming acknowledgements.

82.   Each barrister will be well advised to keep his or her own record in each case in which a note is kept of the list of documents enclosed with each set of instructions, so that if a dispute arises and counsel wishes to withdraw because s/he was not given all relevant available information at the outset, there is no scope for disagreement as to what was sent when.

83.   Dated copies of opinions should be kept.

84.   Advice on settlement in a CFA case should always be given in writing, if at all possible. If, for practical reasons (for example, a settlement at court door), it is not possible to give the settlement advice in the form of a written opinion, then it consideration should be given to putting the essence of the advice into manuscript and ask the lay client to initial the manuscript note. This should be retained. The reason for this is that because of the potential conflict of interest between a client and his lawyers, it is more important to keep a record of advice than in a normally funded case.

85.   Counsel's own file should (subject to confidentiality considerations, which should be addressed with clients) be made available to any other counsel who is requested to accept a return or do interlocutory work. It ought, therefore to include:

(1)   copies of all correspondence leading up to and including the CFA;
(2)   a list of the material considered for deciding to enter a CFA;
(3)   a risk assessment
(4)   if the case has been screened, a note from the 'screener' giving her/his independent assessment.

Screening

86.   Chambers should consider whether, in order to control chambers' risk exposure, they should set up some form of screening of individual tenants' decisions on whether to accept or reject a CFA case. Depending on chambers' resources and its risk exposure, and bearing in mind considerations of confidentiality, suggested methods might be:

(1)   a requirement that a tenant may not take a case until her/his decision has been approved by a 'screening' member of the CFA team, being either a silk of a barrister of 7 years' call or more and of comparable or greater seniority or experience;
(2)   a requirement that a tenant may not reject a case before her/his decision has been approved as above;
(3)   a system whereby tenants may ask a 'screening' member to approve her/his decision to take or reject a case where the individual tenant has doubts about the case.
(4)   a system of random audit on a proportion of cases accepted.
(5)   approval of the screening process should require the consent of the solicitor. This might, in some circumstances, be assumed if the process is described in an agreed chambers' protocol which is given to the solicitor

with the proposed 'Terms of Engagement' and no objection is received. It should be made explicit in such documentation that the 'screener' assumes no duty of care to tenants, solicitors or clients.

Teams

87. Some chambers will establish a CFA team or teams. Tenants who are prepared to take CFA work from approved solicitors in appropriate cases should so inform the Committee, and thereafter consider themselves part of the chambers' 'CFA Team', and bound by the protocol agreed by chambers. This would imply a long-term commitment to do CFA work. That commitment must include agreement by team members, where available and subject to (1) their pre-existing CFA commitments and (2) client approval;

    (1) to accept returns of CFA work from other team members on a 'for better for worse' basis; and
    (2) to do appropriate interlocutory work on a CFA basis where the tenant generally instructed is reasonably thought by the instructing solicitor to be too senior for such interlocutory work, provided that an agreement approved by the CFA Committee applies to such work.

88. A tenant who wishes to cease to undertake CFA work may, on notice to the CFA Committee cease to take new CFA cases immediately, but should be bound:

    (1) to continue existing cases to conclusion
    (2) to accept returns, subject to aforesaid, for (say) 18 months after such notice.

*****

Bar Council Guidance: Conditional Fee Agreement Work on Public Access

1. By s.58(3)(c) Courts and Legal Services Act 1990 (as substituted by the Access to Justice Act 1999) a conditional fee agreement ('CFA') is lawful only if it complies with such requirements as may be specified by the Secretary of State.

2. Pursuant to that section the Conditional Fee Agreement Regulations 2000 (SI 2000 no.692) ('the 2000 Regulations') specified detailed requirements for the contents of CFAs and as to information which was to be given to a client prior to making a CFA.

3. However, many members of the Bar considered that the 2000 Regulations were deficient in failing to require clients to be warned that there is a risk in any case where a CFA has been made of a conflict of interest arising between client and lawyer. This is especially likely to occur if and when a low offer in settlement is made: the lawyer then may have a strong incentive to encourage acceptance, so as to avoid the risk of no payment, and indeed to secure up to double fees, whereas the offer may be at a level which a client would not normally be advised to accept.

4. As is well known, these Regulations spawned much satellite litigation in which defendants, who often consider it unjust that they should pay up to double costs, challenged the lawfulness of CFAs which arguably failed to comply with the Regulations.

5. In the hope of reducing such satellite litigation, with effect from 1 November 2005 the 2000 Regulations were revoked, and no new regulations were put in their place.

6. The specific requirements of the 2000 regulations had by that date been incorporated into the Law Society's Solicitors Costs Information and Client Care Code. Therefore, the revocation of the 2000 Regulations was regarded as altering the mode of enforcement of the requirements rather than their substance: they would in future fall within the purview of Law Society discipline rather than determination by a Cost Judge.

7. When making this change no thought appears to have been given by the Department of Constitutional Affairs to the fact that since July 2004 it had been possible for a barrister to be instructed directly by a member of the public, and that it was theoretically possible for a barrister acting on public access to make a CFA. This oversight may well be attributable to the extreme rarity of a CFA being made by a barrister with a public access client, if, indeed, such a CFA has ever been made at all.

8. Nonetheless, since a CFA is at least theoretically possible between a barrister and a public access client thought has to be given to the manner in which such CFA should be made. This paper sets out the thinking of the Bar Council's Access to the Bar Committee (the 'ABC').

9. The ABC is part of the representational, rather than the regulatory, side of the Bar Council: therefore, this paper is for information only and has no binding effect.

10. The ABC considers that any barrister making a CFA with a public access client should,

    (a) Comply with the requirements as to the formalities of such an agreement set out in the 2000 Regulations with such necessary modifications as are required by the circumstance of the agreement being made by a barrister rather than a solicitor;

    (b) Provide the client, prior to the making of the agreement, with the information required by the 2000 Regulations;

    (c) Provide the client, prior to the making of the agreement, with the information as to costs, mutatis mutandis, contained in the Law Society's Costs Information and Client Care Code and in the Law Society leaflet for clients 'Conditional Fee Agreements: what you need to know';

    (d) Warn the client that there is a risk in any case where a CFA has been made of a conflict of interest arising between client and lawyer;

    (e) Advise the client that making a CFA with a solicitor may have advantages for the client over a CFA direct with a barrister by reason of the procedures for independent assessment of solicitors' fees.

11. With regard to the warning of conflicts, the ABC takes the view that the mere fact that other regimes relating to CFAs provide, in the opinion of barristers, insufficient protection for clients, is no reason why the Bar's practice should also be deficient.

12. The ABC expects that barristers will often advise clients who want to make a CFA to place their instructions via a solicitor. That is because amongst the information which the 2000 Regulations stipulated to be given to a client was information whether other methods of financing were available, and whether a contract of insurance was appropriate; if a contract of insurance was recommended, certain further explanation must be given. Many barristers will not feel themselves to be in a position to provide such information or explanation.

13. Barristers will have in mind that under the Public Access Rules they must consider, before accepting a case on public access, whether it would be in the interests of the client to instruct a solicitor. Unless a barrister feels confident that he can provide all the appropriate information and explanations, he is, therefore, unlikely to be involved in making a CFA on public access, even if, as a matter of business decision, he is willing to undertake a particular case on a CFA.

14. Paragraphs 10 and 11 of this document extend to conditional fee agreements which do not contain any success fee, but by the nature of things the requirements are then more limited. The requirements of the 2000 Regulations for the provision of information are more extensive in the case of success fee CFAs than of CFAs without a success fee. Nor does CPR 44.15 (as to giving notice of a CFA to an opposing party) apply to a CFA without a success fee. The Bar Council is aware that barristers sometimes make CFAs without a success fee in situations where as an act of kindness to an impecunious client they are willing to act without fee, but see no reason why they should not recover normal fees in the event of securing an order for costs against an opposing party. The Bar Council attaches a high priority to extending access to justice, and, subject to necessary safeguards, is not discouraging such arrangements.

15. This document applies, with necessary modifications, to CFAs in which liability for only part of the barrister's fees are subject to the condition, in the same way as CFAs in which the whole of the fee is so subject.

APIL/PIBA 6 Standard Agreement

CFA for use BETWEEN SOLICITORS AND COUNSEL on or after 1 November 2005

This agreement forms the basis on which instructions are accepted by counsel from the solicitor to act under a conditional fee agreement and incorporates the standard terms agreed between APIL and PIBA on 31.10.05, which is available on both the APIL and PIBA websites and is incorporated in, but not annexed to this agreement. *Paragraphs . . . of the standard terms and conditions have been amended as shown and underlined on the copy annexed hereto.

This agreement is not a contract enforceable at law. The relationship of counsel and solicitor shall be governed by the Terms of Work under which barristers offer their services to solicitors and the Withdrawal of Credit Scheme as authorised by the General Council of the Bar as from time to time amended and set out in the Code of Conduct of the Bar of England and Wales, save that where such terms of work are inconsistent with the terms of this agreement the latter shall prevail.

Csl's Ref: . . . .   Sol's Ref . . . .

In this agreement 'Counsel' means: _____ and any other counsel either from Chambers or recommended by counsel in accordance with clause 20 who signs this agreement at any time at the solicitor's request. 'The solicitors' means the firm: _____.

'The client' means: _____
[*acting by his/her Litigation Friend._____]

'Chambers' means members of chambers at   _____

The solicitor provided Counsel with instructions, see copy attached, date stamped __/__/__ and the documents listed there.

What is covered by this agreement

- The client's claim for damages for personal injuries against ———————
  suffered on _____ until the claim is won, lost or otherwise concluded, or this agreement is terminated,* or part only of proceedings as set out below.
  [If either the name of the opponent or the date of the incident are unclear then set out here as much detail as possible to give sufficient information for the client and solicitor to understand the basis of the claim pursued.]

- Part only of proceedings, specifically: _____;
- Any appeal by the opponent(s);
- Any appeal the client makes against an interim order advised by Counsel;
- Negotiations about and/or a court assessment of the costs of this claim.

What is not covered by this agreement

- Any Part 20 claim against the client;
- Any appeal the client makes against the final judgment order;
- Any application under any award of provisional damages that might be obtained in these proceedings or to vary any order for periodical payments that might be obtained in the proceedings.

[NOTE: delete those parts of the proceedings to which the agreement relates or does not relate as appropriate]

The case is likely to be allocated to the *multi-track *fast track and damages are likely to be in excess of *£500,000* £250,000, disregarding any possible reduction for contributory negligence.

DELIVERY OF BRIEF FOR TRIAL: The solicitor agrees to deliver the brief for trial of any issue including the assessment of damages not less than ....
weeks*days before the date fixed for hearing.

COUNSEL'S NORMAL FEES are as follows:

Advisory work and drafting: in accordance with counsel's hourly rate
obtaining for work in this field currently: (hourly rate)   £100.00

Court appearances:–   [insert hourly rate]

Brief fees for a trial (allowing 5 hours per day in court) whose duration
and hours preparation are estimated as follows:

Time estimate for trial	Hours of preparation	Estimated fee
Up to 2 days	6	£1,600.00
3 to 5 days	12	£3,200.00
6 to 8 days	18	£5,050.00
9 to 12 days	24	£7,650.00
13 to 20 days	30	£11,400.00

Brief fees for interlocutory hearings whose duration and hours of
preparation are estimated as follows:

Estimated duration	Hours of preparation	Estimated fee
Up to one hour	2	£300.00
One hour to half a day	3	£450.00
Half a day to one day	4	£650.00

Over one day will be charged as if it were a trial.

Refreshers estimated at 5 hours in court at counsel's hourly rate
currently obtain such work in this field: £500.00

Renegotiating Counsel's fees: the extent that the hours of preparation set out above are
reasonably exceeded then counsel's hourly rate will apply to each additional hour of
preparation. If the case is settled or goes short, counsel will consider the solicitor's reasonable
request to reduce his/her brief fee set out above.

Counsels Success Fees:			Case Concludes:		
		at trial:	14 or 21 days before date fixed for trial	more than 14 or 21 days before date fixed for trial	Applicable row marked with a tick: ✓
CPR	**Track**	**%**	**%**	**%**	
Road Traffic Accident Claims (for accident after 6.10.03)					
45.17	Multi Track:	100	75	12.5	
	Fast Tack:	100	50	12.5	
45.18(2); 45. 19 (over £500,000)		100	75	More than 20 or less than 7.5	
Employers Liability Claims (for injury sustained after 1.10.04)					
45.21	Multi Track:	100	75	25	
	Fast Tack:	100	50	25	
45.22 (over £ 500, 000)		100	75	More than 40 or less than 15	
Employers Liability Disease Claims (when letter of claim sent after 1.10.05)					
45.23 (3)(a) Asbestos	Multi Track:	100	75	27.5	
	Fast Tack:	100	50	27.5	
45.26 Asbestos Over £ 250, 000		100	75	More than 40/ less than 15	
45.23(3)(d) RSI & Stress	Multi Track:	100	100	100	
	Fast Tack:	100	100	100	
45.26 RSI & Stress Over £ 250, 000		100	100	Less than 75	
45.23(e) Other disease claim	Multi Track	100	75	62.5	
	Fast Track	100	62.5	62.5	
45.26 Other disease claim Over £250,000		100	. . .	More than 75 or less than 50	
Other Type of PI Claim					
	Multi Track:	100	. . .	. . .	
	Fast Track:	100	. . .	. . .	

319

The reasons, briefly stated, for counsel's success fee are that at the time of entry into this agreement:

- the percentage increase is fixed by CPR 45. . . . .[specify];
- the percentage increase is fixed by CPR 45. . . . .[specify] but CPR 45.18*, CPR 45.22*, or CPR 45.26* applies to this claim;
- the percentage increase sought is consistent with an industry-wide agreement dated __/__/__ reached by representatives of both Claimants and Defendants under the supervision of the Civil Justice Council and there is no special reason to apply a different uplift in this case;
- the percentage increase reflects the prospects of success estimated in counsel's risk assessment which is* not attached to this agreement
- the length of postponement of the payment of counsel's fees and expenses is estimated at __ year(s), and a further increase of . . . . % relates to that postponement and cannot be recovered from the opponent.

The success fee inclusive of any additional % relating to postponement cannot be more than 100% of counsel's normal fees in total.

Dated:

_____

Signed by counsel

_____

or by his/her clerk [with counsel's authority]

_____

[Additional counsel*]

_____

Date signed   _____

Signed by:

_____

Solicitor/employee in Messrs:

_____

The solicitors firm acting for the client

By signing and today returning to counsel the last page of this agreement the solicitor agrees to instruct counsel under the terms of this agreement and confirms that the Conditional Fee Agreement between the solicitor and client complies with ss. 58 and 58A of the Courts and Legal Services Act 1990 as amended.

DISCLAIMER: Counsel is not bound to act on a conditional fee basis until both parties have signed this agreement.

COUNSEL'S RISK ASSESSEMENT

[To help counsel make a Risk Assessment and give a Statement of Reasons for Conditional Fees in Personal Injury Cases]

1 The Solicitor has agreed with the client a *one-stage uplift, namely . . . . . .% or a two-stage uplift, namely . . . . .% where the claim concludes at trial; or . . . . .% where the claim concludes before a trial has commenced. The solicitor has*not included an element relating to the postponement of payment of basic charges.

2 The following stages of the proceedings have been completed: *pre-action protocol, statements of case, disclosure, exchange of evidence as to fact, exchange of expert evidence, case management conference(s), other (please specify) . . . . Attempts to settle the claim have failed; the defendant's latest offer (if any) was . . . .; the client's latest offer (if any) was . . . . (see letter(s) dated . . . . & . . . .).

3 Counsel estimates the overall **prospects of success**, taking all risk factors into account, in the region of . . . . .%. This overall assessment is made irrespective of the date for delivery of the brief.

4 Csl's reasons for setting the % increase at the level(s) stated in the agreement are:

[N.B. The ordinary risks of litigation and facts set out elsewhere in this form are deemed to be incorporated into this statement of reasons and do not need to be repeated here.]

5 **Further considerations**:
Current APIL/PIBA 5 Agreement?   ✓/✗
Case requiring screening?   ✓/✗
Csl has reason to believe the client is/may be, a child or patient ✓/✗
A leader is likely to be needed   ✓/✗
This Statement of Reasons is to be attached to the CFA?   ✓/✗

6. Csl's **decision**: *Accepted; Rejected &/or advised alternative funding / ADR

7. Csl's note of the **next step** due to be taken (if instructed on conditional fees) & any comment:

. . . .
. . . .

Screened by . . . . on . . . .   Signed by screener . . . .

Signed by Csl. . . . .   *Dated* . . . .

The ready reckoner is included for use only as a familiar aide-memoire when assessing a one stage uplift from the overall prospects of success:

READY RECKONER

Prospects of 'Success'	% Increase
100%	0%
95%	5%
90%	11%
80%	25%
75%	33%
70%	43%
67%	50%
60%	67%
55%	82%
50%	100%

NB: The way in which fees are estimated is a matter for counsel to agree with the solicitor on a case by case basis. The layout of the new agreement is immaterial and the risk assessment can be placed on a separate page if required, eg for non-disclosure to a client.

APPENDIX 14

APIL/PIBA 6 Standard Terms and Conditions

ANNEXED TO THE CONDITIONAL FEE AGREEMENT BETWEEN SOLICITOR AND COUNSEL FOR USE AFTER 1 NOVEMBER 2005

PART ONE

CONDITIONS PRECEDENT

Papers provided to Counsel

1. The solicitor should have provided counsel with the following documents:

    1) a copy of the conditional fee agreement between the solicitor and the client and the Law Society's Conditions as they apply to the claim;
    2) written confirmation that 'after the event' or other similar insurance is in place, or a written explanation why it is not;
    3) all relevant papers and risk assessment material, including all advice from experts and other solicitors or barristers to the client or any Litigation Friend in respect of the claim, which is currently available to the solicitor; and
    4) any offers of settlement already made by the client or the defendant.

Solicitor's Compliance with Statute

2. The solicitor confirms that the conditional fee agreement between the solicitor and the client complies with sections 58 and 58A of the Courts and legal Services Act 1990 and the Conditional Fee Agreements Order 2000.

PART TWO

OBLIGATIONS OF COUNSEL

To act diligently

3. Counsel agrees to act diligently on all proper instructions from the solicitor subject to paragraph 4 hereof.

Inappropriate Instructions

4. Counsel is not bound to accept instructions:

    1) to appear at any hearing where it would be reasonable

     (a)   to assume that counsel's fees would not be allowed on assessment or

     (b)   to instruct a barrister of less experience and seniority, (albeit that counsel shall use his/her best endeavours to ensure that an appropriate barrister will act for the client on the same terms as this agreement);

2)   to draft documents or advise if a barrister of similar seniority would not ordinarily be instructed so to do if not instructed on a conditional fee basis;

3)   outside the scope of this agreement.

PART THREE

OBLIGATIONS OF THE SOLICITOR

5.   The solicitor agrees:

    1)   to comply with all the requirements of the CPR, the practice direction about costs supplementing parts 43 to 48 of the CPR (PD Costs), the relevant pre-action protocol, and any court order relating to conditional fee agreements, and in particular promptly to notify the Court and the opponent of the existence and any subsequent variation of the CFA with the client and of this agreement and whether he / she has taken out an insurance policy or made an arrangement with a membership organisation and of the fact that additional liabilities are being claimed from the opponent;

    2)   promptly to apply for relief from sanction pursuant to CPR part 3.8 if any default under part 44.3B(1)(c) or (d) occurs and to notify counsel of any such default;

    3)   to act diligently in all dealings with counsel and the prosecution of the claim;

    4)   to liaise with or consult counsel about the likely amount of counsel's fees before filing any estimate of costs in the proceedings, and to provide a copy of any such estimate to counsel;

    5)   to consult counsel on the need for advice and action following:

     (a)   the service of statements of case and if possible before the allocation decision; and

     (b)   the exchange of factual and expert evidence;

    6)   to deliver within a reasonable time papers reasonably requested by counsel for consideration;

    7)   promptly to bring to counsel's attention:

     (a)   any priority or equivalent report to insurers;

     (b)   any Part 36 or other offer to settle;

     (c)   any Part 36 payment into Court;

     (d)   any evidence information or communication which may materially affect the merits of any issue in the case;

     (e)   any application by any party to have the client's costs capped;

     (f)   any costs capping order;

     (e)   any other factor coming to the solicitor's attention which may affect counsel's entitlement to success fees whether before or after the termination of this agreement;

    8)   promptly to communicate to the client any advice by counsel:

     (a)   to make, accept or reject any Part 36 or other offer;

     (b)   to accept or reject any Part 36 payment in;

     (c)   to incur, or not incur, expenditure in obtaining evidence or preparing the case;

     (d)   to instruct Leading counsel or a more senior or specialised barrister;

(e)   that the case is likely to be lost;

(f)   that damages and costs recoverable on success make it unreasonable or uneconomic for the action to proceed;

9) promptly to inform counsel's clerk of any listing for trial;

10) to deliver the brief to counsel in accordance with the agreement between the solicitor and counsel;

11) to inform Counsel promptly if the case concludes 14 days before the date fixed for trial if the claim is allocated to the fast-track or 21 days if allocated to the multi-track;

12) if any summary assessment of costs takes place in the absence of counsel, to submit to the court a copy of counsel's risk assessment and make representations on counsel's behalf in relation to his/her fees;

13) to inform counsel in writing within 2 days of any reduction of counsel's fees on summary assessment in the absence of counsel and of any directions given under PDCosts 20.3(1) or alternatively to make application for such directions on counsel's behalf;

14) where points of dispute are served pursuant to CPR part 47.9 seeking a reduction in any percentage increase charged by counsel on his fees, to give the client the written explanation required by PDCosts 20.5 on counsel's behalf;

15) where more than one defendant is sued, the solicitor will write to the 'after the event' insurers clarifying whether and when defendants' costs are to be covered if the claimant does not succeed or win against all of the defendants, and send that correspondence to counsel; and

16) when drawing up a costs bill at any stage of the case to include in it a claim for interest on counsel's fees.

PART FOUR

TERMINATION

Termination by Counsel

6.   Counsel may terminate the agreement if:

1) Counsel discovers the existence of any document which should have been disclosed to him under clause 1 above and which materially affects Counsel's view of the likelihood of success and/or the amount of financial recovery in the event of success;

2) Counsel discovers that the solicitor is in breach of any obligation in paragraph 5 hereof;

3) the solicitor client or any Litigation Friend rejects counsel's advice in any respect set out in paragraph 5(8) hereof;

4) Counsel is informed or discovers the existence of any set-off or counter-claim which materially affects the likelihood of success and/or the amount of financial recovery in the event of success;

5) Counsel is informed or discovers the existence of information which has been falsified or should have been but has not been provided by the solicitor, client or any Litigation Friend, of which counsel was not aware and which counsel could not reasonably have anticipated, which materially affects the merits of any substantial issue in the case;

6) Counsel is required to cease to act by the Code of Conduct of the Bar of England and Wales or counsel's professional conduct is being impugned; provided that counsel may not terminate the agreement if so to do would be a breach of that Code, and notice of any termination must be communicated promptly in writing to the solicitor;
7) A costs capping order is made which counsel reasonably believes may adversely affect the recoverability of his or her normal fees and/or his or her percentage increase.
8) If the opponent receives Community Legal Service funding.

Termination by the Solicitor

7. The solicitor may terminate the agreement at any time on the instructions of the client or any Litigation Friend.

Automatic Termination

8. This agreement shall automatically terminate if:
   1) Counsel accepts a full-time judicial appointment;
   2) Counsel retires from practice;
   3) the solicitor's agreement with the client is terminated before the conclusion of the case;
   4) Legal Services Commission funding is granted to the client;
   5) the client dies;
   6) the court makes a Group Litigation Order covering this claim.

Client becoming under a Disability

9. If the client at any time becomes under a disability then the solicitor will:
   1) consent to a novation of his Conditional Fee Agreement with the client to the Litigation Friend and
   2) where appropriate, apply to the Court to obtain its consent to acting under a conditional fee agreement with the Litigation Friend.
   Thereafter, the Litigation Friend shall, for the purposes of this agreement, be treated as if he/she was and has always been the client.

Counsel taking Silk

10. If counsel becomes Queen's Counsel during the course of the agreement then either party may terminate it provided he/she does so promptly in writing.

PART FIVE

COUNSEL'S FEES AND EXPENSES

Counsel's Normal Fees

11. 1) Counsel's fees upon which a success fee will be calculated (the normal fees) will be calculated on the basis of the figures contained in the agreement between the Solicitor and Counsel.

2) To the extent that the hours of preparation set out in that agreement are reasonably exceeded then counsel's hourly rate will apply to each additional hour of preparation.

3) If the case is settled or goes short counsel will consider the solicitor's reasonable requests to reduce his/her brief fees as set out in the agreement.

4) Counsel's normal fees will be subject to review with effect from each successive *anniversary of / * first day of February from the date of this agreement but Counsel will not increase the normal fees by more than any increase in the rate of inflation measured by the Retail Prices Index.

Counsel's Success Fee

12. The rate of counsel's success fee and reasons will be as set out in the agreement between the Solicitor and Counsel.

Counsel's Expenses

13. If a hearing, conference or view takes place more than 25 miles from counsel's chambers the solicitor shall pay counsel's reasonable travel and accommodation expenses which shall:

1) appear separately on counsel's fee note;
2) attract no success fee and
3) subject to paragraph 16 be payable on the conclusion of the claim or earlier termination of this agreement.

PART SIX

COUNSEL'S ENTITLEMENT TO FEES

(A) If the Agreement is not Terminated

Definition of 'success'

14. 1) 'Success' means the same as 'win' in the Conditional Fee Agreement between the solicitor and the client.
2) Subject to paragraphs 15, 18 & 21 hereof, in the event of success the solicitor will pay counsel his/her normal and success fees.
3) If the client is successful at an interim hearing counsel may apply for summary assessment of solicitor's basics costs and counsel's normal fees.

Part 36 Offers and Payments

15. If the amount of damages and interest awarded by a court is less than a Part 36 payment into Court or effective Part 36 offer then:

1) if counsel advised its rejection he/she is entitled to normal and success fees for work up to receipt of the notice of Part 36 payment into Court or offer but only normal fees for subsequent work;
2) if counsel advised its acceptance he/she is entitled to normal and success fees for all work done.

Failure

16. Subject to paragraph 17 (1) hereof, if the case is lost or on counsel's advice ends without success then counsel is not entitled to any fees or expenses.

Errors and Indemnity for Fees

17. 1) If, because of a breach by the solicitor of his/her duty to the client, the client's claim is dismissed or struck out:
     a) for non compliance with an interlocutory order; or
     b) for want of prosecution, or
     c) by rule of court or the Civil Procedure Rules; or
     becomes unenforceable against the MIB for breach of the terms of the Uninsured Drivers Agreement:
     the solicitor shall (subject to sub paragraphs (3) – (6) hereof) pay counsel such normal fees as would have been recoverable under this agreement.
    (2) If, because of a breach by counsel of his/her duty to the client, the client's claim is dismissed or struck out:
     a) for non compliance with an interlocutory order; or
     b) for want of prosecution, or
     c) by rule of court or the Civil Procedure Rules
     counsel shall (subject to sub paragraphs (3)–(6) hereof) pay the solicitor such basic costs as would have been recoverable from the client under the solicitor's agreement with the client.
    (3) If, because of non-compliance by the solicitor of the obligations under sub-paragraphs (1), (2), (11), (12) or (13) of paragraph 5 above, counsel's success fee is not payable by the Opponent or the client then the solicitor shall (subject to sub-paragraphs (5) to (7) hereof) pay counsel such success fees as would have been recoverable under this agreement.
    (4) No payment shall be made under sub paragraph (1), (2) or (3) hereof in respect of any non-negligent breach by the solicitor or counsel.

Adjudication on disagreement

    (5) In the event of any disagreement as to whether there has been an actionable breach by either the solicitor or counsel, or as to the amount payable under sub paragraph (1), (2) or (3) hereof, that disagreement shall be referred to adjudication by a panel consisting of a Barrister nominated by PIBA and a solicitor nominated by APIL who shall be requested to resolve the issue on written representations and on the basis of a procedure laid down by agreement between PIBA and APIL. The costs of such adjudication shall, unless otherwise ordered by the panel, be met by the unsuccessful party.
    (6) In the event of a panel being appointed pursuant to sub paragraph (5) hereof:
     a) if that panel considers, after initial consideration of the disagreement, that there is a real risk that they may not be able to reach a unanimous decision, then the panel shall request APIL (where it is alleged there has been an actionable breach by the solicitor) or PIBA (where it is alleged that the has been an actionable breach by counsel) to nominate a third member of the panel;
     b) that panel shall be entitled if it considers it reasonably necessary, to appoint a qualified costs draftsman, to be nominated by the President for the time being of the Law Society, to assist the panel;

c)   the solicitor or counsel alleged to be in breach of duty shall be entitled to argue that, on the basis of information reasonably available to both solicitor and barrister, the claim would not have succeeded in any event. The panel shall resolve such issue on the balance of probabilities, and if satisfied that the claim would have been lost in any event shall not make any order for payment of fees or costs.

Cap

(7)   the amount payable in respect of any claim under sub paragraph (1) or (2) or (3) shall be limited to a maximum of £25,000.

(B)   On Termination of the Agreement

Termination by Counsel

18.   (1)   If counsel terminates the agreement under paragraph 6 then, subject to sub-paragraph 2 hereof, counsel may elect either:
    a)   to receive payment of normal fees without a success fee which the solicitor shall pay not later than three months after termination: (**'Option A'**), or
    b)   to await the outcome of the case and receive payment of normal and success fees if it ends in success: (**'Option B'**).

(2)   If counsel terminates the agreement because the solicitor, client or Litigation Friend rejects advice under paragraph 5(8) (e) or 5(8)(f) counsel is entitled only to **'Option B'**.

Termination by the Solicitor

(4)   If the solicitor terminates the agreement under paragraph 7, counsel is entitled to elect between **'Option A'** and **'Option B'**.

Automatic Termination and Counsel taking silk

(5)   If the agreement terminates under paragraphs 8 or 10 counsel is entitled only to **'Option B'**.

Challenge to fees

19.   If the client or any Litigation Friend wishes to challenge:
    a)   the entitlement to fees of counsel or the level of such fees following termination of the agreement ;or
    b)   any refusal by counsel after signing this agreement to accept instructions the solicitor must make such challenge in accordance with the provisions of paragraphs 14 and 15 of the Terms of Work upon which barristers offer their services to solicitors (Annexe D to the Code of Conduct of the Bar of England and Wales).

Return of Work

20.   If counsel in accordance with the Bar's Code of Conduct is obliged to return any brief or instructions in this case to another barrister, then:

1) Counsel will use his/her best endeavours to ensure that an appropriate barrister agrees to act for the client on the same terms as this agreement;
   If counsel is unable to secure an appropriate replacement barrister to act for the client on the same terms as this agreement counsel will not be responsible for any additional fee incurred by the solicitor or client.

2) Subject to paragraph 20(3) hereof, if the case ends in success counsel's fees for work done shall be due and paid on the conditional fee basis contained in this agreement whether or not the replacement barrister acts on a conditional fee basis; but

3) If the solicitor or client rejects any advice by the replacement barrister of the type described in paragraph 5(8) hereof, the solicitor shall immediately notify counsel who shall be entitled to terminate this agreement under paragraph 6(3).

PART SEVEN

ASSESSMENT AND PAYMENT OF COSTS / FEES

Costs Assessment

21. 1) If:
   (a) a costs order is anticipated or made in favour of the client at an interlocutory hearing and the costs are summarily assessed at the hearing; or
   (b) the costs of an interlocutory hearing are agreed between the parties in favour of the client; or
   (c) an interlocutory order or agreement for costs to be assessed in detail and paid forthwith is made in favour of the client:
      then
      (i) the solicitor will include in the statement of costs a full claim for counsel's normal fees; and
      (ii) the solicitor will promptly conclude by agreement or assessment the question of such costs; and
      (iii) within one month of receipt of such costs the solicitor will pay to counsel the amount recovered in respect of his/her fees, such sum to be set off against counsel's entitlement to normal fees by virtue of this agreement.

Solicitor's Obligation to pay

22. 1) The amounts of fees and expenses payable to counsel under this agreement
   (a) are not limited by reference to the damages which may be recovered on behalf of the client and
   (b) are payable whether or not the solicitor is or will be paid by the client or opponent.

   2) Upon success the solicitor will promptly conclude by agreement or assessment the question of costs and will pay Counsel promptly and in any event not later than one month after receipt of such costs the full sum due under this agreement.

Interest

23. The solicitor will use his best endeavours to recover interest on costs from any party ordered to pay costs to the client and shall pay counsel the share of such interest that has accrued on counsel's outstanding fees.

Challenge to Success Fee

24. 1) The solicitor will inform counsel's clerk in good time of any challenge made to his success fee and of the date, place and time of any detailed costs assessment the client or opponent has taken out pursuant to the Civil Procedure Rules and unless counsel is present or represented at the assessment hearing will place counsel's risk assessment, relevant details and any written representations before the assessing judge and argue counsel's case for his/her success fee.

    2) If counsel's fees are reduced on any assessment then:
      a) the solicitor will inform counsel's clerk within seven days and confer with counsel whether to apply for an order that the client should pay the success fee and make such application on counsel's behalf;
      b) subject to any appeal or order, counsel will accept such fees as are allowed on that assessment and will repay forthwith to the solicitor any excess previously paid.

Disclosing the reasons for the success fee

25. 1) If (a) a success fee becomes payable as a result of the client's claim and
      (b) any fees subject to the increase provided for by paragraph 12 hereof are assessed and
      (c) Counsel, the solicitor or the client is required by the court to disclose to the court or any other person the reasons for setting such increase as the level stated in this agreement, he/she may do so.

Reduction on Assessment

26. If any fees subject to the said percentage increase are assessed and any amount of that increase is disallowed on assessment on the ground that the level at which the increase was set was unreasonable in view of the facts which were or should have been known to counsel at the time it was set, such amount ceases to be payable under this agreement unless the court is satisfied that it should continue to be so payable.

Agreement on Fees

27. If the Opponent offers to pay the client's legal fees or makes an offer of one amount that includes payment of Counsel's normal fees at a lower sum than is due under this agreement then the solicitor:
    (a) will calculate the proposed pro-rata reductions of the normal and success fees of both solicitor and counsel, and

    (b)   inform counsel of the offer and the calculations supporting the proposed pro-rata reductions referred to in paragraph (a) above, and

    (c)   will not accept the offer without counsel's express consent.
    If such an agreement is reached on fees, then counsel's fees shall be limited to the agreed sum unless the court orders otherwise.

APPENDIX 15

Example risk assessments

EXAMPLE 1

SCHEDULE 1 – Reasons for level of success fee

The success fee

The success fee is set at:
(a) 67 per cent of the basic charges, assuming the case settles at any time prior to three months before the date fixed for the trial or the first date of the trial window (whichever is the earlier); or
(b) 100 per cent if the case settles at any time thereafter.

The risk assessment

The percentage success fee shown at (a) above reflects our assessment of the risks of your case, based purely on the information available to us at the time of entering into this agreement. This includes those specific issues which we regard as relevant and appropriate to take into account and which are set out in the table below.

The percentage success fee shown at (b) above reflects all of the risks in the table below which would be enhanced considerably should your case not settle prior to three months before trial. The enhanced risks at trial are due to the potential risk of failing to establish one or more fundamental elements of your case in respect of which the judge prefers the opponent's evidence, and also the significant risk that you may fail to beat an offer or Payment into Court made by your opponent (see Condition 3(k) – Part 36 Offers or Payments of your Agreement).

Particular issue	Risk
Limitation/Date of knowledge **Diagnosis in March 2006 following pleural biopsy.**	Low
Type of disease **Mesothelioma**	High
Claimant's evidence **Claimant has provided a detailed witness statement recounting exposure**	Medium

Particular issue	Risk
Independent witness **No witnesses identified to date**	Medium
Liability **Although Claimant's exposure was relatively light and he was provided with a thin paper mask it was late-1979–1988 (approx).**	Medium
No of defs/Periods of exposure **One defendant, one period of exposure**	High
Def's means to pay **Defendant is dissolved (2004)**	Low
Identity of insurers for period of exposure **None traced**	High
Diagnosis confirmation **GP records confirming diagnosis have been received**	High
Causation **No obvious competing causation.**	Medium
Quantum **Claimant is a widower and quantum will be severely diminished should he die prior to settlement**	Medium
Expert evidence **None obtained to date**	High
Documents available **Letter from employment pension scheme. IR schedule awaited**	High

EXAMPLE 2

SCHEDULE 1 – Reasons for level of success fee

Name of client

Date of accident

The success fee

The success fee is set at:
(a) 67 per cent of the basic charges, assuming the case settles at any time prior to three months before the date fixed for the trial or the first date of the trial window (whichever is the earlier); or
(b) 100 per cent if the case settles at any time thereafter

The risk assessment

The percentage success fee shown at (a) above reflects our assessment of the risks of your case, based purely on the information available to us at the time of entering into this agreement. This includes those specific issues which we regard as relevant and appropriate to take into account and which are set out in the table below.

The percentage success fee shown at (b) above reflects all of the risks in the table below which would be enhanced considerably should your case not settle prior to three months before trial. The enhanced risks at trial are due to the potential risk of failing to establish one or more fundamental elements of your case in respect of which the judge prefers the opponent's evidence, and also the significant risk that you may fail to beat an offer or Payment into Court made by your opponent (see Condition 3(k) – Part 36 Offers or Payments of your Agreement).

335

Particular issue	High risk	Med risk	Low risk	Comments
Limitation			☐	Normal PI claim with a three-year limitation period.
Type of accident			☐	Road traffic accident with our client as a passenger.
Claimant's evidence	☐			We have not yet seen a copy of the police report.
Independent witness	☐			There are no independent witness statements available as we pursue a claim against the driver of the vehicle.
Liability			☐	Liability is admitted.
Identity/No of defs			☐	We already established who the insurers of the driver (defendant) are.
Def's means to pay			☐	One of the biggest liability insurers in Germany.
Identity of insurers			☐	Identity known (see above)
Contrib negligence		☐		Possible that the defendant's insurers argue that client did not wear a seatbelt.
Causation	☐			No medical report available to date.
Quantum	☐			High value claim – brain injury
Expert evidence	☐			Unclear whether the German insurers accept that we pursue this claim in England in accordance with English law. Therefore also uncertain whether they accept our experts.
Documents available	☐			No documents yet available.
Part 36 offer			☐	Defendant's insurers have no means to make an offer and as German insurers, they are also unfamiliar with Part 36 offers.

EXAMPLE 3

CONDITIONAL FEE AGREEMENT RISK ASSESSMENT

PERSONAL INJURY/CLINICAL NEGLIGENCE

Fee Earner: H/Rate: £85

File Ref:

Client Name:

Address: Date of First Interview: 21/9/04

                                        4 Months Expire: 16/1/04

Postcode: Accident Date: 13/9/04

Referral Source: Date of Risk Assessment: 28/9/04

Likely Damages: (1)   General   £ 2,000

                         (2)   Special   £ 500

                         (3)   Futures   £

Total Likely Damages
(less likely contributory negligence and likely CRU clawback):   £ 2,500

Best Estimate as to percentage prospects of success: 65 %

Premium Rate:-

RTA Fast Track Driver	£394.00 inc IPT (reduced to £336.00 if liability admitted within 6 months of policy start date)	(1)
RTA Passenger	£336.00 inc IPT	(2)
Other Fast Track	£997.50 inc IPT (reduced to £593.25 if liability admitted within 6 months of policy start date)	(3)
All Multi Track	On application to Allianz Cornhill	(4)

NAT009/00024/DOC 1662 docLEM:005.DR6

337

APPENDIX 15

Are we sending a Prior Authority request Form ?   Yes/No

(a)   Any multi Claimant or multi Defendant claim

(b)   Any Multi Track claim

(c)   Proceedings already issued

(d)   Industrial disease / Stress at work Case

(e)   Accident is over 2 years old

Enclosures:-

1.   Statement

2.   Attendance note

3.   Other evidence (please specify) ....

Disbursements:-

1.   Client to pay

2.   Firm to pay

Level of Success Fee

Success Fee in respect of Risk Factors
(Not including Funding Only General Risk factors 3&4)   60   %

Success Fee in respect of Funding Only General Risk Factors 3 & 4   10   %

TOTAL SUGGESTED SUCCESS FEE: 70   %

NAT009 00024 DOC 1662 docLEM 1995 DRA

338

COMMENTS OF CFA RISK ASSESSMENT PANEL :

Review closely at end of protocol.

APPROVED   **REJECTED**

SUCCESS FEE: *70*   %

Specify breakdown of Success Fee if different from the above:

Signed ....
(By person/team considering Conditional Fee Agreement)

CFA RISK ASSESSMENT - APPEAL

COMMENTS BY APPEAL CTTEE:

APPROVED   **REJECTED**

SUCCESS FEE   %

Specify breakdown of Success Fee if different from the above:

Signed ....
(By person/team considering Conditional Fee Agreement)

NAT909/00024 DOC 1662.docLBM 1095 DRA

339

APPENDIX 15

FACTORS DETERMINING SUCCESS FEE

Risk factors specific to this case (tick box if issue applies, and if   *% Risk*
relevant, explain why. Also please put down the percentage risk
in respect of each issue):-

1.   Limitation issues   — no

2.   Witnesses problems — no, however unknown whether they will wait   10%.

3.   Accident not reported at the time or shortly afterwards? not been copy of   10%.
         (e.g. to police, local authority or accident report book) accident book

4.   Causation difficulties? (e.g. pre-existing condition) – no

5.   Complex medical issues? ~no

6.   Did the accident occur more than 6 months ago?   Yes/**No**

7.   Is the correct Defendant identifiable ?   **Yes**/No

8.   Is there any doubt as to whether the Defendant has
         the means to pay ?   Yes/**Not known**

9.   Is it a multi-party non- RTA claim? no

10.   Does the type of injury raise any specific   no
       risk (e.g. RSI)?

11.   Is the 100% cap going to apply in this case
       (issues relating to proportionality)?   yes

ASSESSMENT OF OTHER RISK FACTORS SPECIFIC TO THIS CASE :

1. *Dy to raise issue wording - failure to look where going / allegation* 10%. *Incorrect footnead.*

2. *witnesses may not co-speak of all work by transco* 20%.

3. *Not seen accidat report form ∴ may have not something different in there to what client y saying* 10%.

GENERAL RISK FACTORS

1. Outcome of Litigation is always uncertain. We need to spread the risk of losses in individual cases across the working case load of the firm. **5%**

2. Although this may appear a strong case in relation to ability, a greater risk often arises in relation to dealing with Part 36 Offers and payments, which cannot be predicted in advance. **10%**

3. Delay until payment of the firms' costs (5% per annum x years to estimated date of payment) (FUNDING ONLY) 5%

4. Extra costs of CFA work (non-payment for risk assessment calculation; non-recovery of part or all of success fees; additional administrative work) (FUNDING ONLY) **5%**

5. We generally enter into Conditional Fee Agreements with clients at an early stage, because clients do not want to pay investigation costs. We take the risk of that investigation. The cost of us investigating cases which do not eventually proceed is part of our risk assessment procedure which has to be reflected in our success fees. 5%

EXAMPLE 4

CONDITIONAL FEE AGREEMENT RISK ASSESSMENT

PERSONAL INJURY/CLINICAL NEGLIGENCE

Fee Earner: H/Rate: £150

File Ref:

Client Name:

Address: Date of First Interview: 12/2/07

                                             4 Months Expire: 12/6/07

Postcode: Accident Date: 7/12/06

Referral Source: Recommended   Date of Risk Assessment: 16/2/07

Likely Damages: (1)   General   £ 4,000

                       (2)   Special   £500

                       (3)   Futures   £

Total Likely Damages
(less likely contributory negligence and likely CRU clawback):   £ 4,500

Best Estimate as to percentage prospects of success: 80 %

Premium Rate:-

RTA Fast Track Driver	£394.00 inc IPT (reduced to £336.00 if liability admitted within 6 months of policy start date)	(1) ✓
RTA Passenger	£336.00 inc IPT	(2)
Other Fast Track	£997.50 inc IPT (reduced to £593.25 if liability admitted within 6 months of policy start date)	(3)
All Multi Track	On application to Allianz Cornhill	(4)

GRM 1905 DRA

Are we sending a Prior Authority request Form ?   Yes No

(a)   Any multi Claimant or multi Defendant claim

(b)   Any Multi Track claim

(c)   Proceedings already issued

(d)   Industrial disease / Stress at work Case

(e)   Accident is over 2 years old

Enclosures:-

1.   Statement ✓

2.   Attendance note

3.   Other evidence (please specify) ....

Disbursements:-

1.   Client to pay

2.   Firm to pay ✓

Level of Success Fee

Success Fee in respect of Risk Factors
(Not including Funding Only General Risk factors 3&4)   %

Success Fee in respect of Funding Only General Risk Factors 3 & 4   10   %

TOTAL SUGGESTED SUCCESS FEE: 12 ½%

increasing to 100% if proceed to trial

FEE EARNERS VIEW ON STRENGTHS / WEAKNESSES OF THE CASE:

S -   Third party insurers have admitted liability
         to client's employer re vehicle damage

    -    Police accident should be available

W -   client has no memory of the accident

LRS1 04E58 x

343

APPENDIX 15

<u>COMMENTS OF CFA RISK ASSESSMENT PANEL</u> :

<u>AUTHORITY</u>

You have authority to: obtain medical records   ✓   i
obtain medical report   ✓   i
obtain police accident report   i
amend review date to:-   _____
other (*please specify*)   _____

APPROVED ✓   **REJECTED**

SUCCESS FEE: 12 1/2 % uncreasing to 100% if proceed to trial

Specify breakdown of Success Fee if different from the above:

Signed .... : Vallere ....
(By person/team considering Conditional Fee Agreement)

<u>CFA RISK ASSESSMENT - APPEAL</u>

<u>COMMENTS BY APPEAL COMMITTEE:</u>

APPROVED   REJECTED   .

SUCCESS FEE   %

Specify breakdown of Success Fee if different from the above:

Signed ....
(By person/team considering Conditional Fee Agreement)

FACTORS DETERMINING SUCCESS FEE

Risk factors specific to this case (tick box if issue applies, and if   *% Risk*
relevant, explain why. Also please put down the percentage risk
in respect of each issue):-

1.   Limitation issues

2.   Witnesses problems

3.   Accident not reported at the time or shortly afterwards?
      (e.g. to police, local authority or accident report book)

4.   Causation difficulties? (e.g. pre-existing condition)

5.   Complex medical issues?

6.   Did the accident occur more than 6 months ago?   Yes/No

7.   Is the correct Defendant identifiable ?   Yes/No

8.   Is there any doubt as to whether the Defendant has
      the means to pay ?   Yes/Not known

9.   Is it a multi-party non- RTA claim?

10.   Does the type of injury raise any specific
      risk (e.g. RSI)?

11.   Is the 100% cap going to apply in this case
      (issues relating to proportionality)?

345

<u>ASSESSMENT OF OTHER RISK FACTORS SPECIFIC TO THIS CASE :</u>

GENERAL RISK FACTORS

1. Outcome of Litigation is always uncertain. We need to spread the risk of losses in individual cases across the working case load of the firm.   **5%**

2. Although this may appear a strong case in relation to ability, a greater risk often arises in relation to dealing with Part 36 Offers and payments, which cannot be predicted in advance.   **10%**

3. Delay until payment of the firms' costs (5% per annum x years to estimated date of payment) (FUNDING ONLY)   **5%**

4. Extra costs of CFA work (non-payment for risk assessment calculation; non-recovery of part or all of success fees; additional administrative work) (FUNDING ONLY) **5%**

5. We generally enter into Conditional Fee Agreements with clients at an early stage, because clients do not want to pay investigation costs. We take the risk of that investigation. The cost of us investigating cases which do not eventually proceed is part of our risk assessment procedure which has to be reflected in our success fees. **5%**

LEMC-095-F2RA

EXAMPLE 5

CONDITIONAL FEE AGREEMENT RISK ASSESSMENT

PERSONAL INJURY/CLINICAL NEGLIGENCE

Fee Earner: H/Rate: 115.00

File Ref:

Client Name:

Address: Date of First Interview: 16 | 3 | 04 (LAS)

                                               4 Months Expire: 16 | 7 | 04

Postcode: Accident Date: 20 | 1 | 04

Referral Source: Date of Risk Assessment: 31 | 3 | 04

Likely Damages: (1)   General   £   4,000

                         (2)   Special   £

                         (3)   Futures   £

Total Likely Damages
(less likely contributory negligence and likely CRU clawback):   £ 4,000

Best Estimate as to percentage prospects of success: 65 %

Premium Rate:-

RTA Fast Track Driver	£394.00 inc IPT (reduced to £336.00 if liability admitted within 6 months of policy start date)	(1)
RTA Passenger	£336.00 inc IPT	(2)
Other Fast Track	£997.50 inc IPT (reduced to £593.25 if liability admitted within 6 months of policy start date)	(3)
All Multi Track	On application to Allianz Cornhill	(4)

LEM1095.DRA

347

APPENDIX 15

Are we sending a Prior Authority request Form ?   Ye̷s/No

(a)   Any multi Claimant or multi Defendant claim

(b)   Any Multi Track claim

(c)   Proceedings already issued

(d)   Industrial disease / Stress at work Case

(e)   Accident is over 2 years old

Enclosures:-

1.   Statement

2.   Attendance note

3.   Other evidence (please specify) ....Sketch.................................

Disbursements:-

1.   Client to pay

2.   Firm to pay

Level of Success Fee

Success Fee in respect of Risk Factors
(Not including Funding Only General Risk factors 3&4)   50   %

Success Fee in respect of Funding Only General Risk Factors 3 & 4   10   %

TOTAL SUGGESTED SUCCESS FEE: 60   %

LED41985.DBA

348

COMMENTS OF CFA RISK ASSESSMENT PANEL :

APPROVED   REJECTED

SUCCESS FEE: 60   %

Specify breakdown of Success Fee if different from the above:

Signed .... J. Vallance ....
(By person/team considering Conditional Fee Agreement)

CFA RISK ASSESSMENT - APPEAL

COMMENTS BY APPEAL CTTEE:

APPROVED   REJECTED

SUCCESS FEE   %

Specify breakdown of Success Fee if different from the above:

Signed ....
(By person/team considering Conditional Fee Agreement)

LEM-0395-DRA

349

FACTORS DETERMINING SUCCESS FEE

Risk factors specific to this case (tick box if issue applies, and if   % Risk
relevant, explain why. Also please put down the percentage risk
in respect of each issue):-

1.   Limitation issues

2.   Witnesses problems   - unclear if they will assist   10%.

3.   Accident not reported at the time or shortly afterwards?
   (e.g. to police, local authority or accident report book)

4.   Causation difficulties? (e.g. pre-existing condition)

5.   Complex medical issues?

6.   Did the accident occur more than 6 months ago?   Yes/No

7.   Is the correct Defendant identifiable ?   Yes/No

8.   Is there any doubt as to whether the Defendant has
   the means to pay ?   Yes/Not known

9.   Is it a multi-party non- RTA claim?

10.   Does the type of injury raise any specific
    risk (e.g. RSI)?

11.   Is the 100% cap going to apply in this case
    (issues relating to proportionality)?

LEAD1095.DRA

ASSESSMENT OF OTHER RISK FACTORS SPECIFIC TO THIS CASE :

Accident involves a complicated system of work which may be difficult for the Court to understand   10%

Unclear if client's previous complaints about the system of work will have been recorded   10%

GENERAL RISK FACTORS

1. Outcome of Litigation is always uncertain. We need to spread the risk of losses in individual cases across the working case load of the firm.   **5%**

2. Although this may appear a strong case in relation to ability, a greater risk often arises in relation to dealing with Part 36 Offers and payments, which cannot be predicted in advance.   **10%**

3. Delay until payment of the firms' costs (5% per annum x years to estimated date of payment) (FUNDING ONLY)   **5%**

4. Extra costs of CFA work (non-payment for risk assessment calculation; non-recovery of part or all of success fees; additional administrative work) (FUNDING ONLY) **5%**

5. We generally enter into Conditional Fee Agreements with clients at an early stage, because clients do not want to pay investigation costs. We take the risk of that investigation. The cost of us investigating cases which do not eventually proceed is part of our risk assessment procedure which has to be reflected in our success fees. **5%**

LEN1095 DRA

351

APPENDIX 16

The Chancery Bar Association's Conditional Fee Agreement (with introductory Note)

[This CFA was drafted by a sub-committee on behalf of the Chancery Bar Association in the light of statutory provisions in force as at 23 December 2005. As at that date, the pre-existing regulations had been revoked with effect from 1 November 2005 so that from 1 November parties could enter into CFAs based only on the primary legislation in the Courts and Legal Services Act 1990 as amended.

Nevertheless, the Chancery Bar Association draft is based upon both the primary legislation and the previous regulations, as it is still thought that compliance with the previous regulations represents good practice.

It is up to those using the Agreement to satisfy themselves as to its appropriateness and legality. In this respect it is stressed that the legislative and regulatory framework is subject to rapid change and any CFA which does not comply with that framework may be unenforceable.

The documents can be downloaded from the CBA website: www.chba.org.uk.]

NOTE

1. The Chancery Bar Association's Conditional Fee Agreement is a relatively short agreement which incorporates the Chancery Bar Association's Conditional Fee Conditions 2005. The Agreement itself will require considerable amendment to fit the circumstances of the particular case. It is unlikely that the Conditions will require amendment but if any amendments are appropriate, these can be dealt with in the Agreement.
2. There are two clauses numbered 2 in the Agreement. The first is appropriate where no fee is payable if the Action ends in Failure. The second is appropriate if a reduced fee is payable in any event. One of the two clauses should be deleted.
3. There are also two clauses numbered 3. The first will create a contract between Counsel and the Solicitor but the second will not. Again, one of the two alternatives should be deleted.
4. Clauses 4–9 and 11–13 need completing as the circumstances of the case require.
5. Clause 10 is optional and can be deleted, if desired.
6. Clause 14 should be deleted if Parts 1 and 2 of the Conditions are incorporated but should be completed if Parts 1 and 3 are incorporated in the Agreement.
7. Further clauses, adding provisions or varying the Conditions, can be included after Clause 14, or elsewhere if appropriate. If the Conditions, in particular Condition 16, are altered in any material respect, you may not be fully insured by Bar Mutual Indemnity Fund Ltd and its approval should be obtained to any such alterations.

8. This CFA was drafted by a sub-committee on behalf of the Chancery Bar Association in the light of statutory provisions in force as at 23 December 2005. As at that date, the pre-existing regulations had been revoked with effect from 1 November 2005 so that from Nov 1 parties could enter into CFAs based only on the primary legislation in the Courts and Legal Services Act 1990 as amended. Nevertheless, the Chancery Bar Association draft is based upon both the primary legislation and the previous regulations, as it is still thought that compliance with the previous regulations represents good practice. It is up to those using the Agreement to satisfy themselves as to its appropriateness and legality. In this respect it is stressed that the legislative and regulatory framework is subject to rapid change and any CFA which does not comply with that framework may be unenforceable.

9. The Chancery Bar Association would be grateful for any comments you may have in the light of your experience. It is intended to update the Agreement and the Conditions in the light of experience. If you have any comments these should be addressed to Charles Purle QC, New Square Chambers, 12 New Square, London WC2A 3SW.

10. Finally, the Agreement and the Conditions have been drafted by volunteers with, perhaps, no greater expertise than any counsel using them for the purposes of a conditional fee agreement. As previously stated, you must satisfy yourself that the Agreement and the Conditions are lawful and are appropriate for the particular circumstances of the relevant proceedings. The Chancery Bar Association and the draftsmen of the Agreement and the Conditions assume no responsibility to you or anyone else. The draftsmen will only accept responsibility if instructed in the usual way.

December 2005

THE CHANCERY BAR ASSOCIATION'S CONDITIONAL FEE AGREEMENT

THIS AGREEMENT is made   20

between

('Counsel') and ('the Solicitor')

1. This agreement contains the terms and conditions upon which Counsel agrees to act in the Action on behalf of the Client.
2. Parts 1 and 2 of the Chancery Bar Association's Conditional Fee Conditions 2005 annexed hereto ('the Conditions') are incorporated in this agreement.
2. Parts 1 and 3 of the Chancery Bar Association's Conditional Fee Conditions 2005 annexed hereto ('the Conditions') are incorporated in this agreement.
3. This agreement is a contract enforceable at law.
3. This agreement is not a contract enforceable at law.
4. The Action is
5. The Base Rate for Counsel's fees to which the Uplift for the Uplifted Rate is to be applied is as follows:

(1) as regards all work other than Court appearances, in accordance with his/her hourly rate applicable to the type of work involved in the Action, currently

£ per hour,

(2) for an interlocutory hearing, the fee will be based on the number of hours which Counsel reasonably considers are required for preparation plus the number of hours which Counsel reasonably considers that the hearing is due to last, charged at the rate of £ per hour,

(3) for the trial, the brief fee will be £

based on an estimated duration of days but in the event that the estimated duration is greater or less than days the brief fee will be increased or decreased by £ for each day the estimated duration is greater or less than days,

(4) as regards refreshers, in accordance with his/her daily rate for the type of work involved in the Action, currently £ per day, and

(5) in the event of the trial being adjourned for more than one month, a re-reading fee based on the hourly rate specified in subclause (1) above will be charged.

6. The Client is
7. The Opposing Party is
8. The Uplift which is to apply to Counsel's fees is %.
9. The reason for setting the Uplift at that rate are:

and the cost to Counsel of the postponement of the payment of his/her fees and expenses.
% relates to the cost to Counsel of the postponement of the payment of his/her fees and expenses.

10. In the event Counsel does not appear at any interlocutory hearing in the circumstances referred to in Condition 4 or returns any brief or instructions in the Action in the circumstances set out in Condition 5, Counsel shall use reasonable endeavours to arrange that Other Acceptable Counsel will take over and act on a conditional fee basis but Counsel does not warrant that he/she will be able to arrange for other Acceptable Counsel to take over and if other Acceptable Counsel does not agree for whatever reason to act on a conditional fee basis, that will not be a breach of this agreement or retainer by Counsel.
11. Relief for the purposes of Success means
12. The rate of interest for the purposes of Condition 22 shall be %.
13. The period for the purposes of Condition 23 shall be .
14. The Reduced Rate is % of the Base Rate

Signed

Counsel   the Solicitor

THE CHANCERY BAR ASSOCIATION'S CONDITIONAL FEE CONDITIONS 2005

PART 1

1. The following expressions used in these Conditions have the following meanings:

the Action	the action or proposed action referred to in the Agreement including any appeal or proceedings to enforce judgment or any other order but not any counterclaim
the Agreement	the agreement between Counsel and the Solicitor incorporating these Conditions
the Base Rate	the rate of Counsel's fees described in the Agreement which would be payable if there was not a conditional fee agreement
Becomes Insolvent	(1) in the case of an individual, when the individual is made bankrupt or an individual voluntary arrangement is approved in respect of the individual,
	(2) in the case of a corporation, when a winding up order or an administration order is made against the corporation, or a resolution is passed for its voluntary winding up, or administrative receivers are appointed over the property of the corporation or a company voluntary arrangement is approved in respect of the corporation, and
	(3) in the case of a partnership, when a winding up order or partnership administration order is made against the partnership or when a partnership voluntary arrangement is approved in respect of the partnership
the Client	the client referred to in the Agreement
Condition	a particular condition of these Conditions
these Conditions	the Chancery Bar Association's Conditional Fee Conditions 2005
Counsel	the barrister defined as Counsel in, and who is a party to, the Agreement
Failure	the Action is concluded without qualifying under the head of Success
Normal Litigation Practice	the normal practice adopted in litigation in the Chancery Division which is not carried out under a conditional fee agreement
the Opposing Party	the other party or parties to the Action identified in the Agreement
Other Acceptable Counsel	counsel other than Counsel whom the Solicitor has agreed or does agree is acceptable for the purposes of the Agreement

Solicitor	the solicitor or firm of solicitors defined as the Solicitor in, and who or which is *a* party to, the Agreement
the Solicitor's Conditional Fee Agreement	the conditional fee agreement entered into between the Solicitor and the Client
Success	the Client becoming entitled, whether pursuant to a decision of the Court or agreement between the parties, to the relief referred to in the Agreement and where the Client's entitlement to that relief is pursuant to a decision of the Court, the Opposing Party, or, in the case of multi party litigation, any Opposing Party is not allowed to appeal against the Court decision or has not appealed in time or has entered into a settlement agreement
the Uplift	the percentage by which the Base Rate is to be increased under the Agreement
the Uplifted Rate	means the Base Rate as increased by the Uplift

2. The relationship between Counsel and Solicitor shall be governed by the Terms of Work under which barristers offer their services to solicitors and the Withdrawal of Credit Scheme as authorised by the General Council of the Bar as from time to time amended and set out in the Code of Conduct of the Bar of England and Wales, save that where such Terms of Work and such Scheme are inconsistent with the terms of the Agreement the latter shall prevail.

3. Subject to Conditions 4 and 5, Counsel will diligently perform in accordance with his/her instructions any tasks in or related to the Action which in Normal Litigation Practice would be performed by a barrister of his/her seniority.

4. In particular, Counsel is not bound:

   (1) to appear at any interlocutory hearing for which he/she reasonably believes that:
       (a) counsel of lesser experience and seniority would ordinarily be instructed; or
       (b) the Court would conclude that the hearing was not fit for the attendance of one or, in the case where two or more Counsel are instructed, two or more Counsel;
   (2) to draft documents such as schedules, letters, summonses or witness statements or to advise orally or in writing or perform any other task if such would not be expected of counsel in Normal Litigation Practice;
   (3) to accept instructions outside the scope of the Agreement; or
   (4) to accept any brief or instructions where he/she is required or permitted to refuse such brief or instructions.

5. If Counsel is, in accordance with the Bar's Code of Conduct, obliged or permitted to return any brief or instructions in the Action to another barrister or not to accept any brief or instructions in the Action, then:

   (1) it will not be a breach by Counsel of the Agreement to return or not to accept such brief or instructions, and
   (2) in the event of Success, Counsel shall still be entitled to his/her fees in accordance with the Agreement at the Uplifted Rate on all work done.

6. Subject to subcondition (5) below, the Solicitor will perform any tasks in or related to the Action which in Normal Litigation Practice would be performed by a solicitor. Without prejudice to the generality of the foregoing, the Solicitor will:

    (1) prosecute and prepare the Action promptly, diligently and carefully and take all necessary procedural steps in time;

    (2) provide Counsel with, or make available to Counsel, copies of all documents relevant to the Action as soon as possible after they become available to the Client or the Solicitor;

    (3) inform Counsel of all material developments and information relevant to the Action as soon as possible after they become known to the Client or the Solicitor;

    (4) acquire and provide Counsel with or make available to Counsel any other documents or information relevant to the Action which Counsel reasonably requests and which are available to or known to the Client or the Solicitor;

    (5) consider with Counsel the need for Counsel to advise on evidence, merits and quantum or to perform any other tasks and the need for any further procedural steps which Counsel may consider necessary at, at least, each of the following stages of the action:

        (a) on first instructing Counsel,

        (b) upon service of any statement of case or application by the Opposing Party,

        (c) upon completion of disclosure and inspection of documents,

        (d) the preparation of witness statements, affidavits, instructions to experts and/or expert's reports,

        (e) upon exchange or service of any witness statement or affidavit,

        (f) upon exchange or service of any expert's report, and

        (g) at any other time when Counsel considers it expedient,

    and shall instruct Counsel to advise or to act accordingly, provided that such advice or task would be given or performed by Counsel in Normal Litigation Practice;

    (6) communicate Counsel's advice on, at least, the following matters to the Client forthwith at whatever stage the Action has reached:

        (a) the merits or quantum of the Action, including in particular that the Action is not likely to end in Success,

        (b) the appropriate terms, if any, under which the Action ought to be settled, and whether any Part 36 Payment into court or offer or analogous type of offer should be made or accepted,

        (c) the likelihood that the value of any recovery in the Action likely to be made by the Client together with the costs recoverable on Success are such that they are not likely to exceed the Client's legal costs and disbursements likely to be allowed following an assessment of such costs and disbursements,

        (d) the expenditure which should or should not be incurred instructing leading counsel or a more senior or specialised barrister, or instructing experts or otherwise obtaining evidence or preparing the Action;

    (7) agree (where possible) with Counsel's clerk in good time the date, place and time of any hearing fixed in the Action or otherwise inform Counsel's clerk in good time of such matters, and instruct Counsel and provide all necessary papers for the hearing within a reasonable time before the hearing or, where appropriate, within a reasonable time before the date on which Counsel's skeleton argument is due to be lodged and/or exchanged;

357

(8) deliver the brief (and, where appropriate, agree stage accrual of brief fees) for any hearing within a reasonable time before the hearing;

(9) forthwith upon receipt of any Part 36 or other offer to settle the Action or any issues in it, communicate immediately the terms of the offer to Counsel and seek his/her advice on whether to accept or reject the offer or as to the appropriate terms, if any, under which the Action or issues ought to be settled;

(10) forthwith upon receipt of notice of a Part 36 payment into court, inform Counsel of such payment in and seek his/her advice on whether to accept or reject the Part 36 payment;

(11) give to any other party to the Action such information relating to the Agreement as required by the Civil Procedure Rules and/or any Practice Direction; and

(12) in any case where the amount of Counsel's fees falls to be assessed by the Court, notify Counsel immediately of any appointment or hearing when the amount of Counsel's fees falls to be assessed, take reasonable steps to assist Counsel in preparation of his/her argument in support of his/her fees, including obtaining information reasonably required by Counsel for that purpose and otherwise use best endeavours to ensure that Counsel's fees are allowed.

7. The Solicitor confirms that he/she/they has/have brought the terms of the Agreement to the attention of the Client and has explained to the Client the Client's responsibilities and liabilities under the Agreement and the Client has consented to the terms and conditions of and incorporated in the Agreement in so far as they relate to the Client.

8. Subject to clause 9 below, the Solicitor may terminate Counsel's retainer at any time

(1) without cause, or

(2) if the Solicitor has good reason to believe the relationship of trust between the Solicitor and Counsel has irretrievably broken down,

then, in either of those events, Counsel shall be entitled, at his/her option, to one of the following, namely, either:

(a) his/her fees accrued to the date of termination at the Base Rate in full, or

(b) in the event only of Success, his/her fees at the Uplifted Rate.

9. The Solicitor shall not have the right to terminate Counsel's retainer on any ground once Counsel has fully performed his/her obligations under the Agreement.

10. Counsel may terminate his/her retainer if

(1) he/she reasonably believes that the relationship of trust between the Solicitor and Counsel or between Counsel and any other Counsel instructed in the Action has irretrievably broken down;

(2) the Solicitor and/or the Client and/or more senior Counsel instructed in the case rejects Counsel's advice about the appropriate terms under which the Action ought to be settled and/or any Part 36 payment into court or any Part 36 offer should be made, accepted or rejected;

(3) the Solicitor has failed to comply with any obligation under the Agreement;

(4) Counsel is informed of or discovers the existence of an actual or likely defence or counterclaim or of information which is not correct or has not been provided which he/she reasonably believes materially affects the likelihood of Success in the Action and/or the amount or value of any recovery likely to be made by the Client in the event of Success but of which he/she was not aware and which he/she could not reasonably have anticipated from the information before him/her at the date of his/her entry into the Agreement;

(5) the Client dies;

(6) the Client Becomes Insolvent; or

(7) the Opposing Party Becomes Insolvent;

and must terminate his/her retainer if:

(8) funding is granted to the Client by the Legal Services Commission in respect of the Action; or

(9) the Solicitors Conditional Fee Agreement is terminated before the conclusion of the Action;

then, in any of those events, Counsel shall be entitled, at his/her option, to one of the following, namely, either:

(a) his/her fees accrued to the date of termination at the Base Rate in full, or

(b) in the event only of Success, his/her fees at the Uplifted Rate.

11. If the Solicitor or Counsel terminates Counsel's retainer, they must do so by notice in writing giving the reasons, if any, relied upon.

12. Where the Uplift becomes payable as a result of the Action then, if any fees subject to the Uplift are assessed and Counsel, the Solicitor or the Client is required by the Court to disclose to the Court or to any other person the reasons for setting the Uplift at the level stated in the Agreement, that person may do so.

13. Subject to Condition 14 below, upon Success Counsel will be entitled to be paid his/her fees at the Uplifted Rate.

14. If the amount of damages and interest awarded by the Court qualifies as Success but is less than a Part 36 payment into Court or effective Part 36 offer then:

(1) if Counsel advised its rejection he/she is entitled to his/her fees at the Uplifted Rate for the work done up to the receipt of the notice of the Part 36 payment into Court or offer but fees at the Base Rate only for subsequent work;

(2) if Counsel advised its acceptance, or did not advise whether it should be accepted or rejected, he/she is entitled to his/her fees at the Uplifted Rate for all work done.

15. If the action is dismissed for want of prosecution or because the Client fails to provide security for costs or otherwise ends in Failure as a result of a breach by the Solicitor but not by Counsel of any of the terms of the Agreement or a procedural default by the Solicitor and/or the Client but not by Counsel, the Solicitor shall pay Counsel's fees within three months of the date of dismissal or the ending of the Action at the Base Rate.

16. If, because of a breach by Counsel but not the Solicitor of his/her duty to the Client, the Action is dismissed for want of prosecution or otherwise ends in Failure, Counsel shall, subject to subconditions (1) to (3) below, pay the Solicitor such basic costs, excluding any element of uplift, as would have been recoverable from the Client under the Solicitors Conditional Fee Agreement with the Client but

(1) no payment shall be made under this Condition in respect of any breach by Counsel which would not give rise to a claim for damages if an action were brought by the Client,

(2) in the event of a disagreement as to whether or not there has been an actionable breach by Counsel, or as to causation, or as to the amount payable under this Condition, that disagreement shall be referred to arbitration pursuant to the procedure set out in Conditions 25 to 28 below, and

(3) the amount payable in respect of any claim under this Condition shall be limited to a maximum of £25,000.

17. The Solicitor has the right to challenge Counsel's fees, but not the agreed rates, in accordance with the Terms of Work referred to in Condition 2 above.

18. In the event that Counsel may be entitled (including after termination) to payment in the event of Success, the Solicitor must keep Counsel reasonably informed of the progress of the Action and must promptly inform Counsel of Success if it occurs.

19. If costs are ordered to be paid or are agreed to be paid forthwith to the Client in respect of any interlocutory hearing, Counsel can elect to be paid his/her fees of the application at the Base Rate and the Solicitor will promptly conclude by agreement or assessment the amount of any such costs and enforce such order for costs or such agreement as to costs in respect of any such interlocutory hearing and within one month after receipt of any such costs will pay to Counsel the amount recovered in respect of his/her fees. If costs are not ordered to be paid or are not agreed to be paid to the Client in respect of any interlocutory hearing, or Counsel does not elect to be paid his/her fees at the Base Rate, in the event of Success, Counsel shall be entitled to his/her fees in accordance with the Agreement at the Uplifted Rate.

20. If any fees subject to the Uplift are assessed and any amount in respect of the Uplifted Rate is disallowed on assessment on the ground that the level at which the Uplift was set was unreasonable in view of facts which were or should have been known to Counsel at the time it was set, such amount ceases to be payable under the Agreement, unless the Court is satisfied it should continue to be so payable.

21. Where Condition 20 does not apply, if Counsel agrees with any person liable as a result of the Action to pay his/her fees subject to the Uplift that a lower amount than the amount payable in accordance with the Agreement is to be paid instead, then the amount payable under the Agreement in respect of those fees shall be reduced accordingly, unless the Court is satisfied that the full amount should continue to be payable under it.

22. In the event that Counsel's fees are not paid in due time under the Agreement, the Solicitor will pay Counsel interest on those fees at the rate specified in the Agreement.

23. Whenever Counsel is entitled to payment under this Agreement, payment must be made within the period specified in the Agreement.

24. The Solicitor will pay Counsel's fees in accordance with this Agreement whether or not the Solicitor is or will be paid by the Client or the Opposing Party.

25. Any dispute arising out of or in connection with the Agreement shall be referred to arbitration by a panel consisting of a barrister nominated by the Chairman of the Bar Council and a solicitor nominated by the President of the Law Society, who shall act as arbitrators in accordance with the Arbitration Act 1996. The arbitrators so appointed shall have power to appoint an umpire.

26. The arbitrators so appointed and where applicable the umpire shall be entitled to act with or without charge. In the event that any one or more of them choose to

charge for their services, the fees and expenses of such arbitrator (s) and/or umpire shall be paid by one or both of the parties as the panel, in their discretion, shall direct. The panel shall not have power to make any order in respect of the costs of the parties.

27. In the event of a reference to arbitration pursuant to paragraph 16 above, Counsel alleged to be in breach of duty shall be entitled to argue that the claim in the Action would not have succeeded in any event. The panel shall resolve such issue on the balance of probabilities and, if satisfied that such claim would not have succeeded in any event, shall not make any order for payment of the Solicitor's fees or costs incurred in relation to the Action.

28. The right to refer any dispute to arbitration must be exercised promptly by either the Solicitor or Counsel. In the event of termination it must be exercised at the latest within three months of

   (1) receipt of notice of such termination or
   (2) receipt of the fee note for the fees being subjected to challenge,

   failing which the right of challenge shall become irrevocably barred.

PART 2

29. Subject to Condition 9 above, the Solicitor may terminate Counsel's retainer with cause in any of the following circumstances:

   (1) Counsel becomes unavailable for the trial of the Action, or
   (2) the Solicitor has good reason to believe that Counsel, in breach of his/her duty to the Client, has manifested such incompetence so as to justify the termination of his/her retainer,

   then, in either of those events, Counsel shall be entitled to be paid any fees which he/she has elected to receive at the Base Rate pursuant to Condition 19 and (in the event only of Success) his/her fees accrued to the date of termination at the Uplifted Rate.

30. Counsel may terminate his retainer in any of the following circumstances:

   (1) Counsel is required to cease to act by the Code of Conduct of the Bar of England and Wales or Counsel's professional conduct is impugned;
   (2) Counsel becomes Queen's Counsel during the course of the Agreement;

   and must terminate his/her retainer in the following circumstances:

   (3) Counsel accepts a full time judicial appointment; or
   (4) Counsel ceases to practice as a barrister;

   then, in any of those events, Counsel shall be entitled to be paid any fees which he/she has elected to receive at the Base Rate pursuant to Condition 19 and (in the event only of Success) his/her fees accrued to the date of termination at the Uplifted Rate.

31. In the event that the Action ends in Failure no fees will be payable to Counsel other than in the circumstances referred to in conditions 8, 10, 15 or 19 above,

PART 3

32. In this Part of these Conditions the following expression shall have the following meaning:

   the Reduced Rate   the rate of Counsel's fees specified as such in the Agreement.

33. Subject to Condition 9 above, the Solicitor may terminate Counsel's retainer with cause in any of the following circumstances:

    (1) Counsel becomes unavailable for the trial of the Action, or
    (2) the Solicitor has good reason to believe that Counsel, in breach of his/her duty to the Client, has manifested such incompetence so as to justify the termination of his/her retainer,

    then, in either of those events, Counsel shall be entitled to be paid any fees which he/she has elected to receive at the Base Rate pursuant to Condition 19 and both of the following, namely:

    (a) his/her fees accrued to the date of termination at the Reduced Rate, and
    (b) in the event of Success, the difference between the Reduced Rate and the Uplifted Rate.

34. Counsel may terminate his retainer in any of the following circumstances:

    (1) Counsel is required to cease to act by the Code of Conduct of the Bar of England and Wales or Counsel's professional conduct is impugned;
    (2) Counsel becomes Queen's Counsel during the course of the Agreement;

    and must terminate his/her retainer in the following circumstances:

    (3) Counsel accepts a full time judicial appointment; or
    (4) Counsel ceases to practice as a barrister;

    then, in any of those events, Counsel shall be entitled, to both of the following, namely:

    (a) his/her fees accrued to the date of termination at the Reduced Rate, and
    (b) in the event of Success, the difference between the Reduced Rate and the Uplifted Rate.

35. In the event that the Action ends in Failure Counsel will be entitled to his/her fees only at the Reduced Rate other than in the circumstances referred to in conditions 8, 10, 15 or 19 above.

36. The Solicitor will every three months during the Action pay

    (1) Counsel's fees for work done at the Reduced Rate to that date;
    (2) the difference between his/her fees already paid at the Reduced Rate and his/her fees at the Uplifted Rate, whenever Counsel is entitled pursuant to the Agreement to be paid his/her fees at the Uplifted Rate; and
    (3) the difference between his/her fees already paid at the Reduced Rate and his/her fees at the Base Rate, whenever Counsel is entitled pursuant to the Agreement to be paid his/her fees at the Base Rate.

APPENDIX 17

Draft deeds of rectification

DRAFT DEED OF RECTIFICATION

(Original erroneously referring to the wrong jurisdiction)

DATED   [*year*]

[NAME OF FIRM]

and

[NAME OF CLIENT]

DEED OF RECTIFICATION

THIS DEED OF RECTIFICATION is made on [*date*]

BETWEEN:

(1)   *[NAME OF FIRM]* Solicitors of *[ADDRESS]* ('the Firm')
(2)   *[NAME OF CLIENT]* of *[ADDRESS]* ('the Client')

RECITALS:

(1)   This Deed is supplemental to a Conditional Fee Agreement ('the Agreement') made on [*date*] between the Firm and the Client regarding the Client's claim for damages plus interest and costs due to her as a consequence of the opponent's breaches of the European Convention on Human Rights.
(2)   The Firm and the Client intended that the Agreement would conform in all respects with all requirements regarding an agreement of that kind including those contained in the Conditional Fee Agreements Regulations 2000 in particular the correct description of the proceedings. The Agreement correctly indicated at the top of the document (where there is a reference to 'EUROPEAN COURT OF HUMAN RIGHTS') that the proceedings covered by the Agreement were intended to be the proceedings undertaken by the firm in the European Court of Human Rights. However, the definition in 'Proceedings' on the second page of the Agreement failed to state that the Agreement covers proceedings undertaken in the European Court of Human Rights, but refers instead to proceedings undertaken in the 'County Court or High Court'.
(3)   Prior to the making of the CFA it was made clear to the Client that the proceedings intended to be covered by the Agreement were proceedings undertaken by the firm in the European Court of Human Rights, not in the County Court or High Court. Therefore the parties to the Agreement were clear in relation to their understanding of the proceedings covered by the Agreement.

(4)   Accordingly the parties to this Deed have agreed that the Agreement does not accurately set forth the true arrangements between them as regards the particulars mentioned below and wish to rectify the Agreement as appears below.

NOW THIS DEED WITNESSETH as follows:

1.   The Agreement is to be read and construed as if the definition of 'Proceedings' on the second page of the Agreement should read as follows:

> '"Proceedings" – Any legal action undertaken by the firm in European Court of Human Rights excluding any appeal in connection with the client's prosecution of the claim including all work undertaken by the firm for the client between 1 October 2003 and the issue of proceedings concerning taking instructions, assessment of the merits, preparation of the claim and preparing and negotiating this agreement; including any work necessary to secure an order for costs and to deal with all issues of assessment of cash costs, including any appeal.'.

2.   A copy of the Agreement is annexed to this Deed showing in red the amendments referred to in clause 1.

3.   The parties to this Deed declare first that the Agreement shall be read and construed as if from the date of the Agreement it had been in a form which includes such amendments and secondly that the Agreement and every part of it is to continue to have full effect and be binding on the parties.

IN WITNESS whereof these presents have been entered into as a Deed.

EXECUTED AS A DEED by a Partner of   )

the Firm having authority to execute   )

this Deed on behalf of the Firm   )

in the presence of:

Witness Signature: ....

Witness Name: ....

Witness Address: ....

....

....

Witness Occupation: ....

EXECUTED AS A DEED by   )

NAME OF CLIENT   )

in the presence of:

Witness Signature : ....

Witness Name: ....

Witness Address: ....

....

....

Witness Occupation: ....

DRAFT DEED OF RECTIFICATION

(Original erroneously including work covered by a prior investigative CFA)

DATED   [*year*]

[NAME OF FIRM]

and

[NAME OF CLIENT]

_____

DEED OF RECTIFICATION

_____

THIS DEED OF RECTIFICATION is made on [*date*]

BETWEEN:

(1) *[NAME OF FIRM]* Solicitors of *[ADDRESS]* ('the Firm')
(2) *[NAME OF CLIENT]* of *[ADDRESS]* ('the Client')

RECITALS:

(1) This Deed is supplemental to a Conditional Fee Agreement ('the Agreement') made on 8 April 2002 between the Firm and the Client regarding the Client's claim for damages against Boggis Ltd arising out of his development of an asbestos-related condition.
(2) The Firm and the Client intended that the Agreement would conform in all respects with all requirements regarding agreements of that kind including those contained in the Conditional Fee Agreements Regulations 2000 in particular the correct stipulation of the particular proceedings (or parts of them) to which the CFA relates.
(3) The Agreement incorrectly described the proceedings to which the CFA relates under the heading 'What is covered by the Agreement' as 'Your Claim for damages against Boggis Ltd arising out of his development of an asbestos-related condition including all work undertaken on your behalf from the date when we first took instructions from you on 4 February 2002'. The words 'including all work undertaken on your behalf from the date when we first took instructions from you on 4 February 2002' were included in this part of the agreement by mistake.
(4) Prior to the making of the Agreement it had been made clear to the Client and it was understood by both the Client and the Firm that the Client's costs between the date on which the Firm first took instructions on 4 February 2002 and 8 April 2002 were governed by a conditional fee agreement dated 25 February 2002, and that these costs continued to be governed by this earlier agreement.
(5) Accordingly the parties to this Deed have agreed that the Agreement does not accurately set forth the true arrangements between them as regards the particulars mentioned below and wish to rectify the Agreement as appears below.

NOW THIS DEED WITNESSETH as follows:

1. The Agreement is to be read and construed as if the wording in the first bullet point under the Heading 'What is covered by the Agreement' reads 'Your Claim for damages against Boggis Ltd arising out of his development of an asbestos-related condition' without the addition of the words 'including all work undertaken on your behalf from the date when we first took instructions from you on

4 February 2002'. The words 'including all work undertaken on your behalf from the date when we first took instructions from you on 4 February 2002' were included in this part of the agreement by mistake.

2. A copy of the Agreement is annexed to this Deed showing in red the amendments referred to in clause 1 [*PLEASE ADD WITH AMENDMENT*].

3. The parties to this Deed declare firstly that the Agreement shall be read and construed as if from the date of the Agreement it had been in a form which includes such amendments and secondly that the Agreement and every part of it is to continue to have full effect and be binding on the parties.

IN WITNESS whereof these presents have been entered into as a Deed.

EXECUTED AS A DEED by a Partner of)

the Firm having authority to execute)

this Deed on behalf of the Firm)

in the presence of:

Witness Signature: ....

Witness Name: ....

Witness Address: ....

....

....

Witness Occupation: ....

EXECUTED AS A DEED by)

NAME OF CLIENT)

in the presence of:

Witness Signature : ....

Witness Name: ....

Witness Address: ....

....

....

Witness Occupation: ....

APPENDIX 18

Useful contacts

LEGAL EXPENSES INSURANCE, ATE BROKERS AND INSURERS

Abbey Legal Protection
Minories House
2–5 Minories
London
EC3N 1BJ
Tel: 0870 600 1480
E-mail: **sales@abbeylegal.com**
Web: **www.abbeylegal.com**

Allianz Cornhill Legal Protection
Redwood House
Brotherswood Court
Great Park Road
Bradley Stoke
Bristol
BS32 4QW
Tel: 0870 243 4340
Fax: 01454 455601
E-mail:
aclp-marketing@allianzcornhill.co.uk
Web:
www.allianzcornhilllegalprotection.co.uk

Amicus Legal Ltd
The Old Exchange
64 West Stockwell Street
Colchester
CO1 1HE
Tel: 01206 366 500
E-mail: **enquiries@amicuslegal.co.uk**
Web: **www.amicuslegal.co.uk**

ARAG plc
Froomsgate House
Rupert Street
Bristol
BS1 2QJ
Tel: 0117 917 1680
Fax:0117 917 1699
E-mail: **enquiries@arag.co.uk**
Web: **www.arag.co.uk**

ATE Business Solutions
50 Algitha Road
Skegness, Lincs
PE25 2EW
Tel: 01754 760377
E-mail: **enquiries@atebusiness.co.uk**
Web: **www.atebusiness.co.uk**

Box Legal
Tel: 0870 7669997
Fax: 0870 7669998
E-mail: **info@boxlegal.co.uk**
Web: **www.boxlegal.co.uk**

Capita Insurance Services
71 Victoria Street
Westminster
London
SW1H OXA
Tel: 020 7799 1525
Web: **www.capita.co.uk**

Collegiate Claims
Tel: 020 7459 3459
Fax: 020 74593454
Web: **www.collegiate.co.uk**

Complete Claims
Tel: 0161 817 7764
Fax: 0161 817 7762
Web: **www.bwise.uk.com**

Composite Legal Expenses Ltd
Suffolk House, Trade Street
Cardiff
CF10 5DT
Tel: 02920 222033
Fax: 02920 222044
E-mail: **enquiries@composite-legal.com**
Web: **www.composite-legal.com**

DAS/80e
DAS House, Quay Side
Temple Back
Bristol
BS1 6NH
Tel: 0117 934 0087
Fax: 0117 934 2109
E-mail: **admin@80e.com**
Web: **www.80e.com**

Elite Litigation Services
Newton Chambers
Newton Business Park
Isaac Newton Way
Grantham
NG31 9RT
Tel: 0845 601 1221
Fax: 01925 244802
E-mail: **enquiries@elite-insurance.co.uk**
Web: **www.elite-insurance.co.uk**

Financial & Legal
Tel: 0161 603 2230
E-mail: **info@financialandlegal.co.uk**
Web: **www.financialandlegal.co.uk**

First Assist Insurance Services
Tel: 020 8763 3333
Web: **www.firstassist.co.uk**

Funding & Insurance Solutions
Suite 28 Strathclyde Business Centre
Pottery Street
Greenock
PA15 2UH
Tel: 01475 806690
Fax: 01475 806033
Web: **www.fandisolutions.co.uk**

Ibex Legal Ltd
Trafalgar House
5–7 High Lane
Manchester
M21 9DJ
Tel: 0161 860 4945
E-mail: **info@ibexlegal.co.uk**
Web: **www.ibexlegal.co.uk**

Lamp Services Limited
Chester House
Harlands Road
Haywards Heath
West Sussex
RH16 1LR
Tel: 01444 444957
Fax: 01444 450872
E-mail: **info@lampinsurance.com**
Web: **www.lampinsurance.com**

Law Assist
Arundel Court
Park Bottom
Arundel, West Sussex
BN18 0AA
Tel: 01903 883811
Fax: 01903 885611
E-mail: **enquiries@lawassist.co.uk**
Web: **www.lawassist.co.uk**

Lowton Ellenbrook
Astley Park Estate
Kennedy Road
Astley
Manchester
M29 7JY
Tel: 0161 707 3400

Motor Accident Solicitors Society
54 Baldwin Street
Bristol
BS1 1QW
Tel: 0117 929 2560
Fax: 0117 904 7220
E-mail: **office@mass.org.uk**
Web: **www.mass.org.uk**

Mount Grace Insurance
Wansbeck Business Centre
Rotary Parkway
Ashington
Northumberland
NE63 8QZ
Tel: 01670 528295
Fax: 01670 528286
E-mail: **insurance@mount-grace.co.uk**
Web: **www.mount-grace.co.uk**

National Accident Helpline
1430 Montagu Court
Kettering Parkway
Kettering
Northants
NN15 6XR
Tel: 0800 376 0150
E-mail: **enquiries@nahl.co.uk**
Web: **www.national-accident.co.uk**

QLP Ltd
40 Lime Street
London
EC3M 7AW
Tel: 020 7626 0191
Fax: 020 7220 7759
Web: **www.qlp.ltd.uk**

Stirling Legal Services
Stirling House
501 Green Place, Walton Summit
Preston, Lancs
PR5 8AY
Tel: 01772 628900
Fax: 01772 312675
E-mail: **mail@stirlinglegal.com**
Web: **www.stirlinglegal.com**

Temple Legal Protection
Portsmouth House
1 Portsmouth Road
Guildford
GU2 4BL
Tel: 01483 577877
Fax: 01483 300943
E-mail: **info@temple-legal.co.uk**
Web: **www.temple-legal.co.uk**

The Judge Brokering Service
7 Warwick Street
Worthing
West Sussex
BN11 3DF
DX 3770 Worthing
Tel: 01903 23 22 55
Fax: 01903 23 22 54
E-mail: **info@thejudge.co.uk**
Web: **www.thejudge.co.uk**

RVM Assist Ltd
Westbourne House
60 Bagley Lane
Farsley
Leeds
LS28 5LY
Tel: 0870 4002 300
Fax: 0870 4002 301
E-mail: **operations@rvmuk.com**
Web: **www.rvmassist.co.uk**

DISBURSEMENT FUNDING ONLY

Bluestone Litigation Funding
Suite 1, Brownbridges Estate
East Peckham
Kent
TN12 5HF
Tel: 0845 222 5050

Excel Disbursement Funding
Westgate
17 Foley Road East
Sutton Coldfield
B74 3HP
Tel: 0121 3233755
Web:
www.exceldisbursementfunding.co.uk

Hampshire Trust
Fareham House
69 High Street
Fareham
PO16 7BB
Tel: 01329 234294
Web: **www.litigationfunding.co.uk**

Exclusivebenefits plc
Somerset Court
Brinsea Road
Congresbury
Bristol
BS49 5JL
Tel: 01934 853333
Fax: 01934 853444
Web: **www.exclusivebenefits.co.uk**

PROFESSIONAL INDEMNITY INSURANCE

PYV Group
No. 10 St. Mary at Hill
London
EC3R 8EE
Tel: 020 7626 6789
Web: **www.pyv.co.uk**

OTHER ADDRESSES

Academy of Experts
3 Gray's Inn Square
London
WC1R 5AH
Tel: 020 7430 0333
Fax: 020 7430 0666
E-mail: **admin@academy-experts.org**
Web: **www.academy-experts.org**

Action for the Victims of Medical Accidents
44 High Street
Croydon, Surrey
CR0 1YB
Tel: 020 8667 9065
Helpline: 0845 1232352
Web: **www.avma.org.uk**

Association of Personal Injury Lawyers
11 Castle Quay
Castle Boulevard
Nottingham
NG7 1FW
Tel: 0115 958 0585
Fax: 0115 958 0885
Web: **www.apil.org.uk**

The Bar Council
289–293 High Holborn
London
WC1V 7HZ
Tel: 020 7242 0082
Web: **www.barcouncil.org.uk**

Centre for Effective Dispute Resolution (CEDR)
70 Fleet Street
London
EC4Y 1EU
Tel: 020 7536 6000
Web: **www.cedr.co.uk**

Chancery Bar Association
21 Goodwyns Vale
London
N10 2HA
Tel: 020 8883 1700
Web: **www.chba.org.uk**

Child Poverty Action Group
94 White Lion Street
London
N1 9PF
Tel: 020 7837 7979
Web: **www.cpag.org.uk**

Commerce and Industry Group
Woodbank House
80 Churchgate
Stockport
SK1 1YJ
Tel: 0161 480 2918
Web: **www.cigroup.org.uk**

Expert Witness Institute
7 Warwick Court
London
WC1R 5DJ
Tel: 0870 366 6367
Web: **www.ewi.org.uk**

Forum of Insurance Lawyers
The Law Society's Hall
113 Chancery Lane
London
WC2A 1PL
Tel: 020 7323 4632
Web: **www.foil.org.uk**

Legal Aid Practitioners Group
Top Floor
103 Borough High Street
London
SE1 1NL
Tel: 020 7183 2269
Fax: 020 7183 2270
Web: **www.lapg.org.uk**

The Law Society
113 Chancery Lane
London
WC2A 1PL
Tel: 020 7242 1222
Web: **www.lawsociety.org.uk**

Legal Services Commission
85 Gray's Inn Road
London
WC1X 8TX
Tel: 020 7759 0000
Web: **www.legalservices.gov.uk**

Pan-European Organisation of Personal Injury Lawyers (PEOPIL)
Imperial House
31 Temple Street
Birmingham
B2 5DB
Tel: 0121 643 5009
Fax: 0121 643 9405
E-mail: **admin@peopil.com**
Web: **www.peopil.com**

Personal Injuries Bar Association (PIBA)
Web: **www.piba.org.uk**

Society of Expert Witnesses
PO Box 345
Newmarket
Suffolk
CB8 7TU
Tel: 016 3866 0684
Helpline: 084 5702 3014
Web: **www.sew.org.uk**

Index